WILFRID SELLARS

Wilfrid Sellars:

Fusing the Images

JAY F. ROSENBERG

OXFORD
UNIVERSITY PRESS

OXFORD

UNIVERSITY PRESS

Great Clarendon Street, Oxford OX2 6DP

Oxford University Press is a department of the University of Oxford.
It furthers the University's objective of excellence in research, scholarship,
and education by publishing worldwide in

Oxford New York

Auckland Cape Town Dar es Salaam Hong Kong Karachi
Kuala Lumpur Madrid Melbourne Mexico City Nairobi
New Delhi Shanghai Taipei Toronto

With offices in

Argentina Austria Brazil Chile Czech Republic France Greece
Guatemala Hungary Italy Japan Poland Portugal Singapore
South Korea Switzerland Thailand Turkey Ukraine Vietnam

Oxford is a registered trade mark of Oxford University Press
in the UK and in certain other countries

Published in the United States
by Oxford University Press Inc., New York

British Library Cataloguing in Publication Data

Data available

Library of Congress Cataloging in Publication Data

Data available

Typeset by Laserwords Private Limited, Chennai, India
Printed in Great Britain
on acid-free paper by
Biddles Ltd., King's Lynn, Norfolk

ISBN 978-0-19-921455-6

Preface

Forty-three years ago, in 1963, I began my doctoral studies in philosophy at the University of Pittsburgh. That was the same year that Wilfrid Sellars moved from Yale to Pittsburgh, where he would spend the last third of his life as University Professor of Philosophy. My undergraduate degree in philosophy was from Reed, a first-rate small liberal arts college in Portland, Oregon, already one of the most civilized municipalities in the United States, but in those days also something of an isolated backwater. Reed's academic programs in the humanities were long on tradition. For our year-long introduction to philosophy, we plunged into the discipline with Socrates and, after exploring a goodly cross-section of the historical canon, surfaced gasping for air somewhere this side of Kant. Primary sources only, of course. For introductory ethics, we read Hume, Kant, Hegel, and Kierkegaard! Contemporary philosophy was largely a *tabula rasa*. I had a passing acquaintance with the work of A. J. Ayer and Gilbert Ryle. I had never heard of Wilfrid Sellars.

Just three years later, I had participated in at least a half-dozen of his seminars, completed a Ph.D. dissertation (on the determinable-determinate relation) under his direction, and read pretty much everything that he had written, published or in process. And while it would be an exaggeration to say that those three years at Pittsburgh had brought me entirely up to date in contemporary philosophy, they had certainly brought me up to speed. When I left Pittsburgh in 1966 to become an Assistant Professor at the University of North Carolina at Chapel Hill, where I was to remain for the next forty years, I had been exposed to the most influential contemporary literature and its proximate historical antecedents, become familiar with the range of questions and problems then currently under active investigation, and already begun producing my own publishable contributions to the centuries-old ongoing philosophical conversation. Sellars, of course, deserves a great deal of the credit, but I can't move on without taking the opportunity to mention, and thank, the other members of the faculty who guided my studies at Pittsburgh: Kurt Baier, Adolph Grünbaum, Nick Rescher, Nuel Belnap, Jerry Schneewind, Richard Gale, Bruce Aune, and Storrs McCall.

(A note from the winged chariot: When I submitted my doctoral dissertation back in 1966, it was in the form of an original typescript and three *carbon copies*. Xerographic reproductions were first accepted at Pittsburgh the following year. Forty years later, my own university in Chapel Hill has just gone paperless. Dissertations may now be submitted *only* electronically, as word-processor document files. How time flies when you're having fun!)

My relationship to Sellars was, in the best sense, an intellectual apprenticeship. His works supplied the systematic framework within which I initially situated philosophical questions and the methodological framework in terms of which I initially approached them. He showed me how to recognize the problem spaces of our historical predecessors that had been transposed into contemporary settings and idioms and how one can appreciate and appropriate their insights while understanding and avoiding their confusions. His personal philosophical productivity continued unabated until his death in 1989, paralleled by my own abiding engagement, both interpretive and critical, with his writings, which, sustained and extended during the subsequent years, finds its current consummation in this collection. The present volume thus represents a kind of provisional closure on one of my ongoing intellectual life projects.

The theme of closure is growing increasingly salient in my life. It's been a busy two years since I sat down to write my last free-wheeling, self-indulgent book preface (for *Accessing Kant*, Oxford University Press, 2005). I've finally made it to Rome, in the course of a Mediterranean cruise that also included stops at Corsica, Cannes, and Barcelona—"Everyone soon or late comes round by Rome" (Robert Browning)—and in the process discovered that traveling to Rome by cruise ship is a really stupid idea, since Rome doesn't have a harbor. (The ship anchors at Civitavecchia, whence Rome is then a $1\frac{1}{2}$-hour bus ride away.) I've had my first angiogram and echocardiogram—with comfortingly unproblematic results—and developed a nasty bursitis in my right shoulder. And I've become a grandfather! Elena Kate Faltin, in every way a superior child, came into the world on 25 August 2005. I'm now 64 years old, and I will shortly begin my last semester of classroom teaching before full retirement. When you read this, I will be *emeritus*. A good time to think about closure, and about whatever comes next.

Jay F. Rosenberg

Bielefeld,
November 2006

Acknowledgements

1. Jay F. Rosenberg, "Fusing the Images: *Nachruf* for Wilfrid Sellars", *Journal for General Philosophy of Science* (*Zeitschrift für allgemeine Wissenschaftstheorie*), 21/1 (1990), 3–25. © 1990 Kluwer Academic Publishers, with kind permission of Springer Science and Business Media.
2. "Sellars and Quine: Compare and Contrast", previously unpublished.
3. Jay F. Rosenberg, "The Elusiveness of Categories, the Archimedean Dilemma, and the Nature of Man", in *Action, Knowledge, and Reality: Studies in Honor of Wilfrid Sellars*, H.-N. Castañeda (ed.) (Bobbs-Merrill, Inc, 1975); 147–84.
4. Jay F. Rosenberg, "Comparing the Incommensurable: Another Look at Convergent Realism", *Philosophical Studies*, 54 (1988), 163–93. © 1988 Kluwer Academic Publishers, with kind permission of Springer Science and Business Media.
5. "Sellarsian Picturing", previously unpublished.
6. Jay F. Rosenberg, "Linguistic Roles and Proper Names", *The Philosophy of Wilfrid Sellars: Queries and Extensions*, J. Pitt (ed.), 189–216. © 1978 D. Reidel Publishing Co., with kind permission of Springer Science and Business Media.
7. Jay F. Rosenberg, "Wilfrid Sellars' Philosophy of Mind", *Contemporary Philosophy, 4: Philosophy of Mind*, Guttorm Floistad (ed.), 417–39. © 1983 Martinus Nijhoff Publishers, with kind permission of Springer Science and Business Media.
8. Jay F. Rosenberg, "Ryleans and Outlookers: Wilfrid Sellars on 'Mental States'", in *The American Philosophers*, Peter A. French and Howard K. Wettstein (eds.), *Midwest Studies in Philosophy*, 28 (2004), 239–65. © 2004 Blackwell Publishing, Inc.
9. "The Place of Color in the Scheme of Things: A Roadmap to Sellars' Carus Lectures", by Jay F. Rosenberg, *Monist*, 65/3 (1982), 315–35. © 1982 *THE MONIST: An International Quarterly Journal of General Philosophical Inquiry*, Peru, Illinois, USA 61354. Reprinted by permission.
10. "Still Mythic After All Those Years: On Alston's Latest Defense of the Given", *Philosophy and Phenomenological Research*, 72/1 (2006), 177–93.
11. "Perception *vs.* Inner Sense: A Problem about Direct Awareness", *Philosophical Studies*, special issue on The Philosophy of Wilfrid Sellars, Mark Lance (ed.), 101 (2000), 143–60. © 2000 Kluwer Academic Publishers, with kind permission of Springer Science and Business Media.

12. Jay F. Rosenberg, "Sellarsian Seeing: In Search of Perceptual Authority", in Ralph Schumacher (ed.), *Perception and Reality* (Paderborn, 2004), 263–86. © 2004 mentis Verlag.

13. "Divergent Intuitions: McDowell's Kant and Sellars' Kant", previously unpublished.

Appendix: Sellars-Rosenberg Correspondence on Ontology, 1972–3. Originally published over the Internet: http://www.ditext.com/sellars/.

Contents

Introduction

Among the Anglophone philosophers whose work helped to set and decisively shaped the philosophical agenda in the English-speaking world during the second half of the twentieth century, Wilfrid Sellars bids fair to leave the deepest and most lasting impact. The central theses of his acknowledged masterwork, "Empiricism and the Philosophy of Mind", published fifty years ago and now engaging the attention of a third generation of readers, are still very much the focus of spirited debate. While the work of the contemporary colleagues with whom he actively entered into dialogue—W. V. O. Quine, Nelson Goodman, Gustav Bergmann, Roderick Chisholm—is fading from view, interest in Sellars' writings has never been stronger. New systematic introductions to his work are freshly published[1] and the list of influential philosophers who express a debt to that work continues to grow.[2]

I studied under Sellars at the University of Pittsburgh in the early 1960s and have been continuously engaged with his work for over forty years. During those years, I have evidently come to be regarded as its foremost expositor[3] and, for better or worse, although my engagement has not been slavishly uncritical, also as Sellars' truest disciple. I am, in any case, happy to think of myself as a Sellarsian, and much of my own work has indeed been devoted to supporting, refining, and extending the insights and arguments that I have found in his. The fiftieth anniversary of the publication of "Empiricism and the Philosophy of Mind",[4] coinciding with the fortieth anniversary of my doctorate, supervised by Sellars, seemed an appropriate occasion for collecting my essays on his work in one volume and taking a careful retrospective look at what, over the years, I have had to say.

---

[1] Willem A. deVries, *Wilfrid Sellars* (Philosophy Now) (Acumen Publishing/McGill-Queen's University Press: 2005); James O'Shea, *Wilfrid Sellars* (Key Contemporary Thinkers) (Blackwell/Polity Press: 2006).

[2] Richard Rorty, Daniel Dennett, Paul Churchland, Michael Williams, Robert Brandom, and John McDowell, to name a few of the most prominent.

[3] As witnessed by my invited entries on Sellars in the *Routledge Encyclopedia of Philosophy*, the *Stanford Encyclopedia of Philosophy*, the Blackwell *Companion to Analytic Philosophy*, the *Biographical Dictionary of Twentieth Century Philosophers*, and the *Encyclopedia Britannica*.

[4] Commemorated by a major conference at the University of London, where Sellars originally presented his groundbreaking work as "The Myth of the Given: Three Lectures on Empiricism and the Philosophy of Mind". A full conference program, copies of several of the presentations, and interesting archival material are available at http://philosophy.sas.ac.uk/Empiricism_Mind_Sellars.htm.

The process has been a rewarding one. On the one hand, what emerges is a relatively comprehensive picture of the central themes of Sellars' theoretical philosophy, accompanied and shaped by my own periodic attempts to respond to some of his critics and extend some of his insights. (In contrast, his perceptive and provocative, but less fully developed, views in moral philosophy are only briefly sketched, and, except for his interpretation of Kant, his considerable, and not yet fully appreciated, contributions to the history of philosophy remain almost entirely off stage.) On the other hand, I have used the opportunity to rethink, and somewhat amend, one of my central long-term disagreements with Sellars, and to continue my ongoing dialogue with John McDowell, his successor at the University of Pittsburgh, over the proper interpretation and appraisal of key elements of Sellarsian epistemology. The results are presented here in two of the three substantial previously unpublished essays. Here, in brief compass, is a survey of the book's contents.

1. "FUSING THE IMAGES: *NACHRUF* FOR WILFRID SELLARS"

A *Nachruf* is a traditional German form of intellectual obituary, combining biographical information and personal memories with a comprehensive overview and reflective appreciation of the deceased's scholarly and creative work. This essay is consequently largely expository, but it also offers a useful orientation to the central themes and theses of Sellars' philosophy. The title "Fusing the Images", which I have also adopted for this collection, comes from Sellars' explicit conception of a central goal of contemporary philosophy being that of reaching a "stereoscopic understanding" of the possibility of reconciling and combining competing "manifest" and "scientific" images of man-in-the-world into a single "synoptic vision" of persons and their place in nature.

2. "SELLARS AND QUINE: COMPARE AND CONTRAST"

Appearing in the 1950s, Quine's "Two Dogmas of Empiricism" and Sellars' "Empiricism and the Philosophy of Mind" (henceforth 'EPM'), both decisively influenced the course and character of subsequent philosophical inquiry in ways which continue to resonate five decades later. Quine's work unquestionably had the stronger initial impact, but as I read the current philosophical scene, Sellars' influence is now waxing and Quine's waning—and that, I think, is as it should be. In this previously unpublished essay, I attempt both to explain and to support this conviction through a comparative study that, in particular, emphasizes what Sellars has explicitly had to say about the central themes of Quine's seminal essay.

3. "THE ELUSIVENESS OF CATEGORIES, THE ARCHIMEDEAN DILEMMA, AND THE NATURE OF MAN"

This sprawling multi-part study of interlocking themes from Sellars' ontology, philosophy of language, and philosophy of science originally appeared in a 1975 Festschrift for Sellars edited by Hector-Neri Castañeda, who, although his own philosophical views often diverged dramatically from those of his teacher, remains one of Sellars' most distinguished students.[5] The Festschrift appeared when Sellars was in his mid-sixties, at the peak of productivity and includes Sellars' 1971 Machette Foundation Lectures, "The Structure of Knowledge", and a brief intellectual autobiography.

In my essay, actually written five years earlier in 1970, I ventured three theses, two critical and one constructive. One critical thesis (the "Elusiveness of Categories") probed a tension between his nominalistic analyses of Platonistic discourse and his implicit categorial assay of linguistic expressions; the other (the "Archimedean Dilemma") explored the difficulty of appealing to (Tractarian) "picturing" to give content to the (Peircean) notion of a "limit of theories". The constructive thesis attempted to provide a sense for "theory convergence", and so for Peirce's limit concept, that was not similarly vulnerable to criticism. During 1972–3, I conducted an extended correspondence with Sellars, included in this volume as an Appendix, on the relationships between language and ontology, some of whose conclusions were implicitly incorporated into my first book, *Linguistic Representation*, published in 1974. The other two theses, however, subsequently received a more public airing.

4. "COMPARING THE INCOMMENSURABLE: ANOTHER LOOK AT CONVERGENT REALISM"

The University of Pittsburgh's Center for the Philosophy of Science honored Sellars on the occasion of his seventy-fifth birthday with a Colloquium on Sellarsian Philosophy. Versions of most of the papers presented there were subsequently collected and published as a sort of Proceedings in a special edition of *Philosophical Studies*, a journal that Sellars himself, together with Herbert Feigl, had founded in 1950.

In "Coupling, Retheoretization, and the Correspondence Principle", which appeared in *Synthese* in 1980, I had already elaborated the views on theory

---

[5] Castañeda wrote his doctoral dissertation on "The Logical Structure of Moral Reasoning" under Sellars' direction at the University of Minnesota in 1954. He died of brain cancer in 1991 after a distinguished and productive scholarly and administrative career. While an important legacy lives on in the form of the journal *Noûs*, which he founded in 1967 and edited for over twenty years, it is depressing to observe that the discipline has meanwhile completely lost sight of his own original and significant *philosophical* contributions.

succession and theory convergence that I had developed a decade earlier in response to the "Archimedean dilemma". Those views had subsequently been vigorously critically engaged by Larry Lauden and Jarrett Leplin, both colleagues in a Virginia–North Carolina Piedmont Philosophy of Science Discussion Group, both of whom had also published significant challenges to the very notion of a Peircean "convergent realism". I used the occasion of the seventy-fifth birthday Colloquium both to refine and extend my position and to respond to those critical challenges. This paper is the result.

5. "SELLARSIAN PICTURING"

Although I had put some critical pressure on Sellars' endorsement of picturing in "The Elusiveness of Categories, the Archimedean Dilemma, and the Nature of Man", my 1974 *Linguistic Representation* still operated within the Tractarian framework. By 1980, which saw the publication of my *One World and Our Knowledge of It*, however, without having given the matter much more thought, I had effectively abandoned it. This previously unpublished essay takes up the question twenty-five years later. In retrospect, there turns out to be much more to be said for Sellars' position than I would have suspected.

6. "LINGUISTIC ROLES AND PROPER NAMES"

The volume in which this essay originally appeared was the precipitate of a conference on Sellars' philosophy held at the Virginia Polytechnic Institute (VPI) in Blacksburg in 1976. Sellars had by then published a number of increasingly-detailed expositions of his non-relational analysis of semantic discourse in terms of the *roles* played by linguistic expressions, roles normatively-individuated by "language-entries" (perceptual responses), "language-exits" (intentional actions), and "intra-linguistic moves" (material and formal inferences). His analysis had found some resonance as a possible account of the senses of various *descriptive* expressions, but Saul Kripke's recent publications had convinced many, perhaps even most, philosophers that "Descriptivist" accounts of *proper names* were beyond any salvaging. According to the "direct reference" theories which quickly supplanted them, proper names have *no* senses; their references depend only on the way in which their uses are (ultimately) *causally* related to objects. In this paper, I sketch a fully Sellarsian alternative, according to which proper names have *many* "idiolectic" senses, collected through *anaphoric* chains, and commensurated through shared epistemic procedures, an account which I subsequently developed in detail and presented at length in 1994 in *Beyond Formalism: Naming and Necessity for Human Beings*.

7. "WILFRID SELLARS' PHILOSOPHY OF MIND"

This largely expository essay briefly surveys Sellars' views regarding five central topics in the philosophy of mind: the Cartesian self, thoughts, sensations, the identity theory of mind and body; and the concept of a person. Like Kant, Sellars regarded Descartes' reasoning in support of substance dualism as "paralogistic", i.e., formally fallacious. He argued that, in the first instance, a person is not a Cartesian ego, but a multiply-competent living organism understood along broadly Aristotelian lines, themes that I myself subsequently pursued in two books, from a late-Wittgensteinian perspective in *Thinking Clearly About Death*, first publishing in 1983, and from a Kantian perspective, in depth and detail, in my 1986 *The Thinking Self*.

Like Kant, too, Sellars deconstructed Descartes' unitary category of "*cogitationes*", distinguishing the aboutness of (conceptual) thoughts from the of-ness of (non-conceptual) sensations. Thoughts and sensations, he argued, pose radically different challenges for the construction of an acceptable "identity theory", i.e., the satisfactory accommodation of persons within the scientific image. These were themes that Sellars had originally creatively engaged in EPM. They had consequently already generated a considerable independent literature, and, indeed, continue to do so—but, unfortunately, it is a literature which often fails effectively to take into account the essential continuity and the continued development of Sellars' views. The next few essays address some of these issues.

8. "RYLEANS AND OUTLOOKERS: WILFRID SELLARS ON 'MENTAL STATES' "

This essay explores Sellars' relationships to the so-called " 'theory'-theory" (which he is sometimes credited with having originated) and the recently popular "simulation theory" of our self- and other-ascriptions of "propositional attitudes", paradigmatically beliefs and desires. In particular, it critically addresses Robert Gordon's claim that Sellars mislocates the intersubjectivity of such "mental state" attributions. Both authors illustrate their views by considering how mentalistic notions would or could function in an idealized hypothetical community. Sellars' "Ryleans", introduced in EPM, lack all mentalistic idioms, but command a full mastery of subjunctive (counterfactual) conditionals and semantic discourse. Gordon's "Outlookers" are so-called "because they are always looking outward to the world, never inward to the mind of the agent". I defend Sellars' conclusions by carefully exploring his account of the relations between thought and action and, in particular, bringing into proper focus his analysis of the various senses in which language and conduct can be said to *express* thoughts or beliefs and intentions or desires.

9. "THE PLACE OF COLOR IN THE SCHEME OF THINGS: A ROADMAP TO SELLARS' CARUS LECTURES"

Sellars' Carus Lectures, "Foundations for a Metaphysics of Pure Process" were published in 1981 in volume 64 of the *Monist*. A year later, volume 65/3 was devoted to The Philosophy of Wilfrid Sellars, in which this paper appeared. In it, I offer a detailed reconstruction of Sellars' argumentation in the first and third Carus Lectures with the ancillary aim of demonstrating that, despite minor corrections, major refinements, and significant differences in emphasis, his views on givenness and mind-body identity had remained essentially unchanged over 35 years. His first lecture, "The Lever of Archimedes", addressed the basic conceptual structure of sensory predicates and the epistemic terms correlative to them (e.g., 'sees' and 'looks'); his third lecture, "Is Consciousness Physical?", argued that a satisfactory solution to the "sensorium-body problem" ultimately requires the introduction of a monocategorial ontology of "pure processes" (whose fundamental notions had been sketched in the second lecture).[6] Each has a complex logical and motivational structure which my exposition explicitly highlights. My "roadmap" has since been regarded as giving the "standard reading" of Sellars' difficult text.

10. "STILL MYTHIC AFTER ALL THOSE YEARS: ON ALSTON'S LATEST DEFENSE OF THE GIVEN"

Sellars characterized his project in EPM as "a general critique of the entire framework of givenness". His conclusion that "the Given" is a "Myth" quickly elicited philosophical opposition, and it has remained contentious during the ensuing fifty years. William Alston is prominent among the philosophers who have challenged Sellars' account of sensory appearing and attempted to devise an acceptable account of perception committed to the givenness of perceived objects. Here I argue that his latest attempt fails on all fronts.

11. "PERCEPTION VS. INNER SENSE: A PROBLEM ABOUT DIRECT AWARENESS"

This paper was first presented at a conference on Sellars' philosophy held in Dunabogdany, Hungary, in 1996 before finding its way into a special issue of *Philosophical Studies*. Sellars concludes EPM with the story of a mythical genius, Jones, who introduces the notions of thought episodes and sensory states in

---

[6] Johanna Seibt, Sellars' last doctoral student, has made this facet of Sellars' ontology the central theme of her own extraordinarily creative research program. Her insightful survey of Sellars' philosophy—*Properties as Processes. A Synoptic Study of Wilfrid Sellars' Nominalism*, (Ridgeview Publishing Co.; Reseda, CA: 1990)—*inter alia* conveys her sense of the centrality of process ontology to his systematic projects.

the context of separate explanatory theories. He then teaches his compatriots to respond directly (i.e., non-inferentially) to the occurrence of such episodes or states with the appropriate concepts. The concepts thereby acquire a "reporting role", and their users gain a (limited, non-Cartesian) form of "privileged access" to their thoughts and sensations. I argue here that the case of sensations differs significantly from that of thoughts in a way which implies that we have no experience of sense impressions *as such*. Surprisingly, the case of *pains* proves exceptionally problematic and difficult to accommodate within Sellars' "Myth of Jones".

11. "SELLARSIAN SEEING: IN SEARCH OF PERCEPTUAL AUTHORITY"

John McDowell and Robert Brandom are especially prominent among the many philosophers whose work has been significantly influenced by Sellars. Both have explicitly reacted to his account in EPM of the relationship between perceptual experience and epistemic justification, and each has offered a critical alternative to it (and criticized the alternative presented by the other). I here defend Sellars against his admirers, arguing that his own original account is preferable in its essentials to both Brandom's and McDowell's alternatives. However, some of Brandom's ideas, I suggest, can be usefully deployed in response to a further important critical challenge to Sellars' views that has been convincingly pressed by Ernest Sosa.

12. "DIVERGENT INTUITIONS: McDOWELL'S KANT AND SELLARS' KANT"

John McDowell's 1997 Woodbridge Lectures, subsequently published in the *Journal of Philosophy*, represent his most extensive and detailed attempt to spell out his philosophical differences with Sellars regarding the way in which "thought and language are directed toward the world", fruitfully using as an expository medium their divergent interpretations of the notion of an *intuition* that Kant develops in the First Critique. In this previously unpublished essay, presented in an abridged version at the international conference "Empiricism and the Philosophy of Mind after 50 years" held at the University of London in June 2006, I take a careful critical look at McDowell's project and its outcome. While remaining fairly neutral on questions of Kant exegesis—my recently-published *Accessing Kant* (Oxford University Press; Oxford: 2005) presents and defends my own best reading—I conclude that Sellars' philosophical theory of sensory perception is preferable to McDowell's, in particular in coming to terms with the problematic of non-veridical perception. McDowell's account of veridical perception, in contrast, is arguably haunted by the specter of Givenness.

APPENDIX: SELLARS–ROSENBERG CORRESPONDENCE ON ONTOLOGY, 1972–3

This correspondence, previously available only over the Internet, pursues the issues concerning language and ontology that I had raised in 1970 under the rubric "the Elusiveness of Categories". The discussion presupposes a fairly extensive acquaintance with Sellars' adaptation and extensions of Wittgenstein's Tractarian theory of predication and Carnap's account of "pseudo-object sentences" in the "material mode". It will consequently likely be of interest only to a reader who is especially interested in the technical details of his unique form of "linguistic nominalism".

Like many Sellarsians, I have adopted the salutary habit of framing citations in terms of brief mnemonic abbreviations—e.g., EPM, AE, and LTC—in preference to the widespread but comparatively uninformative author-plus-date system—e.g. (Sellars 1956), (Sellars 1963*b*), and (Sellars 1969*c*). This custom has been usefully aided and abetted by Jeff Sicha's practice of including a comprehensive list of Sellars' philosophical publications, complete with canonical mnemonics, as an appendix to each of Sellars' books issued by his Ridgeview Publishing Co.,[7] but the practice has not been limited to citations of Sellars' work. To aid the reader, I have consequently compiled a Master Bibliography of all the works cited anywhere in the essays collected here, indicating the mnemonics that have been employed (alas, not always completely consistently) in those citations.

The essays collected here, of course, all represent Sellars' work, so to speak, only at one remove, and should certainly not be regarded as a satisfactory alternative to engaging with that work itself. There is no substitute for encountering a great philosopher in his own words. Nevertheless, Sellars is also notorious for the difficulty and dialectical intricacy of his philosophical prose, and over the years many of these essays have proved useful in helping others to understand what Sellars' own words were actually trying to *say*. Since Sellars' work still very much deserves to be read, discussed, and taken seriously, it is my hope that they will continue to serve at least in that more modest capacity.

---

[7] Jeff Sicha founded Ridgeview Publishing Co. (http://www.ridgeviewpublishing.com/) with the express purpose of keeping as much of Sellars' work as possible inexpensively in print and available. His efforts have proved extraordinarily successful. He has recovered the rights to and reissued three of the four book-length works by Sellars first appearing under other imprints (SPR, PP, and S&M; EPH remains firmly in expensive Dutch hands), and issued five more under the Ridgeview imprint (N&O, PPPW, ME, KPT, and KTM). At some point the mailing address of Ridgeview Publishing changed from Reseda, CA, to Atascadero, CA. Depending upon the date of publication, either city can appear in a bibliographic reference.

1

Fusing the Images: *Nachruf* for Wilfrid Sellars

WITH the death of Wilfrid Sellars at age 77 in July 1989, we have lost one of the great creative, synthetic, and systematic philosophical talents of our century. His published scholarly work, a corpus including three independent books but dominated by well over one hundred substantial essays, has helped to set and shape the Anglo-American philosophical agenda over a period of forty years and has earned him worldwide recognition and justified acclaim as one of the most consequential and, indeed, definitive figures of postwar Western philosophy. In this *Nachruf*, I shall first present a whirlwind survey of the major academic and scholarly stations of Sellars' long intellectual career as a distinguished teacher, an influential editor, and an innovative philosopher of the first rank, at the end of which I shall permit myself a brief personal reminiscence. Only then will I embark on the much more difficult and demanding task of attempting systematically to articulate and assess the many lasting contributions that his work has made to the 3000-year-old conversation that is philosophy *per se*. Here I shall often let Sellars speak for himself.

OVERVIEW: SELLARS' CAREER

Sellars' intellectual career can be usefully divided into three major periods. The *early period* begins with his philosophical education—as an undergraduate at the University of Michigan, as a graduate teaching assistant at the University of Buffalo, as a Rhodes Scholar in Oriel College, Oxford, and as a doctoral student at Harvard University—and continues through 1955. It encompasses the initial stages of what was to become an extraordinarily distinguished academic career—first, interrupted by the War, at the University of Iowa and later, decisively, at the University of Minnesota, where the synergistic influence of the young and flourishing Center for the Philosophy of Science provided the final catalyst needed to bring his philosophical gifts to full expression.

This essay was completed while its author was spending the academic year 1989–90 as an Alexander von Humboldt Fellow at the Center for Interdisciplinary Research (ZiF) in Bielefeld, West Germany. Thanks are gratefully extended to the Alexander von Humboldt-Stiftung and to the ZiF for their support.

This early period saw the appearance in print of over two dozen substantial essays, typically manifesting singularly demanding levels of dialectical and expository complexity that rapidly earned Sellars the widespread reputation of being "difficult to read". (In 1980, J. Sicha collected, edited, and reprinted nine of the most important of these early essays as a book, *Pure Pragmatics and Possible Worlds*.) It was not, however, as an author but rather as an *editor* that Sellars during this period first began to exert a profound influence on the course of postwar American philosophy. The publication of *Readings in Philosophical Analysis*, coedited with Herbert Feigl, in 1949, and *Readings in Ethical Theory*, coedited with John Hospers, three years later, proved to be seminal events. The "philosophical analysis" represented in these volumes, transplanted from its origins and early development at Cambridge and Oxford and enriched by generous cross-fertilization from the "logical empiricism" of a largely-expatriate Vienna Circle, took strong root in an American philosophical soil that had already been nourished, not only by the pragmatisms of Peirce, James, and Dewey, but also by indigenous schools of "critical realism" and "evolutionary naturalism", in which Wilfrid's father, Roy Wood Sellars, had in fact played a major and distinguished role. With continuing support and encouragement from the first scholarly journal deliberately and explicitly created as a forum for the new hybrid, "analytic philosophy"—*Philosophical Studies*, founded by Feigl and Sellars in 1950, and edited by them jointly until 1971 and by Sellars alone for a further three years—the methodological initiatives and the leading problems and programs of this "analytic" style of philosophizing rapidly came to dominate the American academic scene.

Sellars' *middle period* finds him in full command of a philosophical vision of remarkable scope and depth. Professionally, this period includes Sellars' last years at the University of Minnesota, his short tenure as a professor at Yale University, and the first part of his long and fruitful relationship with the University of Pittsburgh, where, beginning in 1963, he was to spend the balance of his academic life as a distinguished University Professor. The publication in 1956 of his revolutionary essay 'Empiricism and the Philosophy of Mind', immediately acknowledged as a contemporary classic, marks the start of this exceptional period of fecund and influential scholarly productivity, which may (somewhat arbitrarily) be seen as culminating sixteen years later, in 1972, with the publication of his 1970 Presidential Address to the Eastern Division of the American Philosophical Association on the Kantian text, " ... this I or he or it (the thing) which thinks". These middle years saw the appearance of some fifty important essays—most of which were subsequently assembled in three collections: *Science, Perception, and Reality*, 1963; *Philosophical Perspectives*, 1967; and *Essays in Philosophy and Its History*, 1974—innovatively and insightfully addressing themes across the whole spectrum of classical and contemporary philosophical concerns. In addition, an invitation to deliver the John Locke Lectures for 1965–66 resulted in the publication one year later of Sellars' first self-contained book, *Science and Metaphysics: Variations on Kantian Themes.*

The seventeen years from his sixtieth birthday to his death, constitute Sellars' *late period,* not in the sense of being marked by any fundamental shift in his philosophical outlook, but in the sense of being a period of consolidation, refinement, and deepening of mature theses and insights that, at the same time, were coming to be both more fully appreciated and explicitly appropriated by a new philosophical generation. Sellars' own scholarly productivity continued largely unabated well into this late period, with increasing frequency in form of contributions to major established lecture series, including the 1971 Matchette Foundation Lectures at the University of Texas (first published in Castañeda, 1975), the 1974 John Dewey Lectures at the University of Chicago (appearing in 1979 as the book *Naturalism and Ontology*), and the Carus Lectures for 1977–78 (published as a special issue of the *Monist* in 1981). What was significantly new during this period, however, was that, parallel to these publications, there emerged a series of symposia, colloquia, and critical studies explicitly devoted to Sellars' philosophical work: a "mini-*Festschrift*" in *Noûs* (1973); a full-fledged *Festschrift, Action, Knowledge, and Reality,* edited by Castañeda, in 1975; a fairly comprehensive and systematic critical study, *The Synoptic Vision,* from Delaney *et al.* at Notre Dame University, in 1977; a volume of colloquium proceedings, *The Philosophy of Wilfrid Sellars: Queries and Extensions,* edited by Pitt, in 1978; a special issue of the *Monist* in 1982; and, most recently, a special issue of *Philosophical Studies* in 1988, devoted to the proceedings of a colloquium held in 1987 in honor of Sellars' seventy-fifth birthday by another institution that he had also helped to found and to guide for more than two decades, the Center for the History and Philosophy of Science at the University of Pittsburgh.

A PERSONAL REMINISCENCE

I first met Sellars in 1963, when I arrived at the University of Pittsburgh to begin my doctoral studies. Sellars himself had just come to Pittsburgh from Yale, along with Nuel Belnap and Jerome Schneewind—Alan Anderson would follow in 1964—and with Kurt Baier, Adolph Grünbaum, and Nicholas Rescher already in residence, the Pittsburgh philosophy department was just coming into its full flourishing.

As luck would have it, this exceptionally gifted faculty found itself confronted in the early- and mid-sixties by an unusually talented group of doctoral students, including, besides myself, Brian Skyrms, Ernest Sosa, Bas van Fraassen, Michael Dunn, Richard Burian, Louis Goble, Paul Churchland, and Patricia Smith (later Churchland). This group supplied the core membership for what can best be described as an extraordinary continuing seminar—offered from trimester to trimester, to be sure, under nominally different titles, course numbers, and descriptions—whose shifting topics were determined primarily by the philosophical problems that happened to have engaged the attention of its instructor, Wilfrid Sellars.

Life in a Sellars seminar was both stimulating and stressful. Apart from delivering an opening lecture each trimester, with which he brilliantly introduced the next set of problems in their historical and dialectical contexts, Sellars' typical style was not so much to teach us as to help us to teach one another. Each session consequently saw a different student in the "hot seat", responsible for presenting and commenting on some classical or contemporary work, with Sellars presiding socratically over the ensuing, consistently vigorous, philosophical debates, goading and guiding us with pointed questions and brief penetrating remarks to new insights and understanding.

The great exception was the famous Kant course. Here Sellars indeed lectured, lucidly, with great animation and élan—and with pictures! Beginning as a simple circular mind, from week to week the synthetic unity of experience came graphically to life on the chalkboard as, step-by-step, the contributions of sensibility, the forms of outer and inner sense, the productive and reproductive imagination, the Categories, and even the transcendental unity of apperception successively found their places in a series of increasingly intricate and wonderfully enlightening diagrams.

Sellars' own philosophical works were never on the reading list, but if you asked him about his personal views on some issue, you were promptly referred to one of his many essays for your answer. What happened next was utterly predictable. The text indeed answered your original question—but you found yourself with three or four new ones, and when you asked Sellars about them, he straightaway happily referred you to *another* three or four of his essays. The options quickly became clear: surrender immediately, or read them *all*. I have never regretted my own choice.

AN EXPLORATION OF SELLARS' PHILOSOPHY

A. Metaphilosophical Perspectives

"The aim of philosophizing," Sellars wrote in 1971, "is to become *reflectively* at home in the full complexity of the multi-dimensional conceptual system in terms of which we suffer, think, and act" (SK, 295). This image of the philosopher as a *reflective generalist* is a recurrent theme in Sellars' occasional observations on his own discipline or, perhaps more accurately, his own calling. Nine years earlier, he had put it this way:

The aim of philosophy, abstractly formulated, is to understand how things in the broadest possible sense of the term hang together in the broadest possible sense of the term. Under "things in the broadest possible sense" I include such radically different items as not only "cabbages and kings," but numbers and duties, possibilities and finger snaps, aesthetic experience and death. To achieve success in philosophy would be ... to "know one's way around" with respect to all these things, not in that unreflective way in which the centipede of the story knew its way around before it faced the question, "how do I walk?" but in that reflective way which means that no intellectual holds are barred. (PSIM, 37)

True to this vision of philosophy over a period of forty years, Sellars proceeded to make substantial and systematic contributions to metaphysics and epistemology, to moral philosophy and the theory of action, to philosophy of mind and philosophy of language, to philosophy of science, and always to the interpretation and appreciation of the discipline's great historical figures from Plato to Kant and beyond. One of the *leitmotifs* centripetally organizing all these systematic reflections was Sellars' standing conviction that scientific discourse, as he put it in 1956, is not "so to speak, a peninsular offshoot from the mainland of ordinary discourse" (EPM, 304), but rather "a continuation of a dimension of discourse which has been present in human discourse from the very beginning" in consequence of which there is a sense in which "the scientific picture of the world *replaces* the commonsense picture; a sense in which the scientific account of "what there is" *supersedes* the descriptive ontology of everyday life" (EPM, 302).

Sellars, in fact, saw contemporary philosophy as confronted

... not by one complex many-dimensional picture, the unity of which ... he must come to appreciate; but by *two* pictures of essentially the same order of complexity, each of which purports to be a complete picture of man-in-the-world, and which ... he must fuse into one vision. (PSIM, 40–1)

The first of these, the "*manifest image*", is, in first approximation, that conception of the world and the place of persons in it that has been the focal concern of the "perennial philosophy", from the great speculative systems of Plato and Aristotle to their humbler descendants in the Moorean-Austinian-Strawsonian dimensions of contemporary Anglo-American thought that emphasize "ordinary usage" and "common sense". The manifest image delineates "the framework in terms of which man came to be aware of himself as man-in-the-world" (PSIM, 42), and there is thus "an important sense in which the primary objects of the manifest image are *persons*" (PSIM, 46), beings who, *inter alia*, reflectively conceive of themselves *as* being in the world both as thinkers and as doers, as sentient perceivers and cognitive knowers *of* the world, and as agents capable of affecting it through deliberate and rational elective conducts.

The "*scientific image*", in contrast, is the complex projection of man-in-the-world on the human understanding still in the process of emerging from the fruits of *theoretical* reasoning, in particular, from the processes of postulational theory construction. Although this image is "*methodologically* dependent on the world of sophisticated common sense", Sellars argues,

... it purports to be a *complete* image, i.e., to define a framework which could be the *whole truth* about that which belongs to the image. Thus although methodologically a development *within* the manifest image, the scientific image presents itself as a *rival* image. From its point of view the manifest image on which it rests is an 'inadequate' but pragmatically useful likeness of a reality which first finds its adequate (in principle) likeness in the scientific image. (PSIM, 57)

Since, however, man is the being who *essentially* encounters himself in terms of the categories of the manifest image, competitive tension between the two images threatens to undermine the integrity of conceptions that, in an important sense, are constitutive of our very existence as persons. A leading challenge for contemporary philosophy consequently becomes to show how that tension can properly be resolved, not by asserting the exclusivity of one image or the other but by a "stereoscopic understanding" in which the two images come to be "fused" into a single *synoptic vision* of man-in-the-world. One way of understanding Sellars' philosophy is as both a fuller articulation of this confrontation of the images and the difficult and detailed working through of the philosophical agenda that it straightaway entails: that places be found within the sought synoptic image for the *intentional contents* of language and thought, for the *sensuous contents* of perception and imagination, and for the *normative dimensions* of knowledge and action.

B. Theories

Sellars' interpretation of the essential *epistemology* of natural science decisively departed from the received, Positivist, view according to which explanation was identified with derivation—singular matters of empirical fact being explained by deriving descriptions of them from ("inductive") empirical generalizations (along with appropriate statements of initial conditions), and these "empirical laws" in turn being explained by deriving them from theoretical postulates and correspondence rules. On the Positivist view, in consequence, *theories* (e.g., microtheories) explain observational matters of fact only *indirectly*, by implying the (observation-language) generalizations that explain them directly.

This "levels picture" of theories, Sellars proposed, was fundamentally misleading. Theories do not explain laws by entailing them. Rather, "theories explain laws by explaining why the objects of the domain in question obey the laws that they do to the extent that they do" (LT, 123).

[That is,] they explain why individual objects of various kinds and in various circumstances in the observation framework behave in those ways in which it has been inductively established that they do behave. Roughly, it is because a gas is … a cloud of molecules which are behaving in certain theoretically defined ways, that it obeys the *empirical* Boyle-Charles Law. (LT, 121)

This understanding of the epistomology of scientific inquiry is robustly realistic. On Sellars' view, stories that postulate "theoretical entities" are not merely manageable second-class surrogates for more complicated and unwieldy stories about entities that we have good, i.e., observational, reasons to believe actually exist. Theoretical entities, rather, are those entities we warrantedly believe

(margin note: D - N model of explanation *)*

to exist for good and sufficient *theoretical reasons*. The results of scientific inquiry, in fact, are ontologically definitive:

[In] the dimension of describing and explaining the world, science is the measure of all things, of what is that it is, and of what is not that it is not. (EPM, 173)

(Sellars' "*scientia mensura*".) Scientific theories, on this understanding, explanatorily "save the appearances" precisely by characterizing the reality *of which* the appearances *are* appearances.

Sellars' *metaphysical* perspectives have always been informed by the fundamental conviction that to be is to make a difference, more precisely, by the (essentially Platonic) idea that the distinguishing mark of real things is the power to act or be acted upon. The concrete reflection of this root conviction was a thoroughgoing *naturalism* that placed strong constraints, not only on the determinate project of achieving a synoptic fusion of the manifest and scientific images, but also on the potential reach of a traditional categorial ontology in general. On the former front, Sellars' naturalism implied the need for a synoptic story to find a place for mind without assigning an independent autonomous ontological status to *intentional entities* (or relations); on the latter, the unacceptability of any ontological view which conceived of *abstract entities* as real objects without offering an adequate account of their place within the causal order, broadly construed.

C. Meaning

Sellars' response to both of these naturalistic challenges was to develop a sophisticated theory of *conceptual roles*, concretely instantiated in the conducts of representers and transmissible by modes of cultural inheritance. The heart of this theory was a subtle understanding of the way in which linguistic conduct is rule-governed and its keystone an increasingly refined account of *meaning* as *functional classification*, more precisely, of the "meaning" idiom as, in the first instance, a context of *translation* in terms of which structurally distinct "natural-linguistic objects" (e.g., utterings or inscribings) are classified in terms of their roles or functions vis-à-vis the organized behavioral economies of families of speaking organisms. 'Means', in short, was to be interpreted as a specialized form of the copula, tailored to metalinguistic contexts, according to which the right side of the superficially relational form

_____ means ...

is properly understood as mentioning or exhibiting a linguistic item.

On Sellars' view, such special copulae and metalinguistic indicators develop out of a need to abstract from our parochial sign designs in order to classify items of different languages on the basis of functional criteria. In this project, ordinary quotation suffers from a systematic ambiguity regarding the criteria—structural (e.g., geometric, acoustic) or functional—according to which linguistic tokens are classifiable as belonging to this or that linguistic type. Accordingly, Sellars introduced a more straightforward device of two separate styles of quotation marks—star-quotes and dot-quotes—tied respectively to the structural and functional modes of sorting and individuating lexical items. Both star- and dot-quotes are *illustrating*, and thus *indexical*, devices, but dot-quotes are, in a sense, doubly so. For, whereas star-quotes form a common noun that is true of inscriptions (empirical structures) appropriately design-isomorphic to the token exhibited between them, dot-quotes form a common noun true of items in *any* language that play the role or do the job performed in *our* language by the token exhibited between them. In terms of this notational apparatus, then, such semantic claims as, for example,

> (1s)   (In German) 'rot' means *red*

and

> (2s)   (In German) 'Schnee ist weiss' means *snow is white*

can be more perspicuously expressed by

> (1*)   (In the German linguistic community) *rot*s are ·red·s

and

> (2*)   (In the German linguistic community) *Schnee ist weiss*s are ·snow is white·s

D. Categorial Ontology

Classical conceptualism had always exploited the parallels between semantic discourse and the categorial ontological idioms of Platonistic discourse ostensibly adverting to abstract entities. Thus, for example, corresponding to the semantic claims (1s) and (2s) are ontological claims on the model of

> (1a)   (The German word) 'rot' stands for (the property) *redness*

and

> (2a)   (The German sentence) 'Schnee ist weiss' expresses (the proposition) *that snow is white.*

Sellars, too, exploited these parallels, but, consistently with his commitment to naturalism, in precisely the opposite direction. Espousing a form of *linguistic nominalism* according to which

> ... the abstract entities which are the subject matter of the contemporary debate between platonistic and anti-platonistic philosophers—qualities, relations, classes, propositions, and the like—are linguistic entities. (AE, 229)

Sellars proposed to reconstruct (1a) and (2a) too as, in first approximation, the classificatory claims (1*) and (2*). Like Carnap, in other words, Sellars undertook to treat categorial ontological discourse as the classificatory discourse of a functional metalanguage, transposed into the "material mode of speech". Unlike Carnap, however, Sellars refused to (theoretically) *identify* the formally definable constructs of a "pure" syntax or semantics with the syntactical and semantical terms in everyday, pre-philosophical usage having corresponding extensions, arguing that such a facile interpretation of the relationship between "pure" and "descriptive" syntactic and semantic discourses seriously failed to do proper justice to the crucial *normative* aspects of the latter. Thus, while Sellars is prepared to reconstruct such categorial ontological notions as "universal", "individual", "kind", "quality", "proposition", and "fact" in terms of syntactic and semantic counterparts—e.g., 'predicate', 'singular term', 'common noun', 'monadic predicate', 'sentence', and 'true sentence'—he insists that such syntactical and semantical words functioning as such

... have a conceptual role which is no more reducible to [non-syntactical and] non-semantical roles than the role of prescriptive terms is reducible to non-prescriptive roles. ... [The] empirical (in the broad sense) character of statements in descriptive (historical) [syntax and] semantics does not entail that [syntactical and] semantical concepts, properly so called, are descriptive. (EAE, 459)

E. Thoughts

The categorial apparatus of abstract entities has traditionally been invoked to characterize and account for, not only semantical facts, but also, crucially, *mental* facts as well, paradigmatically recorded in claims including a verb of "propositional attitude" (e.g., 'believes', 'hopes', 'realizes', 'wishes').

Realists from the time of Plato on have claimed that facts such as these involve a mental "perception" of abstract entities, traditionally universals, more recently propositions as well. (EAE, 444)

As one would expect, at this point in the dialectic Sellars embraces a "*psychological nominalism*" correlative to his ontological "linguistic nominalism". The *leitmotif* of psychological nominalism is

... the denial of the claim, characteristic of the realist tradition, that a "perception" or "awareness" of abstract entities is the root mental ingredient of mental acts and dispositions. (EAE, 445)

Instead, like the proper account of the entities and categories of classical ontology, the proper account of the distinctive intentionality of thought is also to be drawn in terms of the forms and functions of natural linguistic items. The *positive* thesis correlative to psychological nominalism, consequently, is modeled by what Sellars came to call "*verbal behaviorism*".

According to VB [verbal behaviorism], thinking 'that-*p*,' where this means 'having the thought occur to one that-*p*,' has as its *primary* sense [an event of] *saying* 'p'; and a *secondary* sense in which it stands for a short term proximate propensity [disposition] to say 'p'. (MFC, 419)

The origins of Sellars' mature forms of verbal behaviorism lie in the revolutionary theses of his classic essay "Empiricism and the Philosophy of Mind", and, in particular, in his mythical story of our Rylean ancestors and the genius Jones. The story begins *in medias res* with humans who have mastered a "Rylean language", a sophisticated expressive system, including logical operators and subjunctive conditionals, whose fundamental descriptive vocabulary pertains to public spatio-temporal objects. This hypothetical Rylean language has been enriched by the fundamental resources of semantical discourse—enabling our ancestors to say of the verbal productions of their peers that they *mean* this or that, that they stand in various logical relations to one another, that they are true or false, and so on—but it lacks any resources for speaking of inner episodes, thoughts or experiences. In this milieu now appears the genius Jones.

> [In] the attempt to account for the fact that his fellow men behave intelligently not only when their conduct is threaded on a string of overt verbal episodes ... but also when no detectable verbal output is present, Jones develops a *theory* according to which overt utterances are but the culmination of a process which begins with certain inner episodes.
> ... [His] *model for these episodes* which initiate the events which culminate in overt verbal behaviour *is that of overt verbal behavior itself*. (EPM, 186)

Although the primary use of semantical terms remains the semantical characterization of overt verbal episodes, this Jonesean theory thus carries over the applicability of those semantical categories to its postulated inner episodes. i.e., to (occurrent) *thoughts*.

The point of the Jonesean myth is to suggest that the *epistemological* status of thoughts (*qua* inner episodes) vis-à-vis candid public verbal productions is most usefully understood as analogous to the epistemological status of, e.g., molecules vis-à-vis the public observable behavior of gases.

> [Thought] episodes are 'in' language-using animals as molecular impacts are 'in' gases, not as 'ghosts' are in 'machines'. (EPM, 187)

The import of this epistemic strategy becomes clear when we recognize that, although, *qua* acoustic disturbances, the items of the *model* for Jones's theory have a determinate intrinsic nature, the thought episodes postulated by that theory as covert states of persons are introduced by a purely *functional* analogy. The concept of an occurrent thought is not that of something encountered *propria persona* but rather that of a causally-mediating *logico-semantic role player*, whose determinate ontological character is so far left open.

> [The] fact that [thoughts] are not introduced as physiological entities does not preclude the possibility that at a later methodological stage they may, so to speak, 'turn out' to be such. Thus, there are many who would say that it is already reasonable to suppose that

these *thoughts* are to be 'identified' with complex events in the cerebral cortex ... (EPM, 187–8)

It follows, inter alia, that the manifest image's conception of persons as thinkers can fuse smoothly with the scientific image's conception of persons as complex material organisms having a determinate physiological and neurological structure. On Sellars' account, the concept of a thought is fundamentally the concept of a *functional* kind, and consequently no ontological tensions are generated by the identification within the scientific image of items belonging to that functional kind with states and episodes of an organism's central nervous system.

His conviction that what is fundamentally characteristic of semantic discourse is its ineliminable appeal to functional considerations, and his correlative pioneering analyses of the intentional categories of the mental in terms of epistemologically theoretical transpositions of the semantic categories of public language grant Sellars a definitive place in contemporary analytic philosophy of mind. As Dennett puts it,

Thus was contemporary *functionalism* in the philosophy of mind born, and the varieties of functionalism we have subsequently seen are in one way or another enabled, and directly or indirectly inspired, by what was left open in Sellars' initial proposal ... (MTE, 341)

F. Linguistic Roles

A perspicuous reconstruction of both categorial ontological and mental intentional discourses in terms of a semantic discourse conceived in terms of linguistic functions or roles is, of course, possible only if the notion of a linguistic item's having a role or function can itself be explicated without recourse to irreducibly Platonistic or mentalistic idioms. The exquisite care with which Sellars consequently proceeds to locate the normative conceptual order within the causal order and to interpret the modes of causality exercised by linguistic rules is one of the remarkable strengths of his philosophical system.

The key to Sellars' analysis of the normative dimension of language lies in his account of *pattern-governed behavior*. The general concept of pattern-governed behavior is, roughly,

... the concept of behavior which exhibits a pattern, not because it is brought about by the intention that it exhibit this pattern, but because the propensity to emit behavior of the pattern has been selectively reinforced, and the propensity to emit behavior which does not conform to this pattern selectively extinguished. (MFC, 423)

Pattern-governed behavior characteristic of a species—e.g., the dance of the bees—can, of course, arise from processes of natural selection on an evolutionary time scale. Crucially, however, pattern-governed behavior can be developed in individuals, "trainees", by deliberate and purposive selection on the part of other individuals, the trainers.

Sellars distinguishes in this connection between two sorts of linguistic rules: "rules of action" and "rules of criticism". Rules of action are *ought-to-do*'s—e.g., "*Ceteris paribus*, one ought to say such and such if in circumstances C"—and as such they can be efficacious in guiding linguistic activity only to the extent that their subjects already possess the relevant concepts, e.g., concepts of "saying such-and-such", of "being in circumstances C", and, indeed, of obeying a rule (i.e., doing something *because* it is enjoined by a rule). Rules of criticism, in contrast, are *ought-to-be*'s—e.g., "Westminster clock chimes ought to strike on the quarter hour" (LTC, 95)—whose subjects, although their performances may be *appraised* according to such rules, need not themselves have the concept of a rule nor, indeed, any concepts at all. Thus a trainer can be construed as reasoning

Patterned-behavior of such and such a kind *ought to be* exhibited by trainees, hence we, the trainers, *ought to do* this and that, as likely to bring it about that it *is* exhibited. (MFC, 423)

And, in consequence of the conducts of trainers under the guidance of such rules of action, the behavior of a language-learner can come to *conform* to the relevant rules of criticism without his grasping them, in any other sense, himself. "Trainees conform to *ought-to-be*'s because trainers obey corresponding *ought-to-do*'s" (MFC, 423).

[The] members of a linguistic community are *first* language *learners* and only potentially 'people', but *subsequently* language *teachers* possessed of the rich conceptual framework this implies. They start out being the *subject matter* of the ought-to-be's and graduate to the status of agent subjects of the ought-to-do's. (LTC, 100)

Essential to *language* are three types of pattern-governed behavior:

(1)   Language Entry Transitions: The speaker responds to objects in perceptual situations, and in certain states of himself, with appropriate linguistic activity.
(2)   Intra-linguistic Moves: The speaker's linguistic conceptual episodes tend to occur in patterns of valid inference (theoretical and practical), and tend not to occur in patterns which violate logical principles.
(3)   Language Departure Transitions: The speaker responds to such linguistic conceptual episodes as 'I will now raise my hand' with an upward motion of the hand, etc. (MFC, 423–4)

Although these transitions—respectively the essential elements of perceptual takings, inferences, and volitions—are acts, they are not *actions*. They do not become deliberate obeyings of ought-to-do's but are acquired as and *remain* pattern-governed activities. Nevertheless, these linguistic "non-actions" are what underlie and make possible the domain of actions proper, not only non-linguistic actions, but linguistic actions as well. For

... the trainee acquires not only the repertoire of pattern-governed linguistic behavior which is language about non-linguistic items, but also that extended repertoire which is language about linguistic as well as non-linguistic items. He is able to classify items in linguistic kinds, and to engage in theoretical and practical reasoning about his linguistic behavior. (MFC, 425)

Linguistic roles or functions, finally, are individuated in terms of the structure of positive and negative uniformities generated in the natural order by these pattern-governed activities of perception, inference (both formal and material), and volition. Sameness of function, role, or office amounts to sameness of place in the complex relational structure ("logical space") generated by conducts that are in these ways causally shaped by systems of espoused linguistic norms. It follows, inter alia, that Sellars' functional conception of semantics neither presupposes nor unavoidably leads back into the domains of abstract ontological or intentional mental discourse which he proposes to elucidate by its means.

G. The Myth of the Given

The proposal to illuminate the *epistemic* status of mental concepts by an appeal to the contrast between theoretical and non-theoretical discourse, in turn, makes sense only against the background of another central element of Sellars' philosophical thought which, although it is perhaps the philosophical view most frequently associated with his name, has so far gone unremarked, his thoroughgoing and general critique of the "Myth of the Given". The philosophical framework of givenness historically takes on many guises, of which classical sense-datum theory is but one. More generally, the very idea that empirical knowledge rests on a foundation at all, of *whatever* kind, is a manifestation of the Myth of the Given, as is, significantly, the assumption that the "privacy" of the mental and one's "privileged access" to one's own mental states are primitive features of experience, logically and epistemologically prior to all intersubjective concepts pertaining to inner episodes.

On the contrary, in the case of inner episodes, Sellars argues, what begins as a language with a purely theoretical use can *acquire* a first-person reporting role. For it can turn out to be possible to train people, in essence by a process of operant conditioning, to have "privileged access" to some of their inner episodes, e.g., to respond directly and non-inferentially to the occurrence of one thought with another (meta-) thought to the effect that one is thinking it. It is a special virtue of the Jonesean story that it shows how the essential intersubjectivity of language can be reconciled with the "privacy" of inner episodes, i.e.,

... that it helps us understand that concepts pertaining to such inner episodes as thoughts are primarily and essentially *inter-subjective*, as inter-subjective as the concept of a positron, and that the [first-person] reporting role of these concepts ... constitutes a dimension of [their] use ... which is *built on* and *presupposes* this inter-subjective status. (EPM, 189)

This latter conclusion is nothing but the particularization to "avowals" of a family of *general* considerations that Sellars mobilizes against the Myth of the

Given. At the heart of these considerations is his articulate recognition of the irreducibly normative character of epistemic discourse.

The essential point is that in characterizing an episode or a state as that of *knowing*, we are not giving an empirical description of that episode or state, we are placing it in the logical space of reasons, of justifying and being able to justify what one says. (EPM, 169)

Once it is acknowledged that the senses *per se* grasp no facts, that all knowledge that something is such-and-so (all "subsumption of particulars under universals") presupposes learning, concept formation, and even symbolic representation, it follows that

... instead of coming to have a concept of something because we have noticed that sort of thing, to have the ability to notice a sort of thing is already to have the concept of that sort of thing, and cannot account for it. (EPM, 176)

H. Sensations

Sellars follows Kant in rejecting the Cartesian picture of a sensory-cognitive continuum. The "of-ness" of sensations—e.g., a sensation's being *of a red triangle* or *of a sharp shooting pain*—he insists, is not the intentional "of-ness" ("aboutness") of thoughts.

The "rawness" of "raw feels" is their non-conceptual character. The sense in which "raw feels" are "of something" is not to be assimilated to the intentionality of thoughts. (IAMBP, 376)

Consequently, while his *epistemological* views regarding sensory inner episodes are essentially parallel to his treatment of the epistemology of occurrent thoughts, Sellars' account of the *ontology* of sensations diverges from his semantic and functionalist account of thoughts in important respects.

   Like his account of thoughts, Sellars' theory of sensations begins with a strategic appeal to the unique epistemic status of postulated theoretical entities. In a final episode of the Jonesean myth, as elements of an explanatory account of the occurrence in various circumstances of perceptual cognitions, having determinate *semantic* contents,

... the hero ... postulates a class of inner—theoretical—episodes which he calls, say, *impressions*, and which are the end results of the impingement of physical objects and processes on various parts of the body ... (EPM,191)

This time, however, the *model* for Jones's theory is not that of functionally-individuated families of sentences, but instead

... the model is the idea of a domain of 'inner replicas' which, when brought about in standard conditions share the perceptible characteristics of their physical sources. (EPM,191)

Here Sellars is careful to stress, first, that the leading idea of the model is the occurrence 'in' perceivers of "replicas" *per se*, not of *perceivings* of "replicas" (which would mistakenly inject into the account of impressions the intentionality of thought), and, second, that although the entities of the *model* are particulars, the entities introduced by the *theory* are not particulars but *states* of a perceiving subject. Thus, although talk of the "of-ness" of sensations, like that of the "of-ness" of thoughts, is, on Sellars' view, fundamentally classificatory, the classification at issue is based not on a functional (logical, semantic) analogy but rather on analogies that are (although, in the first instance, extrinsic and causal) ultimately *intrinsic* and *contentive*.

In the first instance, the concept of a person's *having an of-a-red-triangle sensation* (a parsing that highlights the classificatory role of "of-ness"), or, even more perspicuously (reflecting the status of 'sensation' as a "verbal noun"), of her *sensing [red triangle]ₛly*, is the concept of her being in the sort of state that is brought about in normal perceivers in standard conditions by the action of red triangular objects on the eyes. The point of the model of "inner replicas", however, is to insist that such states can discharge their *explanatory* jobs in relation to cognitive perceptual takings (and especially non-veridical perceptual judgments) only if they are conceived as having themselves determinate *intrinsic* characters and, in particular, as resembling and differing from other sensory states—e.g., *sensing [green triangular]ₛly, sensing [red square]ₛly*, etc.—in a manner *formally* analogous to the way in which objects of the "replica" *model*—e.g., red and triangular, green and triangular, and red and square "wafers"—are conceived to resemble and differ from one another.

If that were the end of Sellars' ontological story regarding sensations, matters would be complicated enough. But Sellars proceeds to develop this core account in two different directions, in consequence of which his full theory of sensations has emerged as being one of the most difficult and controversial aspects of his philosophy.

The *first* line of development turns on the conclusion that (within the manifest image) the fundamental *concept* pertaining to color is that of a kind of *stuff*. Our "ur-concept" of red, for example, "has the form of a mass term, the predicative concept *is red* having the form *is an expanse of red*" (CL, I, 46). It is the concept of a quantum of red in space, an expanse or volume consisting of red. The concept is *basic* in the sense that there is "no ... determinate category prior to the concept of red as a physical stuff, as a matter for individuated physical things" (CL, I, 84). When the dialectical pressures that lead us to distinguish *seeing* from (merely) *ostensibly seeing* generate worries about the ontological status of the redness which one ostensibly sees when it is *not* a constituent redness of a physical object, we cannot suppose that a categorial alternative is available which can simply be "read off" from an introspective scrutiny of color quanta. The idea that, if a person is directly aware of an item which has a certain categorial

status, then he is aware of it *as* having that categorial status, argues Sellars, is only
another form of the Myth of the Given.

All that is available is such transcendentals as *actual, something* and *somehow*. The red is
something actual which is *somehow* a portion of red stuff, *somehow* the sort of item which
is suited to be part of the content, of a physical object, but which, … is not, in point of
fact, a portion of physical stuff. (CL, I, 90)

In this situation, according to Sellars, it becomes the job of *analogical* thinking
to construct new categorial forms of concept pertaining to color.

It does this by forming a proto-theory in which items which satisfy an axiomatics of shape
and color play roles which promise to account for the fact in question. (CL, I, 93)

The *first* complication of Sellars' theory of sensation results from his conviction
that, in the case of sensations, Jones's theory takes this *interpretive* form. It does
not introduce new domains of entities, but rather new forms of concepts.

[The] theory of sense impressions does not *introduce*, for example, cubical volumes of
pink. It reinterprets the *categorial status* of the cubical volumes of pink of which we are
perceptually aware. Conceived in the manifest image as, in standard cases, *constituents*
of physical objects and in abnormal cases, as somehow 'unreal' or 'illusory', they are
recategorized as sensory states of the perceiver and assigned various explanatory roles in
the theory of perception. (CL, III, 44)

The relevant intrinsic characteristic of a state of, e.g., *sensing pink$_S$ly*

… is 'analogous' to the pinkness of a manifest pink ice cube, not by being a *different
quality* which is in some respects analogous to pinkness … , but by being the same
'content' in a different categorial 'form'. (CL, III, 47)

The crux of the Jonesean theory, in other words, is the thesis that the very color
quanta of which we are perceptually aware as being in space are *instead* actually
states of persons-qua-perceivers. It follows that, already within the manifest
image, the ontological status ultimately accorded to sensory "content qualia" is,
in fact, *incompatible* with their being instantiated in physical space.

[The] *esse* of cubes of pink is *percipi* or, to use a less ambiguous term, *sentiri*. Of course,
.. we are not perceptually aware of cubes of pink *as* states of ourselves, thought that is in
point of fact what they are. (CL, III, 66)

The *second* complication of Sellars' theory of sensations arises from the further
conclusion that it is *this* manifest image conception of sensory contents as *states of
perceivers* which must ultimately be synoptically "fused" with the scientific image,
and that the latter's commitment to the idea that those perceivers themselves are
complex systems of micro-physical particles constitutes a barrier to doing so in
any straightforward way.

On the one hand, claims Sellars, the states of persons (*qua* single logical
subjects) that are the final ontological locus of sensory contents within the

manifest image formally preserve the *ultimate homogeneity* of those contents as originally categorially conceived (i.e., as space-filling stuffs), and no (defined) states of a *system* or *multiplicity* of logical subjects could continue to do so. On the other hand, since only a further categorial *re-interpretation* of those sensory states as *actual* items within the scientific image properly respects the demands of an adequate sensory phenomenology, we cannot simply adopt a "reductive materialist" view according to which

... what really goes on when a person senses a-cube-of-pinkly consists in [a certain] system of micro-physical particles being in a complex physical-2 state (CL, III, 79)

where "physical-2" states are definable in terms of theoretical predicates necessary and sufficient to describe *non-living* matter. (To be "physical-1", in contrast, is simply to belong in the space-time network.) For such reductive materialism, by proposing to identify manifest image and scientific image *circumstances* or *states-of-affairs*, amounts to the rejection of the idea that a (Jonesean-theoretical) state of, e.g., sensing a-cube-of-pinkly is *itself* something actual in *any* categorial guise.

Sellars concludes, therefore, that sensory contents can be synoptically integrated into the scientific image only after both they and the currently-fundamental micro-physical particulars of that image as well undergo yet another categorial transposition. What is required is a categorially monistic ontology whose fundamental entities are all *"absolute processes"*. Once perceivers themselves have been reconceived as systems or "harmonies" of absolute processes, the way would be cleared for a unitary "image" which could achieve global explanatory closure by assigning the conceptual descendents of mechanistic parameters and the conceptual descendents of sensory contents *essentially correlative* roles in the nomologicals that ultimately were genuinely explanatory of sensory consciousness. Sensings *qua* absolute processes would then be *physical*

... not only in the weak sense of not being mental (i.e., conceptual), for they lack intentionality, but in the richer sense of playing a genuine causal role in the behavior of sentient organisms. They would, as I have used the terms, be physical-1 but not physical-2. Not being epiphenomenal, they would conform to a basic metaphysical intuition: to be is to make a difference. (CL, III, 126)

I. Justification

Consonant with his thoroughgoing rejection of the Myth of the Given, Sellars interprets a person's first-person epistemic authority with respect to the sensory aspects of his or her own experience as built on and presupposing an intersubjective status for sensory concepts *per se*. Correlatively, Sellars rejects the idea that sensory consciousness supplies a form of knowledge of empirical facts that (1) is immediate (i.e., non-inferential); (2) presupposes no knowledge of other matters of fact, particular or general; and (3) constitutes the ultimate court of appeals for all factual claims. (EPM,164) Thus, although he is prepared to agree that a person can *directly know* an empirical fact in a sense which implies that he has not inferred what he justifiedly believes from other propositions, Sellars insists that it does not follow that the belief constituting such direct knowledge must somehow be *self*-justifying, *self*-warranting, or *self*-authenticating. Rather,

> ... to say that someone directly knows that-*p* is to say that his right to the conviction that-*p* essentially involves the fact that the idea [belief] that-*p* occurred to the knower in a specific way. I shall call this kind of credibility 'trans-level credibility', and [speak of] the inference schema ... to which it refers, as trans-level inference. (P, 88)

The *epistemic authority* of a non-inferential perceptual belief, proposes Sellars, can be traced to the fact that, in the course of learning perceptual language, the believer has acquired propensities for the reliable use of the relevant concepts in perceptual situations. What is more, in order to have *full* mastery of perceptual language, a person must himself know what is involved in learning to use perceptual sentences reliably in perceptual contexts. Thus, when someone, for example, sees there to be a red apple in front of him—a perceptual taking which can be modeled according to the conventions of Sellars' "Verbal Behaviorism" by a candid, spontaneous thinking-out-loud of the form: "Lo! Here is a red apple"—then,

> ... given that he has learned how to use the relevant words in perceptual situations, he is justified in reasoning as follows:

> > I just thought-out-loud 'Lo! Here is a red apple' (no countervailing conditions obtain); So, there is good reason to believe that there is a red apple in front of me. (SK, 341–2)

This reasoning does *not* have the original perceptual judgment as its conclusion, but is rather an inference from the character and context of the original non-inferential experience to the existence of a good reason for accepting it as veridical. What gives this justificatory argument its peculiar "trans-level" character, and, correlatively, conveys the impression that the spontaneous non-inferential belief thereby warranted is *self*-justifying, is the fact that its main premiss asserts the occurrence of precisely that belief in a specific context.

It is central to Sellars' thoroughgoingly holistic view of cognition and warrant that the reasonableness of accepting even *first* principles is a matter of the availability of good arguments warranting their acceptance. What is definitive of *first* principles, FP, is the *un*availability of sound reasonings in which they are derived from still more basic premises, thus of arguments of the form:

(A1)   ... ...
          ... ...
          ... ...
          _____

Therefore, FP

Here, too, Sellars invokes the notion of a "trans-level" inference. The unavailability of sound reasonings of the form (A1), he proposes, is entirely compatible with the existence of good arguments of the form:

(A2)   ... ...
          ... ...
          ... ...
          _____

Therefore, *it is reasonable to accept* FP

the conclusion of which is not FP itself, but in whose conclusion the principle FP is, in essence, *mentioned*.

Since accepting principles is something that persons *do*, observes Sellars, the conclusion of (A2), in turn, amounts to the claim that a particular course of *epistemic conduct* can be supported by adequate reasons and thus suggests the existence of yet another argument, a sound *practical* argument whose conclusion expresses an *intention* to engage in just such conduct, thus:

(A3)   I shall achieve desirable epistemic end E
          Achieving E implies accepting principles of kind K
          The principle FP is of kind K
          _____

Therefore, I shall accept FP

J. Induction

It is at this point that we can finally achieve closure on Sellars' philosophy of science. On Sellars' view, the forms of justificatory reasoning governing the acceptance of lawlike generalizations (both universal and statistical) and theoretical systems alike are all at base such patterns of practical inference. Thus Sellars sees adopting a systematic theoretical framework as ultimately justified by an appeal to the epistemic end of "being able to give non-trivial explanatory accounts of established laws" (IV, 384). And he sees the adopting of statistical nomologicals which project the observed frequency of a property in a class (including the special case in which this frequency $= 1$) to unobserved finite samples of the class, in turn, as ultimately justified by the epistemic end of

... being able to draw inferences concerning the composition with respect to a given property Y of unexamined finite samples ... of a kind, X, in a way which also provides an explanatory account of the composition with respect to Y of the total examined sample, K, of X. (IV, 392)

It is crucial to Sellars' account that these epistemic *ends* controlling the acceptance of new laws and theories are concerned with

... the realizing of a logically necessary condition of being in the framework of explanation and prediction, i.e., being able to draw inferences concerning the unknown and give explanatory accounts of the known. (IV, 397)

Since, on his view, inductive reasoning does not need to be *vindicated*, i.e., shown to be truth-preserving, but is rather itself fundamentally a form of *vindication*, i.e., (deductive) practical reasoning justifying our engaging in determinate (epistemic) conducts, the ends-in-view to which it appeals must be the sort of things that can be *known* to obtain or be realized. The end of being in possession of laws and principles that enable one to draw predictive inferences and to produce explanatory accounts satisfies this practical constraint; such Reichenbachian ends-in-view as being in possession of limit-frequency statements which are within a certain degree of approximation of the truth, where such limits exist, do not.

K. Practical Action

The challenge of integrating *actions*, that is, conducts informed by practical thinkings, into the synoptic fusion of the manifest and scientific images is not fundamentally an ontological challenge. From the ontological point of view, intentions and volitions are simply species of occurrent thinkings, although, from the functional point of view, they are thoughts of a special kind. They are *practical* cognitions, whose unique functional role within the total cognitive and behavioral economy of persons is thus to be understood in terms of their special relationships to conducts, analogously to the manner in which the role of cognitions in perceptual judgments is understood in terms of their status as non-inferential responses to sensations.

Sellars signals the special conduct-structuring role of practical cognitions by a contrived use of the auxiliary verb '*shall*' as an operator on sentential thinkings. Categorical *intendings* are time-determinate first-person future-tensed practical thinkings of the form:

(IT)   Shall(I will do X at t).

Willings (volitions, "acts of will") are special cases of such intendings in which the time determination becomes the indexical present:

(VT)   Shall(I will *now* do X).

On Sellars' view, such practical thinkings mediate between reasoning (delib-eration) and conduct (behavior). They relate to behavior by being caught up in a network of acquired causal propensities which guarantee, roughly, that intendings of the form (IT) regularly give rise, at time t, to volitions of the form (VT), which, in turn, barring paralysis and the like, regularly give rise, then and there, to bodily movements that *are* (further circumstances being appropriate) the initial stages of a doing of X. And they relate to deliberation according to a single principle which unites practical and theoretical reasoning:

If p implies q, then Shall(p) implies Shall(q).

The manifest image's conception of an intention or a volition, in other words, is once again the functional conception of a causally-mediating logico-semantic role player, *not* the concept of something with a determinate intrinsic character given *propria persona*. The ontological accomodation of practical thinkings within the scientific image can consequently proceed along the lines already sketched for cognitive thought in general.

But such ontological accomodation cannot be the end of the story here. Taking seriously the idea that the scientific image purports to be a *complete* image of man-in-the-world and a candidate ultimately to *replace* the manifest image requires that the categories pertaining to persons reappear within the sought synoptic fusion *as such*. The question becomes, in other words, whether we can perform

... the task of showing that categories pertaining to man as a *person* who finds himself confronted by standards (ethical, logical, etc.) which often conflict with his desires and impulses, and to which he may or may not conform, can be reconciled with the idea that man is what science says he is. (PSIM, 38)

On Sellars' view, the concept of a person is irredeemably social. To think of an entity as a person is essentially to think of it as actually or potentially a member of a *community*, "an embracing group each member of which thinks of itself as a member of the group" (PSIM, 39).

It is the most general common *intentions* of a community that fundamentally define the structure of *norms* and *values* in terms of which the conducts of its members come to be appraised as "correct" or "incorrect" or "right" or "wrong".

Roughly, to value from a moral point of view is to value *as a member of the relevant community* ... (S&M, 220)

Categorical *'ought'*s are categorically valid intersubjective intentions that anyone in a certain kind of circumstance do (or refrain from) a certain kind of action.

It follows that to recognize a featherless biped or dolphin or Martian as a person requires that one think thoughts of the form 'We (one) shall do (or abstain from doing) actions of kind A in circumstances of kind C.' To think thoughts of this kind is not to *classify* or *explain*, but to *rehearse an intention*.

Thus the conceptual framework of persons is the framework in which we think of one another as sharing the community intentions which provide the ambience of principles and standards (above all, those which make meaningful discourse and rationality itself possible) within which we live our own individual lives. (PSIM, 39–40)

Within the manifest image, the framework of *thoughts* is founded on a series of functional analogies, ontological promissory notes for which we can readily imagine an emerging scientific understanding progressively supplying structural (e.g., neurophysiological) cash. The accommodation of the manifest image's *sensory contents* within a synoptic fusion, on the other hand, requires the conceptual transposition of some of its ontologically basic entities into new categorial forms enabling their integration with the explanatory nomologicals of a hitherto purely mechanistic scientific image. Unlike the frameworks of thoughts and sensations, however, Sellars argues, the conceptual framework of *persons* as such "is not something that needs to be *reconciled* with the scientific image, but rather something to be *joined* to it" (PSIM, 40). To achieve a genuinely synoptic vision of man-in-the-world, we need to *enrich* the scientific image

> ... *not* with more [or different] ways of saying what is the case, but with the language of community and individual intentions, so that by construing the actions we intend to do and the circumstances in which we intend to do them in scientific terms, we *directly* relate the world as conceived by scientific theory to our purposes, and make it *our* world and no longer an alien appendage to the world in which we do our living. (PSIM, 40)

A CONCLUDING REMARK

The scope and depth of Sellars' philosophical vision far exceeds what any such summary encounter can possibly provide. Lengthy though my own explorations here have been, there remains much of great value in Sellars' work that has nevertheless gone unmentioned—inter alia, his significant contributions to ethical theory and his masterful interpretations of the work of many of the discipline's great historical figures, not as academic museum exhibits, but always and characteristically from the standpoint of his own systematic work, as active contributors to a continuing and contemporary philosophical dialectic. Most unfortunately of all, however, it belongs to the essential nature of such a summary that it presents the *what* of Sellars' philosophical views and theses in abstraction from their *why*, i.e., in abstraction from the extraordinarily powerful, subtle, and sophisticated dialectical structure of evidence and argumentation with which he *supports* his substantive claims and conclusions. It is consequently my hope that this *Nachruf* will at the same time serve as an *Aufruf* to a wider philosophical community to dedicate to the work of Wilfrid Sellars the detailed and penetrating intellectual engagement that it so richly deserves.

GENERAL BIBLIOGRAPHY

Works by Wilfrid Sellars

Pure Pragmatics and Possible Worlds—The Early Essays of Wilfrid Sellars [PPPW], ed. Jeffrey F. Sicha (Ridgeview Publishing Co; Reseda, CA, 1980). [Also contains a long introductory essay by Sicha and an extensive bibliography of Sellars' work through 1979.]

Science, Perception and Reality [SPR] (Routledge & Kegan Paul Ltd; London, and The Humanities Press; New York, 1963).

Philosophical Perspectives [PP] (Charles C. Thomas; Springfield, IL, 1967); repr. in two volumes, *Philosophical Perspectives: History of Philosophy* and *Philosophical Perspectives: Metaphysics and Epistemology* (Ridgeview Publishing Co.; Reseda, CA; 1977).

Science and Metaphysics: Variations on Kantian Themes [S&M] (Routledge & Kegan Paul Ltd; London, and The Humanities Press; New York, 1968). [The 1966 John Locke Lectures.]

Essays in Philosophy and Its History [EPH] (D. Reidel Publishing Co.; Dordrecht, Holland, 1975).

Naturalism and Ontology [N&O] (Ridgeview Publishing Co.; Reseda, CA, 1979). [An expanded version of the 1974 John Dewey Lectures.]

The Metaphysics of Epistemology, Lectures by Wilfrid Sellars, ed. Pedro Amaral (Ridgeview Publishing Co.; Reseda, CA, 1989). [Also contains a complete bibliography of Sellars' published work through 1989.]

Major Critical Studies

Castañeda, H-N., ed. *Action, Knowledge, and Reality* (Bobbs-Merrill; Indianapolis, IN, 1975). [Also contains an extensive bibliography of Sellars' work through 1974, Sellars' intellectual autobiography, and 'The Structure of Knowledge' (see below).]

Delaney, C.F., Loux, Michael J., Gutting, Gary, and Solomon, W. David, *The Synoptic Vision: Essays on the Philosophy of Wilfrid Sellars* (University of Notre Dame Press; Notre Dame. IN, 1977). [Also contains an extensive bibliography.]

Pitt, Joseph C., ed., *The Philosophy of Wilfrid Sellars: Queries and Extensions* (D. Reidel Publishing Co.; Dordrecht, Holland, 1978). [Revised proceedings of a workshop on the Philosophy of Wilfrid Sellars held at Virginia Polytechnic Institute and State University in Blacksburg, VA, in Nov. 1976.]

Pitt, Joseph C., *Pictures, Images, and Conceptual Change: An Analysis of Wilfrid Sellars' Philosophy of Science* (D. Reidel Publishing Co.; Dordrecht, Holland, 1981).

Noûs, 7/2 (1973). [Special issue devoted to the philosophy of Wilfrid Sellars.]

Monist, 65/3 (1982). [Issue devoted to the philosophy of Wilfrid Sellars.]

Philosophical Studies, 54/2 (1988). [Revised proceedings of a colloquium on Sellars' philosophy held in Oct. 1987 at the University of Pittsburgh's Center for Philosophy of Science.]

REFERENCES

Dennett, Daniel C. [MTE], 'Mid-Term Examination: Compare and Contrast', in *The Intentional Stance* (Bradford Books, The MIT Press; Cambridge, MA; 1987), 339–50.

Sellars, Wilfrid [AE], 'Abstract Entities', *Review of Metaphysics*, 16 (1983); repr. in [PP], pp. 229–69.

_____ [CL], The Carus Lectures for 1977–78, published in *Monist* 64/1 (1981). (Citations by lecture and numbered paragraph.)

_____ [EAE], 'Empiricism and Abstract Entities', in *The Philosophy of Rudolph Carnap*, ed. P.A. Schilpp (Open Court; LaSalle, IL; 1963); repr. in [EPH], pp. 245–86.

_____ [EPM], 'Empiricism and the Philosophy of Mind', in *The Foundations of Science and the Concepts of Psychology and Psychoanalysis*, Minnesota Studies in the Philosophy of Science, vol. I, ed. H. Feigl and M. Scriven (University of Minnesota Press; Minneapolis, MN; 1956); repr. in [SPR], 127–96.

_____ [IAMBP], 'The Identity Approach to the Mind-Body Problem', *Review of Metaphysics*, 18 (1965); repr. in [PP], 370–88.

_____ [IV], 'Induction as Vindication', *Philosophy of Science*, 31 (1964); repr. in [EPH], 367–416.

Sellars, Wilfrid [LT], 'The Language of Theories', in *Current Issues in the Philosophy of Science*, ed. H. Feigl and G. Maxwell (Henry Holt, Rhinehart and Winston; New York, NY; 1961); repr. in [SPR], 106–26.

――― [LTC], 'Language as Thought and Communication', *Philosophy and Phenomenological Research*, **29** (1969); repr. in [EPH], 93–117.

――― [MFC], 'Meaning as Functional Classification', *Synthese*, **27** (1974) 417–37.

――― [P], 'Phenomenalism', in [SPR], 60–105.

――― [PSIM], 'Philosophy and the Scientific Image of Man', in *Frontiers of Science and Philosophy*, ed. Robert Colodny (University of Pittsburgh Press; Pittsburgh, PA; 1962); repr. in [SPR], 1–40.

――― [SK], 'The Structure of Knowledge', The Matchette Foundation Lectures for 1971, published in Castañeda, ed., *Action, Knowledge, and Reality* (see above).

2

Sellars and Quine: Compare and Contrast

W. V. O. Quine and Wilfrid Sellars are arguably the most important and influential American philosophers of the second half of the twentieth century. The publication of Quine's "Two Dogmas of Empiricism" in 1951[1] and Sellars' "Empiricism and the Philosophy of Mind" in 1956[2] were watershed events that significantly shaped the subsequent course of philosophical inquiry. In certain respects, these two seminal essays have much in common. Each is structured around a central negative thesis—respectively, that the received distinction between analytic and synthetic statements is ill-founded and that the received notion of empirical givenness is a myth—and each reaches a holistic conclusion. Thus Quine argues that "our statements about the external world face the tribunal of sense experience not individually but only as a corporate body" (TDE, 38), and Sellars, that "the metaphor of 'foundation' is misleading in that it keeps us from seeing that if there is a logical dimension in which other empirical propositions rest on observation reports, there is another logical dimension in which the latter rest on the former" (EPM §38, 170).[3]

Quine's work initially evoked a more substantial discussion than Sellars', and, some fifty years later, this continues to be the case. A topic search of the *Philosopher's Index*, for example, yielded 31 entries for 'Sellars' during the period 1999–2005, and 168 entries for 'Quine'. But this disparity admits of various explanations, and I will want to suggest that it is by no means indicative of the likely lasting philosophical influence of these two thinkers. For, despite the noted similarities of their seminal essays, the differences between them are both profound and crucial. I shall begin by mentioning three such differences of increasing significance.

To begin with, Sellars is notoriously difficult to read. True to his conception of a philosopher as a reflective generalist who aims to "understand how things in the broadest possible sense of the term hang together in the broadest possible

---

[1] Originally appearing in *Philosophical Review*, 60 (1951), 20–43. Cited henceforth as 'TDE'.

[2] Originally appearing in 1956, in vol. I of the *Minnesota Studies in the Philosophy of Science*. Cited henceforth as 'EPM' from the canonical version appearing in Sellars' *Science, Perception and Reality* (SPR) (Ridgeview Publishing Co.; Atascadero, CA: 1963, 1991), 127–96.

[3] With a slightly different emphasis: "For empirical knowledge, like its sophisticated extension, science, is rational, not because it has a *foundation* but because it is a self-correcting enterprise which can put *any* claim in jeopardy, though not *all* at once" (EPM §38, 170).

sense of the term" (PSIM, 37),[4] his writing is dialectical and multi-layered. Grasping the 'what's and 'why's of a Sellarsian text is normally a challenging task, making substantial demands on a reader's attention, time, and patience. Quine, in contrast, is a gifted prose stylist with an exceptional talent for turning a memorable phrase. His texts are consequently not only often enjoyable to read but also convey the impression of being comparatively easy to access—an impression that sometimes misleads, however, since there is a standing risk that the smooth flow of Quine's writing will carry a reader inattentively past important nuances and even lacunae in his reasoning.

A second observation, not unrelated to the first, is that Quine is largely an a-historical philosopher. His retrospective vision rarely extends beyond Frege, and his working understanding of philosophical problems is fundamentally shaped by his proximate colleagues and adversaries, C. I. Lewis and, especially, Rudolf Carnap. His conceptual armamentarium is correlatively austere, drawing heavily from mathematical logic and empirical psychology. In contrast, the whole history of philosophy is the medium within which Sellars' dialectics live and move. He regularly situates his own work against the background of what he calls the "perennial philosophy", and his conception of philosophical problems is correspondingly multi-perspectival and evolutionary, decisively shaped by an understanding of his historical predecessors from Plato and Aristotle through Wittgenstein and H. H. Price. Critical expositions of their views characteristically become the *lingua franca* within which he presents and defends his own.

Most significantly, however, whereas Sellars consistently aims to be a *constructive* philosopher, Quine's work always remains fundamentally critical. Already in EPM, Sellars sketched out the rudiments of an internalist normative epistemology, a role-classificatory account of meaning, a functionalist theory of thoughts, a postulational account of sensory content, a realist understanding of theoretical posits, and a non-Cartesian view of first-person privileged access. He famously saw contemporary philosophy as still struggling with the problematic of modernism, confronted by two "images"—the "manifest" and the "scientific"—which needed to be "fused" into a unified "synoptic vision" of persons in the world.

Quine's rejection of the received analytic-synthetic distinction, on the other hand, is only the first in a long series of denials. His philosophical message characteristically has the form: "We can do without ... ", and the list of traditional notions that he argues we can and should do without is a long one, including universals, propositions, intentions, *de re* modalities, meanings, synonymy, determinate reference, categorial ontology, and normative epistemology. His explicit paradigm of a philosophical achievement is the eliminative analysis of ordered pairs in terms of unordered sets. If we have the latter, we can do our

---

[4] 'Philosophy and the Scientific Image of Man' (PSIM), in Robert Colodny (ed.), *Frontiers of Science and Philosophy*, (University of Pittsburgh Press; Pittsburgh, PA; 1962); repr. in [SPR], pp. 1–40. Citations to the latter.

mathematics without the former. And as Quine himself demonstrated, if carried through with sufficient resolve, eliminative analyses in this spirit can be pushed to the neo-Pythagorean conclusion that such sets are all the ontology we need, not just for mathematics, but for natural science as well.

The differences between the two philosophers stands out in sharp relief when we examine how Sellars deals with the themes that Quine critically addresses in TDE. Like Quine, Sellars rejects the "Positivist" or "logical empiricist" interpretation of the epistemology of natural science in favor of a more holistic picture. But where Quine focuses on the "dogma" that individual statements are the units of confirmation or disconfirmation, Sellars turns his critical attention to the received identification of *scientific explanation* with logical derivation, according to which singular matters of empirical fact are explained by deducing descriptions of them from "inductively-established" empirical generalizations along with appropriate statements of initial conditions, and such "empirical laws" in turn are explained by deducing them from theoretical postulates and correspondence rules. On this view, theories (e.g., micro-theories) explain empirical matters of fact only indirectly, by implying generalizations framed in an observation-language that explain them directly.

Sellars regarded this "levels picture" of theories as fundamentally misguided. He argued that there is no epistemologically *autonomous* stratum of empirical counterparts to theoretical laws, but that the empirical generalizations corresponding to theoretical laws rather become salient only from the theoretical perspective. Since the generalizations arrived at inductively at the observational level, however reliable, are ultimately not laws of nature, postulational theories cannot be in the business of explaining such lower-level generalizations by entailing them. Rather, "theories explain laws by explaining why the objects of the domain in question obey the laws that they do to the extent that they do" (LT, 123).[5]

[That is,] they explain why individual objects of various kinds and in various circumstances in the observation framework behave in those ways in which it has been inductively established that they do behave. Roughly, it is because a gas is ... a cloud of molecules which are behaving in certain theoretically defined ways, that it obeys the empirical Boyle-Charles Law. (LT, 121)

On Sellars's view, in short, postulational theories are not merely manageable second-class surrogates for more complicated and unwieldy stories about the behavior of the "real" items that we can observe "directly". Posited theoretical entities are themselves items whose reality we can properly acknowledge for good and sufficient theoretical, i.e., explanatory, reasons.

---

[5] "The Language of Theories" (LT), in H. Feigl and G. Maxwell (eds.), in *Current Issues in the Philosophy Science* (Henry Holt, Rhinehart and Winston; New York, NY; 1961); repr. in SPR, 106–26.

In sharp contrast, the notion of explanation plays no significant role in Quine's epistemology of science. "As an empiricist," he writes, "I continue to think of the conceptual scheme of science as a tool, ultimately, for predicting future experience in the light of past experience" (TDE, 41), where _experience_ was to be understood austerely, as "a continuing barrage of sensory stimulations" or "sensory promptings" (TDE, 43). From this perspective, "physical objects are conceptually imported into the situation as convenient intermediaries ... as irreducible posits comparable, epistemologically, to the gods of Homer" (TDE, 41), and "objects at the atomic level and beyond are posited to make the laws of macroscopic objects, and ultimately the laws of experience, simpler and more manageable" (TDE, 42). Indeed, even "the abstract entities which are the substance of mathematics—ultimately classes and classes of classes and so on up—are another posit in the same spirit" (TDE, 42). It is only residual allegiance to the analytic-synthetic distinction that keeps us from recognizing that _class_ and _number_ fall on a continuum with _atom_ and _electron_, the differences being only matters of intra-systematic interconnections and remoteness from the sensory periphery.

For a variety of reasons, Sellars strongly resists the suggestion that physical objects are "posits" subserving the prediction and systematization of sensations. His notion of an _experience_ is, from the beginning, the richer Kantian conception of an ostensible perceptual encounter with persisting and causally-interactive objects in space and time, and he argues in EPM that our sensation-concepts _per se_ are analogically derivative from, and hence methodologically dependent on, a prior conception of the objective characteristics and relationships of such items. His critique of the "levels picture" of theoretical explanation applies here as well, since, like classical phenomenalism, the Quinean alternative presupposes a stratum of epistemologically autonomous sensory regularities which, Sellars argues, is demonstrably not available. Experiential regularities in Quine's sense of the term can become salient only from the perspective of a perceiver who thinks of himself as determinately situated in space and time and as entering into causal relationships with independently-real physical objects.[6]

Sellars also rejects Quine's ultra-holistic conclusion that such categorial notions as _number, class, attribute_, and _proposition_ are epistemologically continuous with the posits of theoretical microphysics within the "man made fabric" of "total science", conceived on the model of "a field of force whose boundary conditions are experience" (TDE, 39). His _local_ reason for rejecting that conclusion turns on the observation that the theory-whole of "total science" itself treats the epistemology of, for instance, _protons_ and _neutrinos_ differently from that of such abstracta. Microphysical theory explains how we are _in touch with_ the items that it posits. It has specific things to say about the determinate, instrument-mediated, causal relations that connect microphysical objects with the sensory

---

[6] Sellars' arguments to this point are set out in "Phenomenalism", pp. 60–105 of SPR.

stimulations of human perceivers. Nothing like that is available in the case of traditionally-conceived abstract entities.[7]

This ostensible discontinuity reflects Sellars' second, *global* reason for rejecting Quine's epistemological continuum, a consideration which arises directly from Sellars' own views regarding the problematic of analyticity. Like Quine, Sellars is deeply influenced by the work of Rudolf Carnap, and, like Quine, he is sympathetic to Carnap's suggestion that acknowledging a category of entities is ultimately an "external question", a matter of the adoption of a particular language-system. Carnap's own account of categorial concepts paired them with the analytic sentence-forms of such a language system, and Quine predictably resists *this* aspect of the proposal.

Now Carnap has maintained that [e.g., the question of whether to countenance classes as entities] is a question not of matters of fact but of choosing a convenient language form, a convenient conceptual scheme or framework for science. With this I agree, but only on the proviso that the same be conceded regarding scientific hypotheses generally. Carnap has recognized that he is able to preserve a double standard for ontological questions and scientific hypotheses only by assuming an absolute distinction between the analytic and the synthetic; and ... this is a distinction which I reject. (TDE, 43)

In a certain sense, Sellars accepts Quine's proviso here, but his more complex and sophisticated understanding of the nature and import of theoretical reasoning in natural science enables him to develop a systematic naturalistic alternative to Quine's influential critique of Carnapian logical empiricism. In particular, Sellars' epistemological contrast between two sorts of empirical generalizations—those adopted on narrowly empirical, i.e., *inductive* grounds and those expressing constitutive principles of postulational theories, themselves adopted on broadly empirical, i.e., *explanatory* grounds—equips him with the resources to distinguish among three different grades of "experiential involvement": (1) statements reporting observations and those general claims individually validated "inductively" by way of direct appeals to observational backing; (2) the constitutive posits of postulational theories, holistically validated by way of indirect, explanatory appeals to such observations and generalizations; and (3) purely formal claims, expressing necessary conditions for the formulation of scientific hypotheses in general.

Consequently, where Quine simply rejects the received Kantian analytic-synthetic dichotomy out of hand, Sellars argues[8] that two quite different distinctions are tangled up in the single dichotomy that Carnap had inherited from the Kantian tradition—the distinction between logical claims and empirical or matter-of-factual claims (analytic$_2$ *vs.* synthetic$_2$), and the distinction between

---

[7] See *Naturalism and Ontology* (Ridgeview Publishing Co.; Atascadero, CA: 1979), ch. 1, §§ 32–4, pp. 15–16.

[8] In "Empiricism and Abstract Entities" (EAE), in P. A. Schilpp (ed.), *The Philosophy of Rudolph Carnap* (Open Court; LaSalle, IL; 1963); repr. in *Essays in Philosophy and Its History* (D. Reidel Publishing Co.; Dordrecht, Holland; 1975), 245–86.

claims whose revision requires a correlative abandonment or modification of the system of (e.g., theoretical) concepts in terms of which they are framed and claims that are revisable on the basis of observations framed in terms of a system of concepts which remain fixed throughout (analytic$_1$ *vs.* synthetic$_1$). Like Quine, then, Sellars moves decisively away from classical Kantian rationalism, but in the direction of a *Kantian* empiricism which preserves logical space for a theory of semantic meaning and the correlative distinctions between individual matter-of-factual truths, e.g., that an electron just passed through this cloud chamber, and truths which, although belonging to theoretical systems that are themselves adopted on broadly empirical (synthetic$_2$) grounds, were, relative to such a system, true *ex vi terminorium* (analytic$_1$), e.g., that electrons have a negative charge.

Sellars thus concludes that Quine blurs a vital distinction. Although observational justification is not *irrelevant* to the adoption of analytic$_2$ sentence forms and the categorial concepts which, on Carnap's account, correspond to them—e.g., *particular, property, relation, proposition, state of affairs*—and there is consequently a sense in which even such categorial posits can be "justified by an appeal to experience", this concession gives no support to Quine's epistemological continuum, for it means only that scientific hypotheses cannot be formulated in a language which lacks a suitable *formal* richness. The justification of our use of specific analytic$_1$ but not analytic$_2$ sentence forms in science clearly involves syntactical relations between the descriptive terms used to frame theoretical hypotheses and the vocabulary of observation, but no *additional* machinery of this sort is involved in the justification of our use of the corresponding analytic$_2$ sentence forms. Categorial ontologies are not further theories *within* scientific theories. Rather, if we're justified in accepting certain analytic$_2$ resources—an acceptance that is justified by pointing out that, without such resources, certain *empirical* statements could not be made—we can then, as Carnap showed, mobilize them by purely nominal means into a corresponding framework of abstract entities.

A *Platonistic* account of abstract entities treats them as independently existing items which figure indispensably and irreducibly in certain *explanations*. The earliest such stories invoked abstract entities in explanations of similarities and differences among concrete individuals and of the lawfulness of laws of nature, but, as Sellars stresses, contemporary strains of Platonism assign explanatory roles to abstracta primarily in connection with mental and, especially, semantic facts. Carnap's nominalistic therapy with respect to abstract entities was in essence to invert this direction of explanation. The terms of traditional Platonistic ontology—e.g., 'property' and 'proposition'—do not designate independently existing entities, but are properly interpreted as transpositions of metalinguistic syntactic categories—e.g., 'predicate' and 'sentence'—into the "material mode of speech". As Sellars puts it, "What Carnap believed ... was that he had shown that ontological categories are *shadows* of syntactical distinctions" (EAE, 443).

Sellars himself in effect adopts this Carnapian strategy, but transforms it in a distinctive way. For where Carnap argued that all one needs to know in order to introduce, e.g., the framework of propositions (or properties) into a language, L, is that L contains at least one sentence (one predicate), Sellars observed that a Platonist might well counter that a sentential expression isn't a sentence (a predicative expression isn't a predicate) unless it's meaningful, and, in that case, there must exist a proposition that it expresses (a property that it stands for). And while he was not prepared to grant the Platonist's contentions in just those terms, Sellars was nevertheless convinced that they pointed the way toward an important insight.

Carnap proposed to interpret his nominalistic reductions in terms of a theory of "pure syntax" according to which syntactic categories could be explicitly defined within an extensional metalanguage, e.g.,

> (1)   x is a predicate of L $=_{df}$ x = 'ϕ' or x = 'ψ' or ...,

but this *modus operandi*, Sellars argued, rides roughshod over a crucial distinction. He had no quarrel with the formal procedure of introducing a combinatorial category of object-language expressions by such extensional means, e.g.,

> (2)   x is a P-expression-of-L $=_{df}$ x = 'ϕ' or x = 'ψ' or ...,

and then elucidating its relationship to syntactic concepts by an appropriate biconditional,

> (3)   x is a predicate of L *if and only if* x is a P-expression-of-L.

But Sellars insisted that a statement is not properly *syntactical* unless it uses syntactical expressions in their ordinary sense, and one can no more *define* the ordinary sense of 'predicate' by such a disjunction than one can define, for instance, the ordinary sense of 'U.S. senator' by the disjunction

> (4)   x is a U.S. senator $=_{df}$ (x = Ted Kennedy) *or* (x = Hillary Clinton)
> *or* ...

The insight that Sellars found implicit in the Platonistic counter to Carnap's nominalistic therapy, in other words, was that, as he put it, 'predicate', like all syntactic terms, is a *role word*, and that specifying the role-*players* doesn't define the role (EAE, 455). The corresponding Platonistic *impulse* is to define an expression's predicative role in terms of its standing in a kind of *sui generis* representing relation to a kind of independently-existing entity, but just here the Carnapian therapy suggests an alternative strategy. We can instead see the syntactic roles of various categories of expressions as implicitly defined by the *formation rules* of the calculus (the grammatical rules of the language) to which they belong, in a manner analogous to the way that the role words 'pawn', 'knight', 'bishop', etc. are implicitly defined by the rules of chess, rules which specify which moves (cf. combinations of signs) are permissible or forbidden (cf. well- or ill-formed). On this view, ordinary syntactic terms will resist reductive extensional definition by virtue of having *normative import*.

Up to a point, the same line of reasoning applies, *mutatis mutandis*, to semantic terms. "The essential concern of *philosophical* semantics", Sellars maintained, "is with semantical words, not as they function as defined expressions in pure semantical systems, but as they function in the assertions of descriptive semantics, i.e., in actual usage, *per se*", and Carnap's own treatment of the relationship between pure and descriptive semantics, he argued, was "much too perfunctory" (EAE, 462).

On Carnap's account, pure semantics is logically prior to descriptive semantics. In essence, he held that the operative terms of descriptive semantics, e.g., 'means', can be defined in terms of expressions of an appropriately-interpreted pure semantic system construed as a formal calculus. Thus we would have, for instance,

(5)   x means y (in German) $=_{df}$ (x = 'rot' and y = red) *or* (x = 'blau' and y = blue) *or* ... ,

which, Sellars argues, suffers from precisely the same defect as its ostensibly descriptive syntactic counterpart (1). Here, too, Sellars has no initial objection to defining, e.g.,

(6)   x Des-in-G y $=_{df}$ (x = 'rot' and y = red) *or* (x = 'blau' and y = blue) *or* ... ,

and, correspondingly, to acknowledging the correctness of

(7)   x means y (in German) *if and only if* x Des-in-G y,

i.e.,

(8)   x means y (in German) *if and only if* (x = 'rot' and y = red) *or* (x = 'blau' and y = blue) *or* ...

In this instance, however, the Carnapian therapy arguably fails effectively to address the impulse toward Platonism. For if we think of (8) on the model of

(9)   x is the uncle of y *if and only if* (x = Tom and y = Bill) *or* (x = Dick and y = John) *or* ...

(EAE, 464), it is hard to avoid seeing the descriptive terms 'red', 'blue', etc. which occur unquoted in (8) as *standing for properties*, i.e., redness, blueness, etc. In this case, it evidently does not suffice to point out (albeit correctly) that, like syntactic terms, semantic terms resist reductive extensional definition by virtue of having normative import. And so it is precisely here that Sellars finds the underlying motive of Quine's repudiation of meanings and, correlatively, of attempts to elucidate the notion of analyticity in terms of "truth by virtue of meaning".

It is the idea that the 'means' or 'designates' of semantical sentences in a framework of abstract entities is a descriptive or factual relation such that [(8)] is true, but [(5)] false, which leads ... the tough-minded to a rejection ... of these sentences, of semantics, of the "theory of meaning," and of the framework of abstract entities. It is this idea ... which is the source of nominalistic anxieties. For if an adequate theory of language required us to hold that linguistic expressions stand in such a relation to abstract entities, how could ... the thesis that linguistic phenomena can, in principle, be described and causally accounted for without using semantical or prescriptive expressions, be true? (EAE, 464–5)

What is fundamentally needed to address such "nominalistic anxieties" is consequently an alternative, non-Platonistic, explication of the context 'x means y', e.g., of such true claims as

(10)   (In German) 'Aachen' means *Aix-la-Chapelle*,

(11)   (In German) 'rot' means *red*,

(12)   (In German) 'und' means *and*.

Sellars' well-known strategy for providing such an explication begins by denying that 'means' is a relation, i.e., that the job of (10), (11), and (12) is to assert that two items stand in *either* an analyzable descriptive *or* an unanalyzable semantic relation. Rather,

the term 'means' as it occurs in [(10), (11), and (12)] communicates the information that the words 'Aachen,' 'rot,' and 'und' respectively play the same roles in German that 'Aix-la-Chapelle,' 'red,' and 'and' play in English. It does not, however, specify what this role is, *nor, in particular, does it claim that it is the same role in the case of all three pairs.* Clearly in each case the role is a different one. (EAE, 466)

This is the point of departure for Sellars' positive account of meaning as *functional classification.*[9] According to this account, we can think of the meaning of a linguistic expression as the "functional role" it plays within the language to which it belongs, in particular, its *causal* (occasioning) role with respect to sensory inputs ("language-entries"), inferential transitions ("intra-linguistic moves"), and behavioral outputs ("language-exits"). The context 'x means y' then *classifies* the functional role of a *mentioned* expression, x, as being (to a sufficient degree of approximation) the same as that of an *exhibited* expression, y, belonging to the language within which the meaning-claim is framed.

To render the account notationally perspicuous, Sellars introduced his apparatus of dot- and star-quotes, each a device for forming *illustrating common nouns*, sortal terms for variously classifying inscriptions and utterances. Dot-quotes form common nouns correctly applicable to expressions belonging to any linguistic framework which play the functional role played in our language by the expression occurring between them, and star-quotes form common nouns correctly applicable to expressions appropriately *structurally* (e.g., geometrically or acoustically) similar to the expression occurring between them. In terms of these conventions, (10), (11), and (12) amount to

---

[9] Sellars' own clearest compact exposition of this view is doubtless ch. 4, "Meaning and Ontology", of *Naturalism and Ontology*, a reworked version of his "Meaning as Functional Classification", *Synthese*, 27 (1974), 417–37.

(10′)   German *Aachen*s *are* ·Aix-la-Chapelle·s,
(11′)   German *rot*s *are* ·red·s,
(12′)   German *und*s *are* ·and·s.

On this view, 'means' turns out to be just a specialized form of the copula, tailored for contexts of linguistic classification.

Sellars thus reconstructs talk about "semantic properties and relations" as a kind of shorthand for talk about norm-governed linguistic role-players. And this puts him in a position to implement the Carnapian strategy by reconstructing talk about "abstract entities" using precisely the *same* resources. Accordingly, the cash value of talk about, e.g., properties is *also* ultimately a matter of norms governing linguistic correctness. In first approximation, for instance,

　　　　　　triangularity = the ·triangular·
and　　redness = the ·red·,

where the definite article is here used to form what Sellars calls "distributive singular terms" on the model of 'the lion' and 'the pawn' in

　　The lion is a carnivore
　　　　[= Lions are carnivores = (x)(x is a lion → x is a carnivore)], and
　　The pawn captures diagonally
　　　　[= Pawns capture diagonally = (x)(x is a pawn → x captures
　　　　diagonally)].

On this reconstruction, such "metaphysically charged" claims as

　　　　　　Triangularity is a property
and　　Blood exemplifies redness

are innocuously explicated in terms of the syntactic roles of linguistic expressions and the truth of sentences, thus

　　·triangular·s are monadic predicates　[*via*: The ·triangular· is a monadic
　　　　predicate], and
　　·Blood is red·s are true　[*via*: The ·red· is true of blood; The ·Blood is red·
　　　　is true].[10]

Sellars thus proposes to understand talk ostensibly referring to abstract entities as a contrived idiom for communicating facts about the normative proprieties that shape the use of expressions within natural languages.

It is, of course, often difficult (and sometimes impossible) to specify explicitly the rules and practices that are constitutive for some item's being, e.g., a ·red·, but

---

[10] Analogously, "That blood is red is a proposition" will be explicated by "·Blood is red·s are sentences" [*via*: The ·Blood is red· is a sentence]. Thus "'Blut ist rot' (in German) expresses the proposition that blood is red" will simply amount to "German *Blut ist rot*s are ·Blood is red·s".

The applications and implications of this strategy are worked out in exquisite detail in Sellars' essays "Abstract Entities" and "Classes as Abstract Entities and the Russell Paradox", both repr. in *Philosophical Perspectives: Metaphysics and Epistemology* (Ridgeview Publishing Co.; Atascadero, CA: 1967), and given a few additional twists in chs. 2–4 of his *Naturalism and Ontology*.

that creates no special problems of understanding, since the *illustrating* functional sortal itself in effect specifies the role ostensively. Sellars can also concede that such classifications are always shaped by implicit idealizations and approximations, and so always a matter of degree. Whether German *rot*s qualify as ·red·s—or, more precisely, the extent to which the linguistic jobs performed in German by tokenings of *rot*s correspond to the linguistic jobs performed by tokenings of *red*s in our own language—is open to both disagreement and investigation, but such investigations and disagreements, to the extent that they occur, reflect only the familiar challenges of effective translation, i.e., the hermeneutic character of all linguistic interpretation.[11]

Quine and his disciples would, of course, find many elements of Sellars' story deeply problematic. Once it is no longer simply identified with logical derivation, for example, the notion of *explanation* clearly stands in need of further elucidation. Similarly, although the notion of a normatively characterized role is clear enough in the case of pieces in a game such as chess, whose rules are explicitly codified as such, the idea of classifying linguistic items according to rule-constituted functional roles plainly presupposes that uses of such items are subject to proprieties governed by *rules of language*, and more needs to be said about what form(s) such rules might take and how they might be empirically identified.[12] Sellars and *his* disciples have, of course, offered further elucidations of these notions, sometimes in considerable detail,[13] but since a keystone of the Sellarsian view is the irreducibility of norms to facts ('ought's to 'is's; practical to theoretical reasoning), they have predictably proved unsatisfying to Quineans.[14]

Yet it is hard to see how anyone can avoid availing himself of *something* like the fact-norm distinction. In particular, it is hard to see how Quine himself can do so, given the terms in which he frames his own positive account.

[11] Quine notoriously and controversially argued, originally in ch. 2 of *Word and Object* (MIT Press; Cambridge, MA: 1960), that translation was deeply and irremediably indeterminate, reference consequently "inscrutable", and ontological questions therefore always "relative to some background language". (The last in "Ontological Relativity", *Journal of Philosophy*, 65 (1968), 185–212.) Pursuing these issues here would take us too far from our central themes. I survey the controversy over the first of these claims in "The Dispute on the Indeterminacy of Translation", in M. Dascal *et al.* (eds.), *Sprachphilosophie/Philosophy of Language*, vol. 2 (Walter de Gruyter; Berlin and New York: 1996), 1050–57; and critically address all three of them from a Sellarsian perspective in ch. 4 of *Linguistic Representation* (D. Reidel Publishing Co.; Dordrecht, Holland: 1974).

[12] Quine himself criticized Carnap's attempt to elucidate "the unexplained word 'analyticity'" by appealing to "an unexplained phrase 'semantical rule'" (TDE 33).

[13] See, e.g., Sellars' "Some Reflections on Language Games", repr. as ch. 11, pp. 321–58, of SPR, and "Language as Thought and Communication", *Philosophy and Phenomenological Research*, 29 (1969), 506–27, repr. in *Essays in Philosophy and Its History* (D. Reidel Publishing Co.; Dordrecht, Holland: 1974), 93–117.

[14] Not that Quineans are all of a piece. The best of them understand Sellars' considerations perfectly well and make an effort, in various ways and often quite helpfully, to take them into account. In connection with this essay, for example, I have profited greatly from some insightful unpublished material, written in a spirit of reconciliation, by Robert Kraut, with whom I have, as he once put it, been dancing this particular dance for several decades. What follows, however, will make it clear that we are still a long way from a thoroughgoing rapprochement. The dance goes on.

The totality of our so-called knowledge or beliefs ... is a man-made fabric which impinges on experience only along the edges. ... A conflict with experience at the periphery occasions readjustments in the interior of the field. Truth values have to be redistributed over some of our statements. Re-evaluation of some entails re-evaluation of others, because of their logical interconnections—the logical laws being in turn simply certain further statements of the system, certain further elements of the field. Having re-evaluated one statement we must re-evaluate some others, whether they be statements logically connected with the first or whether they be the statements of logical connections themselves. (TDE, 39)

But absent some sufficiently stable concept of representational correctness, what are we to make of the notion of a "conflict with experience"? And absent sufficiently robust principles of inference, how is a "re-evaluation" of statements and a "redistribution of truth values" to proceed?

If there can be such a thing as a "recalcitrant experience" (TDE, 40 ff.), then *experience* must surely be more than just "a continuing barrage of sensory stimulations" or "sensory promptings" (TDE, 43). As Sellars stresses with reference to classical sense-datum theories (EPM §3, 128), only an experience which in some way *makes a claim* can literally conflict with some element of "our so-called knowledge or beliefs". And as Lewis Carroll long ago charmingly reminded us,[15] a "logic" consisting *only* of statements is impotent to guide any form of reasoning.

Quine famously rejected the idea that analytic statements are distinguished by a special epistemological status by arguing that "any statement can be held true come what may, if we make drastic enough adjustments elsewhere in the system" and that "conversely, by the same token, no statement is immune to revision" (TDE, 40). I have already surveyed Sellars' local and global criticisms of this ultra-holistic epistemological continuum, but from the present perspective there remains, I think, something more to be said. For if truth is supposed to be a species of representational correctness and "adjustment" or "revision" a principled affair, i.e. not *utterly* arbitrary, then Quine's bold claims begin to elicit the same sorts of worries and reservations that would attach to, e.g., the claim that "any piece can move and capture in any direction, if we make drastic enough adjustments in the rules of chess". Yes, one is inclined to say, indefinitely many such "drastic adjustments" are always *possible*, but all but a handful of them would have the result that the "revised" game of chess would lose its *point*.

Empirical inquiry, to be sure, is not a game with codified rules. But, even by Quine's lights, it does have a *point*. "As an empiricist," he writes, "I continue to think of the conceptual scheme of science as a tool, ultimately, for predicting future experience in the light of past experience" (TDE, 41).

---

[15] "What the Tortoise Said to Achilles', *Mind*, 4 (1895), 278–80; variously reprinted.

Total science, mathematical and natural and human, is ... extremely underdetermined by experience. The edge of the system must be kept squared with experience; the rest, with all its elaborate myths or fictions, has as its objective the simplicity of laws (TDE, 42).

Now one can seriously interrogate the notion of "experience" at work in this passage, and one can quarrel with the purely instrumentalist understanding of science that it expresses. Sellars, as we have seen, does both. But, be that as it may, the aims and objectives of scientific inquiry, *even as Quine conceives of them*, surely already impose constraints on what statements it is *reasonable* to "hold true" in the face of "recalcitrant experience" and on what "adjustments" and "revisions" it is *reasonable* to make "elsewhere in the system". And while it is indeed always *possible* to "plead hallucination" or to "amend certain statements of the kind called logical laws" (TDE, 40), given the aims and objectives of inquiry, even as Quine conceives of them, it will *make sense* to do so only in very limited particular circumstances.

For the notion of matter-of-factual truth is itself conditioned by such considerations of reasonableness and the procedural constraints correlative to them. That is, there must be a difference between merely *holding on* to a statement, i.e., continuing to assert it come what may (a form of fanaticism), and holding the statement to be *true*, i.e., holding it for the right kind of reasons, e.g., because it belongs to a system of beliefs that has proved itself to be an *efficient* and *effective* "tool ... for predicting future experience in the light of past experience" (a form of rationality). Otherwise, as Wittgenstein pithily observed, "What is correct is whatever will seem correct to me. And that just means that there can be no talk of 'correct' here" (*Philosophical Investigations*, §258).

I began this study by observing that, although Quine's and Sellars' seminal essays had much in common, the differences between the systematic views of these two philosophers were both deep and important. The ensuing discussion has explored a number of those differences, and the result of that exploration is instructive, for it has repeatedly identified the theme of *normativity* as lying decisively at their center. As Sellars maintained,

the question inevitably arises, Is it proper to ask of a decision to accept a framework of entities [a form of language, a postulational theory] "Is it reasonable?" "Can this decision be justified, and if so, how?" This is the crux of the matter ... (EAE, 433)

To such questions, he lamented, Carnap offered no useful answers, and it is easy to imagine him registering an analogous complaint regarding Quine. For Quine's philosophical vision is, as it were, purely descriptive. His is a world of 'is's without 'ought's, and of regularities without rules. It is, one might say, a *de facto* world. And that makes it, in one clear sense, a world without *us* in it. For, as Sellars also rightly insisted,[16] "it is no merely incidental feature of man that he has a conception of himself as man-in-the-world", and

---

[16] In what, for reasons of "political correctness", has now become a rather archaic idiom.

anything which can properly be called conceptual thinking can occur only within a framework of conceptual thinking within which it can be criticized, supported, refuted, in short, evaluated. To be able to think is to be able to measure one's thoughts by standards of correctness, of relevance, of evidence. (PSIM, 6)

Hence, although, as I also observed early on, Quine's philosophical message characteristically has the form: "We can do without ... ", the discussion has now arrived at the point at which this impetus to austerity necessarily finds its limit. For *we* cannot do without normativity. Without normativity, there is no *we*. And that is why, *pace* Quine, Sellars properly concluded that philosophy still confronts

the task of showing that categories pertaining to man as a *person* who finds himself confronted by standards (ethical, logical, etc.) ... to which he may or may not conform, can be reconciled with the idea that man is what science says he is. (PSIM, 38)

3

The Elusiveness of Categories, the Archimedean Dilemma, and the Nature of Man: A Study in Sellarsian Metaphysics

I

1. The ontological enterprise is the attempt to delineate the most general complete answer to the question "What is there?". The enterprise has two dimensions. Positively, it rests upon epistemology. Viewing "What is there?" as a question among questions, the philosopher produces an account of the epistemological grounds of an adequate answer. We *discover* what there is. How we discover it, what we have discovered, and, perhaps, what we are likely to discover, form the subject matter of positive ontology. Negatively, the enterprise rests upon analysis. Philosophers discourse about entities or putative entities more or less problematic in nature—numbers, qualities, classes, propositions, facts, and the like. Whether the entities be putative merely and, if so, what such discourse amounts to is the subject matter of negative ontology. In his positive ontology, Sellars is a scientific realist, in his negative ontology, what I shall call a linguistic nominalist. The two stances are, of course, not unrelated. Thereby hangs a long tale, much of which will emerge as we proceed. Let me begin, then, by picking up some of the threads of Sellars' negative ontology. Since he is a synoptic and systematic thinker, following them will take us a considerable distance—and in some unexpected directions.

II

2. The thesis of linguistic nominalism may be succinctly stated in first approximation thus:

... that the abstract entities which are the subject matter of the contemporary debate between platonistic and anti-platonistic philosophers—qualities, relations, classes, propositions, and the like—are linguistic entities. They are linguistic expressions. ([10]; [16]: 229)

3. Like Carnap, Sellars sees discourse putatively about abstract entities as discourse in the material mode of speech. Thus,

(1) Redness is a quality

is viewed, roughly, as a transposed version of something like

(2) 'red' is a monadic predicate.

As anyone who has worked with the basic Carnapian move will recognize, *caveats* are essential. The fundamental difficulty (first raised by Church) can be sketched in connection with translation. (1) is transcribed, for example, in German by

(1g) Die Röte ist eine Qualität,

while (2) translates as

(2g) 'red' ist ein monadisches Prädikat.

The invariance of the quoted item in (2) and (2g) highlights the fact that (2) is a claim about a specific word of the *English* language. Like (2) and (2g), (1) and (1g) are true or false together. (1g), however, could be used to make a true statement even if there were no English language. The truth of (1g) does not turn on the existence of any English word. Hence, since (1g) and (1) say the same thing, neither does the truth of (1). Since (1) would, but (2) would not, be true in the absence of an English language, (1) and (2) evidently have different subject matters. Discourse putatively about universals, therefore, apparently cannot be discourse about linguistic expressions. The traditional conclusion has been that (1) concerns itself with a totally non-linguistic subject matter, e.g., the entities of a platonic realm of subsistents.

4. Sellars, however, does not accept the traditional conclusion. He sees (1) as independent of *specific* linguistic forms not by virtue of its relation to a totally non-linguistic subject matter, but rather by virtue of the fact that its mode of reference to language abstracts from what is idiosyncratic to the specific expressions of determinate historical languages. It is directed, rather, to the role or functions served in common by the different concrete linguistic materials of historical languages regarded as "materially different varieties of one and the same 'language game'" ([10]; [16]: 239). Thus, according to Sellars, (1) is insulated from the idiosyncrasies of translation not by being *non*-linguistic, but rather by being *inter*-linguistic to begin with. (1) adverts to a function shared by 'red's in English, 'rot's in German, and 'rouge's in French. Sellars uses dot-quotation to form common nouns subsuming linguistic materials thus functionally individuated. Thus ·red·s are items in *any* language which have the function (play the role, do the job) which the token exhibited between the dot-quotes has in *our* language, i.e., in the language of *use*. As translation represents a move from one language of use to another, the material between *dot*-quotes—being relativized to the *used* language—is thus translated as well. Asterisk-quotes, by contrast, form common nouns subsuming linguistic materials as *structurally* individuated. *rot*s, thus, are items having the *shape* of

the token exhibited between the asterisks. In English, *rot*s are ˙rot˙s, while, in German, *rot*s are ˙red˙s. Thus Sellars sees ordinary quotation, relatively innocuous in *intra*-linguistic contexts where structure and function run parallel, as systematically ambiguous between structure and function in *inter*-linguistic contexts, where a single structure may answer to diverse functions (as *rot*s may be ˙rot˙s or ˙red˙s) and a single function may be served by items of various structures (as *red*s, *rot*s, and *rouge*s may all be ˙red˙s). And he sees the ontological idiom as our ordinary language resource for coping with this ambiguity. But, being framed in terms appropriate to discourse about objects, it, too, misleads, though in a wholly different way.

5. In second approximation, then,

(1) Redness is a quality

is to be analyzed as

(3) ˙red˙s are monadic predicates.

Bits of language considered simply as belonging to the natural order—inscriptions and utterances viewed solely in terms of "empirical properties and matter-of-factual relations"—Sellars calls 'natural-linguistic objects' ([21]; [18]: 212). Viewed externally, then, the proximate subject matter of philosophers' ontological discourse is such natural-linguistic objects. But the discourse is discourse about them not *qua* natural-linguistic objects but rather as *functionally* individuated items and fit subjects for *normative* claims. Philosophers' ontological discourse is the classificatory discourse of a functional metalanguage transposed into the material mode of speech, but the proximate subject matter of that discourse is the *tokens*—inscriptions and utterances—over which, for example, the universal quantifier implicit in (3) ranges:

(4) $(x)(x$ is a ˙red˙ $\supset x$ is a monadic predicate).

Thus the rubric "linguistic nominalism". 'Linguistic', since, *à la* Carnap, Sellars analyzes ontological discourse as a transposed form of metalinguistic discourse. 'Nominalism', since, according to Sellars, the proximate subjects of that discourse properly analyzed are, considered externally, particulars only—utterance tokens and inscriptions.

III

6. But what is it for some natural-linguistic object to have a role or function? If to be a ˙red˙ is to be an item in any language which has the function which the exhibited token has in our language, are we not then committed to an ontology embracing, at least, functions or roles? The answer, of course, is that we are not, and to see it, we need only pursue a favorite Sellarsian analogy a bit. What is it to be a pawn in chess? It is surely *only* to be subject to chess-normatives in the appropriate way.

A pawn is any item which may advance along a file one square at a time, capture diagonally, queen at the eighth rank, and so on. *Which* items of the natural order (pieces of wood or ivory, configurations of electrons in a computer) are pawns will vary from time to time, and what natural order goings-on *count* as moving, capturing, queening—indeed, what counts as a square, rank, or file—from occasion to occasion will also vary. What is invariant is the set of rules or normatives espoused by the players and the *regularities* in the natural order which are generated in response to these espoused normatives. The *esse* of a game, as Sellars puts it, is *ludi*, to be played. To play a game is to do what one does subject to the constraints of various normatives espoused as action-guiding policies and with a specifiable end-in-view. Externally, what is manifested is regularities *in re*. 'Square' becomes colored cardboard; 'pawn' becomes piece of wood of such-and-such a shape; 'moving' becomes transportation of wood from point to point; and 'capturing' becomes physical displacement and replacement. Thus a game of chess is played out.

7. With language there are both tensions and affinities.

> ... If all rules of language were ought-to-do's, we would be precluded from explaining what it is to have concepts in terms of rules of language. Now many rules of language *are* ought-to-do's thus,
>
> (Other things being equal) one ought to say such and such, if in C
>
> and as such they can be efficacious in linguistic activity only to the extent that people have the relevant concepts. It is therefore of the utmost importance to note that many of the rules of language which are of special interest to the epistemologist are ought-to-be's rather than ought-to-do's. ([14]: 510)

8. Linguistic normatives, in the primary sense, are ought-to-be's, what Sellars calls "rules of criticism". Conceptual activity (covert or overt) is through-and-through rule-governed, not in the sense of being guided by explicitly espoused rules of *action* (ought-to-do's) which require of the agents a rich prior conceptualization of the rules *qua* rules and of the evoking situations as falling under the rule-descriptions and *thus* as reasons for the actions which the rules enjoin, but rather, in the first instance, by being relevantly *assessable* according to rules of criticism the subjects of which need *not* have the concept of a rule as a rule, nor, indeed, any concepts at all. (Sellars' example: Clock chimes ought to strike on the quarter hour ([14]: 508).)

9. But, further,

> ... the members of a linguistic community are *first* language *learners* and only potentially 'people', but *subsequently* language *teachers* possessed of the rich conceptual framework this implies. They start out being the *subject matter* of the ought-to-be's and graduate to the status of agent subjects of the ought-to-do's [the rules of action enjoining, among other things, the *bringing about* of what the rules of criticism posit ought to be]. Linguistic ought-to-be's are translated into *uniformities* by training. ([14]: 512)

In the second instance, then, conceptual activity—and most notably and to the point, linguistic activity—is rule-governed by being the product of agents who are trained to conform to ought-to-be's which are posited by the rules of criticism by their predecessors and teachers who espoused as action-guiding policies the correlative ought-to-do's relating to the bringing about of behavior conforming to those ought-to-be's. It is as rule-governed in this second sense that language makes contact with the chess analogy. As the espoused rules of chess constrain an agent's chess activity and precipitate from time to time uniformities of relational structure among the current physical embodiments of the chess roles constituted by those normatives, so the rules of language are reflected in the natural order by the uniform practices of the trained language users and the uniformities of relational structure among the natural-linguistic objects which are the manifestations *in re* of their conceptual activity and collectively constitute the evolving world-story. "Espousal of principles is reflected in uniformities of performance" ([21]; [18]: 216).[1]

10. The relevant uniformities, Sellars tells us, are of three types:

> I. Language-entry transitions (world → language), e.g., the responses with ·red·s to red objects in daylight;
> II. Intra-linguistic moves (language → language), e.g., the correlations of ·a is north of b·s with ·b is south of a·s or ·thunder at t·s with ·lighting at $t - \Delta t$·s;
> and III. Language-exit transitions (language → world), e.g., the doings of A consequent upon ·I shall now do A·s.
> (See [17]: 114; [20]; [18]: 329 ff; [21]; [18]: 216)

11. Notice that, since ·red·s, ·a is north of b·s, ·I shall now do A·s, and the like are all, considered in themselves, natural-linguistic objects—inscriptions, i.e., piles of ink or chalk, or utterance tokens, i.e., disturbances in the air—the uniformities canvassed here are all world-world uniformities, correlations between relational structures of objects *all of which* are members of the natural order. The picture Sellars gives us, then, is one of agent-persons producing and structuring systems of natural-linguistic objects in a manner which is characterizable as *rule-governed* in at least three dimensions:

first, as performances *assessable* by reference to linguistic ought-to-be's (rules of criticism);

second, by mature language users, as performances responsive to *autonomous* linguistic ought-to-do's (rules of action) espoused as explicit behavior-guiding policies (i.e., rules conceived *as* rules); and

third, again by mature language users, as performances responsive to *derivative* linguistic ought-to-do's pertaining to the bringing about of linguistic ought-to-be's conceived as explicit behavioral constraints (again, rules conceived *as* rules).

12. Sameness of function, role, or office, then, amounts to sameness of place in the "logical space" or relational structure generated by this system of linguistic normatives which finds its total *ontological* reflection in the world-world

---

[1] For a more leisurely and detailed development of this theme, see my [9].

uniformities which are the linguistic actions of persons and their natural-order consequences. Synonymy, to put it crudely, is substitutability *salve* uniformities. Terms which make the same contribution to the system of language-entry, language-exit, and intra-language uniformities are terms having the same function. For that function is individuated by the relational structure induced by the total set of linguistic normatives, and the world-world uniformities resulting from the linguistic actions of persons is the total reflection *in re* of the structure.

IV

13. So much, for now, for the ontology of language. What of its epistemology? We have been taking the semantical rules of criticism, the normatives formulating linguistic ought-to-be's, as given. But, of course, they are not. In a deep sense, the correlation of relational structures, the world-world uniformities, which we have been discussing will prove to be their Sellarsian *raison d'être*. But that is a point which we must approach gradually. More immediately, we must begin to make contact with positive ontology. Sellars, recall, is in his positive ontology a scientific realist. It is to science that he turns also for the epistemological underpinnings of linguistic ought-to-be's. Briefly and roughly put, for Sellars, *laws of nature* and *semantical rules of criticism* are one and the same. In more detail:

> ... law-like propositions tell us how we ought to think about the world. They formulate rules of criticism, and if, as such, they tell us what ought or ought not to be the case, the fact that it is what ought or ought not to be the case with respect to *our beliefs about* the world suffices to distinguish them from those rules of criticism which tell us what ought or ought not to be the case in the world. ([17]: 117)
> ... law-like statements are, in our sense of the phrase, 'semantical rules', and are, *ceteris paribus*, reflected in uniformities pertaining to the verbal behaviour (and conceptual acts) of those who espouse them. ([17]: 118)

14. Thus, for Sellars, evolution of theories and evolution of concepts go hand in hand. Theory change *is* concept change, either in the *limited* sense of introducing new intra-language moves governing old "pieces"—new language → language inferential connections—as when a new law is formulated in an old theoretical vocabulary, or in the more *radical* sense of introducing wholly new "pieces" into the game—a new theoretical vocabulary including ·molecule·s or ·gene·s, for example—in postulational theory formation. Even in the latter case, however, Sellars sees the change as, in an important sense, gradual and evolutionary, for the new theoretical predicates are introduced in the first instance as *analogical* predicates, where the relevant analogies occur at the level

of second-order attributes, analogies which it is the function of the *model* to control.

As I see it, … models provide a basis for a more or less vague and open-textured reference to a framework of propositional functions which the predicates of a theory are to satisfy. They are specified as *the functions which* hold, with certain qualifications, of the predicates which apply to the entities of the model. I say "with certain qualifications" because the reference to a model is accompanied by what I have called a "commentary" which eliminates specific functions from the analogy and modifies others. ([19]; [16]: 348)

15. Like Feyerabend, Sellars sees observationality as a *de facto* property of a system of predicates at a time. But, unlike Feyerabend, Sellars sees also that the essential role of the concepts of the framework of common sense (e.g., colored physical objects, extended in space and enduring through time), in controlling the analogies in terms of which theoretical predicates are in the first instance introduced, gives those concepts a *methodological* bindingness which precludes the *piecemeal* abandonment of common sense for theoretical concepts and, thus, precludes acceptance of the full-fledged Feyerabendian "pragmatic theory of observation".

16. Hence, while Sellars assents to the contention that

The framework of common sense is radically false (i.e., there *really* are no such things as the physical objects and processes of the common sense framework) ([19]; [16]: 354)

he insists that this idea be clarified

… in terms of the concept of its being reasonable *at some stage* to abandon the framework of common sense and use only the framework of theoretical science, suitably enriched by the dimension of practical discourse. ([19]; [16]: 354)

It is only when the conceptual space of the theory has acquired a status which is *fully* non-analogical and, thus, not parasitic on the framework of common sense, however, that such an abandonment would not result in conceptual loss.

It is the rock bottom concepts and principles of common sense which are binding until a total structure which can do the job better is actually at hand—rather than a "regulative ideal". ([19]; [16]: 355)

17. Nevertheless, it is clear that such methodological bindingness is compatible with the *eventual* abandonment and replacement of any set of concepts, however observational (i.e., governed by language-entry semantical rules) they may currently be. Hence, for Sellars, the observational concepts of the common sense framework are *epistemologically* on a par with the concepts of developed postulational theories and, thus, *consonance* with such common sense observations cannot be the fundamentum of the acceptability of new laws and theories. Rather, for Sellars, the ends controlling the scientific enterprise are basically and centrally the ends of *explanation*.

V

18. On Sellars' view, accepting a new law-like statement is espousing a new principle of inference (semantical rule) as a behavior-guiding policy resulting in modification of the world-world regularities consequent upon conceptual—paradigmatically, linguistic—activities. This view places the epistemology of science squarely in the realm of human conduct, and so it is not surprising to find Sellars arguing that the fundamental forms of reasoning governing the acceptance of new laws and theories are one and all forms of *practical* reasoning. An inductive argument emerges as a schematized practical argument.

The major premiss of the first level probability argument, i.e., briefly,

> a proposition is probable$_M$ if it satisfies condition C

has the sense of

> there is a good argument of kind M for accepting a proposition if it satisfies condition C

and, hence, since the conclusion of this argument is a practical one, the sense of

> there is a good argument of kind M which has as its conclusion 'I shall accept a proposition, if it satisfies condition C'.

In short, the major premise of the first order probability$_M$ argument tells us that the *complete* practical reasoning which culminates in

> I shall accept h

(where this acceptance is bound up with probability$_M$), has the form

> I shall bring about E
>
> (but bringing about E implies accepting a proposition, if it satisfies condition C)
>
> so, I shall accept a proposition, if it satisfies condition C
>
> h satisfies condition C
>
> so, I shall accept h.

Thus,

> h is probable$_M$

where the subscript indicates a specific mode of probability, asserts the availability of a good argument for 'I shall accept h', the ultimate major of which is the intention to achieve a certain end, and the proximate major is the appropriate intention to follow a certain policy with respect to accepting propositions. ([12]: 207–8)

19. What are these epistemic ends which govern the various modes of probability and, hence, the scientific enterprise as a whole? Two cases are of central concern here—the probability of *theories* and the *nomological* probability,

or probability of law-like propositions, upon which it is grounded. To fix the relevant ends, Sellars first examines the policies of action which they are to justify. Let us consider the probability of theories first. The appropriate practical reasoning for the probability of theories, according to Sellars, concludes thus:

T is the simplest available framework which generates new testable lawlike statements, generates acceptable approximations of nomologically probable lawlike statements and generates no falsified lawlike statements (from now on, the statement that T has this complex property will be represented by '$\phi(T)$').
    Therefore, I shall accept T. ([12]: 209)

The policy, then, is accepting frameworks which are ϕ. What is the end, E, which justifies the policy?

But why should one accept the policy? By what end is it analytically implied? Surely the state of being in possession of such frameworks logically implies accepting such frameworks *if one does not already have them.* And that this state is the end in question is supported by the fact that it simply unpacks the concept of *being able to give non-trivial explanatory accounts of established laws.* ([12]: 210; second italics mine)

20. For the nomological probability which is presupposed by the probability of theories, the results are similar. The policy to be justified in this case is the adoption of rules of inference which project the observed frequency of a property in a class to unobserved finite samples from the class (with "universal" laws being that special case in which the observed frequency = 1). And the epistemic end, E, which justifies the policy,

... is the state of being able to draw inferences concerning the composition with respect to a given property Y of unexamined finite samples (Δ K) of a kind, X, *in a way which also provides an explanatory account* of the composition with respect to Y of the total examined sample, K, of X. ([12]: 215; italics mine)

In more detail, the practical reasoning underlying nomological probability runs:

I shall be able to draw inferences concerning the composition with respect to a given property Y of unexamined finite samples (ΔK) of a kind, X, in a way which also provides an explanatory account of the composition with respect to Y of the total examined sample, K, of X.
    Being able to do this involves coming to have (where I do not already have) principles of inference which accord with the evidence in the sense that they project the composition of the evidence in a way which generates an explanatory account of this composition.

n/m of all examined As is B.

The implication 'that ΔK is a finite unexamined class of As implies that approximately n/m ΔK is B' accords in the above sense with the evidence.
    Therefore I shall accept this principle of inference. ([12]: 216–17)

21. The epistemic ends controlling the acceptance of new laws and theories, then, are ends concerned with "the realizing of a logically necessary condition of being in the very framework of explanation and prediction, i.e. being able to draw inferences concerning the unknown and give explanatory accounts of the known" ([12]: 219). Roughly, we accept the law or theory which permits inferences to new cases or laws while providing the *best explanatory account* of the cases or laws which we already know.[2]

22. Now this conclusion may seem peculiar. Surely, it will be objected, the epistemic end controlling the scientific enterprise can be nothing less than the possession of *empirical truth*. The relevant epistemic states must surely be, not merely the ability to give explanatory accounts, but rather the ability to give *explanations*, i.e., *true* explanatory accounts; not merely the ability to infer predictions, but rather the ability to infer *true* predictions. To cut the scientific enterprise off from the quest for empirical truth as Sellars does is not only to falsify radically the essential character of that enterprise, but surely also to undermine the very possibility that science can be the fundamentum of the claims of positive ontology, the prime thesis of Sellars' scientific realism.

23. To this objection, Sellars offers both a negative and a positive reply. Negatively, his reply is to insist that the epistemic ends controlling the scientific enterprise must be the sort of things that can be known to be realized, be known to obtain. While this condition is met by the ends in terms of which Sellars analyzes the acceptability of theories and laws, in light of the standing possibility that any theory may be superseded by a better theory, however, it is *not* similarly met by the proposed end-in-view of the possession of empirical truth.

24. Positively, however, Sellars replies that the assertions licensed by an acceptable semantical rule *are* true, and, indeed, it is a mere tautology to say so. For the generic concept of truth—the *meaning* of 'true', on Sellars' account—precisely *is* correct assertibility, that is, assertibility "in accordance with the relevant semantical rules, and on the basis of such additional, though unspecified, information as these rules may require... 'True', then, means *semantically* assertible ('S-assertible') and the varieties of truth correspond to the general varieties of semantical rule" ([17]: 101). Thus, for Sellars, while the epistemic end-in-view *controlling* the scientific enterprise cannot be the possession of empirical truth (for a state which cannot be known to be realized cannot ground a valid practical reasoning), that the scientific enterprise *issue in* empirical truth is itself a necessary truth, for the products of that enterprise are precisely semantical rules, assertibility in accordance with which *is* truth.

---

[2] For a similar conclusion, see [3] and [2]. I have applied this point to the philosophy of linguistics in [6] and [7].

25. But, to cast a finer net, while the *generic* concept of truth is S-assertibility, its specification for the primary concept of *empirical* or *matter-of-factual* truth leads to a deeper set of considerations grounded in an analysis of the distinctive *function* of first-level factual discourse. Like Wittgenstein in the *Tractatus*, Sellars sees this function as one of *picturing*. The primary concept of *factual* truth, for Sellars, is truth as correct picture. Atomic statements are pictures which are

... correct or incorrect in terms of the semantical rules of the framework within which they are statements. They are true (S-assertible) if correct, false if incorrect. ([17]: 119)

The *criterion* of the correctness of the performance of asserting a basic matter-of-factual proposition is the correctness of the proposition *qua* picture, i.e. the fact that it coincides with the picture the world-cum-language would generate in accordance with the uniformities controlled by the semantical rules of the language. Thus the *correctness* of the picture is not defined in terms of the *correctness* of a performance but vice versa. ([17]: 136)

VI

26. Picturing, for Sellars, is not a semantic relation, but a relation *in re*, a relation between two relational structures. It is, in fact, precisely that correlation of natural-linguistic objects and non-linguistic objects, that set of world-world uniformities, to which we have already adverted. To say that first-level factual discourse pictures the world is, roughly, to say that the system of linguistic productions *qua natural-linguistic objects* forms a relational structure isomorphic to the system of items in the natural order which *qua semantical objects* those linguistic productions are about. Thus,

A statement to the effect that a linguistic item pictures a non-linguistic item ... is, in an important sense, an object language statement, for even though it mentions linguistic objects, it treats them as items in the order of causes and effects, i.e. *in rerum natura*, and speaks of their functioning in this order in a way which is to be sharply contrasted with the metalinguistic statements of logical semantics, in which the key role is played by abstract singular terms. Thus it is essential to note that whereas in

'*a*' (in L) denotes O

the 'O' of the right-hand side is a metalinguistic expression, in

'*a*'s (in L) represent O

it is not. ([17]: 137)

The former is roughly equivalent to

For some INSENSE, *a*s (in *L*) are INSENSE's and INSENSE's are (equivalent to) ·O·s (where 'INSENSE' is a metalinguistic variable taking dot-quoted individual constants as substituends—see [17]: 137–38), while the latter corresponds rather to something like

> The regularities involving *a*s (produced by *L*-speakers) are isomorphic to the regularities involving *O* (in the world).

27. I have been speaking of *isomorphism*, but the 'fit' between systems of natural-linguistic objects and systems of non-linguistic objects, like any correlation of relational structures, is one which admits of degrees.

> [P]ictures, like maps, can be more or less adequate. The adequacy concerns the 'method of projection'. A picture (candidate) subject to the rules of a given method of projection (conceptual framework), which is a correct picture (successful candidate), is S-assertible with respect to that method of projection. ([17]: 135)

28. A conceptual framework (system of semantical normatives) controls the production of natural-linguistic objects, the regularities of relation among which then correspond more or less to the regularities among the non-linguistic objects which they variously represent. Since the picturing relation thus generated admits of degrees, it follows that

> ... one conceptual framework can be more 'adequate' than another, and this fact can be used to define a sense in which one proposition can be said to be 'more true' than another. ([17]: 134)

Less metaphorically, responsive to the earlier identification of theoretical evolution and conceptual evolution, we can distinguish

> ... between the conceptual structure to which a proposition *belongs* and the conceptual structure *with respect to which its truth is defined*. ([17]: 134)

In other words, while the so-called 'absolute' sense of 'true'—and the *ultimate* cash value of 'S-assertibility'—remains assertibility in *our* conceptual structure, here and now, it makes sense to view our conceptual structure as merely one stage in the evolution of a series of conceptual frameworks which are, in the picturing sense adumbrated above, increasingly adequate. Consequently, we may consider the assertibility—in accordance with the semantical rules of conceptual structures which are more or less evolved *counterparts* of our own—either of propositions belonging to our current conceptual structure or of propositions which are themselves more or less evolved counterparts of those which we can formulate with our current conceptual resources.

29. And now we are in the position to take the last step and

> ... conceive of a language which enables its users to form *ideally* adequate pictures of objects ... ([17]: 140)

This language (which Sellars naturally enough calls "Peirceish") forms the *fundamentum* of a notion of *ideal* truth. What is true, then, *in the last analysis* is what would be correctly S-assertible according to the semantical rules of the *Peirceish* conceptual framework, and 'what really exists', in the sense of Sellars' scientific realism, is what the Peirceish conceptual structure would posit as the ultimate furniture of the world, what is correctly pictured by first-level factual statements of Peirceish.

30. Peirceish, of course, is but a regulative ideal.

Although the concepts of 'ideal truth' and 'what really exists' are defined in terms of a Peircean conceptual structure they do not require that there ever be a Peirceish community. ([17]: 142)

Nevertheless, Sellars insists that it is an *intelligible* regulative ideal, given literal content by the notion of the adequacy of a conceptual framework *qua method of projecting more or less adequate pictures.*

Peirce himself fell into difficulty because, by not taking into account the dimension of 'picturing', he had no Archimedean point outside the series of actual and possible beliefs in terms of which to define the ideal or limit to which members of this series might approximate. ([17]: 142)

VII

31. This, then, is a sketch—and, let me emphasize, *only* a sketch—of one strand of Sellars' deep and intricate philosophy. It leads from ascent to the formal mode through linguistic rules of criticism, natural laws as semantical rules, practical reasoning and the epistemic ends of scientific inquiry, and the conception of factual discourse as picturing the world to a renovated Peircean conception of ideal truth. While fascinating sideroads—many of which Sellars himself has fruitfully explored—lead off from each juncture of this path, the path itself provides more than enough discussible topography. In what follows, I should like to pick up three themes for further exploration. I will first raise a problem from the beginning, from negative ontology. Call it "The Elusiveness of Categories". Wittgenstein has a 'solution' of sorts for it, and while I'm not at all happy with his solution, I don't myself have a better one, so I shall leave this issue as an open question. Second, I will discuss a theme from the end, theory convergence and Peircean limit concepts. There is a problem here too. Call it "The Archimedean Dilemma". For this one, I have a solution which I shall do my best to lay out. These two discussions bring pressure to bear from two different directions on Sellars' account of the picturing relation, exploring its limitations, first from the standpoint of negative ontology and, then, from the standpoint of positive. Finally, I shall return to the middle and say a bit about epistemic ends. Here I intend to indulge my propensity for speculative metaphysics. Call it a study of "The Nature of Man". But first things first.

VIII

32. Consider the following ontological thesis:

(T) Facts are not objects.[3]

Sellars, as I understand him, would assent to two claims about (T)—first, that it is misleadingly put, being the material mode transposition of a thesis perspicuously formulated in a functional metalanguage, but, second, that it is *true*. Or, more precisely, the metalinguistic thesis for which it is a material mode surrogate is true. What metalinguistic thesis? Well, 'fact', in this truth-neutral sense, is the material mode counterpart of 'sentence', and 'object' of 'name' ('referring expression', 'individual constant'), so (T) puts unperspicuously roughly the metalinguistic thesis that

(T*) Sentences are not names.

And that Sellars accepts (T*) is clear enough.

33. What is important to us here, however, is that (T*) *is* contentious. Not all philosophers would accept it. Frege, for example, held that sentences *are* names—specifically, names of truth-values. According to Frege, every well-formed sentence has, in addition to a sense, a referent. It denotes either the True or the False. (T*), then, is not only disputable; it has been disputed. And so arguments are called for. Are there relevant arguments concerning the putative distinction between sentences and names claimed by (T*)?

34. Of course there are such arguments, deep and cogent arguments deriving from Wittgenstein's *Tractatus*. But, and this is the heart of the matter, the arguments turn upon drawing a categorial *ontological* distinction between sentences and names. Indeed, they turn upon the very ontological distinction with which we began. Briefly, sentences are not names because names are natural-linguistic *objects* and sentences are natural-linguistic *facts*. And facts are not objects. This, in broad outline, is the structure of the problem which I call the Elusiveness of Categories. Let us look at the details.

35. How is it possible to use language to make claims about the world? A classical, though unacceptable, answer appeals to *reference*. Language is about the world by virtue of the fact that bits of language (names) *stand for* bits

---

[3] Two comments: First, the choice of thesis is not crucial. Any of several others would have done as well. Second, as always in ontological discourse, a few cautionary terminological remarks are in order. Here I am using 'fact' in the *truth-neutral* sense of the Tractarian '*Sachlage*'. In this sense of 'fact', both true and false sentences may be used to state facts. Thus, 'situation' or 'state of affairs' would do as well as 'fact'. On the other hand, I do *not* intend that objects be conceived as "ontologically simple", Tractarian '*Gegenstände*'. Thus, 'things' or 'particulars' would do as well as 'objects'. (But *not* 'individuals'. There is *a* reading of (T) on which "Facts are not individuals" comes out false—cf. [10]; [16]: 253—and I need a thesis which is unambiguously Sellarsianly *true*.)

of the world (objects). If that were the *whole* story, however, there would be no essential difference between a sentence and a mere list of names. Yet a mere list makes no claim. So a sentence cannot be a mere list of names. Here the road forks. Frege hews to the referential model. But recognizing the need to differentiate a sentence from a list, Frege insists, too, that a sentence contains at least one *non-name*. Yet his semantics undermines his good intentions. Frege multiplies relations of *standing for*—an expression *denotes* its referent and *expresses* its sense—but he applies all of them across the whole range of linguistic forms. Subjects, predicates, and sentences alike—all of them have *both* senses *and* referents. True, the referents of predicate expressions are concepts—*'ungesättigt'* entities categorially different from the objects which are the referents of subject terms—but that is a difference in the world where we need a difference in the words. Functionally, however, subject and predicate expressions are alike—both relate to the world by the twin ties of sense and reference. A Fregean *non-name*, thus, turns out to be a name after all, but the name of a *non-object*. On the side of ontology, Frege gives us only the metaphor of "unsaturatedness", and on the side of language, no functional difference at all. However ingeniously modified, the referential model remains a dead end.

36. Wittgenstein's answer is one which we have already met. Language (and here let us limit ourselves to first-level matter-of-factual language) represents the world by *picturing* it. The picturing theme is a vast one, of course, but its primary impact for our current discussion can be spelled out quickly.[4] Let me quote Sellars' exposition:

What Wittgenstein tells us is that while superficially regarded the statement [aRb] is a concatenation of the three parts 'a', 'R', and 'b', viewed more profoundly it is a *two-termed fact*, with 'R' coming in to the statement … as bringing it about that the expressions 'a' and 'b' are related as having an 'R' between them. And he is making the point that what is essential to any statement which will say that aRb is not the names 'a' and 'b' have a relation word between them … but that these names be related (dyadically) *in some way or other* whether or not this involves the use of a third sign design. ([15]; [18]: 226; first italics mine)

37. Now Sellars rejects the *full* Tractarian view that the only *essential* feature of the picturing relation is that *n*-adic atomic facts be pictured by *n*-adic configurations of names (i.e., by *n*-adic *linguistic* facts).

It was, indeed, a significant achievement to show that it is *n*-adic configurations of referring expressions that represent *n*-adic states of affairs. But of itself this thesis throws no light on the crucial question: What is there about *this specific n*-adic configuration of referring expressions that makes the configuration say that the items referred to are related in *that specific n*-adic way? ([21]; [18]: 213–14)

---

[4] For a more extended discussion, see my [5], [9], and [8].

38. For the Tractarian schema

Linguistic fact pictures non-linguistic fact,

Sellars substitutes the richer scheme

(natural-linguistic objects) $O_1', O_2', \ldots, O_n'$ make up a picture of [objects] $O_1, O_2, \ldots, O_n$ by virtue of such and such facts about $O_1', O_2', \ldots, O_n'$. ([21]; [18]: 215)

Yet this account "preserves in a modified way the Wittgensteinian theme that it is configurations of names that picture configurations of objects" for "the occurrence of an elementary statement is to be construed as the occurrence *in a certain manner* of the names of the objects referred to" ([21]; [18]: 215). Pursued directly, this Sellarsian modification of the Tractarian account would bring us, again, to the correlations of relational structures, the world-world uniformities, consequent upon the linguistic activities of persons controlled by a "method of projection" which is a system of semantical normatives constituting a conceptual framework.[5] But enough has been said for our purposes here to see that the features of the picturing account which generated our initial puzzle are still with us. For Sellars accepts the view that a *necessary* condition of picturing is a categorial *ontological* distinction between names and sentences. And whether that distinction be described as one between linguistic objects and linguistic facts, between natural-linguistic objects and configurations of such objects, or between names and names occurring in a certain manner, it does not alter the essential point—that the distinction is precisely the categorial ontological distinction between objects and facts with which we began, though now restricted to the domain of language as it is manifested in the natural order.

39. This, then, is the Elusiveness of Categories. The rock-bottom categorial distinctions of ontology cannot be elucidated by metalinguistic ascent because the *truth* of the very metalinguistic claims proposed as analyses of the material mode ontological theses ultimately *presupposes* the very distinction putatively drawn by those theses. And here, I think, we reach the deepest understanding of Wittgenstein's thesis that "What *can* be shown, *cannot* be said". This, of course, is the Wittgensteinian 'solution' which I alluded to earlier. According to it, ultimate categorial distinctions belong to the realm of what is showable only. They "make themselves manifest", but any attempt to render them explicit is futile. In Sellarsian-Carnapian terms, if we attempt to *state* a categorial distinction, we find ourselves talking in the material mode. And this is misleading. So we ascend to a functional metalanguage—the formal mode—transposing our putative ontological thesis into a putatively metalinguistic one. But the resulting metalinguistic thesis is contentious. *And the correct defense of that thesis turns upon our ability to draw the very categorial distinction with which we began.* Our attempt to give explicit statement to a categorial thesis of ontology has met with futility.

[5] For the corresponding earlier Sellarsian version of this story, see [21]; [18]: 215–22.

40. The only alternative, then, seems to be Wittgenstein's—relegate categorial ontological distinctions to a special realm which we *call* the realm of the merely showable, recognizing thereby that any attempt to state such a distinction will meet with *just this sort* of futility. Now this seems to me an alternative which is as defeatist as it is unenlightening. As I said earlier, I am not at all happy with it. But at this point I see no other, better, alternative, and so I must be content simply to commend this difficult question of categorial distinctions to your attention.

IX

41. We have not yet finished putting pressure on Sellars' version of *picturing*, however, and a second look at the proposed role of the picturing relation as a fundamentum for first-level matter-of-factual truth provides a convenient place to begin the development of our second problem. Recall that Sellars insists that the correctness of an elementary proposition as a picture is *criterial* for the correctness of the assertion-performance which, *qua* justified by semantical rules, constitutes the truth of that proposition. "Thus the *correctness* of the picture is not defined in terms of the *correctness* of a performance but vice versa" ([17]: 136).

42. The point is a delicate one and it has its consequences. For while the correctness of an assertion-performance *with respect to a system of semantical rules* is something which can be judged from *within* the conceptual structure constituted by those semantical rules, Sellars' requirement, that the adequacy of the semantical rules themselves ultimately be measured by the adequacy *as pictures* of the first-level assertions which they license, suggests that we need a standpoint which is *neutral* as among diverse conceptual structures from which we can judge the degree of fit between a system of natural-linguistic objects and a system of non-linguistic objects in a way which does not *presuppose* that one conceptual framework is more adequate than another.

43. And, indeed, this is a consequence to which Sellars appears to assent, for, recall, he characterizes the notion of correctness of picture as an Archimedean standpoint *outside* the Peircean series of actual and possible beliefs, intending thereby to provide some non-metaphorical *content* for Peirce's notion of a limit point for scientific inquiry. Thus Sellars hopes to answer the challenge of such philosophers as Quine, who find the Peircean model intrinsically unintelligible:

Peirce was tempted to define truth outright in terms of scientific method, as the ideal theory which is approached as a limit when the (supposed) canons of scientific method are used unceasingly on continuing experience. But there is a lot wrong with Peirce's notion besides its assumption of a final organon of scientific method and its appeal to an infinite process. There is a faulty use of numerical analogy in speaking of a limit of theories, since the notion of limit depends on that of "nearer than," which is defined for numbers and not for theories. ([4]: 23)

44. But can Sellars' conception of the picturing role of first-level matter-of-factual discourse thus provide content for the Peircean limit notion? That the matter is doubtful may be brought into sharper relief by reemphasizing another Sellarsian point, that statements to the effect that a natural-linguistic object, *X*, represents a non-linguistic object, *Y*, (briefly, that *X* pictures *Y*) are wholly in the object language ([17]: 137). Here, however, we must surely ask *which* object language, and it seems inevitable that any answer will again tie us down to one specific conceptual framework or another. A conception of *what* is pictured, in other words, seems to be available only from *within* a *single* conceptual scheme, and that will not do for an Archimedean standpoint.

45. Now Sellars recognizes this difficulty, and in a single passage of *Science and Metaphysics* he attempts to meet it:

Are the individual variables we use tied exclusively to the individual senses of our current conceptual structure? Are the predicate variables we use tied exclusively to our conceptual resources? It is obvious that the only *cash* we have for these variables is to be found in our current conceptual structure, but it is a mistake to think that the substituends for a variable are limited to the constants which are here-now possessions of an instantaneous cross-section of language users. The identity of a language through time must be taken seriously, and a distinction drawn between the *logical* or 'formal' criteria of individuality which apply to any descriptive conceptual framework, and the more specific (material) criteria in terms of which individuals are identified in specific conceptual frameworks; and, similarly, between the logical criteria which differentiate, say, *n*-adic from *m*-adic predicates generally, from the conceptual criteria (material rules) which give distinctive conceptual content to predicates which have the same purely logical status.

Thus the purely formal aspects of logical syntax, when they have been correctly disentangled, give us a way of speaking which abstracts from those features which differentiate specific conceptual structures, and enables us to form the concept of a domain of objects which are pictured in one way (less adequately) by one linguistic system, and in another way (more adequately) by another. And we can conceive of the former (or less adequate) linguistic system as our current linguistic system. ([17]: 139–40)[6]

46. But, as suggestive as this passage is, it seems evident that "the purely formal aspects of logical syntax" are just not rich enough to do the requisite job. The easiest way to highlight the limitations of Sellars' proposal is to recognize that the *counterpart* in a more-highly-evolved conceptual framework of a predicate in our, or some other, "less adequate" conceptual framework may well turn out to be a relation of *different polyadicity*. There is every indication, for example, that the counterpart concepts of our common-sense color concepts will be, minimally, dyadic, rather than the strictly monadic predications of the physical-object framework. "Logical criteria which differentiate, say, *n*-adic from *m*-adic

---

[6] For a heroic early attempt to actually *carry out* parts of such a program, see Sellars' [11].

predicates generally" give us no hold on the problem of *identifying* counterpart predicates of *different* polyadicities in different conceptual frameworks. Again, as Sellars himself recognizes, it is entirely possible for the counterpart concept of some *individual* sense in our conceptual scheme to belong to a logical category which is distinct from that which is occupied by the less-well-developed concept. Indeed, Sellars deems it likely that objects in our conceptual framework will have as counterparts in successor frameworks not objects but, rather, *virtual classes* of objects ([17]: 149–50). If a particular conceptual framework is an explanatory dead-end, we shall even find within it concepts which have *no* counterparts in highly developed conceptual schemes which are "on the right track". Thus no predicate in current science is a more highly evolved counterpart of 'phlogiston'. If such fundamental matters as the *number* of objects available *in re* to be pictured and the polyadicities of the relations into which they enter are open to reconceptualization in successive conceptual frameworks, we must surely conclude that logical syntax alone, however thoroughly disentangled, is inadequate to the task of guiding the formation of "the concept of a domain of objects which are pictured in one way ... by one linguistic system and in another way ... by another" ([17]: 140). The only alternative is to grant that there can be *no* system of concepts which is *both* framework-neutral *and* descriptive. The myth of the *gettable*, in that sense, must be recognized as being as pernicious as the myth of the *given*.

47. But if this is so, Quine's criticisms of the Peircean notion of ideal truth would seem to carry the field. For we have lost the "Archimedean standpoint" from which we could view Peirce's limit concepts as more than mere metaphors. This is the problem which I call the Archimedean Dilemma. How, if there is no framework-neutral standpoint from which to assess the relative adequacy as pictures of the systems of propositions generated in accordance with the semantical rules of different conceptual schemes, are we to give content to the Peircean notion of a limit toward which successive conceptual systems evolve?[7]

X

48. To begin to approach this problem, let us return to the primary and natural home of limits and convergence and examine the nature of convergence to a limit for number series. What does it mean to say that the infinite series of rationals

1/2, 2/3, 3/4, 4/5, ...

---

[7] The Archimedean Dilemma has a strict counterpart as an *internal* problem of philosophical methodology. Hall has called it 'the categorio-centric predicament'. See [1] for an extended discussion.

converges to the number 1? It means that, as you go out in the series, the individual members of the series get arbitrarily close to 1. More precisely, if we represent the members of our series by 'A_1', 'A_2', ..., etc., to say that the limit of the A_i-series is 1 ($\lim\limits_{n\to\infty} A_n = 1$) is to say that

$$(\epsilon)(\exists N)(n)(n > N \supset |A_n - 1| \leq \epsilon).$$

In general, a series $S_1, S_2, \ldots$ converges to the limit L, ($\lim\limits_{n\to\infty} S_n = L$), if and only if

$$(\epsilon)(\exists N)(n)(n > N \supset |S_n - L| \leq \epsilon).$$

(For every increment, ϵ, there is a point in the series, N, beyond which every member, S_n, of the series is within ϵ of the limit L.) This is the *Weierstrass condition* for convergence. Notice that, even though the limit of the series of A_i is not a *member* of the series of A_i, in order to make use of the Weierstrass definition of convergence *we must know, and be able to say, what that limit is*. The model of convergence which Sellars utilizes is a model based upon Weierstrass' definition. Consequently, in order to give content to the notion that conceptual frameworks converge to a limit, Sellars finds it necessary to attempt to specify, from without, the character of the limit to which the series of frameworks is to converge. This is the demand for a framework-neutral standpoint which gives rise to the Archimedean Dilemma.

49. But we have argued that there is no way of characterizing a limit point for conceptual evolution in framework-neutral terms. Is there any analogue to this difficulty in mathematics? Consider the series of rationals

$$2/1, \ 4/3, \ 10/7, \ 24/17, \ 58/41, \ 140/99, \ldots$$

which converges to the square root of 2. Again, the limit of the series is not a member of the series. But, more significantly, the limit of the series is not even a member of the *system of numbers to which the members of the series belong*. For the square root of 2 is demonstrably irrational, provably incapable of being represented as any ratio of integers. Is there any way in which, while remaining entirely within the system of *rational* numbers, we can demonstrate that this series (call it the B_i-series) converges? That is, can we demonstrate that *there is* a limit to which the B_i-series converges without being able to demonstrate, or even to *state*, that the series converges to the limit L, for any specifiable L? The answer, interestingly enough, is that we can. Rather than using the Weierstrass notion of converges, where members of the series get arbitrarily close to a *known limit*, we can demonstrate simply that the series of B_i converges to *some* limit by establishing, instead, that, as we go out in the series, individual members of the series get arbitrarily close *to each other*. More precisely, the series of B_i converges if and only if

$$(\epsilon)(\exists N)(m)(n)(m > N \& n > N \cdot \supset \cdot |B_m - B_n| \leq \epsilon).$$

(For every increment, ϵ, there is a point in the series, N, beyond which any pair of members, B_m and B_n, are within ϵ of each other.) This is the *Cauchy condition* for convergence. Unlike a case in which use is made of the Weierstrass condition, convergence can be demonstrated by appeal to the Cauchy condition *even if the limit to which a series converges is not capable of being explicated in terms of the concepts governing the members of that series*. The requisite analogue for conceptual frameworks is clear. A temporal series of conceptual systems can be shown to be evolving towards *some* limit if it can be established that pairs of systems grow successively and arbitrarily closer to each other. This is the requirement, but it is still phrased metaphorically. Is there a way of breaking the metaphor and providing a *literal* content for the notion of conceptual systems approaching, not an ideal limit specified in framework-neutral terms, but rather *each other*? To do so requires that we take a closer look at the epistemology of theory succession and, more particularly, at the requirement of explanatory adequacy which is the *sine qua non* of acceptability for a theory. In virtue of what relation between a successor theory and its predecessor(s) is it the case that the new theory can be said to provide an explanatory account of the laws of the old?

50. On the now-classical Hempelian account of explanation, a successor theory provides an explanatory account of a set of predecessor laws if and only if the new theory *entails* the old laws. It is clear, however, that, while deducibility relations will be of crucial importance, this straightforward *identification* of explanation and deducibility cannot hold up under scrutiny. Most significantly, the Hempelian identification fails because it presupposes meaning-invariance of terms between old and new theories, a possibility analytically precluded by our earlier identification of natural laws with a subset of the semantical rules which are constitutive of meanings *qua* linguistic roles or functions. Theory change *is* concept change, and so there can be no question of strict entailment relations between new laws and old. But each old law *will* have a *strict counterpart* in the new theory. Why not require, then, that these strict counterpart laws be deducible from the basic principles of the new theoretical framework? This brings us to the heart of the matter, for it will rather be a consequence of the principles of the new theory that the *strict* counterparts of the old laws are *literally false*.

51. Let me provide a handful of illustrations. Kepler's Laws of Planetary Motion specify that the path of a planet about the sun is an *ellipse*. Yet it is a consequence of Newton's Laws of Motion and Universal Gravitation that the orbit of a planet will *not* be an ellipse, since no planet is subject *solely* to the central gravitational force of the sun as the *total* determinant of its motion. The Law of Universal Gravitation asserts that *every* two bodies attract one another with a determinate gravitational force, and the Second Law of Motion posits that *any* force produces a consequent acceleration in the bodies upon which it acts. It follows that, while roughly elliptical in the large, planetary paths will

necessarily be highly irregular in the small, for each planet is subject not only to the central solar gravitational force, but equally to the perturbational gravitational forces resulting from the presence in the solar system of other planets, satellites, asteroids, and interplanetary gas and dust. Again, Galileo's Law of Falling Bodies specifies that the acceleration in free fall of a body near the surface of the earth is constant. But, according to Newton's theories, acceleration in free fall results from the action of gravitational forces which vary continuously with the changing distance of the falling body from the center of the earth. It follows that the absolute magnitude of the acceleration will *not* be constant, but will rather be a continuously varying function of the distance of fall. Finally, to take an example from another area of science, the Boyle-Charles Gas Law specifies that the volume of a sample of gas of fixed mass varies directly as the temperature of the sample and inversely as the pressure. But the counterpart concepts of temperature and pressure in the kinetic theory (mean kinetic energy of the molecules composing the sample and relative frequency of collisions between those molecules and the walls of the container) are not thus regularly related to volume. Rather, a correction factor must be introduced into the equation, depending, among other things, upon the absolute diameter of the molecules in the sample and the degree to which the collisions between those molecules are not perfectly elastic.

52. The upshot is that the new theories do not provide explanatory accounts of the old laws by entailing their strict counterparts in the successor framework. Rather, it is an analytic consequence of the basic principles of the new framework that the strict counterparts of the predecessor laws are literally false, for the new principles entail laws which are *inconsistent* with the strict counterparts of the old laws. And this basic fact about theory succession is something Sellars himself not only recognized but, indeed, in certain contexts, stressed. As he has put it, theories

> ... *explain empirical laws by explaining why observable things obey to the extent that they do, these empirical laws*; that is, they explain why individual objects of various kinds and in various circumstances in the observation framework behave in those ways in which it is inductively established that they do behave. Roughly, it is because a gas is—in some sense of 'is'—a cloud of molecules which are behaving in certain theoretically defined ways, that it obeys the *empirical* Boyle-Charles law. ([13]; [18]: 121)

53. Strictly speaking, then, theories do not provide a direct explanatory account of their predecessor laws. Rather they provide an *indirect* explanatory account of predecessor laws by providing a *direct* account of the *success* of those laws. And this point is not, as Sellars seems to suggest, limited to the relationship between postulational microtheories and inductively established macro-regularities. It applies to the relationship between *any* pair of theories related as predecessor and successor. Just as it is because a gas is a cloud of molecules that the empirical Boyle-Charles Law is as good an account of the behavior of gases as it is, so

it is because a *molecule* is a system of protons, neutrons, and electrons, with determinate masses and charges, interacting in ways specified by the theory of subatomic particles, that the *kinetic* theory is as good an account of the behavior of gases as *it* is.

54. In general, then, the *prime* explanatory function of a new theory, and, thus, as we have seen, the fundamental constraint on its acceptability, is to account for the *success* of its predecessor(s). And this accounting essentially involves idealizations and limit concepts. Its structure is this: The basic framework principles of the new theory must have three analytic consequences. First, they must have the consequence that the strict counterparts of predecessor laws are literally false. But, second, they must *also* have the consequence that those strict counterparts are *true in the limit.* The orbit of a planet *would* be an ellipse were there no perturbational forces; the acceleration of a freely falling body *would* be constant were its distance from the center of the earth constant; the strict counterpart of the Boyle-Charles Law *would* be literally correct were molecules of zero diameter and collisions between them perfectly elastic. And, finally, the new theory must have the consequence that the relevant limit is one which is *closely approximated* by the world as it is posited in the successor framework to be. The perturbational forces acting upon a planet are *near zero;* the relative change in distance between a falling body and the center of the earth is *near zero;* and molecules have *near zero* diameters, collisions between them being *almost* perfectly elastic. Thus, it follows that the strict counterparts within the successor framework of the old laws are *good approximations* to what the successor theory now asserts to be the actual state of affairs.

55. A successor theory, in other words, allows us to calculate the *magnitude* of the deviation of the accounts provided by its predecessor(s) from what the new theory now tells us is actually the case. And here we have precisely the raw materials which we need to construct a version of Cauchy convergence for scientific theories. The degree to which two theories approach one another can be measured by the absolute numerical magnitude of the correction factors which must be introduced into applications of the strict counterparts of predecessor laws to arrive at the values determined by their successors. Inasmuch as the absolute numerical values of the requisite correction factors become increasingly smaller as we move from successor theory to successor theory, we may say, non-metaphorically, that the theories are approaching each other.

56. This solution to the convergence problem incorporates *both* the insights of Sellars *and* the insights of Quine. For we may now say, with Sellars, that it is the "purely formal aspects of logical syntax"—in this case, the framework-neutral but *descriptively empty* (content-free) concepts of pure mathematics—which enable us to give a non-metaphorical sense to the Peircean limit concept, while *also* agreeing to the Quinean contention that the notion of limit is "defined for numbers and not for theories". For theories generate numbers. And as the

absolute numerical magnitudes of the correction factors introduced by theory succession converge, *in the well-defined sense of pure mathematics*, to zero, so we may say that the theories themselves are growing successively closer to each other.

57. And this shows, too, that it is no mere accident that the notion of scientific progress has been historically tied to the extent to which a discipline projects *quantitative measures* of its theoretical parameters. For, if the argument to this point has not been misguided, it is only after a discipline has introduced quantitative measures over its subject matter that there *can* be any literal sense given to the notion that successive theories within that discipline have a *direction* and represent progress, more or less rapid, in that direction. Since the acceptability of a successor theory turns fundamentally upon its ability to account for the successes of its predecessor(s), since it is essential to such an account that the strict counterparts of old laws in the new framework be *closely approximated* limit cases or idealizations of laws of the new theory, and since the notion of a close approximation makes *literal* sense (is well-defined) only for *numerical measures*, it follows that theories in a non-quantitative discipline cannot be related as predecessor and successor but, at best, merely as *alternatives* to one another.

58. If my colleagues in the social sciences find this "transcendental deduction of 'quantitativism' " objectionable, I can only plead, as Sellars does in connection with his own "transcendental deduction of 'finitism' ", that "I am not alone in thinking that the issue is not an empirical one" ([17]: 148). If we must abandon the myth of the gettable and recognize that no conceptual system can be both framework-neutral and descriptive, as I have argued that we must, then I can see no alternative solution to the Archimedean Dilemma.

XI

59. Before proceeding to my final theme, let me pause to collect a few morals concerning the picturing relation and its role in Sellars' philosophy. Sellars gives picturing two major jobs to do. First, as the sole genuine relation between linguistic and non-linguistic entities (natural-linguistic objects and non-linguistic objects), picturing is to provide the ultimate basis *in re* for the normative claims of a functional metalinguistic discourse. The cash value for the pseudo-relations of functional semantics is to be provided by the regularities of picturing consequent upon the linguistic activities of persons. Indeed, the very possibility that language make claims about the world at all depends, in the last analysis, precisely upon the possibility that first-level statements be related to states of affairs in the world as pictures of them. Further, since the *content* of philosophers' ontological discourse is to be explicated by semantical claims in a functional metalanguage,

the picturing relation is to be the ultimate basis for the analysis of such discourse as well.

60. Second, since the picturing relation is posited to admit of continuous refinement toward a characterizable limit, it is to serve also to supply non-metaphorical content for the Peircean notions of 'completed science' and 'ideal truth', an Archimedean standpoint outside the series of actual and possible conceptual frameworks against which the adequacy of those frameworks may be neutrally measured.

61. That we must appeal to picturing to resolve the first cluster of problems seems to me an unavoidable conclusion. The relation of language to the world cannot be elucidated—indeed, as I see it, cannot even be *understood*—in any other terms. But the problem of the Elusiveness of Categories shows us how little, in the last analysis, such an appeal accomplishes in coping with prime *ontological* concerns. In particular, the need to ground the picturing function of factual discourse by categorial ontological distinctions prevents the metalinguistic ascent of linguistic nominalism from providing a fully formal analysis of philosophers' ontological discourse. Categorial ontological distinctions, while *in one sense* purely formal, emerge as, in another important sense, *real* distinctions, primitive realities so fundamental that they are presupposed by the very functioning of *any* mode of representation, formal or contentive, and, thus, incapable of any representational elucidation in terms still more basic. In the first case, then, Sellars' appeal to picturing, while fundamentally *correct*, is, in a deep sense, *impotent* to provide a path leading totally out of the jungle of classical ontological puzzlements.

62. In the second case, the conclusion is much the reverse. The picturing relation *would* provide the Archimedean standpoint which Sellars sees as a requirement of a non-metaphorical understanding of theory convergence, were it possible to have knowledge of the degree of adequacy of a system of linguistic pictures in a manner *neutral* as among conceptual frameworks. But adequacy of picture *cannot* be thus neutrally assessed and so, I have argued, Sellars' appeal to the picturing relation in the second case is basically *incorrect*. In this case, however, we have an alternative. By attending to the epistemological details of theory succession, we were able to locate a determinate measure of the distance between a *pair* of theories and, thus, to make non-metaphorical sense from within of the tending of the scientific enterprise toward *a* limit, although a limit which there is now no need to formulate, *per impossibile*, in framework-neutral terms.

63. Thus, incorrect in one instance and significantly impotent in another, the conception of picturing central to Sellars' philosophy turns out to be a more limited tool for the unravelling of philosophical perplexities than he believes. Yet, for all that, picturing *is* the ultimate—indeed, the only genuine—relation between language and the world. That Sellars could see this, and see it as clearly as he has, remains a philosophical accomplishment of the first magnitude, an accomplishment that cannot be diminished.

XII

64. And now let me, finally, bring this already unwieldy study to a close by developing a few speculative remarks concerning the epistemic ends-in-view controlling the scientific enterprise and, more broadly, inquiry into the world in general and the representations (pictures) which result from it. The epistemic ends, you will recall, are essentially the ends of explanation. The prime requirement of acceptability for lawlike statements turned out to be the realization of a necessary condition for being in the framework of explanation and prediction, the controlling end-in-view being the possession of principles which license inferences to unknown cases while optimally explaining what is known. Similarly, the epistemic end controlling the acceptance of new theoretical frameworks emerged as the state of "being able to give non-trivial explanatory accounts of established laws" ([12]: 210). Now the question which I wish to pose here is itself the request for an explanatory account. People seek explanations. Their doing so is the ultimate "motive force" of the scientific enterprise and, more broadly, of all representings of the world. But *why* do people seek explanations? Why do people have the epistemic ends which they in fact do have and thus come to produce representations of the world? It is this question which will be exercising us for the balance of the essay.

65. Now a first reaction might well be that the question itself is misguided. It asks for what can't be given. In the case of any *individual* person, perhaps, a psychoanalytic account might be given of why *he* has and pursues the ends with which we find him, but there is no *more general* account to be given of why *people* have and pursue the ends with which we find them. From the philosophical point of view, the most we can say is that people just *do*, generally, have these ends and pursue these activities, and that that must be an end to the matter.

66. While there is doubtless *some* merit to this reaction, I think that we must finally respond to it by dismissing it. First, we must dismiss it because, insofar as it contains merely a polemic against raising questions of a certain sort, it counts as "blocking the road to inquiry", and Peirce's injunction against such epistemological obstructionism is as valid today as when first issued. But, second, we must dismiss it because, insofar as it contains a diagnosis of the putative illegitimacy of our question, the presumptive evidence seems contrary to the grounds of that diagnosis. For the "will to explain" is not, as the reaction seems to suggest, an idiosyncratic feature of isolated persons or groups of persons. Rather the search for explanations seems to be characteristic of man *as a species*. While the nature and sophistication of the particular explanatory accounts offered varies widely from culture to culture and, within a single culture, from epoch to epoch, the *presence* of explanatory accounts seems itself to be a cultural invariant. From the elemental mythologies of primitive man to contemporary

postulational microphysics is a great distance measured in terms of sophistication. But *epistemologically* myth and microtheory are brothers. Each is a system of beliefs and principles accepted because it provides, at the time of its acceptance, the *best available explanatory account* of a range of phenomena. That people's systems of beliefs and representations of the world grow out of and are controlled by the end of explanation is too pervasive a feature of human life to be dismissed as a brute and unexplainable fact.

67. On the other hand, the contrasting immediate reaction that men seek explanations simply because they wish to *understand* their world must also be dismissed. Here, however, the basis of dismissal is not that the proposed reply is incorrect. Rather it is all *too* true. For the connection between explanation and understanding is analytic. What we understand and what we can explain are not just contingently coextensive. Rather, it is a *necessary* truth that we understand *only* what we can explain. The process of explaining a range of phenomena *is* the process of coming to understand those phenomena. And since it is a necessary truth that we understand only what we can explain, to say that men seek explanations *in order* to achieve understanding is itself to offer no explanation but merely a *rephrasal* of our original question. *Why* do people seek to understand the world?

68. An appropriately sophisticated answer sees scientific inquiry as activity in the service of higher ends. What we do not understand, the reply runs, we cannot predict and we cannot control. Only when we understand the world, therefore, can we act most effectively in optimizing all those factors which conduce to the good life for man. The ends of understanding (explanation) are, indeed, the ultimate ends controlling the *scientific* enterprise. But, viewed more broadly, that enterprise itself is but a *means* to a more fundamental end—the achieving of the good life for man. And, thus, in this broader context, the epistemic ends-in-view of understanding are to be seen as merely *proximate* ends, and the belief-systems and representations which they generate are to be seen as means or instruments for the attaining of the *genuinely* ultimate ends of *all* human activity.

59. As attractive as this "epistemological instrumentalism" may seem, I believe that we must finally reject it also. For it does not fairly reflect the essential *autonomy* of the epistemic ends of explanation. And this is so because epistemological instrumentalism mislocates the relation between understanding and the good life. To be sure, there *is* a necessary connection, but it is *not* the relation of necessary means to an autonomous end. It is, in fact, even *closer* than that. What we must recognize is that understanding is an *essential part* of the good life for man. The relation of human understanding to human happiness is not like the relation between buying a car and owning it; it is, rather, much more like the relation between eating an apple and enjoying it. Here the activity is a constituent of the enjoyment. *What* we enjoy is *eating the apple.* If I may be permitted a somewhat archaic mode of expression, the enjoyment is *supervenient* upon the eating, not *consequent* upon it as effect upon cause nor separable from it

as end from means. Human understanding and the good life for man are related in *that* way. The latter is not consequent upon nor separable from the former but, rather, supervenient upon it. Understanding is itself a wholly autonomous human good and, thus, not *merely* a precondition of human happiness but rather a prime constituent of that happiness. Epistemological instrumentalism, therefore, will not do.

60. What alternative, then, is left us? As I see it, our only choice is to begin to take Aristotle seriously: Every man *by nature* desires to know. What I propose is that we must properly regard our explanatory question concerning the epistemic ends controlling the scientific enterprise as an *empirical* question and, thus, one which *falls within the legitimate scope of that enterprise itself.* Thereby we turn the methodology upon itself as subject. And when we do so, we may find that our *problem* undergoes a radical Copernican inversion. Let me briefly explain what I have in mind.

71. We have been asking for an explanation of why, with respect to epistemic ends and, more broadly, with respect to the representations of the world consequent upon the human epistemic activity controlled by those ends, man is as he is. Taken seriously, the Aristotelian proposal suggests that humans seek to understand and thus to represent the world as a matter of *natural* necessity. It is a law of nature that man, as a species, searches for explanations of phenomena and thereby comes to project representations of his world. Since it is the job of *science* to develop theoretical frameworks which provide explanatory accounts of natural laws, it now becomes a part of that enterprise to develop a comprehensive theoretical account of man-in-the-universe from which it will follow that men seek to understand and represent the universe of which they are a part. And the way to do *this* may well be by means of a *total* conception of the *universe* as a physical system which of natural necessity *evolves* subsystems that in turn necessarily project increasingly adequate representations of the whole. Crudely, our universe necessarily "grows knowers" and thereby comes to reflect *itself* (*picture* itself) within itself.

72. Such a theory would treat man and the universe as explanatorily *correlative.* The fundamental nature of man would, of course, be explained by an appeal to the general character of the physical universe of and within which man is an evolutionary product. But, equally, the fundamental nature of the physical *universe* would be explained by showing that in a universe of that sort, and *only* in a universe of that sort, *could* there evolve a species of entities which generate representations of the total physical system of which they are but a part and thereby *come to inquire* into the fundamental nature of that system. "If the universe weren't the way it *is*, there couldn't be anything in it *capable* of asking what it *was* like."

73. Nor is this Copernican explanatory inversion totally alien to the thinking of contemporary physical theorizers. The physicist John Wheeler and his students have recently begun to speculate about just such an account of the "very large

numbers" of physics—the ratio of electrical to gravitational forces, for example. It now begins to appear that, if such fundamental constants were very much different from what they are, the most fundamental physical preconditions of life could not be instantiated within the universe at all. Thus the proposal has been made that we explain the *universe* by reference to *us*. The universe *did* evolve us, after all, and it would not be a trivial result if it could be shown that *only* a universe of this sort (where "this sort" is now to be specified in precise and quantitative theoretical terms) *could* evolve us.

74. Here, indeed, is a synoptic view of man-in-the-world. We cannot understand the universe until we understand it precisely *as* a universe which is such that, within it, a species of entities evolves which seeks to understand and represent it. And we cannot understand *ourselves* and our epistemology until we understand them both as *products* of this total evolutionary system and as *parts* of the very process of its evolution. And is there anything like this in Sellars' philosophy? Well, at one time there *was*. In 1948, Sellars sketched a distinction

... between a broader and a narrower sense of "empirical system." The narrower sense would cover only such relational systems as include "minds" which "know" the system in which they are embedded. The broader sense would cover any systems which could be said to be a system of exemplifications of universals. With this distinction in mind, one might introduce the phrase "concrete system" to stand for this broader sense, and use the phrase "empirical system" for those systems which are "self-knowing", to which alone the term "empirical" is appropriate. An exploration of the concept of self-knowing concrete systems would take us into the heart of epistemology, for, indeed, in the material mode of speech, epistemology is nothing other than the pure theory of such systems. ([11]: 305)

A universe which evolves a subsystem of entities who necessarily generate, within the whole of which they are a part, a representation of that whole is surely nothing other than a "self-knowing concrete system" in this early Sellarsian sense.

75. But we need not turn to Sellars for an anticipation of these speculations. The reader has doubtless been hearing echoes for some time; let me now say that they are intentional. For, although newly clothed in respectability by our appeals to empirical science, our universe thus conceived as understandable only as a total system evolving *within* itself a representation *of* itself is a philosophical old friend: the Hegelian Absolute evolving to self-consciousness. Nor is the turning of the methodology of science in upon itself as subject any different from Hegel's identification of subject matter and method in *Die Phänomenologie des Geistes*. Sellars proposes that we now understand Kantian *noumena* in terms of the posits of postulational microtheory. What I am suggesting here is that we can now understand the self-actualization of the Hegelian Absolute as well, in terms of a synoptic empirical theory of man-in-the-universe which views the epistemic activities of persons and the fundamental nature of the physical arena in which

those activities occur as explanatorily correlative, neither being understandable without recourse to a conception of the other.

76. To pursue this topic further would, I fear, generate quite another study, no shorter surely than the present one. So this is not the place to pursue it. But I firmly believe that it is a topic well worth pursuing. And if my readers do not find such an attempt to resuscitate the central themes of Nineteenth Century Idealism particularly congenial to their contemporary idioms, I can cheerfully reply that it is a habit which, like almost everything else philosophical, I learned from Wilfrid Sellars.[8]

REFERENCES

[1] Hall, Everett, *Philosophical Systems* (Chicago: The University of Chicago Press, 1960).

[2] Harman, Gilbert, "Enumerative Induction as Inference to the Best Explanation", *Journal of Philosophy*, 65 (1968), 529–33.

[3] _____ "Inference to the Best Explanation", *Philosophical Review*, 74 (1965), 88–95.

[4] Quine, W. V., *Word and Object* (Cambridge, Mass.: M.I.T. Press, 1960).

[5] Rosenberg, Jay F., "New Perspectives on the *Tractatus*", *Dialogue*, 4 (1966), 506–17.

[6] _____ "Synonymy and the Epistemology of Linguistics", *Inquiry*, 10 (1967), 405–20.

[7] _____ "What's Happening in Philosophy of Language Today", *American Philosophical Quarterly*, 9 (1972), 101–6.

[8] _____ "Wittgenstein's Self-Criticisms, or 'Whatever Happened to the Picture Theory?' ", *Noûs*, 4 (1970), 209–23.

[9] _____ "Wittgenstein's Theory of Language as Picture", *American Philosophical Quarterly*, 5 (1968), 18–30.

[10] Sellars, Wilfrid, "Abstract Entities", *Review of Metaphysics*, 16 (1963); repr. as ch. IX, pp. 229–69, of [16].

[11] _____ "Concepts as Involving Laws and Inconceivable Without Them", *Philosophy of Science*, 15 (1948), 287–315.

[12] _____ "Induction as Vindication", *Philosophy of Science*, 31 (1964), 197–231.

[13] _____ "The Language of Theories", in *Current Issues in the Philosophy of Science*, Herbert Feigl and Grover Maxwell, eds. (New York: Holt, Rinehart, & Winston, 1961); repr. as ch. 4, pp. 106–26, of [18].

[14] _____ "Language as Thought and Communication", *Philosophy and Phenomenological Research*, 29 (1969), 506–27.

[8] This essay was completed in 1970. The ensuing four years have provided ample opportunity for second, and even third, thoughts. In consequence, much of what I said in this essay I would now say differently, and some of it (Section VIII, for example) I would now not say at all. My current views are comprehensively represented in two forthcoming works: an essay, "The 'Given' and How to Take It—Some Reflections on Phenomenal Ontology" [*Metaphilosophy*, 6/3–4 (1975), 303–37] and a book, *Linguistic Representation* (Philosophical Studies Series in Philosophy, D. Reidel Publishing Company., Dordrecht, Holland [1974, 1981]).

[15] ____ "Naming and Saying", *Philosophy of Science*, 29 (1962): repr. as ch. 7, pp. 225–45, of [18].

[16] ____ *Philosophical Perspectives* (Springfield, Ill.: Charles C Thomas, Publisher, 1967).

[17] ____ *Science and Metaphysics* (London: Routledge & Kegan Paul; New York: Humanities Press, 1968).

[18] ____ *Science, Perception and Reality* (London: Routledge & Kegan Paul; New York: Humanities Press, 1963).

[19] ____ "Scientific Realism or Irenic Instrumentalism: A Critique of Nagel and Feyerabend on Theoretical Explanation", *Proceedings of the Boston Colloquium on Philosophy of Science* (1965); repr. as ch. XIV, pp. 337–69, of [16].

[20] ____ "Some Reflections on Language Games", *Philosophy of Science*, 21 (1954), 204–28; repr. as ch. 11, pp. 321–58, of [18].

[21] ____ "Truth and 'Correspondence' ", *Journal of Philosophy*, 59 (1962); repr. as ch. 6, pp. 197–224, of [18].

4

Comparing the Incommensurable: Another Look at Convergent Realism

In Kant's era, there was only one physical theory—Newton's. Physics was regarded as historically closed. A fundamental fact which epistemologists of science have had to learn to contend with in the (post-Einsteinian) twentieth century is that physical science—and in particular physics, which I shall take as my paradigm—is essentially historically open. Theories succeed one another, and there are compelling reasons to suppose that they will inevitably continue to do so. Our physical theories—our cosmology, dynamics, thermodynamics, and the like—we must now acknowledge, are simply the latest in a long historical sequence of such theories, and will some day be dethroned from their current status as the story of what our world is like, just as Ptolemaic cosmology, Newtonian dynamics, and the classical theory of gases suffered that epistemic fate.

Some of us would like nevertheless to have a *normative* epistemology for natural science.[1] We would like, that is, to be able to go beyond mere historical accounts of theorizing activities and the genesis of theories to make well-founded judgments of *appraisal* with regard to such activities and their products. We would like, that is, to be able to answer such questions as these:

(1) Do historically-evolving sequences of physical theories represent anything which can sensibly be called "progress"? If so, how?

(2) In virtue of what (if anything) can a successor theory be legitimately judged better than (an improvement upon) its predecessor(s)?

(3) When and how is a re-theoretization—the adoption of a candidate successor theory in place of its established predecessor(s)—justified or warranted?

Nowadays, however, it is disputed that such questions have, or can have, anything but empty ("Whiggish") answers. (Rorty, [PMN], is a chief exponent of this view.) Nowadays, in fact, it is disputed that a normative epistemology for natural

---

[1] There are also those, e.g., Richard Rorty, who find this traditional impulse deplorable, although it has really never been clear to me why they so regard it. For some relevant reflections on the matter, see my [PSI].

science—in contrast to a history or sociology of natural science—is possible at all. Of course I demur. But that leaves me with a task, the task of diagnosing and treating the dialectical roots of this contemporary style of epistemological skepticism.

In the golden age of "logical positivism" or "logical empiricism", my normative questions were thought to have clear, straightforward answers. The answers which emerged then have since largely been abandoned by epistemologists of natural science (although in the so-called social and behavioral sciences they continue to exercise a direct and unholy influence), but their abandonment has not broken their power. They have indeed, as I shall try to show, continued to condition almost all subsequent philosophical reflection on the subject. To get beyond them, we must break their power, and that calls for an alternative picture of scientific epistemology. I am convinced that there is one—and that Sellars' work has shown us how to locate it—but, to understand what it is, we need first to understand better what we are leaving behind.

The picture drawn in the golden age of logical positivism and logical empiricism presupposed and rested upon a sharp absolute distinction between theory and observation. Observations delivered us a growing collection of stable phenomena. The goal of theorizing was to equip us to "explain" and "predict" such phenomena.

Both "explanation" and "prediction" were understood in terms of derivation or logical deduction. A theory "explained" an observed phenomenon if a (past-tensed) description of the phenomenon was deductively recoverable from the laws or principles of the theory together with a specification of then-and-there obtaining "boundary conditions", formulated in the vocabulary of that theory. "Prediction" differed from "explanation" only in tense—observations of the (confirming) phenomena coming temporally later than deductions of their (future-tensed) descriptions from theoretical principles and specifications of boundary conditions.

Acknowledged theory-theory relationships, in turn, mirrored these presumed theory-observation relationships. A successor theory was better than some predecessor just in case it "explained" that predecessor, that is, just in case the laws or principles of the successor allowed the laws or principles of the predecessor to be deductively recovered as "special cases" given a successor-theoretic specification of a family of general "boundary conditions".

A picture of scientific progress emerged quite smoothly from these understandings. Physical science was a cumulative enterprise. Progress took the form of increased generality and increased precision. Successively better theories, that is, "fit" more phenomena and fit them more closely, to a greater degree of precision or accuracy. Since both predecessor theories and descriptions of phenomena could be deductively recovered from successor theories, historical theory-sequences took on the form of nested sets, cumulative over the domain of "observable phenomena":

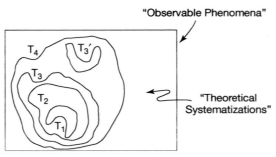

Shortly after the Second World War, however, this comfortable picture was disturbed by a variety of complementary philosophical developments, developments which brought critical pressure to bear on, and ultimately led to the abandonment of, almost every aspect of it.

The collection of "observed phenomena" which formed the fundamentum for all theorizing on the positivist picture was supposed to be recorded in a growing catalogue of "observation statements", reports of the results of "making observations" expressed in an "observation language". The positivist picture of natural science in turn demanded that this catalogue of observation statements be regarded as the record of an epistemological *Given* in the classical sense, a record of cognitions which were both immediate (that is, they were not derived by logical operations from other cognitions) and truth-determinative (that is, the deductive recoverability of these observation statements from theoretical laws and principles was treated as criterial for the epistemic acceptability of all theoretical statements). As a direct consequence of these commitments, it followed that "observations" must be fixed and invariant. Statements ostensibly recording observations could not be revised on the basis of theory—for, since they were truth-determinative, consilience with them was criterial for the acceptability of theories—nor as a result of abandoning other cognitions—for, since they were immediate, they were not logically derived from any other cognitions. In consequence, statements ostensibly recording observations could not be revised at all. They were "indefeasible".

Precisely this picture of an epistemic Given, however, was now subjected to devastating criticism—not least by Wilfrid Sellars (e.g., in [EPM])—the upshot of which was a growing recognition that the very idea of such a Given, of in-principle irrevisable cognitions and in-principle indefeasible judgments, was inherently incoherent. Hanson [PD], among others, was quick to draw the consequences (already anticipated by a heretical Otto Neurath) for the positivist epistemology of natural science: the *absolute* distinction between observation and theory which that epistemology presupposed and required could not be sustained. "All language is theory-laden" became the new parole.

Simultaneously with these developments, a number of philosophers—Quine [TDE] obviously comes to mind—proceeded to mount a successful attack on the interlocking notions of meaning, synonymy, analyticity, and necessity, one upshot of which was a growing acceptance of the conclusion that the very idea of an absolute distinction between change of meaning and change of belief was inherently incoherent.

The consequences for the positivist epistemology of natural science were again promptly drawn, for example, by Feyerabend (see, e.g., [HBGE, AM]): *Any* change of theory could be read as a change of meanings, as "meaning variance". The deductive relationships among predecessor and successor theories required by the positivist picture, however, presupposed and demanded meaning *in*variance, that is, a theory-independent way of fixing the meanings of theoretical terms. In the absence of an epistemic Given to fund such meaning determinations independently of all theories, however, there was no alternative but to treat those theories themselves as the sole (holistic) meaning-determinative units, as "implicit definitions" of their substantive terms. The inevitable consequence, then, was that predecessor-successor theory pairs became radically logically "uncoupled". Statements sharing no terms can stand in no deductive relationships to one another. Feyerabendian talk of "incommensurability" and Kuhnian talk of "revolutions" and "paradigm shifts" became the order of the day.

Its epistemic underpinnings thus demolished, the positivist picture of scientific progress as cumulation by nesting ought rightly to have crumbled as well. Curiously, however, what in fact happened was no such thing. Instead, the *picture* was retained. Only the labels were changed. In place of a fixed domain of "observable phenomena" philosophers began to talk of a fixed domain of *entities*, and in place of successive alternative "theoretical systematizations", they began to talk of successive theoretical *descriptions* or *characterizations*. The banner under which this shift occurred read "theory of reference". A theory of reference was to be the respectable replacement for the theory of meaning. On this new view, the terms of successive theories all "referred" to the same "entities", however differently those theories might proceed to "describe" or "characterize" those entities. The language of theories, in other words, was now to be coupled to the world through a semantic relation of reference. And so the natural next question became, *inter alia, what* relation was this "semantic relation of reference" supposed to be?

As it turned out, there were three possibilities. Reference might be either:

(a)   a "primitive" "non-natural" relation, or

(b)   a "derived" "non-natural" relation, determined (*à la* Frege) by meaning or "sense", or

(c)   a "natural" relation.

Each of these possibilities was in fact tried out.

Option (a) was carried to its inevitable conclusion by Quine (in [W&O] and [OR]). The upshot was "ontological relativity": We can make no absolute sense of the question, "To what does the term 'X' refer?". The most that we can do is show how one theory can be interpreted or reinterpreted in another.[2] Indeed, since, on this view, the interpretation of one theory in another was ultimately a matter of extensional mathematical modeling, the door was opened to some extraordinarily *outré* ontological possibilities, and Quine himself, for example, sometimes came out sounding remarkably like a neo-Pythagorean.

Option (b), of course, was antithetical to the project of substituting a theory of reference for a theory of meaning in the first place. Oddly enough, however, it got tried out too. Davidson objected (in [T&M]) that we had no theory of "senses", but he was wrong. We had *descriptivism*, championed by Russell and, to a certain extent, by Searle—the theory that the sense of a referring expression was captured by a (uniquely individuating) definite description (or family of such descriptions), its referents being the thing or things answering to that description (or a weighted majority of the descriptions). The problem turned out to be that descriptivism was a *bad* theory of senses. The relation of reference which was wanted, that is—as Kripke (see [N&N]), among others, proceeded to show—simply didn't track with "answering to descriptions" in the manner proposed by the descriptivist theory.

Kripke's own alternative—embraced and extended by Putnam$_1$ [MM, WR]—was option (c): a *causal* theory of reference. The referent of a term was whatever was connected to usings of that term by an appropriate set of natural relations, a "causal chain". As Davidson [VICS], Rorty [WWL], and, surprisingly, Putnam$_2$ ([R&R], hence the indexing) were quick to point out, however, the preferred term 'cause' was just as "theory-laden"—and thus the "natural" relation of causation just as theory-*relative*—as any other empirical notion. Appeals to "causal chains", therefore, could not allow us to isolate an invariant domain of referents for our changing theoretical terms. Once again we were back in the land of "ontological relativity". There was no way to "step outside" the *de facto* historical sequence of predecessor and successor theories to locate that supposed domain of entities of which they supposedly were alternative conceptions. Hence, our choices were limited to either stopping with common sense (saying that the world consists of rocks and trees, stars and rivers, ...)—and thus treating theories as at best some sort of useful fictions—or giving the *latest* answer to the question of "what we were talking about all along" (molecules, atoms, electrons, quarks)—an answer for which we could claim no special

---

[2] Otherwise put, there is nothing to choose between talk of "elimination" (e.g., "There really are no gases, only molecules") and talk of "reduction" (e.g., "A gas really is a population of molecules").

epistemic authority but only historical "privilege". What Davidson and Rorty themselves concluded we must do, (see especially [PMN], ch. VI), therefore, is abandon the entire positivist picture, that is, the entire picture of "scheme *vs* content"—an invariant "content" (of phenomena or entities) "supplied by the world", and successive varying "schematizations" (theoretical systematizations or characterizations) "supplied by us"—and, with it, abandon the hope of any normative epistemology of science and (well-founded, non-"Whiggish") notion of scientific *progress* at all.

Interestingly enough, we had seen something quite like this before. Descartes, adopting the mediaeval notions of "objective" and "formal" being, posited a "primitive" "ontological" relationship—a "metaphysical coincidence", as it were—between true thoughts and the world [option (a)]: A thought is true just in case the same entity which exists "objectively" ("in the thought") also exists "formally" ("in the world"). Locke, a good empiricist (and the Kripke of his day), could tolerate no such primitive "non-natural" relation between "ideas" and the world, and so proceeded to offer a "naturalized" alternative [option (c)]: An idea is true if it is *caused by* and *resembles* its material archetype. And then came Berkeley: Either 'causation' and 'resemblance' are terms we can understand, and thus fall *within* the realm of "ideas" (for all our concepts are "derived from experience", and we experience nothing but "ideas"), or they are empty noises. What appeals to "causation" and "resemblance" cannot do, in any case, is lead us out of the field of ideas to entities having an "absolute existence without the mind".

Given the ready availability of this historical object lesson, the recapitulation of its dialectic under the rubric "theory of reference" in the 20th century is an especially striking illustration of the unbroken power of the positivist picture of scientific progress as cumulation by nesting over an invariant domain. But the source of that power is not difficult to diagnose. The picture was thought of as necessary to sustain *realism* in natural science. (Thus $Putnam_1$'s objection that accepting the "meta-induction" leading to the conclusion that "no theoretical term ever refers" would be "disastrous".) The movement to replace "theory of meaning" by "theory of reference" was an attempt to replace the deductive nesting-structures terminating in "axioms" (the "self-evident" or "self-warranting" truths of an epistemic Given) with the nestings arising from the basis + recursion structure of a model-theoretic referential semantics. The picture of an invariant content contributed by the world and increasingly more general and more accurate schematizations of that content contributed by us, however, remained the same.

But Davidson and Rorty are correct. The only way out of the resulting predicaments which has *any* hope of preserving "scientific realism" and an intelligible, non-arbitrary notion of scientific progress is decisively to abandon that picture of progress and, simultaneously, the two subtle but fundamental presuppositions upon which it rests:

(P1) *Epistemic atomism*: The notion that there are *epistemically-criterial* relations between individual representings (ideas, thoughts, words) and individual representeds (phenomena, entities), and

(P2) *Epistemic foundationalism*: The notion that epistemic justification or warrant *must* ultimately make recourse to the possibility of a regress (whether via deduction or via recursion) to something epistemologically "more secure" than what is being justified or warranted.

Curiously enough, both of these presuppositions were in fact abandoned by at least one philosopher long ago—by Kant. Kant abandoned (P1) by drawing a sharp distinction between sensations and cognitions and insisting that it is *forms of judgment* which are crucial for understanding "experience", not the mere having of sense-impressions.[3] He abandoned (P2) by recognizing and applying new "holistic" patterns of justificatory reasoning (his "transcendental deduction"), strategies of embedding problematic concepts and judgments ("categorial" concepts and "synthetic *a priori*" judgments) as *mentioned* (rather than used) in larger contexts which could transmit (independently demonstrable) epistemic authority to the disputed cases.

Kant, indeed, did abandon the picture of "scheme *vs* content" *from below*—an invariant content contributed by the world; various schemes contributed by us—and replaced it with a picture of "scheme *vs* content" *from above*—an invariant *formal* scheme (space, time, and the categories) and potentially-diverse contentive fillings-out of that scheme. But, alas, in Kant's era, physical science was regarded as historically closed. Having no historical experience of "scientific revolutions" and (as Hegel pointed out) no articulate theory of social reality or social practice, but still feeling the need for an "external" contrast to his *theory-relative* "reality *vs* appearance" distinction—the distinction between what is "actual" and what is "illusory or imaginary"—Kant was ultimately unable to free "framework questions" regarding the acceptability of a theoretical or conceptual system as a whole from the Scholastic ontology of "formal *vs* objective being" and so, in end, adopted it—as "noumena *vs* phenomena", "things in themselves" *vs* "appearances"—and, with it, the muddle that has come down to us as his commitment to both "empirical realism" and "transcendental idealism".

What makes Kant's failure all the more unfortunate is the fact that, along the way, he had actually developed the key notion which would have enabled him to avoid it, the notion of a "regulative ideal". It was Peirce, however, who first found the way to exploit this Kantian notion. The Peircean gambit, in essence, was to replace the positivist picture of progress as cumulation by nesting over an invariant domain by the pragmatist picture of progress as convergence by successively better approximations to a limit:

---

[3] In terms of contemporary slogans, the point was that "all seeing is seeing as", and "thinking of" presupposes "thinking that".

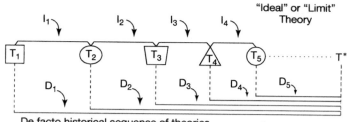

As a picture, this pragmatist alternative to positivism is clear enough. The key question, however, is whether we can here advance beyond a mere picture. Can we give a *sense* to this notion of the "convergence" of theories, and, if so, how?

"Convergence" is a mathematical metaphor. It is only natural, then, to look to mathematics for an interpretive model. What clearly will not do is the model supplied by the notion of "Weierstrass convergence", convergence to a fixed, *known* limit:

$$(\varepsilon)(\exists N)(n)[n > N \rightarrow |T_n - T^*| < \varepsilon]$$

Here, the focus is on the 'D's of our diagram, the diminishing "distances" between successive elements of the convergent sequence (the de facto historical theories, T_n) and a *specified* limit (the "ideal" or "limit" theory, T^*). The difficulty, of course, is that we can make sense of the notion of such diminishing "distances" only if we have some way of specifying T^*, the "limit", independently of our historical embedding in the T_i sequence—and this we do not and cannot have.

Rorty interprets [PMN, 295 ff.] recourse to a "picture theory" of language as just the attempt to produce such an a-historical, extra-sequential specification of T^*—and Sellars has indeed sometimes written in a way which aids and abets this construction:

Linguistic picture-making is not the performance of asserting matter-of-factual propositions. The *criterion* of correctness of the performance of asserting a basic matter-of-factual proposition is the correctness of the proposition *qua* picture, i.e., the fact that it coincides with the picture the world-cum-language would generate in accordance with the uniformities controlled by the semantical rules of the language. Thus the *correctness* of the picture is not defined in terms of the *correctness* of a performance but vice versa. [S&M §57, 136]

Taken at face value, this paragraph appears to be an outright endorsement of (P1), the idea that there are epistemically-criterial relations between individual representings and individual representeds. But if Sellars' term 'criterion' is indeed to be understood as having the sense "*epistemic* criterion", it is clear that the view will not do. If "the correctness of [a] proposition *qua* picture" is "the fact that it coincides with the picture the world-cum-language would generate ...", then that a proposition is correct-qua-picture is not something which we could ever be warranted in asserting from our perspective within the historical sequence of theories. That a proposition is correct-qua-picture, in other words, is something we could know only if we had already arrived at the "limit theory", T^*, (and knew that we had arrived there). Since the notion of correctness-qua-picture thus presupposes the idea of a limit to convergence of theories, it cannot be used to explicate that idea.

The only viable alternative is to abandon (P1) in all its forms decisively and irreversibly, and with it, to abandon the epistemic reading of 'criterion' as well. The correctness of an assertive performance may be *defined* in terms of the correctness of a picture, but the performance cannot be *authorized* (*per impossibile*) by our discovery that the asserted proposition is correct-qua-picture. If "picturing" has a job to do, in other words, it cannot be an epistemic job. Appeals to picturing can explain neither how language is learned, nor how language is understood, nor why inquiry is successful. They do not "handle epistemological problems" at all [Rorty, PMN, 296].[4] The metaphor of "convergence" simply cannot be cashed out on the Weierstrass model, the model of convergence to a fixed and known limit, for the "limit" to which physical theories may converge is not and cannot be "fixed and known" to us, to beings situated discursively within the historical sequence of such theories.

Fortunately, we have an alternative. Rather than focusing on the (unknowable) "distances" from the T^* "limit"—the 'D's of our diagram—what we need to look at are the "intervals" between theories—the intertheoretical "distances" represented by the 'I's of our diagram. If this I-series converges to 0, that is, if the "intervals" between successive theories necessarily diminish, then we may sensibly say that the T-series itself, the series of theories, also "converges" to some "limit", even in the absence of any way to talk sensibly about what that "limit of theories" *is*. The mathematical model for the convergence of theories will then be Cauchy convergence:

$$(\varepsilon)(\exists N)(m)(n)[(m > N \ \& \ n > N) \to |T_m - T_n| < \varepsilon]$$

But finding an appropriate mathematical model for the convergence of theories takes us only part of the way to a usable understanding of this alternative picture. We are, in fact, immediately confronted with two new questions:

(A) How can we make sense of a notion of "inter-theoretical distance" from our historical perspective within an (unending) succession of physical theories?

(B) What reasons, if any, can we have for believing that the sequence of theories does in this sense "converge", necessarily or even in fact?

Question (A) arises when we notice, with Quine [W&O, 23], that such metrical notions as distance and interval are well-defined only for mathematical entities

---

[4] For all that, however, appeals to "picturing" still do have a job to do, a job that belongs to the story of the ontology of representation rather than to that of its epistemology. For a fuller discussion, see, for instance, [LR].

(numbers and equations, for example), but not for theories or representational systems. The solution, naturally enough, is to use just these mathematical metrics—and this implies, in turn, that we will be able to make sense of "convergence", if at all, only for sequences of *quantitative* theories. The insight which allows us to pass beyond question (A), in other words, is that measurements yield numbers (to which equations may be fitted), and that these numbers (and equations) *can* be compared purely mathematically, quite independently of possibly radically differing theoretical conceptions of what is being measured (of what the numbers and equations *represent*), and even of what it is that *constitutes* "measurement".

That and, more importantly, *how* this is the relevant insight, however, becomes clear only when we have a grip on an adequate answer to question (B). As Sellars recognized, the key move in that regard is once again to shift our focus, but this time from theoretical to practical reasoning. Theorizing is an activity; it is something people do. The basic question which needs to be answered is thus: What is the *telos* of this activity, its end, aim, goal, or purpose? The reason is this: We can answer question (B), if at all, only if we can locate a family of *normative* constraints on (successor-) theory acceptability which either imply "convergence" (in our partially clarified sense) for sequences of "qualified" theories or turn out to be compatible with an in-principle perpetual "non-convergence". But only a clear view of the *telos* of theorizing as an activity holds out any hope of giving us what we need to locate such a family of normative constraints.

There are two traditional possibilities. The *telos* of theorizing is either realistic or what I shall call eudaemonistic. On the former conception, theorizing aims at equipping us with an account of "how things really are", of "what our world is really like". In traditional terms, claims expressed in the theoretical vocabulary are advanced as *truths* about the contents and structure of physical reality. On the latter conception, theorizing aims at equipping us with an effective cognitive means for pursuing *extra*-cognitive ends, an instrument for arriving at beliefs about "nature" which will enable us better to anticipate and cope with her vagaries in the interest of a broader human happiness (the "good life for man"). Claims expressed in the theoretical vocabulary are advanced, not as truths, but rather as useful fictions—representational tools which cognitively mediate the drawing of conclusions about "observable" matters of fact from premises describing "observed" matters of fact in ways which allow for and promote the development of effective technological interventions in nature, i.e., the prediction and control of natural phenomena.

I, for one, am convinced that a purely eudaemonistic conception of the *telos* of theorizing activity cannot be sustained, not only because it ultimately presupposes just that sort of "absolute" observational/theoretical distinction which the contemporary critique of positivism has shown to be untenable, but because, in the end, it presupposes realism as well. For what differentiates theories from petitionary prayers or magical incantations as instruments for shaping nature to our ulterior ends of happiness is that theories purport to derive their instrumental utility precisely from the cognitive access which they give us to a reality which underlies and gives rise to that manifest "nature" which we aspire to predict and to control. I am convinced, indeed, that the activity of theorizing *necessarily* has a realist *telos* for such beings as we are—the temporally-discursive, passive, apperceptive intelligences of Kant's First Critique—but I shall not pause to argue the question here. (I have done a good bit of that in [OW].) Rather, for the balance of this essay, I shall simply *assume* (or, if you prefer, *pretend*) that the realist conception of the *telos* of theorizing is correct and try to show that it can supply the resources to yield solutions to our remaining problems, in particular, that it implies a family of precisely the sort of normative constraints on the acceptability of theories that we require in order to arrive at an answer to question (B).

Suppose we take seriously, then, the idea that a new theory epistemically qualifies as an acceptable successor by earning its credentials as a better story than its predecessor(s) of "how things (really) are". What can we then conclude about specific criteria of theoretical acceptability?

To begin with, it seems clear enough that there is something right about traditional appeals to "scope" and "accuracy". One *prima facie* way in which a new theory could be a better "story of reality" than its predecessor—is by supplying either an account of *more* of "reality" or a *more precise* account of the same part of "reality", i.e., accounting for more phenomena than its predecessor or more accurately accounting for those phenomena already subsumed by the predecessor. Traditionally these desiderata have been expressed in terms of "fit": A candidate successor theory is epistemically better than its predecessor just in case it *fits more* phenomena or *better fits* the same phenomena. For reasons which will become clearer as we proceed, however, I shall frame this criterion somewhat differently.

(E1)   A qualified successor theory must explain the *actual explanatory failures* of its predecessor, that is, be able to supply satisfactory explanatory accounts of phenomena which the predecessor could *describe* (in terms of its representational resources) but could not itself *explain* (in terms of its laws and principles).

So far, however, we have not really made use of our "scientific realist" assumption. To do so, we need to look carefully at its notion of "how things (really) are" itself. "How things (really) are" is a term of *contrast*. Its story stands in opposition to another, the story of "how things *seem* to be" or "how things *appear*", and what is important to realize is that these cannot simply be two *unrelated* stories. The story of "reality" (of how things are) has a job to do *vis-à-vis* the story of "appearance" (of how things seem). Appearance and reality are related, and, in fact, they are related precisely by an explanatory '*because*': Things seem as they do *because* things are as they are.[5]

---

[5] For an elaboration of this claim, with examples, see my [SEALA].

In the context of theory-succession, "how things seem" is what the last theory tells us, the predecessor theory for which the new theory is a candidate successor. The extant theory was accepted, when it was accepted, as itself the (then best) account of "how things are". *When* it was accepted, in other words, how it (still) says things are was how it (then) *seemed* things are. But now a candidate successor theory offers itself as a *new* story of "how things are", and it thereby acquires a second epistemic obligation with respect to its predecessor. It must account for how and why it (then) seemed that things are as its predecessor (still) says they are. Otherwise put,

(E2)   A qualified successor theory must explain the *apparent explanatory successes* of its predecessor, that is, enable us to account for the fact that the predecessor, although incorrect, nevertheless appeared to have as much explanatory power as it in fact appeared to have.

This second, crucial, epistemic obligation is precisely what Sellars has in mind in the following seminal passage:

[Theories] about observable things *do not explain empirical laws, they explain why observable things obey, to the extent that they do, these empirical laws*; that is, they explain why individual objects of various kinds and in various circumstances in the observation framework behave in those ways in which it has been inductively established that they do behave. Roughly, it is because a gas is—in some sense of "is"—a cloud of molecules which are behaving in theoretically defined ways, and, *hence*, in particular cases, places and times behaves in a certain way, that it obeys the Boyle-Charles law. [LT, 71–2]

And, since the point is one which pertains to theory succession in general, Sellars proceeds to add, in a footnote, that "The same is true in principle—although in a way which is methodologically more complex—of micro-theories about microtheoretical objects" [LT, 71 n.].

Unfortunately, it has turned out that both of these epistemic constraints on qualified successor theories are all too easily misunderstood. In particular, the expository idiom Sellars adopts in the passage we have just cited unhappily blurs several crucial distinctions. Consider, for example, his talk of things "obeying" laws, for example, his talk of gases "obeying" the Boyle-Charles law. Speaking of things "obeying" laws *to the extent that they do* is clearly speaking of something which is a matter of degree. But can "obedience to a law" be a matter of degree? If gases "obey" the Boyle-Charles law only to a certain extent, then surely, strictly speaking, they do not *obey* that law at all. (Perhaps, for example, they actually obey the van der Waals equation.) Indeed, should we not say, contrary to Sellars, that:

it is because a gas is—in some sense of "is"—a cloud of molecules which are behaving in theoretically defined ways, and, *hence*, in particular cases, places and times behaves in a certain way, that it *does not* obey the Boyle-Charles law (*but rather* obeys the van der Waals equation).

In fact, what is *here* being called a thing's "obedience" to a law is not, as the idiom suggests, an intentional matter of the law *qua* nomological generalization providing a (conceptually and ontologically correct) *explanation* of certain phenomena, but an extensional matter of the law *qua* mathematical formula or equation supplying a (more-or-less accurate) *representation* of certain phenomena. More precisely the *extent* to which a thing "obeys" a quantitative law is the degree of approximation with which the law-*qua*-formula "fits" some relevant observational or phenomenological data-base of *measurements*. Call this "descriptive adequacy". Descriptive adequacy is extensional and comes in degrees.

What is more important to notice, however, is that descriptive adequacy is a purely formal (mathematical) matter and therefore itself conceptually and ontologically *neutral*. Whether or not one mathematical formula or equation is *descriptively* more adequate than another with respect to a specific data-base of measurements is a question which can be framed and answered independently of variant conceptions of *what it is* that one is measuring, and even variant conceptions of the particular world-observer or world-instrument (causal) interactions that in this instance *constitute* observation or measurement. Thus, significantly, it is also a question which can be framed and answered independently of whether the formulae or equations are drawn from one and the same theory or from different *and conceptually incommensurable* theories.

Explanatory success, in contrast, is not a matter of degree. A theory is successful in this sense just in case its explanatory accounts of the phenomena which fall within its scope are (conceptually, semantically, and ontologically) *correct*. A theory that has been judged to be false, consequently, has *eo ipso* been judged to have *no* explanatory successes. Yet, being judged false, it may have had many *apparent* explanatory successes. In its salad days, a now-rejected theory may well have allowed for the formulation of numerous explanatory accounts which *seemed* correct. It is important to be clear, however, that these were not *approximate* explanatory successes, nor could they have been. Unlike formal extensional descriptive adequacy ("fit"), explanatory success is conceptually contentive and intentional. It is consequently an all-or-nothing business. It does not come in degrees, any more than semantic *truth* comes in degrees. An "approximate truth" is not a species of truth, after all, but rather a species of falsehood and, similarly, an "apparent explanatory success" (of an abandoned theory) is not a species of explanatory success at all but rather a species of actual explanatory failure.

But, if this is right, how then does the demand of our first epistemic constraint, that a qualified successor explain the actual explanatory failures of its predecessor, *differ* from the demand of our second, that a qualified successor explain the apparent explanatory successes of that predecessor? Indeed, what can it mean for a successor theory to *explain* either of these things?

In the traditionally-paradigmatic *intra*-theoretical sense, explanation is a matter of deduction or derivation. A theory is *applied* in explanatory accounts of phenomena *conceived in its terms*, and we *apply* the theory precisely by using its laws in derivations of descriptions of individual phenomena from descriptions of specific initial conditions, both characterized in terms of the theory's own parameters. Within the classical theory of gases, for example, we explain the observed pressure of a given volume of gas at a given temperature by using the Boyle-Charles law. Phenomena characterizable in a theory's terms which cannot in this way be explained (e.g., within the classical theory, the observed behavior of gases at extremely high pressures or extremely low temperatures) become the theory's *anomalies*, those "actual explanatory failures" which, according to our first epistemic constraint, it becomes incumbent upon a qualified successor theory (e.g., the kinetic theory) to explain.

But, *if we take "incommensurability" seriously*, it is hard to see how a successor theory could explain such anomalies. Given the "incommensurability" and "meaning-variance" which seem to be inescapable consequences of the lack of any extra-theoretical standpoint from which to "fix" meanings in some theory-neutral way, the laws, principles, and ontological posits of a successor theory will not only not entail those of its predecessors but typically will stand in no deductive logical relationships to those predecessor laws, principles, and posits at all. Within the classical theory, for example, a gas is (conceived as) a continuous homogeneous compressible fluid, and pressure and temperature are among its (theoretically-posited) *primitive* properties. Thermometers and manometers are instruments for measuring these primitive properties. According to the kinetic theory, however, there are no continuous homogeneous compressible fluids and consequently no such *properties* as pressure or temperature, conceived, *as the classical theory conceives them*, as (primitive) properties of such fluids (temperature$_C$ and pressure$_C$). How, then, can the kinetic theory explain what the classical theory failed to explain, e.g., the anomalous measured pressure$_C$ of a particular volume of continuous homogeneous incompressible fluid at a specific extremely low temperature$_C$?

What the kinetic theory can and does explain, in the traditionally-paradigmatic intra-theoretic sense, are phenomena conceived in *its* terms—the observed (mean) frequencies of impact on the walls of a container of a particular volume by molecules (having a certain diameter, elasticity, and inter-molecular attraction) belonging to a population of molecules at specific high or low levels of (mean) kinetic energy. For what a gas *is* (conceived as) within the kinetic theory is a collection of molecules, whose theoretically-posited properties do not include pressure and temperature but rather, for example, size (diameter), mass, velocity, and elasticity. What are *called* "pressure" and "temperature" within kinetic theory (temperature$_K$ and pressure$_K$) are *defined statistical properties* of determinate populations of such molecules, and what our thermometers and manometers (actually) measure are precisely these statistical properties.

Despite such radical differences in conceptualization, however, it seems clear enough how at least casual and informal versions of the explanations demanded by our epistemic constraints (E1) and (E2) would look in this case. The gist of both of them would surely be that the *differences* between the theoretically-projected values for (the primitive properties) temperature$_C$ and pressure$_C$ of a volume of continuous homogeneous compressible fluid *assumed* to obey (in the intentional sense) the Boyle-Charles law and the theoretically-projected values for (the defined statistical properties) temperature$_K$ and pressure$_K$ of a spatially-confined collection of molecules (of a sort characterized by a particular size, mass, elasticity, and inter-molecular attraction) obeying the van der Waals equation are (E2) very small indeed over a wide range of temperatures$_K$ and pressures$_K$ but (E1) become significantly larger at extremely low temperatures$_K$ or extremely high pressures$_K$.

The most important point to be clear about at this juncture is that neither of these "explanations" consists in an *application* of the candidate successor theory. The sense of 'explanation' here, in other words, is *different* from the traditionally-paradigmatic sense in which theoretical appeals can provide explanations of individual empirical phenomena falling within its scope. These explanations belong rather to the level of theoretical appraisal, and *what* in each case is being explained is thus not an empirical phenomenon characterized in terms of the theory's ontological commitments and constitutive principles or laws but a *pragmatic meta-phenomenon*, an actual explanatory failure or apparent explanatory success of the predecessor theory. What it takes to certify the kinetic theory as an epistemically *qualified* successor to the classical theory, to put it paradoxically, are not explanations of the behavior of gases but explanations of the behavior of theories.

In epistemic appraisal, a candidate successor theory is *used* without being *applied*. In this instance, as in many instances, we can even supply a formal account of one way in which the successor theory can be so used. Let me introduce the notion of a *counterpart model*. A counterpart model of a (predecessor) theory T_i within a (candidate successor) theory T_j is a theory T_i' nomologically isomorphic to T_i defined within a "virtual theory" T_j^* produced by adding one or more (T_j-) *countertheoretical* assumptions A_j to T_j. A counterpart model of T_i within T_j is thus formulable and formulated entirely in terms of the conceptual and representational resources of T_j. The picture is this:

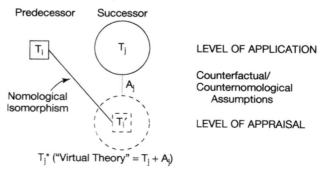

If, for instance, we pretend for a moment that the classical theory simply consists of the Boyle-Charles Law and the kinetic theory of the van der Waals equation, we can illustrate this notion of a counterpart model by the example:

T_i : $P_C V = nRT_C$
T_j : $(P_K + n^2a/V^2)(V - nb) = nRT_K$
A_j : $a = b = 0$
T_j^* : $T_j + A_j$, i.e., $P_K V = nRT_K$.

And here, since we have here collapsed each theory into a single equation, it turns out that T_j^* is also T_i', the desired nomological isomorph to T_i.

Within the kinetic theory, the van der Waals equation contains constants 'a' and 'b' that represent, respectively, the inter-molecular attractive force and the volume and incompressibility of individual molecules within the population composing a sample of some gas. The numerical values of these parameters vary from gas to gas, but what is important is that, for most gases and over a wide range of "medium-sized" pressures, volumes, and temperatures, the computable magnitudes of the terms containing 'a' and 'b' ('n^2a/V^2' and 'nb') remain extremely small, smaller in fact than the characteristic magnitude of *measurement error* of all but the most sensitive instrumentation. Over a wide range of "medium-sized" pressures, volumes, and temperatures, that is, the candidate successor theory T_j is *measurement-indistinguishable* from the *virtual* theory T_j^*, and thus from T_i', the nomological isomorph to T_i definable within T_j^*, and hence from T_i itself.

It is because the *actual* behavior of gases (i.e., populations of molecules), as described by the successor theory T_j, was in this way measurement-indistinguishable from the *ostensible* behavior of gases, as characterized by the predecessor theory T_i, that T_i appeared to have as much explanatory power (*vis-à-vis* the results of specific measurements) as it did. Conversely, it is precisely by providing (conceptual and mathematical) resources for formulating and supporting this very (meta-level) explanatory story that the kinetic theory satisfies the second epistemological constraint, (E2), on *qualified* successor theories with respect to its classical predecessor.

The actual explanatory failures of the predecessor theory, on the other hand, take the form of observational anomalies, characteristically emerging at *extremes of measurement* (both extremes of precision or accuracy and extremes of registration or magnitude. See [CRCP] for details and examples.). Satisfaction of our first epistemological constraint, (E1), will thus be a matter of supplying successor-theoretic descriptions of the anomalous phenomena which bring them under the scope of the successor's explanatory laws and principles, i.e., in the possibility of *applying* the successor theory to such predecessor-anomalous observations. In the absence of any "theory-neutral" way of picking out the phenomena at issue, these descriptions in turn, however, must themselves be determined by the pairings of predecessor and successor *concepts* employed in the satisfaction of constraint

(E2), the explanation of the apparent explanatory successes, pairings which can themselves be either, as in this instance, heterophonic—'temperature' in the classical theory being mapped onto 'mean kinetic energy' in its successor—or homophonic—e.g. 'mass' in Newtonian dynamics being mapped onto 'mass' in the theory of special relativity.[6]

Counterpart modeling thus allows the *inter*-theoretical explanatory relationships called for by our two epistemological constraints to be formal or "logical" even if we grant the theses of theoretical incommensurability and "meaning variance" in their strongest forms, positing a total lack of (material) concept-sharing between predecessor and qualified successor theories. They are relationships which can be explicated in terms of deduction or derivation (of a nomological isomorph to the predecessor within a virtual theory created from the successor) without themselves *being* deductions or derivations of predecessor laws, principles, or posits from those of the successor theory. Incommensurability of theories does not entail *incomparability* of theories. Counterpart models in particular are one way of comparing the incommensurable. Acceptance of our two explanatory constraints on qualified successor theories, in short, does not require that we abandon hard-won insights in either the philosophy of language or the history of science.

Nevertheless, one might well still ask whether it is *reasonable* for a normative epistemology of science to require that candidate successor theories qualify epistemologically by satisfying constraints of these sorts in these ways. Interestingly, there are two diametrically opposed ways of arguing that it is not, and each of them has its advocates. One line of criticism suggests that it requires too little of a candidate successor theory; the other, that what it requires is too much.

The following objection, for example, illustrates the first line of criticism:

Take a familiar example, Newton and Galileo. For sure, we can use Newtonian gravitational theory to derive a version of Galileo's law [of falling bodies, $s = \frac{1}{2}gt^2$], specifically by assuming that the gravitational potential is constant near the surface of the earth. But to derive a version of Galileo's law within Newtonian mechanics is *not* to explain why a *theory* like Galileo's which postulates circular inertia and which denies action at a distance was successful. It is one thing to point out that Galileo's theory of physics has some approximately true consequences (that after all is simply to state the *fact* of its success) but how can we possibly claim to *explain* that success unless we're prepared

---

[6] Why not pick out the phenomena in question by "regress to a shared background language", e.g., descriptions of the states of ordinary "middle-sized" objects such as meters and cloud chambers? The answer is that this sort of "regress to a shared background language" loses both theoretical explanations. For theories do not explain meter readings qua pointer positions but only qua semantic indicators of, e.g., theoretically-conceived states of gases. The classical theory may fail to explain and the kinetic theory may succeed in explaining the distinct anomalous phenomena each respectively takes to be indicated by an initially unexpected pointer position, but neither fails to explain or succeeds in explaining that pointer position conceived and described (in a "shared background language") as such. The classical theory is a theory of the behavior of continuous homogeneous compressible fluids; the kinetic theory, of populations of molecules—but neither is a theory of the behavior of pointers.

to discuss the basic mechanisms which that successful theory postulated? And that, I claim, is precisely what we can't do in terms of the ontology of the successor theory. [Larry Lauden, personal communication, 5 May 1985]

In terms of the distinctions drawn in the present discussion, it is easy enough to say what has gone wrong here. For "to derive a version of Galileo's law within Newtonian mechanics" certainly is to explain why Galileo's theory was *descriptively* successful to the extent that it was, a conceptually and ontologically noncommittal remark about the "fit" between theoretical predictions and actual measurements, but it is not and cannot be to explain why Galileo's theory was *explanatorily* successful (to any "extent") for the simple reason that, from the perspective of Newton's theory (and its successors), Galileo's theory was *not* explanatorily successful. *Sub specie* Newton, there *are no* bodies answering to the theoretical characterizations (as undergoing a uniform and constant centripetal acceleration) invoked by Galileo to *explain* the specific (numerical) outcomes of distance-time measurements performed on falling objects. At best, Newton's theory can be used to construct an explanation of the *apparent* explanatory successes of Galileo's theory, by exhibiting—e.g., by means of a (homophonic) counterpart model—how what was actually being observed and measured, bodies undergoing a continuously variable acceleration due to gravity, could have *appeared* to be what Galileo postulated they were, bodies undergoing a uniform and constant acceleration. But that is all it takes to satisfy the crucial and central second explanatory constraint of this normative epistemology for natural science.

The second, and more interesting, line of criticism, in contrast, can look like this:

My comment on the line of argument [in the essay] is that it at most enjoins *science as such* to seek explanatory accommodations of its (partially) successful but discarded past, and I endorse this requirement. But I oppose sweeping second order accountability as a condition upon particular theories in virtue of their standing as alternatives to theories that have enjoyed some empirical warrant. Of course, a theory which can accommodate none or very few of the empirical successes of a theory it purports to replace lies under a tremendous presumption of inadequacy. But this admission is a far cry from your version of second order accountability. Frequently key empirical successes of discarded theories are *dropped* from the set of expectations reasonably held out for an adequate successor, and there are many possible rationales for dropping them. Nor is it required of the successor theory which fails to recover past explanatory successes that *it itself* provide such a rationale, which could instead come from some remote area of science. Occasionally there is no rationale at all, which may leave science (not any particular theory) with an outstanding problem (of which there are always plenty) but is itself no impediment to progress. Certainly that the T1 → T2 transition be progressive cannot depend either on the satisfaction of your version of second order accountability or on the provision of rationales in every case of failed explanatory accommodation. [Jarrett Leplin, personal communication, 1 July 1985]

Now there is a good bit of summary *reportage* here with which I would not want to quarrel, but I would also stress that history of science, however insightful, is not normative epistemology, and the latter is still what engages me here. The explanatory constraints (E1) and (E2) were not set down arbitrarily but rather themselves emerged from an investigation of the "being *vs* seeming" or "reality *vs* appearance" distinction *pre se*, and from taking seriously the idea that a new theory epistemically qualifies as an acceptable successor by earning its credentials as a better story than its predecessor of "how things (really) are".

The norms of theoretical appraisal which I have been articulating here are, of course, essentially retrospective. We cannot, that is, bring them to bear in a concrete assessment of epistemic adequacy until a determinate candidate successor theory for some specific predecessor is actually in hand. The story I have telling, in other words, belongs essentially to the "logic of appraisal" rather than to the "logic of discovery", and Leplin's talk of "*expectations* reasonably held out for an adequate successor" is therefore, to that extent, out of place. Theories are *de facto* accepted and adopted for all sorts of reasons—scientific and socio-political, good and bad—and about such matters I have deliberately had nothing to say. The explanatory constraints (E1) and (E2) come into play only afterwards, when we, as practicing epistemologists and philosophers of science rather than as historians or sociologists of science, entertain the normative question of whether some determinate *temporal* or *historical* successor to some specific predecessor was or was not (or is or is not) also an *epistemically qualified* successor to that predecessor.

To this question, as Leplin correctly observes, the answer may in fact be a matter of degree. The notion of a candidate successor theory that both explains *all* the actual explanatory failures of its predecessor we happen to have noticed *at the time of that successor's adoption* and explains *all* the (apparent) explanatory successes with which that predecessor was credited *before the time of that successor's adoption* is, indeed, a kind of idealization. But I want to insist that it is not just some arbitrary, "pie in the sky" idealization. Rather, it represents and articulates a *regulative ideal* of theoretical inquiry which is determinative for the (realist) methodology of natural science as such, a norm of epistemological adequacy against which actual historical theories are *appropriately* measured, and which explains *why*, as Leplin himself grants, "a theory which can accommodate none or very few of the empirical successes of a theory it purports to replace lies under a tremendous presumption of inadequacy" and *why* the absence of an adequate rationale for ignoring key empirical (descriptive) successes of a theory when adopting a successor to it leaves science with an outstanding problem.

One thing that makes it worthwhile to insist upon this point is that acknowledgement of the explanatory constraints (E1) and (E2) successfully defuses a fundamental philosophical challenge to the neo-Peircean picture of *theory convergence* that I have argued offers our only hope for a defensible "scientific realism". What I have in mind, of course, is the question of potential "forks" or "splittings" of the historical theory-sequence.

A "fork" or "split" in the historical sequence of successive physical theories looks like this:

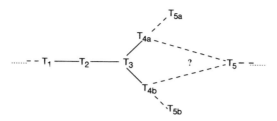

Here 'T_{4a}' and 'T_{4b}' are presumed to represent two *equally-qualified* but incommensurable successors to T_3, that is, two competing theories, each of which satisfies its epistemological responsibilities *vis-à-vis* their common predecessor as well as does the other. The question, then, is this: Must there in principle exist a *single* qualified successor, T_5, which *reconciles* such a split, or could such a splitting prove to be perpetually irreconcilable?

What makes this the central outstanding question for our present inquiry is the connection between the "convergence" picture of scientific progress and realism. For according to the pragmatist ontology which informs this normative epistemology for physical science, "the world" just *is* whatever would be represented as existing at the limit of such a convergent sequence of theories. More precisely, talk about "the world" simply amounts to talk about this temporal sequence of world-stories, and, in particular, to say that there is or exists only *one* world just is to say that the diachronic sequence of pairs of theories related as predecessor and epistemically-qualified successor *does* "converge to a limit". If, therefore, such a sequence of theory-pairs could split perpetually and irreconcilably, it would follow that we could no longer make any *sense* of the claim that there is but one world, and of the notion that our successive theories represent ever-closer approximations to the truth about it, the one non-theory-relative "absolute" truth.

If the relationships between predecessor theories and their epistemologically qualified successors were in fact required to be what they were understood to be in the golden age of logical positivism and logical empiricism, then *demonstrably* irreconcilable splits would indeed be possible, and that would be the end of the matter.[7] Theoretical forks could not be removed through an explanation-preserving reconciliation but only by, so to speak, "breaking one tine", i.e.; by

---

[7] If the relationships between predecessor and qualified successor theories were what positivism took them to be, all theories—and, in particular, the T_{4a} and T_{4b} of our diagram—would be logically commensurable. T_{4a} and T_{4b} would have a "deductive core" in common; the laws and principles of each would entail the laws and principles of T_3 as special cases. If T_{4a} and T_{4b} were nevertheless not complementary partial-successors but rather genuine complete alternatives, then, this could only be by reason of their logical inconsistency, either in the specification of the "boundary conditions" for their respective deductions of the laws and principles of their common

developments that would lead us to simply *abandon* (as false or disconfirmed) all of the theories on one of the branches initiated by T_{4a} and T_{4b}, and thus one of those two theories as well. If, however, those relationships are *not* what the positivists took them to be, but rather consist in the satisfaction of the explanatory constraints (E1) and (E2), for example after the manner of counterpart modeling, such *in-principle* irreconcilability of any *de facto* split cannot be demonstrated, even for arbitrary hypothetical cases.[8] But, for all that, although I do not think any actual historical examples are forthcoming, there is nothing to rule out *a priori* the occurrence of such a split, and the question naturally arises whether there are any constraints supplied by an adequate *normative* epistemology of scientific inquiry which would in-principle militate against any such split's simply getting worse and worse once it had occurred.

If the relationships between predecessor theories and their epistemologically qualified successors are those given by the explanatory constraints (E1) and (E2), the answer is qualified "Yes". For those constraints require that a *fully-qualified* successor theory explain the actual explanatory failures and apparent explanatory successes of *both* of its predecessors, and that is demonstrably sufficient to guarantee that any historical sequence of physical theories, successive pairs of which are related as predecessor and *qualified* successor in the sense of satisfying (E1) and (E2) after the manner of counterpart modeling at least does not *diverge*.[9]

We are thus free to adopt the pragmatist view root and branch, i.e., to hold that the *sense* of our "ontological" claims is epistemic. This is the core of the "pragmatist turn". To say that there is or exists only one world just *is* to say that such an historical sequence of world-stories, of physical theories appraised in accordance with the normative constraints of a realist *telos*, converges. The thesis of "scientific realism" then just *is* the thesis that the enterprise of theorizing is progressive—but progressive in its convergence, not in its cumulation over some fixed and invariant domain. And that is why our chief metaphysical problem has not been to show that the claim that there exists but one world is true, but rather to show how a physical science which, despite "incommensurabilities", remains progressive is *possible*.[10]

---

predecessor from their own or in their respective implications vis-à-vis phenomena falling within the (deductive) explanatory scope of both successors but outside that of the predecessor. On the positivist account, however, any single theory, T_5, could qualify as an acceptable successor to both T_{4a} and T_{4b} only by entailing the laws and principles of both predecessors—and thus only an inconsistent T_5 could in principle qualify at all. But, of course, any inconsistent theory is eo ipso epistemically unacceptable, precisely on account of its inconsistency. It follows therefore that, if the positivists were right about the relationships between predecessor and qualified successor theories, a genuine split in the historical sequence not only could be but necessarily would be in-principle and demonstrably irreconcilable.

   [8] See Appendix 4.1, below.   [9] See Appendix 4.2, below.

   [10] The present essay is a version of an earlier paper, informally circulated under the title "Theory Convergence and the Idea of Scientific Progress", much-revised and expanded on the occasion of the Colloquium on Sellarsian Philosophy held in October of 1987 at the University of Pittsburgh's

REFERENCES

Davidson, Donald, [T&M] 'Truth and meaning', *Synthese*, 7 (1967), 304–323.

_____ [VICS] 'On the very idea of a conceptual scheme', *Proceedings of the American Philosophical Association* 17 (1973–4).

Feyerabend, Paul, [AM] *Against Method* (New York, 1978).

_____ [HBGE], 'How to be a good empiricist—A plea for tolerance in matters epistemological', *Philosophy of Science: The Delaware Seminar II*, B. Baumrin, ed. (New York, 1963).

Hanson, N. R., [PD] *Patterns of Discovery* (Cambridge, 1958).

Kripke, Saul, [N&N] 'Naming and necessity', in *Semantics of Natural Language*, G. Harman and D. Davidson, eds. (Dordrecht, Holland, 1972), 253–355.

Kuhn, Thomas, [SSR] *The Structure of Scientific Revolutions* (Chicago, IL, 1962).

Putnam, Hilary, [WR] 'What is realism?', *Meaning and the Moral Sciences* (London, 1978), chs. II–III.

_____ [R&R] 'Realism and reason', *Proceedings of the American Philosophical Association* 50 (1977).

_____ [MM] 'The meaning of meaning', *Mind, Language, and Reality* vol. 2 (London, 1975).

Quine, W. V. O., [EN] 'Epistemology naturalized', repr. in *Ontological Relativity and Other Essays* [OROE]. (New York, 1969).

_____ [OR], 'Ontological relativity', repr. in [OROE].

_____ [TDE] 'Two dogmas of empiricism', repr. in *From a Logical Point of View* (New York, 1963).

_____ [W&O] *Word and Object* (Cambridge, MA, 1960).

Rorty, Richard, [PMN] *Philosophy and the Mirror of Nature* (Princeton, NJ, 1979).

_____ [WWL] 'The world well lost', *Journal of Philosophy*, 69 (1972), 649–665.

Rosenberg, Jay F., [CRCP] 'Coupling, retheoretization, and the correspondence principle', *Synthese*, 45 (1980), 351–385.

_____ [LR] *Linguistic Representation* (Dordrecht, Holland, 1974, 1981).

_____ [OW] *One World and Our Knowledge of It.* (Dordrecht, Holland, 1980).

_____ [PSI] 'Philosophy's self-image: a reply to Rorty', *Analyse & Kritik*, 4 (1982), 114–128.

_____ [SEALA] 'Science and the epistemic authority of logical analysis', in *Reason and Rationality in Natural Science*, N. Rescher, ed. (Lanham, MD, 1985).

Sellars, Wilfrid, [EPM] 'Empiricism and the philosophy of mind', repr. in *Science, Perception, and Reality* (London, 1963).

Center for Philosophy of Science in honor of Sellars' 75th year. The essay in its present form owes much to the penetrating objections and insightful critical observations raised by members of the Virginia-North Carolina Piedmont Philosophy of Science Discussion Group, especially Larry Lauden, Jarrett Leplin, Dick Burian, and my colleague Bill Lycan. In addition, I have learned a great deal from Lauden's "A Confutation of Convergent Realism" (*Philosophy of Science*, 48 (1981), 19–49) and Leplin's "Reference and Scientific Realism" (*Studies in History and Philosophy of Science*, 10 (1979) 265–284) about what it takes to defend convergent realism nowadays. Inter alia, this paper indicates my responses to both of these important earlier essays.

Rosenberg, J. F., [LT] 'The language of theories', in *Current Issues in the Philosophy of Science*, G. Maxwell and H. Feigel, eds. (New York, 1961).
——— [S&M] *Science and Metaphysics* (London, 1968).

APPENDIX 4.1

To see that the in-principle irreconcilability of any de facto "split" will never be demonstrable what we need to do is to add the level of appraisal to the level of application depicted in our original diagram of the historical T-sequence:

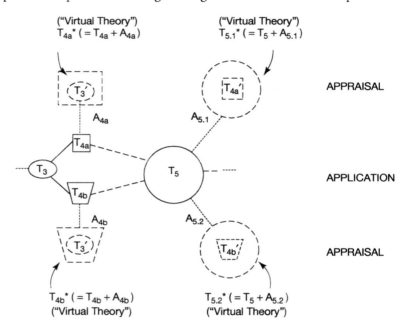

The left side of this diagram depicts the way in which, ex hypothesi, two alternative theories T_{4a} and T_{4b} did fulfill their second explanatory accountability vis-à-vis their common predecessor T_3. By adding (possibly different) countertheoretical assumptions, A_{4a} and A_{4b}, to T_{4a} and T_{4b}, one was able to construct a nomological isomorph to T_3 (T_3') within each of the resultant "virtual theories", T_{4a}^* and T_{4b}^*. Similarly, the right side of the diagram depicts the tests which a single successor theory T_5 would need to pass in order to fulfill its second explanatory accountability vis-à-vis both of its predecessors, T_{4a} and T_{4b}, that is, in order to qualify as a "reconciling successor" for the two branches of our hypothetical split. One would need to be able, by adding countertheoretical assumptions $A_{5.1}$ and $A_{5.2}$ to the candidate-successor T_5, to produce a pair of "virtual theories", $T_{5.1}^*$ and $T_{5.2}^*$, in one of which (say, $T_{5.1}^*$) it was possible to construct a nomological isomorph to T_{4a} (T_{4a}') and in the other of which ($T_{5.2}^*$), a nomological isomorph to T_{4b} (T'_{4b}). Our question is: Could we ever demonstrate, even in principle, that there could not be a single theory T_5 which could pass this test? And the answer clearly is: No.

On the positivist test, T_5 itself must entail nomological isomorphs to both T_{4a} and T_{4b}. As we noted, then, if T_{4a} and T_{4b} were themselves inconsistent, only an inconsistent T_5 could pass that test, but any inconsistent theory fails epistemically to qualify as acceptable simply by virtue of its inconsistency. On our picture, however, it is not T_5 itself but two "virtual theories", $T^*_{5.1}$ and $T^*_{5.2}$, which must severally entail nomological isomorphs of T_{4a} and T_{4b}, and these "virtual theories" are produced from the candidate-successor T_5 through the addition of possibly radically different countertheoretical assumptions, $A_{5.1}$ and $A_{5.2}$. The key point, indeed, is that these countertheoretical assumptions can even themselves quite comfortably be inconsistent—for neither belongs to the candidate-successor theory T_5. Both $A_{5.1}$ and $A_{5.2}$ would be auxiliary hypotheses, introduced for testing purposes as part of the appraisal of T_5, but neither would be part of the story which T_5 itself, the theory being appraised, told about the world. There can be, of course, no a priori guarantee that anyone will ever be clever enough actually to think up a T_5 which qualifies in this way as a "reconciling successor" for any actual historical fork. It does follow, however, that the logical relationships between the predecessor-alternatives, T_{4a} and T_{4b}—whatever they might be, even to the point of inconsistency—can never supply premises adequate for validly concluding that the existence of a qualifying T_5 is impossible, for T_5 itself need not and typically will not stand in any direct logical relationships to T_{4a} and T_{4b} themselves. No hypothetical split, however radical in other words, can be demonstrably irreconcilable.

APPENDIX 4.2

Consider three successive members of an historical sequence of quantitative physical theories, successive pairs of which are related in this way as predecessor and qualified successor—T_x, T_y, and T_z. Since T_y qualifies as a successor to T_x, there are some countertheoretical assumptions A_y, formulable using the representational apparatus of T_y, which allow the construction of a nomological isomorph to T_x(T'_x) within the "virtual theory" T^*_y($= T_y + A_y$). Similarly, since T_z qualifies as a successor to T_y, there will be some countertheoretical assumptions A_z, formulable using the representational resources of T_z, which allow the construction of a nomological isomorph to T_y(T'_y) within the "virtual theory" T^*_z($= T_z + A_z$).

Now, in order for a nomological isomorph of T_y(T'_y) to be constructible within T^*_z, there must exist a mapping which correlates the theoretical primitives of T_y, the representational resources by means of which T_y formulated its own laws and principles, with the terms (either primitive or defined) of T^*_z, and thus, of T_z (since A_z is, ex hypothesi itself formulable using the representational resources of

T_z). Call this mapping "M_{yz}". M_{yz} supplies, so to speak, a "translation manual" for formulating, using the representational resources of T_z, a counterpart to any claim which could be formulated within T_y, using the representational resources of T_y. But among those claims which could be formulated within T_y using the representational resources of T_y are the countertheoretical assumptions A_y which, when added to T_y, issued in the "virtual theory" $T_y^*(= T_y + A_y)$ within which a nomological isomorph to $T_x(T_x')$ could be formulated by appeal to a similar "translation manual", M_{xy}. Call the counterparts of A_y which are thus formulable using the representational resources of T_z "A_y'".

Since the assumptions A_y are countertheoretical within T_y, their T_z-formulable counterparts, A_y', will not belong to the "nomological image" of the theory $T_y(T_y')$ constructible with $T_z^*(= T_z + A_z)$. However, by adding these A_y' to that nomological image of T_y, we can construct within T_z^* a nomological isomorph to the "virtual theory" T_y^*, originally constructed from T_y and A_y for the purpose of qualifying T_y as a successor to T_x. Call this nomological image of T_y^* within T_z^* "$T_y^{*'}$". Finally, within $T_y^{*'}$, we can construct a nomological isomorph to T_x, for $T_y^{*'}$ is adequate for the nomological modeling of whatever T_y^* itself was, and T_y^* itself was created precisely as a "virtual theory" within which T_x could be modeled. Thus the representational resources of the theory T_z are not only adequate to construct a nomological image of $T_y(T_y')$ within the "virtual theory" $T_z^*(= T_z + A_z)$ but also adequate to construct a nomological image of T_x (call it: T_x'') as well. That is, a qualified successor theory not only satisfied the second explanatory accountability vis-à-vis its immediate predecessor, but also vis-à-vis the predecessor of that immediate predecessor (to which the immediate predecessor was, ex hypothesi, a qualified successor) and in fact, by iteration of the reasoning, vis-à-vis all of its predecessors within the historical sequence of successively qualifying physical theories with which we began. Qualified successor theories save all the appearances—but always as appearances. Diagrammatically, our situation looks like this:

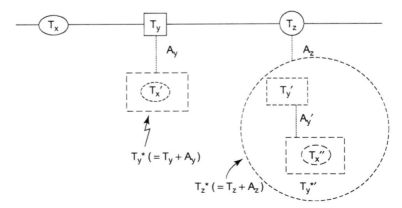

It follows that "inter-theoretic distance" cannot increase. For the "measures" of "inter-theoretic distance" are the successive adjustments, embodied in effect of successive countertheoretical assumptions, which must be made to the laws and principles of qualified successor theories to achieve a "nomological fit" with the laws and principles of their predecessors, and the same countertheoretical assumptions will qualify a successor theory vis-à-vis all of its predecessors if they qualify it vis-à-vis its immediate predecessor. The "intertheoretic distance" between T_y and T_z—measured by effect of the countertheoretical assumptions A_z in our hypothetical example—then, cannot be greater than the "intertheoretic distance" between T_x and T_y—measured by the effect of A_y—since the countertheoretical assumptions A_z alone are adequate to achieve the same degree of "nomological fit" between T_z and T_x (through the construction of a nomological isomorph of T_x—T_x''—within the "virtual theory" T_z^*) that was achieved between T_y and T_x (through construction of a nomological isomorph of T_x—T_x'—within the "virtual theory" $T_y^* = T_y + A_y$).

5

Sellarsian Picturing

Linguistic picture-making is not the performance of asserting matter-of-factual propositions. The *criterion* of the correctness of the performance of asserting a basic matter-of-factual proposition is the correctness of the proposition *qua* picture, i.e. the fact that it coincides with the picture the world-cum-language would generate in accordance with the uniformities controlled by the semantical rules of the language. Thus the *correctness* of the picture is not defined in terms of the *correctness* of a performance but vice versa. (V§57, 136)[1]

Thus Wilfrid Sellars in *Science and Metaphysics*, 1968. Sellars never abandoned the thesis of linguistic picturing. Everyone else did. Although I had strongly endorsed it in *Linguistic Representation* in 1974, I abandoned it myself in 1980, writing, in *One World and Our Knowledge of It* (OW),

That a successor conceptual scheme is more nearly (absolutely) correct than its predecessor(s) *consists* in its adoption or espousal *as* a successor being warranted or justified. The notion of justification is *prior* to the notion of correctness as the notion of correctness was itself prior to that of adequacy to the world. Absolute correctness is nothing but the diachronic limit of justification.[2] (OW, 117)

My proximate difficulty, in other words, was that the picturing relation, as Sellars characterized it, seemed arguably incapable of playing the epistemological role of a *criterion of correctness* in which he evidently proposed to cast it. At least on the face of it, whether or not a proposition (regarded as a picture) "coincides with the picture the world-cum-language would generate in accordance with the uniformities controlled by the semantical rules of the language" doesn't seem to be the sort of thing one could ever be in a position to use as a *reason* for accepting, endorsing, or asserting that proposition. But if a proposition's acceptance could only be epistemically justified independently of establishing its correctness as a picture, then the fact that it *was* a correct picture, even when it obtained, was arguably epistemologically idle.

---

[1] Citations in this form are to Wilfrid Sellars, *Science and Metaphysics* (S&M) (Routledge & Kegan Paul and Humanities Press; London and New York: 1968). The Roman numeral denotes the chapter; the '§' picks out the numbered section within that chapter; and number following the comma gives the page.

[2] An apostasy for which I was warmly commended by Richard Rorty in "Pragmatism, Davidson and truth" (1986).

There was also a more remote difficulty. My problem wasn't that I couldn't make good sense of a picturing relation between elements of *some* representational systems and what they represented. Indeed, I still believed that one could plausibly argue that *some* representational systems *do*, in Sellars' sense, contain pictures of objects in the world. But, as I saw it, one couldn't make good sense of a picturing relation between elements of *theoretical* representational systems and what they represented—and, for us scientific realists, that was the one that ultimately counted. Sellars explicitly disagreed:

The scientific realist must take singular theoretical statements seriously. [Factual] truth in the full sense involves ... a picturing or mapping of events in nature by linguistic or, more generally, conceptual episodes in their own capacity as natural events. ... Thus, to say that theoretical statements are capable of factual truth in the full sense is to say that a stage in the development of scientific theory ... is conceivable in which it would be reasonable to abandon mediation by substantive correspondence rules in favor of a direct commerce of the conceptual framework of the theory with the world. (SRII, 189; cf. 163)[3]

Prima facie, it makes just as much sense to speak of basic singular statements in the framework of micro-physics as pictures, according to a complicated manner of projection, of micro-physical objects, as it does to speak of basic singular statements in the observation framework as pictures of the objects and events of the world of perceptible things and events. (V§88, 145)

These remarks, however, plainly presuppose that the framework of a sophisticated postulational micro-theory *includes* (the possibility of formulating) "basic singular statements", and that seemed to me to be at best a highly problematic thesis.

More than twenty-five years have now elapsed since I last thought seriously about these matters, and it strikes me as appropriate to ask whether my wholesale abandonment of picturing might not have been overly hasty.[4] The picturing thesis was, after all, a central and recurrent motif in Sellars' thought. It is featured in "Truth and 'Correspondence'", published in 1962; he made it the centerpiece of his John Locke Lectures, which appeared as *Science and Metaphysics* in 1968; and he explicitly returned to it in 1978 in chapter 5 of *Naturalism and Ontology* (N&O),[5] the published revision of his 1974 John Dewey Lectures. When a philosopher of Sellars' caliber repeatedly and persistently defends a thesis over

---

[3] "Scientific Realism or Irenic Instrumentalism" (SRII), repr. as ch. 8, pp. 157–89 of Sellars, *Philosophical Perspectives: Metaphysics and Epistemology* (Ridgeview Publishing Co., Atascadero, CA: 1959, 1967).

[4] Not to mention the fact that two colleagues engaged in writing introductions to Sellars' philosophy, Jim O'Shea and Willem DeVries, kept encouraging me to say something useful about picturing.

[5] The concluding pages of which are literally *identical* to the concluding pages of 1962's "Truth and 'Correspondence'", *Journal of Philosophy*, 59 (1962), 29–56, repr. as ch. 6, pp. 197–224 of *Science, Perception and Reality* (SPR) (Ridgeview Publishing Co., (Atascadero, CA: 1963, 1991). Citations as T&C are to the latter.

a period of decades, it is surely reasonable to suspect that he must be on to *something* interesting and important—or, if he is nevertheless mistaken, that it will turn out to be an interesting and important mistake. In either case, the matter deserves a careful second look. And the obvious place to begin is by asking what Sellars means by a *basic singular statement.*

BASIC SINGULAR STATEMENTS

If we suppose that statements are expressed by the formulae of a *formal system*, the answer seems straightforward enough. Here's what Sellars says:

> The key distinction pertaining to matter-of-factual statements of the first level is a familiar one, easy to indicate, but difficult to refine. It is that between atomic and molecular statements. In first approximation it is atomic statements which make up "linguistic pictures" of the world. (V§10, 119)

The answer begins to seem less straightforward, however, when we ask how we are supposed to distinguish atomic from molecular *statements*. Given an effective, typically recursive, specification of the syntax of a formal system, it is a straightforward matter to distinguish atomic from molecular *formulae*, but that isn't yet the distinction that Sellars wants and needs. His explicit concern is with "the distinctive *functions* of first-level matter-of-factual discourse",

> for even within this level essential distinctions must be drawn if we are to grasp the difference between the *primary* concept of factual truth (truth as correct picture), which makes intelligible all other modes of factual truth, and the *generic* concept of truth as S-assertibility, which involves [a] quite different mode of correspondence ... (V§9, 119)

Being *S-assertible*, he has earlier told us, means being "*correctly* assertible; assertible, that is, in accordance with the relevant semantical rules, and on the basis of such additional, though unspecified, information as these rules may require" (IV§26, 101). And *semantical rules*, in turn, are the "rules of criticism" ("ought-to-be" rules)[6] governing demonstrative and sortal linguistic responses to non-linguistic stimuli ("language-entry transitions"), non-linguistic responses to linguistic stimuli ("language-exit transitions"), and formal and material inferences ("intra-linguistic moves") (cf. IV§61, 114). Thereby hangs a long and complicated story, which I shall not attempt here further to

---

[6] The most detailed Sellarsian account of the distinction between rules of criticism—'ought-to-be's—and rules of conduct—'ought-to-do's—can be found in his "Language as Thought and Communication", *Philosophy and Phenomenological Research*, 29 (1969), 506–27; repr. as ch. 5, pp. 93–117 of Sellars, *Essays in Philosophy and Its History* (D. Reidel; Dordrecht, Holland: 1974). Citations as LTC are to the latter. A useful précis of this and other central themes of Sellars' philosophy of language and "Verbal Behaviorism" can be found in my "Ryleans and Outlookers: Wilfrid Sellars on 'Mental States'" (R&O), ch. 8 in this volume.

summarize, but, for future reference, it is important to note that Sellars inter-prets all *lawlike* statements as (expressions of) such semantical rules (V§4–6, 117–18).

From this perspective, then, atomic and molecular statements are presumably *functionally* distinguished by their ways of being S-assertible. The former, Sellars tells us, make up "linguistic pictures" of the world which are "correct or incorrect in terms of the semantic rules of the framework within which they are statements. They are true (S-assertible) if correct, false if incorrect." Molecular statements, he continues, have a different way of being S-assertible. "They pick out sets of pictures within which they play no favorites, and are true if the set of pictures they pick out includes the correct picture, false if they pick out a set of pictures which does not include this picture" (V§10,119).

But when distinguishing atomic from molecular statements is supposed to be the first step toward elucidating the notion of linguistic picturing, such remarks clearly do nothing to advance our understanding. If atomic and molecular statements are distinguished *in terms of* their conditions of correctness, then the relevant, i.e., functional, distinction between them *presupposes* the notion of picturing and cannot be non-circularly used to explain it.

One tempting alternative is to think of the distinction in epistemological terms. Perhaps atomic statements are the ones that express *immediate observations*, i.e., statements manifesting a responsive "language-entry transition", roughly from a sensory stimulus to a representation. Statements that express immediate observations, after all, characteristically have an indexical, "this, here, now", aspect which on the face of it resonates well with the idea of a "basic singular statement". The hallmark of a molecular statement, in contrast, would be its inability to serve as such a language-entry. It would be a statement whose epistemic justification *essentially* involved inferences from premises recording immediate observations.

Unfortunately, Sellars explicitly rejects this interpretation of the distinction, precisely on the grounds that it does not allow for basic singular *theoretical* statements.

[It] might be argued that the requirement that pictures not be molecular or quantified statements … rules out the idea that the language of micro-physics could permit the formulation of pictures. For, it might be said, no singular statement about individual micro-physical particles can occur in a language entry transition. … This objection assumes, however, that statements which are basic as the constituents of pictures must also be epistemically basic in the sense that they formulate observable states of affairs. It is, indeed, true of the common-sense framework that statements which are basic in one sense are also basic in the other. Yet the two senses of 'basic' are different, and a transcendental philosophy which rises to a level of abstraction which distinguishes the generic character of epistemic concepts … from the specific forms they take in common-sense discourse will not assume that the basic constituents of conceptual pictures must be statements of the kind which occur as conceptual responses to sensory stimulation. (V§92, 146–7)

That Sellars frames his discussions of truth and picturing in terms of language reflects his conviction, embodied in his methodological commitment to "Verbal Behaviorism", that, as he put it elsewhere,[7] "in the domain of the mental, language is primary in the order of knowing" (MEV, 325). Correlatively, although in his elucidation of the notion of picturing in "Truth and 'Correspondence'" he invokes the myth of a "super-inscriber" whose inscriptions are, he argues, "projections" of the objects that they represent, he remarks that this "projection exists in any completeness at the level of *acts of thought*" (T&C, 224). In fact, however, the notion of picturing operates at a level of generality which abstracts from the difference between public linguistic events and silent thought episodes. By Sellars' lights, picturing is evidently the fundamental mode of correctness for *any* matter-of-factual representational system, and this suggests that a useful strategy might be to begin by considering his account of representational systems (RSs) too basic for the atomic-*vs.*-molecular distinction to get a foothold in the first place, i.e., *animal RSs*.[8]

ANIMAL REPRESENTATION SYSTEMS

The primary use of our semantic concepts is to classify and characterize elements (items, functions, aspects) of our own *human natural languages*. Their application to animal RSs will consequently be essentially analogical. Sellars' expository strategy is to push the analogy to the hilt. An animal RS will be instantiated in a family of *representational states*, and a state will count as representational just in case—and *because*—it is suitably implicated in analogues to our language-entries, language-exits, and intra-linguistic moves.

The animal RS analogues of our intra-linguistic moves are what Sellars calls "primitive inferences". In first approximation, for both human language-users and animal RSs, an appropriate inferential embedding is what differentiates items (e.g., states, thoughts, or utterances) which count as (representational) awarenesses *of* something *as* something (e.g., *of* an object, a, *as* being F) from items that are mere responses *to* something that *is* something (e.g., *to* an object, a, that *is* F).

Thus a rat's φ-state wouldn't be a state of representing something *as* a triangle, unless it [i.e., the rat] had the propensity to move from the φ-state to another state which counts as a primitive form of representing it [i.e., the "something"] as 3-sided or as having, say, pointed edges. (MEV, 336)

"It is therefore important to realize," Sellars continues, "that inference is, at bottom, the sort of thing Hume had in mind when he speaks of the association of

    [7] In "Mental Events" (MEV), *Philosophical Studies*, 39 (1981), 325–45.
    [8] We human beings, of course, are animals too, but, like Sellars, I here adopt the familiar usage according to which the domain of 'animals' excludes us. When more precision is needed, I shall speak of *primitive* animal RSs.

ideas" (MEV, 336). In particular, the primitive inferences of an animal RS will all be analogues of our *material* inferences.[9] Like our own inferential conduct, the relevant animal behavior will be *pattern-governed*:[10]

[Inferential] patterns are uniformities in the occurrence of representational states. Certain kinds of representational states tend to be followed (or to be followed by the absence of) certain other kinds of representational states. (MEV, 337)

The animal RS analogue to a language-entry (perceptual awareness) straight-forwardly consists in its responding to a sensory stimulus with a representational state. "Clearly a suitably trained RS can come to be in a 'This is a triangle' state by virtue of being irradiated by a triangular object" (MEV, 337). The animal RS analogue to a language-exit (intentional action), in contrast, is arguably more problematic. On Sellars' account,

a RS can represent its own behavior. It can represent itself as, for example, jumping. Under certain conditions the representation of itself as jumping becomes a primitive form of 'choosing to jump'. An adequate theory of RSs will discuss how the action-triggering valence is transmitted along a chain of representational states from 'goal states' to the representation of actions. [Compare the analogy of practical inferences.] (MEV, 338)

Now *I* can certainly represent myself as jumping, e.g., by saying or thinking "I am jumping". I find, however, that it is hard to imagine, for instance, a rat doing anything analogous to *that* because it is hard to imagine a rat's having anything analogous to my *first-person pronoun*. The issue is an extremely complicated one,[11] but, for present purposes, I shall simply bracket this worry and move on, for Sellars explicitly makes *some* sort of self-awareness an indispensable condition of an animal RS.

---

[9] I advance a parallel account of the "inferences" of what I call "Humean creatures" in ch. 8 of *Beyond Formalism: Naming and Necessity for Human Beings* (Temple University Press; Philadelphia, PA: 1994). See esp. pp. 183–91.

[10] Pattern-governed behavior is "behavior which exhibits a pattern, not because it is brought about by the intention that it exhibit this pattern, but because the propensity to emit behavior of the pattern has been selectively reinforced, and the propensity to emit behavior which does not conform to this pattern selectively extinguished". (From p. 423 of "Meaning as Functional Classification", *Synthese*, 27 (1974), 417–36.) More detail can again be found in my R&O.

[11] I think that there are compelling reasons for concluding that rats and their like are rather what I called in *The Thinking Self* (Temple University Press; Philadelphia, PA: 1986) *pure positional awarenesses*, and consequently present "in" their representational states, if at all, only as aspects of their *form*, e.g., spatial perspectivality. The issue of self-awareness becomes an especially pressing one, I there argued, already with the question of *temporal* perspectivality, e.g., the ability to represent past items *as* past. Sellars is unfortunately simply optimistically noncommittal at just this point: "Another dimension is added by memory-retention. But given the rest this seems relatively unproblematic" (MEV, 338). Pages 113–27 of *The Thinking Self* present a significantly more complex picture, and a correspondingly less sanguine assessment, of the matter. (It is instructive to compare Sellars' example of a "smart missile" at N&O, 126–8. The missile represents its own location only *relative* to the objects that it represents, by centering its maps on itself, and its "actions" are triggered by a "program" which includes explicit conditional *imperatives*.)

[To] be a representational state, a state of an organism must be the manifestation of a system of dispositions and propensities by virtue of which the organism constructs *maps* of itself in its environment, and locates itself and its behavior on the map. (MEV, 336)

States of an organism are *representational*, in other words, only if they are appropriately connected, directly or indirectly, to its conduct or behavior. A state, ρ, represents a certain location λ in the environment of a white rat, for example, only if it belongs to "a system of representational states ρ_i, ρ_j ... so related that the system is structurally similar to the spatial structure of its environment, consisting of λ_i, λ_j [...]" *and* "so connected with each other and with the rat's locomotor activity that together they constitute ... a strategy for finding λ". A symbol[12] S represents an object O—referentially "picks it out"—only if "S belongs to a RS in which it is so connected with other features of the system (including *actions*) as to be the focal point of a strategy for finding O". And a state represents an object as being of a certain character, φ, he tells us, only if "the organism has a strategy for finding φ objects" which "essentially involves inferential sequences" (MEV, 337).

On Sellars' account the representational states of an animal's RS are *essentially* connected to behavioral "strategies for finding" locations (e.g., its nest or lair), individual objects (e.g., its mate or offspring), and types of objects (e.g., water, food, or prey). It's in this sense that they constitute a *map*.

One doesn't have to actually use [maps] to go to the places they represent in order for them to be maps, but the point of being a map is to translate into sentences which dovetail with *practical* discourse about getting from point A to point B. (N&O, 134)

Sellars is here talking about the ordinary sort of maps that *we* construct and employ. Their functioning *as* maps, he argues, is parasitic on our ability to "translate" them into the sorts of natural-language sentences that can function as premises in the practical reasoning which shapes, e.g., our automotive travels. An animal RS, in contrast, doesn't *use* a map as we do but rather *instantiates* one in a more direct sense insofar as the representational states that compose it *themselves* function as (analogues to) premises in the (analogues to) practical reasoning that shapes the animal's behavioral interactions with its environment.

PROPOSITIONAL FORM

Sellars' primary aim in these sections of "Mental Events" is to defend two key theses:

---

[12] The text speaks explicitly of a *symbol*, but, since we're in the process of talking about the functions of *states* of an organism that qualify them as representational, what Sellars must have in mind here is surely the aspect or element of such a state that performs the *symbolizing function* of representing an object O.

(1) The representational states involved in primitive inference have propositional form.

(2) Propositional form is more primitive than logical form. (MEV, 336)

Thesis (1) turns on the claim that the basic representational states of a (primitive or sophisticated) RS are *double-aspected*.

A basic representational event is an event which has two characters: one by virtue of which it represents an object in its environment (or itself); another by virtue of which it represents that object as being of a certain character.[13] (MEV, 338)

Thus a *single* (basic representational) *state* performs a *double function*, representing something (e.g., an object O) *as* something (e.g., as being φ) by virtue of its ability to play a role in two "search strategies"—one for finding an *individual* item (e.g., the object O), the other for finding items of particular *type* (e.g., φ items).

The thesis that such basic representational states have *propositional* form, in turn, amounts to the claim that we should interpret, e.g., subject-predicate sentences which express propositions as having the form of such basic representational states, i.e., as themselves also having two characters, one serving a referential function and the other a characterizing function. That this is the *correct* way to interpret certain simple sentences of a natural language (e.g., "Socrates is wise", "Crito blushed", "Meno dislikes Alcibiades") and the atomic formulae of a logical calculus by which we sometimes abbreviate them (e.g., 'Ws', 'Bc', 'mDa') is the leading thesis of Sellars' Tractarian *nominalist account of predication*.[14]

The account takes as its point of departure *Tractatus* 3.1432:

Not: "The complex sign 'aRb' says that *a* stands in the relation R to *b*, but: "*That* 'a' stands in a certain relation to 'b' says *that* aRb."

The nominalist account of predication draws a radically general moral from this remark:

We can *only* say that aRb by placing the names 'a' and 'b' in a certain conventional dyadic relation. (N&O, 57)

---

[13] This is rather messy. For present purposes, I think, we are entitled to treat Sellars' talk of representational *events* here as simply interchangeable with his prior talk of representational *states*. The point of switching to 'event' here is to connect the discussion of RSs with the episodic character of our own representational thoughts, which are the paradigms of the "mental events" that are the nominal topic of MEV. More likely to confuse is the search for pronoun-antecedents, which can lead to the mistaken conclusion that a basic representational event can have a character by virtue of which it represents *itself*. Despite the lack of a proper grammatical antecedent, the 'it's in "its environment (or itself)" surely refer to the represen*ter*, e.g., the white rat, not to its represent*ings*.

[14] Sellars originally outlined this account in "Naming and Saying" (N&S), *Philosophy of Science*, 29 (1962), 7–26, repr. as ch. 7, pp. 225–46 of SPR. It is précised in section III, pp. 332–35 of MEV, and invoked without much discussion in S&M (cf. pp. 108–9, 120–1). The most extensive and detailed exposition is perhaps the one given in ch. 3, pp. 47–71 of N&O.

The moral extends to predications of any polyadicity. In particular, "we can *only* say that Fa by tokening an 'a' in a certain conventional style" (N&O, 61).

On this account, the 'R' in 'aRb' and the 'F' in 'Fa' are dispensable auxiliary symbols. The *functional* role of the 'R' in 'aRb' is only to help bring it about that the two names 'a' and 'b' *do* stand in such a conventional dyadic relation, namely, that of *standing* (respectively) *to the left and right of an 'R'*; that of the 'F' in 'Fa', to bring it about that the 'a' has a certain conventionally-defined property, that of *standing to the right of an 'F'*. In N&S, Sellars envisages a language—he calls it 'Jumblese'—which would make no use of such auxiliary symbols. In Jumblese, one would say, for instance, that a is larger than b, not by putting an 'is larger than' between an 'a' and a 'b', but by *directly* relating the 'a' and the 'b', e.g., geometrically, by writing one above the other: $\begin{smallmatrix}a\\b\end{smallmatrix}$, and one would say that b is red, not by appending an 'is red' to a 'b', but by writing the 'b' itself in a certain style, e.g., in italic script: *b*.

The proper way to relate this nominalist theory of predication to our earlier discussion of representational systems is to see *signs* or *symbols* as playing the role of *states*. The Jumblese sentence '*b*' represents an object, b, as being red by virtue of being a single simple *sign* having two characters, respectively performing the two functions of "referring" and "characterizing". The sign '*b*' represents the *object* b by virtue of *being 'b'-shaped*; it represents b as being red by virtue of *being italicized*. The Jumblese sentence ' $\begin{smallmatrix}a\\b\end{smallmatrix}$ ' represents a as larger than b by virtue of being a single *composite* sign consisting of an 'a'-shaped *part* above a 'b'-shaped *part*.

It is plausible to suppose that the representational states of *animal* RSs resemble sentences of Jumblese more closely than they do sentences of a natural language or formulae of a logical calculus, i.e., that they perform their representational functions without the aid of auxiliary elements. In consequence, like Jumblese sentences, they admit of non-logical amalgamation into *complex representations*.

Let us enrich the Jumblese fragment with which we've been working by supposing that its signs represent objects as *being blue* by virtue of *being in boldface*, that they represent objects as *being triangular* by virtue of *being capitalized*, and that they represent objects as *being square* by virtue of *being in a sans serif script*. Then a *single* simple sign, '*A*', will be able to represent the object a as being *both* red *and* triangular by virtue of being 'a'-shaped *and* italicized *and* capitalized; the *single* simple sign '**b**' will represent the object b as being both blue and square by virtue of being 'b'-shaped and boldface and sans serif; and the single *composite* sign ' $\begin{smallmatrix}A\\b\end{smallmatrix}$ ' will represent the red triangular object a as being larger than the blue square object b by virtue of one of its suitably representing parts being above the other. Thus the complex state of affairs that we might represent in a logical calculus by an extended conjunction—'Ra & Ta & Bb & Sb & aLb'—will be represented in a

Jumblese-style RS by a single composite sign whose mode of composition is a matter of its parts simultaneously instantiating a multiplicity of (representationally relevant) properties and relationships. As Sellars is anxious to stress,

> the mode of composition by virtue of which a number of atomic statements join to make a complex picture must not be confused with the mode of composition by virtue of which a number of atomic statements join to make a molecular statement. In other words, we must distinguish "pictorial" from "logical" complexity. (V§15, 120)

Animal RSs, it is plausible to suppose, exhibit only the first, "pictorial" sort of complexity.

A second significant consideration is that the *properties* of and *relationships* among the representing states of an animal RS by virtue of which they perform their representational functions must presumably be *natural*, as opposed to conventional, properties and relationships. Reflection on the animal RS analogue to language entries suggests that paramount among them will be the properties of and relationships among the *sensory* states with which the organism responds to external stimuli. Putting this point together with the previous one yields a conception of, e.g., an animal's total *visual field* at a given time as a single composite state functioning as a *"pictorially" complex representation of its then and there visual environment.* Insofar as they are appropriately caught up in dispositions to (primitive) inferences and behavior, such sensory states *function* as highly complex Jumblese-style "sentences". To put it metaphorically, the world "speaks" to organisms through their senses.[15]

BASIC SINGULAR REPRESENTATIONS

We began this excursus through the theory of animal RSs in search of a useful elucidation of the notion of a "basic singular statement". The natural suggestion to make at this point, I think, is that a "basic singular *representation*" is just one which performs its representational *function* in the way in which the multiply-aspected representing states of an animal RS do, i.e., "propositionally", by virtue of instantiating both "referential" and "characterizing" properties and relationships. Correlatively, that way of representing states of affairs is what is meant by *"picturing"*.

A statement to the effect that a linguistic item [e.g., a representing state, sign, or event] pictures a non-linguistic item by virtue of the semantical uniformities characteristic of a certain conceptual structure [i.e., representational system] is, in an important sense, an object language statement, for even though it mentions linguistic objects, it treats them as items in the order of causes and effects, i.e., *in rerum natura*, and speaks directly of their

---

[15] As I recall, it was Anton Friedrich Koch who first suggested the ideas in this paragraph to me during the course of one of our spirited philosophical conversations in Tübingen. The image of nature speaking to us in a sensory dialect of Jumblese has haunted me ever since.

function in this order, in a way which is to be sharply contrasted with the meta-linguistic statements of logical semantics ... (V§59, 137)

One significant consequence of our investigation to this point is that *such* basic singular representations can be functionally, and so also empirically, extremely complex. The *double*-aspected (subject-predicate) "basic representational states" highlighted by Sellars in MEV are simply the limiting case. And, correspondingly, one significant moral of the nominalist account of predication will be that *every* RS contains a stratum of such basic singular representations, including those representational systems which, like our own natural languages and symbolic calculi, make liberal use of auxiliary elements.

From this point of view, a sentence or formula will be, in the semantically relevant sense, "atomic" just in case it is, *functionally regarded*, a basic singular representation. An expression that is clearly *syntactically* "molecular", i.e., constructed according to *formation* rules which make use of connective- and quantifier-signs, can thus nevertheless be *semantically* "atomic", i.e., represent by picturing. As Sellars puts it,

logical connectives and quantifiers do not occur *as such* in pictorial complexes. Thus, when the conjunctive statement '*fa · aRb · gb*' is considered *qua* picture the connectives, though physically present, no longer function as such, but become so to speak mere punctuation. (V§18, 121)

It is presumably in this way that *theoretical* representational systems can in principle contain basic singular representations used to make "atomic" statements. The *prima facie* difficulty in representing individual basic theoretical entities—e.g., molecules, electrons, neutrinos, quarks, or quantum fields—is that our theoretical languages characteristically supply no syntactically simple representatives for such entities. But although we have been treating the representatives of individual objects on the model of *proper names* or *individual constants*, our most recent reflections imply that there is no necessity about this.

It is perhaps not unreasonable to assume that we can in principle always identify a basic theoretical item, *b*, by means of a *definite description*, for instance, (where Θ is a basic theoretical kind) as *the Θ that was implicated in theoretical event e at place p and time t*. And the crucial point is that such syntactically complex expressions can, from the point of view of their representational *function*, be "simple signs".

When ... we turn our attention to first-level matter-of-factual statements which resemble the statements we have been calling pictures in every respect *save that the subject term is a definite description*, we need to recognize that although
    The *g* is *f*
can be perspicuously represented as
    $f[(\iota x)gx]$
neither 'the *g*' nor '$(\iota x)gx$' is occurring *as a logically complex expression, but rather as a simple expression which, if the uniqueness condition it indicates is satisfied, can be used to form linguistic pictures of a certain object.* (V§24, 124)

There is thus no obstacle, Sellars concludes, to *introducing* an expression, e.g., '*a*', without internal syntactic complexity by specifying that '*a*' denotes just in case $\exists!(\iota x)gx$, in which case it denotes $(\iota x)gx$. "The difference between '*a*', on the one hand, and 'the *g*' and '$(\iota x)gx$', on the other, is that the latter carry on their sleeve the logical and empirical information relevant to their correct use" (V§26, 124).

Independently of whether they are, *in the natural order*, aspects of the representing states of an animal RS or syntactically simple or complex expressions of a natural language or symbolic calculus, on Sellars' view, the *representative function* of "referring elements" is properly elucidated in terms of the rules and uniformities in which they are implicated.

(1) Non-demonstrative referring expressions must themselves belong to the 'natural' order and be connected with objects in a way which involves language entry transitions, intra-linguistic moves … and language departure transitions …

(2) There must be a relatively stable, if skeletal, framework of propositions (involving those referring expressions) which "describe the spatio-temporal location of these objects with respect to each other".

(3) A proper part of this skeletal framework must "specify [the] location of the language user in his environment".

(4) Rehearsings of this skeletal framework must gear in with the use of demonstratives to "specify the location with respect to *here-now* of the objects with which the referring expressions are correlated". (V§30, 125–6)

If this is right, then there is no *in principle* obstacle to the idea that, for instance, the language of theoretical physics can contain basic singular statements[16] whose role is to represent *by picturing* states of affairs involving individual theoretical objects and events localized in space and time.

Although more remains to be said on the matter, that is enough to suggest that Sellars' account of picturing in fact contains sufficient resources to address what, at the beginning of this essay, I called my "more remote difficulty" with the picturing thesis. It is time, then, to turn to my "proximate difficulty", the notion that the picturing relationship could serve as a criterion of correctness for basic singular representations.

PICTORIAL CORRECTNESS

My reason for appealing to Sellars' account of animal RSs was to attempt to elucidate the idea of picturing in a way that made no use of a prior

---

[16] Sellars gives the notion of "basic singular statements in the language of theoretical physics" a somewhat different gloss in a footnote to VI§55, 171: "By this I do not mean statements about individual micro-physical objects, for statements about wholes can be as basic, in the relevant sense, as statements about their parts." From this perspective, the thesis that elements of theoretical RSs could represent by picturing is even easier to defend.

conception of representational correctness. But if, as Sellars contends, the concept of basic matter-of-factual *truth*—the S-assertibility of a basic matter-of-factual proposition—presupposes and rests on the concept of the *correctness* of a proposition *qua* picture, we clearly need a complementary understanding of what it is in virtue of which a picture is correct. If the representational states of a primitive animal RS are indeed paradigmatic *pictorial* representations, then, it is apposite to ask whether—and, if so, how—they can be correct or incorrect. As soon as we ask the question, however, we find ourselves confronting a number of problems. The following quote cuts to the heart of the matter:

> [The] concept of a linguistic or conceptual picture requires that the picture be brought about by the objects pictured; and while bringing about of linguistic pictures could be 'mechanical' (thus in the case of sophisticated robots), in thinking of pictures as correct or incorrect we are thinking of the uniformities involved as directly or indirectly subject to rules of criticism. (V§56, 136)

The immediate difficulty is that the behavior of primitive animal RSs is evidently not subject to rules of criticism *at all*, directly or indirectly.

Rules of criticism are 'ought-to-be' rules, and while the items to which they apply, their "subject-matter subjects", need not be capable of using them as reasons for acting,[17] it makes no clear sense to posit such rules in the absence of "agent subjects" who, by deriving rules of conduct, i.e., 'ought-to-*do*'s, from them, *can* do so. As Sellars himself has notoriously stressed, characterizing a state, transaction, condition, or episode in normative terms is a matter of locating it in the "logical space of reasons, of justifying and being able to justify what one says" (EPM §36, 169).[18]

> [The] idea that epistemic facts can be analyzed without remainder—even "in principle"—into non-epistemic facts, whether phenomenal or behavioral, public or private, with no matter how lavish a sprinkling of subjunctives and hypotheticals is ... a radical mistake ... (EPM §5, 131)

In training domestic animals, for instance, *we* translate the relevant rules of criticism, e.g., "Dogs ought to defecate only outdoors", into the ought-to-do's guiding the actions of positive and negative reinforcement by which we shape the animals' behavior to exhibit the desired uniformities. Unlike us, however, primitive animal RSs lack the resources to recognize the normative authority of reasons, i.e., to acknowledge and respond to them *as* reasons, and so, if we limit our consideration to such primitive representational systems, the notion that

---

[17] Sellars' elegant example: "Westminster chimes ought to strike on the quarter hour" (LTC, 95).

[18] "Empiricism and the Philosophy of Mind", repr. as ch. 5, pp. 127–96 of SPR. Citations by section and page number to this appearance.

their behavior is subject to rules of criticism will have to be one that applies to them, not literally, but only by analogy.[19]

The analogy which lies closest at hand is that between animal RSs and *maps*, but here we must proceed with great care, for we typically assess maps, not as correct or incorrect, but rather, for instance, as more or less *accurate* or *inaccurate*. In the case of our ordinary maps, we characteristically think of their accuracy or inaccuracy in terms of their degree of correspondence to the territory being mapped, and, since we have map-independent access to that territory, this practice creates no difficulties. It is, rather, simply another expression of the fact that the way in which *we* use our ordinary maps is dependent on our command of natural languages. But insofar as a primitive animal RS does not *use* but only *instantiates* a map of its environment, the accuracy or inaccuracy of that map cannot, *for the organism*, be understood in terms of such correspondence relationships. Rather we need to attend to the mapping *function* of an animal RS, and that, Sellars has proposed, is a matter of its representational states being essentially related to behavioral "strategies for finding" locations, individual objects, and types of objects.

In fact, however, we normally also don't think of such strategies as correct or incorrect. A strategy is rather more or less *effective* or *ineffective*, depending upon the proportion of its implementations that are *successful* and *unsuccessful*, where pursuing a strategy S for achieving an end, E, is successful just in case behaving in accordance with it results in E's being realized. The ends of primitive animal RSs, in turn, and so the "strategies for finding" that they *need*, are essentially limited to the evolutionarily-conditioned requirements for individual survival and species reproduction, and so we can also think of their "internal environmental maps" and corresponding "search strategies" teleologically, as *functional adaptations* in the biological sense. But that seems to be the end of this analytical road. When the chips are down, the concept of a strategy's "effectiveness" is purely statistical—a matter of the frequency with which its behavioral implementations prove successful—and, by Sellars' own lights, there is nothing *normative* about that. For primitive animal RSs, the *teleology* of representational states is evidently as close as we can come to their normativity.

But if this is right, then we are not going to be able to elucidate the notion of pictorial correctness solely by reference to primitive animal RSs. On the contrary, the representational states of such a system will be correct or incorrect only in the analogical sense that we can think of them as "anticipations" of basic singular representations which, like our own, are *literally* subject to rules of criticism. And this brings us to the closest approximation to such an elucidation in Sellars' text. The claim,

---

[19] This point is clearly related to the worries expressed earlier about a primitive animal RS's self-representations. See n. 11 above.

(p1)   '*fa*'s (in L) correctly picture O as ϕ,

he writes,

tells us that (in L) utterances consisting of an '*f*' concatenated with an '*a*' are correlated with O, which is ϕ, in accordance with the semantic uniformities which correlate utterances of lower-case letters of the alphabet with objects such as O, and which correlate utterances of lower-case letters of the alphabet which are concatenated with an '*f*' with objects which are ϕ. These correlations involve the complex machinery of language entry transitions (noticings), intra-linguistic moves (inference, identification by means of criteria) and language departure transitions (volitions pertaining to epistemic activity) … (V§58, 136)

The essentially conjunctive character of this elucidation comes into view when we ask, for instance, whether, assuming that the semantic uniformities of L also correlate utterances of lower-case letters of the alphabet which are concatenated with a '*g*' with objects which are ψ, we would also be entitled to the claim that,

(p2)   '*ga*'s (in L) *incorrectly* picture O as ψ.

The answer, surely, is that it depends upon whether or not O *is* ψ. If it is not, then (p2) is perhaps in order, but if O is *both* ϕ *and* ψ, then presumably both '*fa*'s and '*ga*'s will *correctly* picture O.

If this is right, then we can comfortably retain the account of picturing as a *mode of representation* that we extracted from our exploration of animal RSs and other dialects of Jumblese. *What* is pictured by a multiply-aspected basic singular propositional representation (e.g., state or statement) is determined by the correlations between representing aspects with represented locations, objects, and types of objects that are generated by the (analogues to the) rules of criticism shaping the representer's (analogues to) language-entries, language-exits, and intra-linguistic moves. But these correlations do not yet determine whether that picture is *correct* or *incorrect*. That is, (p1) and (p2) are more perspicuously expressed by

(p1*)   '*fa*'s (in L) picture O as ϕ. &. O *is* ϕ,   and
(p2*)   '*ga*'s (in L) picture O as ψ. &. O *is not* ψ.

This makes it clear why Sellars insists on replacing the Tractarian schema "Linguistic fact pictures nonlinguistic fact" by the schema

[natural linguistic objects] O'_1, O'_2, …, O'_n, make up a picture of [objects] O_1, O_2, …, O_n by virtue of such and such facts about O'_1, O'_2, …, O'_n. (T&C, 215; N&O, 139)

For (applying the nominalist account of predication) it is a fact about the '*a*' in any instance of '*ga*' (belonging to L) that it has the property of *standing to the right of a* '*g*' and thereby, we are supposing, pictures O *as* being ψ, whether or not it is also a fact that O *is* ψ. The interpretation of pictorial *correctness* at which we have arrived, however, is nevertheless Tractarian root and branch.

2.21 A picture agrees or disagrees with reality; it is correct or incorrect, true or false.

2.22 A picture represents what it represents through its form of depiction, independently of its truth or falsity. ...

2.223 In order to tell whether a picture is true or false we must compare it with reality.

2.224 From the picture alone one cannot tell whether it is true or false.[20]

This interpretation can perhaps also help us come to terms with Sellars' contention that "the *criterion* of the correctness of the performance of asserting a basic matter-of-factual proposition is the correctness of the proposition *qua* picture" (V§57, 136), but only after we have first dealt with some exegetical matters. To begin with, it is not entirely obvious what it is for a *performance* to be correct in the first place. We might call the performance of, say, an actor or a musician "correct" if the words that the performer says or the notes that she plays correspond to those specified by the script or score, but that sense of "correctness" does not seem to be what is at issue. At its core, Sellars' contention rather seems to amount to the claim that we are, in some sense, *entitled* to assert a basic singular proposition only when it is a correct picture. But in what sense?

Recall, too, that Sellars characterizes a proposition as *S-assertible* just in case it is "*correctly* assertible; assertible, that is, in accordance with the relevant semantical rules, and on the basis of such additional, though unspecified, information as these rules may require" (IV§26, 101). In the case of a basic singular proposition, the "relevant semantical rules" can only be the rules of criticism ('ought-to-be's) which give rise to the uniformities of language-entries, language-exits, and intra-linguistic moves by virtue of which that proposition pictures what it does. Since, however, asserting is something we *do* and such 'ought-to-be' rules are not themselves rules of conduct, it is also not entirely obvious what it means for a proposition to be assertible "in accordance with them". Nor is it clear why assertibility "in accordance with" such 'ought-to-be' rules should amount to *correct* assertibility. That expression again seems to suggest some form of entitlement, but rules of criticism do not as such convey entitlements.

The most straightforward suggestion is surely that the entitlements in question are *epistemic*, and that is the interpretation that I propose to endorse. Here it is helpful to observe that Sellars thinks of *asserting* a matter-of-factual proposition as entering it into an evolving *world story*. At any given time,

the living language involves a *commitment* to one world story, however schematic and fragmentary. This commitment, however, is provisional. The story is the ship which is being built (and, of course, re-built) by those who live on it. (N&O, 129)

Matter-of-factual representings are consequently, as Sellars puts it, "Janus-faced" in that they belong to "both the causal order and the order of reasons".

[The] causal aspect of perceptual takings, introspective awarenesses, inferences, and volitions accounts for the selecting of *one* world story *rather than another* and connects

---

[20] The translations are my own.

the 'is' of this selecting with the rule-governed or 'ought to be' character of the language. (N&O, 130)

The uniformities manifested in a language's entry and exit transitions and intra-linguistic moves are governed by rules of criticism expressible by the 'ought-to-be' propositions of a normative semantic meta-language, but our acceptance of such propositions, in turn—crucially including both *lawlike* statements and specific principles concerning *normal conditions* for perception (cf. N&O, 121–2)—is governed by the ought-to-be's and ought-to-do's of correct *inquiry*. The concept of a world story is thus "an *epistemic* concept, the concept of a story which is generated by (is) and required by (ought) the rule governed involvement of a language in the world it is about" (N&O, 131).

It is thus correct, Sellars observes, to say, for instance, that "it is *because* a is red that it is (semantically) correct to token 'a is red' " (N&O, 131). But, as we have seen, it is also correct to say that 'a is red' pictures (the object) a as being red *because* (in our language, we are supposing) 'a'-shaped tokens are correlated with the object a and tokens standing to the left of an 'is red' are correlated with red objects in accordance with the semantic uniformities generated by the relevant semantic rules. Since, on the interpretation I have offered, 'a is red' *correctly* pictures a as being red only if, in addition, a *is* red, we can conclude that it is (semantically) correct to token 'a is red' only if 'a is red' correctly pictures a as being red, that is, that the correctness of the proposition *as a picture* is a necessary condition of the correctness of the correlative tokening *performance*.

That, I suggest, is how we should understand Sellars' claim that "the *criterion* of the correctness of the performance of asserting a basic matter-of-factual proposition is the correctness of the proposition *qua* picture", which, on this interpretation, turns out to be rather less momentous than it might initially appear to be. For the concept of picturing *per se* is the concept of a mode of representation, not a mode of correctness, and so has no independent *epistemic* function. In order to determine whether, e.g., the proposition 'a is red' is correct *qua* picture, we do not need first to find out *what* it pictures. Since (as we are assuming) 'a is red' belongs to *our* representational system, its picturing, so to speak, takes care of itself. In order to determine whether 'a is red' is a *correct* picture, and hence S-assertible (i.e., true), then, the only thing that we need to *find out* is whether a *is* red—but that hardly comes as a surprise.

If that were all that Sellars had to say about the picturing relation, we could stop here, but, as he himself remarks, in philosophy one thing always leads to another, and so, of course, there is more work to do. For Sellars also contends that

pictures, like maps, can be more or less adequate. The adequacy concerns the "method of projection". A picture (candidate) subject to the rules of a given method of projection (conceptual framework), which is a correct picture (successful candidate), is S-assertible with respect to that method of projection. (V§56, 135)

The "dimension of 'picturing' ", he suggests, supplies "the Archimedeian point outside the series of actual and possible beliefs" that one needs to make proper sense of Peirce's notion of the ideal limit of inquiry (V§75, 142). And that brings us to the central Sellarsian theme of *alternative conceptual structures*.

PICTORIAL ADEQUACY

Sellars introduces the notion of a *conceptual structure* (CS) as a generalization of the notion of a natural language, as "the common game" which is played by speakers of, e.g., English, French, and German (V§49, 132). It is clear enough, however, that other, quite different, forms of *propositional* representational systems can also qualify as instances of a CS, and Sellars also invites us to think of *scientific theories* as, in essence, thematically compact CSs. Since the semantical rules governing the elements of representational systems can and do change over time, an individual CS is an evolving system, consisting of different *stages* at different times. These notions are, of course, vague and "open-textured" in various ways, but—especially in the case of scientific theories, where we can explicitly track significant changes in the semantical rules (lawlike statements) governing such concepts as *oxidation, mass,* and *simultaneity*—at least initially, they are clear and determinate enough for our present purposes.

As we have seen, Sellars identifies truth with S-assertibility, and, since any assertion mobilizes the resources of some CS to which the asserted proposition belongs, the fundamental form of a truth-ascription is 'true in conceptual structure CS_i'. The "unqualified" or "absolute" sense of 'true' "pertains to the special case where CS_i is *our* [current] conceptual structure (abbreviated, in what follows, as CSO) ..." (V§50, 133). To call a matter-of-factual proposition 'true' *simpliciter*, in other words, is to say that it is S-assertible by us, here and now.

Sellars introduces two ways of relating the alethic status of propositions belonging to different CSs. Both make use of the concept of a *family* of propositions (abbreviated 'PRFAM'), which are *counterparts* of each other at different stages in the development of a CS across time. The notion of the truth (i.e., S-assertibility) of a proposition belonging to an earlier stage (CS_1) of our conceptual structure (CSO) can then be defined in terms of the truth (*simpliciter*) of its counterpart in CSO. In Sellars' formulation (V§52, 133):

> $PROP_j$ (in CS_1) is true ↔ for some PRFAM and for some PROP, PROP belongs to CSO, $PROP_j$ (in CS_1) ⊂ PRFAM, PROP ⊂ PRFAM, and PROP is true.

In this way, to the extent that we can think of a primitive animal RS as such a CS_1, instantiating an earlier stage of our own CS, we can think of its propositional representational states as true and thereby, since truth is S-assertibility, i.e., assertibility in accordance with the relevant semantical rules, as falling within the scope of rules of criticism whose normative authority *we*, but not such primitive representers, are (in principle) in a position to acknowledge.

Correlatively, Sellars proposes (V§53, 134) to define a sense in which a proposition in our current conceptual structure, CSO, is true *with respect to* an earlier conceptual structure, CS_1 — in his terminology, true *quoad* CS_1:

> $PROP_k$ (in CSO) is true *quoad* CS_1 $\leftrightarrow$ for some PRFAM and for some PROP, PROP belongs to CS_1, $PROP_k$ (in CSO) $\subset$ PRFAM, PROP (in CS_1) $\subset$ PRFAM, and PROP is true *quoad* CS_1.

This is plainly a recursive definition, and so we would expect Sellars to supply a basis clause, but curiously he does not. It would presumably look like this:[21]

> $PROP_i$ (*in* CS_1) is true *quoad* CS_1 $\leftrightarrow$ $PROP_i$ (in CS_1) is S-assertible by users of CS_1.

In this case, the representational activities of users of CS_1 must fall directly within the scope of rules of criticism whose normative authority *they themselves* are (in principle) in a position to acknowledge. Where CS_1 is a primitive animal RS, then, propositions belonging to CSO could not literally be true *quoad* CS_1.

Analogously, Sellars argues, "we can define a sense in which expressions in a different but related conceptual structure can be said to refer to or denote that which is denoted by expressions in our conceptual structure" (V§62, 138). The operative notion here is that of a family (INFAM) of *counterpart individual senses* (INSENSE).

> $INSENSE_j$ (in CS_i) denotes O $\leftrightarrow$ for some INSENSE and for some INFAM, INSENSE belongs to CSO, $INSENSE_j$ belongs to CS_i, INSENSE $\subset$ INFAM, $INSENSE_j$ $\subset$ INFAM, and INSENSE materially equivalent to ·O·.[22]

"The importance of this analysis," Sellars suggests,

lies in the fact that it permits the extension of epistemic notions to conceptual items in a framework which is other than, but related to, the conceptual structure which is embedded in our language as it now stands. In other words, the connection of these epistemic notions with our current conceptual structure … is loosened in a way which makes meaningful the statement that our current conceptual structure is both more adequate than its predecessors and less adequate than certain of its potential successors. (V§63, 138)

Finally, Sellars invites us to imagine a language, Peirceish, "which enables its users to form *ideally* adequate pictures of objects" (V§69, 140). Identifying the truth of propositions in the Peirceish conceptual structure, CSP, with their S-assertibility by users of CSP, it is then a straightforward matter for him to define

---

[21] By analogy to the basis clause of the recursive definition of 'true *quoad* CSP' at V§73, 141.

[22] (S&M, V§62, 138). A brief reminder: Sellarsian dot-quotes form common nouns applying to items in other RSs which do the same job or play the same role as the "sign-design" between the dots does in CSO. Two individual senses, e.g., ·a· and ·b·, are materially equivalent just in case (f)(fa ≡ fb). Cf. III§63, 84.

truth *quoad* CSP for propositions in less developed, less adequate conceptual structures, including CSO (V§73, 141):

> PROP$_j$ (in CS$_i$) is true *quoad* CSP $\leftrightarrow$ for some PROP and for some PRFAM, PROP belongs to CSP, PROP belongs to PRFAM,[23]PROP$_j$ (in CS$_i$) $\subset$ PRFAM, and PROP is true *quoad* CSP

In the case of *basic* matter-of-factual propositions, he suggests, two principles plausibly relate 'true *quoad* CSP to other senses of 'true':

(a) If a proposition in CSO is true its counterpart in CSP is true *quoad* CSO, and true *quoad* CSP. (Roughly, if a system of natural linguistic objects tokening a proposition in CSO pictures certain objects, then tokens of the counterpart proposition in CSP also picture these objects.)

(b) If a proposition in CSP is true *quoad* CSP its counterparts in such frameworks (CS$_i$) as contain a counterpart are true *quoad* CSP, but not necessarily true *quoad* CS$_i$, though not false *quoad* CS$_i$. (V§74, 141–2)

Principle (b) explicitly acknowledges the possibility that objects pictured by propositions belonging to a "more developed" CS may not be pictured *at all* by *any* proposition of a "less developed" one. This seems plausible enough. (Think, e.g., of neutrinos or quarks and eighteenth- or-nineteenth-century physics.) Principle (a) makes a specific application of "the concept of a domain of objects which are pictured in one way (less adequately) by one linguistic system, and in another way (more adequately) by another" (V§67, 140). In contrast to principle (b), however, it also evidently presupposes that any objects pictured ("less adequately") by propositions of our current conceptual structure *will* be ("more adequately") pictured by counterpart propositions in "more developed" successors to it. This condition arguably imposes significant constraints on the notion of a counterpart proposition. To see what they are, however, we must first get clear about something else.

Sellars is remarkably noncommittal about the notion of pictorial *adequacy*. "Pictures, like maps, can be more or less adequate" (V§56, 135), he casually remarks, and that is all the elucidation we are offered. But just as it was unclear how we were to understand the notion of a map's being correct or incorrect, it is equally unclear how we are to understand the notion of one map's being more or less adequate than another.

"The adequacy," Sellars tells us, "concerns the 'method of projection' " (V§56, 135). This most naturally invites us to consider different forms of *ordinary* map projection, e.g., cylindrical, conic, azimuthal, etc. But there does not seem to be any clear sense in which a map of a given territory constructed according to one such "method of projection" is more or less adequate than one constructed according to another. Different forms of projection have different strengths and

---

[23] Since Sellars elsewhere uses 'belongs to' to assign propositions to CSs and the subset operator to relate propositions to proposition families, this clause is presumably to be read as 'PROP $\subset$ PRFAM'.

weaknesses, and the same form of projection can be applied to produce maps having different cartographic properties. A *conformal* projection, for instance, maintains the correct shape of small regions, so that angles at any point are correct, although sizes will be distorted. An *equal-area* projection, in contrast, properly represents relative sizes, but at the expense of distorting correct shape. For some uses, such as navigation, conformality is absolutely necessary; for others, e.g., in statistical mapping, the equal-area property is crucial.

The talk of "correctness", "accuracy", and "distortion" here, of course, again presupposes our map-independent access to the territories being mapped, and so again cannot serve as a useful model for the comparative assessment of conceptual frameworks or of propositions *qua* pictures. But these considerations do serve to remind us that anything that might properly be called the *adequacy* or *inadequacy* of a map is necessarily always relativized to some *purpose* for which the map is to be used. A map that is an adequate resource for someone planning to drive from Maine to Georgia will likely be entirely inadequate to serve the needs of someone who intends to traverse the same territory by hiking the Appalachian Trail (and conversely). Since the "adequacy" of systems of basic matter-of-factual propositions *qua* pictures is supposed to be analogous to the "adequacy" of maps, this suggests that what we need to ask next is *why* we engage in such matter-of-factual picture-making *per se*, i.e., what are the ends or aims of *empirical inquiry*.

That, of course, is a topic worthy of more than one extended study on its own. Here, alas, I can only be brief and dogmatic. In any event, Sellars' views on the matter are clear enough: Inquiry aims at the explanatory accommodation of perceptual experience. One useful indicator is his notorious *scientia mensura*:

[In] the dimension of describing and explaining the world, science is the measure of all things, of what is that it is, and of what is not that it is not. (EPM §42, 173)

Another is his rejection of the "levels picture" of theories, which identified explanation with derivation. On Sellars' account, theories do not explain laws by entailing them. Rather, "theories explain laws by explaining why the objects of the domain in question obey the laws that they do to the extent that they do" (LT, 123).[24] What challenges us to develop new and better theories, on this account, are perceived *irregularities* by which our experience anomalously departs from provisionally accepted lawfulnesses. Theories, that is, have a *double* explanatory accountability. They

not only explain why observable things obey certain laws [to the extent that they do], they also explain why in certain respects their behavior obeys no inductively confirmable generalization in the observation framework. (LT, 121)[25]

---

[24] "The Language of Theories", repr. as ch. 4, pp. 106–26 of SPR. Cited as 'LT'.

[25] "The same is true in principle," he adds in a footnote, "of micro-microtheories about microtheoretical objects." That is, theories also explain why *unobservable* things obey certain laws

On this understanding, scientific theories "save the appearances" *as such* by characterizing the reality *of which* the appearances *are* appearances.[26]

This double explanatory accountability of theories is what guarantees that the objects pictured ("less adequately") by propositions of a given conceptual structure will be ("more adequately") pictured by counterpart propositions in "more developed" successors to it. Sellars is as noncommittal about "counterparts" as he is about "adequacy", but now we are in a position to see that, like the correctness of basic singular representations, the counterpart relation is properly understood *epistemologically*. A successor theory can discharge its explanatory accountabilities with respect to a predecessor only by aligning primitive predecessor-theoretic concepts (including object-concepts) with primitive or defined successor-theoretic concepts and basic predecessor-theoretic principles with basic or defined successor-theoretic laws. Such alignments *constitute* the counterpart relation which groups individual senses and propositions belonging to different conceptual structures into families (INFAM, PRFAM). The proper understanding of the counterpart relation, in short, *presupposes* a correct epistemology of empirical inquiry.

The analogy between sophisticated postulational theories and ordinary maps is necessarily somewhat attenuated. "The point of being a map," we recall, "is to translate into sentences which dovetail with *practical* discourse about getting from point A to point B" (N&O, 137). The key to understanding the analogy, I suggest, is to emphasize the *testability* of theories. If we think of "point A" as an experimental setup and "point B" as the expected outcome of carrying out the experiment, then the "inadequacy" of our current theoretical "map" will manifest itself as a crisis of failed expectations, i.e., the failure of the *perceived* outcome to correspond to the *theoretically-predicted* outcome.

The end of an explanatory hypothesis, Peirce once wrote, is "through subjection to the test of experiment, to lead to the avoidance of all surprise and to the establishment of a habit of positive expectation that shall not be disappointed".[27] It is perhaps not too difficult to discern in this formulation the notion of a "map" which would be "ideally adequate" in that, by facilitating the explanatory accommodation of *whatever* perceptual experiences we might find ourselves having, it would provide representational resources sufficient to guide us "from

---

to the extent that they do and depart from such lawfulness when and where they do. Compare too: "Thus, microtheories not only explain why observational constructs obey inductive generalizations, they explain what, as far as the observational framework is concerned, is a random component in the behavior, and, in the last analysis it is by doing the latter that microtheories establish their character as indispensable elements of scientific explanation and ... as knowledge about what *really* exists" (LT, 122).

[26] I have developed this account of theory-succession in more detail in "Coupling, Retheoretization, and the Correspondence Principle", *Synthese* 45 (1980), 351–85, and "Comparing the Incommensurable: Another Look at Convergent Realism", ch. 4 in this volume.

[27] Charles Hartshorne and Paul Weiss (eds.), *Collected Papers of Charles Sanders Peirce*, 6 vols. (Harvard University Press; Cambridge, MA: 1931–5). The passage here cited is from vol. 5, p. 197.

point A to point B" in *any* "territory". This notion of "ideal adequacy", of course, can ultimately be only a *regulative* ideal of inquiry, enjoining us to respond to anomalous experiences by attempting to construct new theories that satisfy the demands of a double explanatory accountability.

RETROSPECT

Rather surprisingly, then, it turns out that most of what Sellars had to say about picturing admits of a defensible interpretation. The verdict is a guarded one, because it also turned out to be remarkably easy to interpret Sellars' claims about picturing quite differently, in a way which indeed makes them properly contentious. The strategy which I have here pursued divests picturing of immediate epistemological significance by interpreting it as a functional mode of representation, rather than as a mode of correctness. Being in the "picturing line of work" is the determinative function of matter-of-factual representational systems *per se*, and so, *trivially*, the correctness of a basic matter-of-factual representation will be its correctness as a picture—but, crucially, the priority expressed here is conceptual and *not* epistemological.

We were also able to make good sense of Sellars' conception of "more developed" conceptual structures—paradigmatically, better theories—as "more adequate" pictures. Here again, however, a correct epistemology of empirical inquiry turned out to be, not constituted by, but rather presupposed by the notion of "more adequate" picturing. The idea of an "ideally adequate" picture determines an "Archimedean point outside the series of actual and possible beliefs" *not* by specifying, as it were, an *object of comparison* against which the relative "adequacy" of conceptual structures could (even in principle) be measured, but only insofar as it transposes into the functional idiom of pictorial representation the *regulative* ideal which properly informs matter-of-factual inquiry as such.

Properly interpreted, then, Sellars' conception of "linguistic picture making" is one that we can in fact maintain and even endorse. But we can do so only if we recognize, so to speak, the autonomy of epistemology. Twenty-five years ago, I wrote that "the notion of justification is *prior* to the notion of correctness as the notion of correctness was itself prior to that of adequacy to the world." (OW, 117). I still think that is right. But, in light of this "second look", I now no longer think that Sellars would disagree—and that comes as a rather pleasant surprise.

6

Linguistic Roles and Proper Names

1

Sellars' philosophy forms an extraordinarily complex and thoroughly interconnected systematic unity. If only tangentially, it touches every major concern
of the philosophical community. On some of these concerns, Sellars has both
thought long and written extensively; on others, while he has thought no less
long, much of what he has to say he has so far said largely by implication. In
this essay, I want to address a theme from the second group. Specifically, I want
to try to develop an appropriately Sellarsian understanding of proper names, to
locate and assess their place in the broader context of his semantic theories. In
pursuing this goal, I shall presuppose enough acquaintance with his views and
principles to justify my footnoting only explicit quotations and omitting more
extensive citations. Most of what I say will be familiar enough to anyone familiar
with Sellars' work, and all of it is documentable from the four books which form
the centerpiece of his current corpus.[1] To set my problematic, then, I shall begin
by assembling a few reminders.

2

One central and fundamental theme of Sellarsian philosophy is that meaning
is not a relation. Sellars holds, in fact, that semantic discourse in general
is not relational but rather classificatory. He sees 'means' as a special form
of the copula, one especially tailored for metalinguistic contexts. Essential to
this thesis is his further contention that the right side of the basic meaning
context:

_____ means . . . .

is properly understood as mentioning the linguistic item which occurs there or,
more precisely, as exhibiting it.

---

[1] *Viz:* SPR, PP, S&M, and EPH. These, and later, abbreviations are decoded in the References, below.

3

Classical conceptualism has always exploited the parallels between semantic idioms and Platonistic discourse ostensibly 'about abstract entities'. To the meaning claim

    (1) (In German) 'rot' means *red*

for example, there corresponds the Platonistic

    (2) (The German word) 'rot' stands for redness.

Sellars' strategy is to construe this parallelism as an identity. He regards 'stands for', like 'means', as a special form of the copula, and treats such abstract-singular-forming suffixes as '—ness', '—hood', '—ship', '—kind', and '—ity' as metalinguistic indicators, functioning, like quotation marks, to mention or exhibit lexical items.

4

This metalinguistic ascent is signaled in semantic discourse by a breakdown of normal syntactic forms. Thus the 'red' in (1), for example, is neither an attributive adjective nor a predicate adjective (its standard syntactic roles) but occupies instead a position syntactically suited to a predicate nominal, ostensibly that of a direct object.

5

Analogously, the meaning idioms adapted to whole-sentence contexts have as their Platonistic counterparts abstract discourse ostensibly 'about propositions'. Thus,

    (3) 'Schnee ist weiss' means *snow is white*

parallels

    (4) 'Schnee ist weiss' expresses the proposition that snow is white.

Here, too, Sellars carries through his strategy consistently. He treats 'expresses (the proposition)' as a classificatory idiom, a tailored copula, and takes 'that' to signal metalinguistic ascent, that-clause formation being viewed as a special form of quotation. And here too, he finds a clue in the syntactic breakdown of the semantic claims: (3), for example, contains two verbs without subordination.

6

According to Sellars, ordinary quotation suffers from a certain systematic ambiguity—not merely the classical type-token ambiguity, but one which infects the very criteria for classifying tokens as of this or that type. It is an ambiguity of structure *vs* function. To be a 'red' ('a token of that type' in traditional terms) may be, for example, to be a sign-design of that shape. That is, it may be to be an item sorted and individuated by inscriptional or geometrical criteria.[2] On the other hand, to be a 'red' may be to be an item which does a certain job—a job which may be done in other languages by quite different looking inscriptions.

7

On Sellars' view, our special copulae and metalinguistic indicators have evolved out of a need to abstract from our parochial sign-designs in order to classify lexical items of diverse languages on the basis of functional criteria. Sellars instead introduces the more straightforward device of two separate styles of quotation marks, pinned to the two varieties of criteria for sorting and individuating lexical items: star-quotes and dot-quotes. To be a *red* is to be an inscription appropriately design-isomorphic to the token exhibited between the stars, for example, while to be a ·red· is to be an item which plays the role or does the job played or done in *our* language by *red*s.[3] Thus we can put

(5) *rot*s (from the pens of Germans) are ·red·s,

on Sellars' view, for either (1) or (2). 'Means', 'stands for', and 'expresses' all become transformed into the simple plural copula 'are',[4] while items formed by employing the abstract suffixes, 'that', and other indicators of implicit metalinguistic ascent become explicitly metalinguistic with the appearance of dot-quotation.

8

This account does not, of course, commit Sellars to roles or jobs—hitherto unsuspected abstract entities standing in the 'play' or 'do' relations to English-speakers' *red*s and German-speakers' *rot*s. Explicit talk of roles or jobs is

---

[2] Allowing, of course, for complications of size, type-face, handwriting, and the like. That the criteria are inscriptional or geometrical does not imply, alas, that they are simple and straightforward—a truth familiar to anyone who has tried to implement a pattern-recognition program on a computer.

[3] Items between dot-quotes, being tied in this way to the *use*-language (*our* language), change appropriately when the use-language changes. Thus, unlike star-quoted items, dot-quoted items are translated when passing from language to language.

[4] And so, ultimately, into a quantified conditional form:

(t)(t is a German *rot* → t is a ·red·)

where the quantifier, as one says, 'ranges over' tokens.

itself putatively relational semantic or abstract discourse and so, on Sellars' view, is itself to be understood as metalinguistic, classificatory, and functional. Talk of roles or jobs may form a part of our informal exposition of the apparatus of dot-quotation, but the apparatus itself is logically primary. The *analysis* of our 'role-playing' discourse, like that of any other semantic or Platonistic idiom, is to be given by means of the very dot-quote apparatus which we may use that discourse, ladderwise, to elucidate.

9

In this respect, roles are like *lengths*. They are merely nominal objects. '*x* is the same length as *y*' is the *basic* form, not to be 'analyzed' as '($\exists L$) (L is a length & *x* has L & *y* has L)'. Isometry is a relation between objects. To understand it, we need to understand the processes of measurement and comparison which give metric talk its sense. The cash value for talk ostensibly about lengths is not found in Platonistic entities but in particular human activities.

10

So, too, for roles. The *basic* notion is sameness of function (role-isomorphism), and to understand it, what we need to explore is not Plato's heaven but the dimensions of human (cognitive) activity in which these variously classifiable linguistic sign-designs are caught up.

11

Sameness of function or role-isomorphism is a holistic notion, the counterpart relation between a pair of *items* being derivative from a counterpart relation between a pair of *systems* to which the items respectively belong. An item, *i*, belonging to one system is the functional isomorph of an item, *j*, belonging to another if *i* is related to the balance of items comprising the first system in a manner suitably analogous to the way in which *j* relates to the balance of items constituting its system. The fundamental unit of language is thus *a language*, a theme to which Sellars repeatedly returns. You cannot know one word unless you know many.[5]

---

[5] Analogously, on Sellars' view the fundamental unit of knowledge is a *theory*. You cannot know one fact unless you know many. Indeed, 'analogously' is a bit weak here. It is the same point. I shall have more to say about this later, but for immediate lengthy elaboration see my LR.

12

At issue in the case of linguistic roles are systems of conducts or behaviors. Sellars calls our attention to three families of these, which he calls

      (α) language entries
      (β) intra-linguistic moves
and (γ) language exits.

(α) consists, roughly, of our linguistic responses to non-linguistic stimuli (whether those responses be overt or covert, spoken or thought—a complication which I shall, for the most part, avoid); (β), of linguistic responses to linguistic stimuli; and (γ), of non-linguistic responses to linguistic stimuli. Couched in more traditional vocabulary these turn out, in fact, to be three old friends: (α) is perception, (β) is inference, and (γ) is volitional action.[6]

13

It is crucial to realize that intra-linguistic moves possess a sort of logical or conceptual centrality in this picture. The notion of an entry presupposes something to be entered; that of an exit, something to be departed. A move can be a *language* entry, after all, only if what is entered is a language. It can be a language exit only if the stimulus triggering our non-linguistic behavior is itself linguistic. It follows that the inferential performances constituting (β) are primary. They are what determine items *as linguistic*. A move will be a language entry only if the position occupied in consequence of the move is marked by an item which can play a premissory role. It will be a language exit just in case the stimulus triggering our non-linguistic activity itself occupies a position in a family of (potentially) inferentially interconnected items.

14

The picture Sellars offers us, then, is of a complex structure of items among which we are prepared to make inferential transitions and which, as a whole, is 'fitted' to the world in perception and action. Learning to perceive is coming to occupy points of this network, non-inferentially, when suitably stimulated, items which admit of subsequent inferential elaboration (and possible ultimate rejection). Learning to act (volitionally) is coming to follow the occupying of certain points of this network (conclusions of practical deliberations, for example)

---

[6] Very roughly speaking, to be sure. Much of Sellars' work consists of the sensitive and detailed elaboration of these schematic core insights.

by suitable non-linguistic behavior. It is the inferential connections *among* the items constituting the network, however, our readiness to proceed from point to point *within* the structure, which provide the primary conditions for their functional individuation.

15

What stand in such inferential relations and thereby constitute the nodes or points of this network are essentially what are traditionally called 'statements' or 'propositions' (on some interpretations of those terms). For expository neutrality, I usually choose to speak of *claims*, a practice which I shall adopt here. The inferential relationships in question are both formal and material, material inferences being those in which, roughly speaking, descriptive terms occur non-vacuously. That x is east of y, to take a favorite example, implies that y is west of x, that x is on the right if one is facing north between x and y, that facing x from y at dawn the sun rises in front of one, and so on, for arbitrary x and y. Some species of necessity attaches to these implications. They support appropriate counterfactuals, for example (e.g., 'if a had been east of b, then b would have been west of a'), and their corresponding conditionals are perennial candidates for classification as 'analytic truths'. In addition, such relationships enjoy a relatively privileged epistemological status. The corresponding general conditionals are not accepted as the result of, nor are they further confirmed by, processes traditionally characterized as enumerative induction—elaborate series of compass readings taken in pairs of cities, for example. Nor are they straightforwardly defeasible by individual observations. Rather these families of inferential interrelationships have a thoroughgoing holistic character. To abandon such principles is to abandon our whole *system* for assigning directions. It is in this sense that they are constitutive of such terms as 'east', 'west', 'north', and 'south', individuating their roles through a complex inferential interlocking with one another, with 'right', 'left', 'between', 'in front', and 'behind', and ultimately with the fundamental posits of our geophysical and astronomical theorizing.[7]

16

Impetus for a metalinguistic analysis is provided, in the case of 'means', by breakdowns of our normal syntactic forms; in the case of 'stands for', by abstract-singular suffixing; and in the case of 'expresses', by that-clause formation. In addition, however, all three cases bear the characteristic mark of intentionality, the non-intersubstitutivity of co-extensive terms. Although whatever is triangular is (necessarily) trilateral

---

[7] For a detailed elaboration of these themes, consult my LR.

'dreieckig' means *triangular*

is true, while

'dreieckig' means *trilateral*

is not. Similarly, 'dreieckig' stands for triangularity, but not for trilaterality, and 'Hans ist dreieckig', while it expresses the proposition that Hans is triangular, does not express the proposition that Hans is trilateral. There is another family of ostensibly relational semantic idioms, however, which provides none of these motivations for metalinguistic treatment:

—— names . . . .
—— denotes . . . .
—— designates . . . .
and   —— refers to . . . .

When employed in connection with proper names and singular descriptions, these forms preserve normal syntax, requiring and receiving nominal expressions on the right. They demand no special linguistic devices, no suffixes or 'that's. And they are 'referentially transparent'. Since Socrates was Plato's mentor, for example, from

(6) 'Sokrates' (in German) refers to [names, denotes, designates] Socrates

we can correctly infer that

(7) 'Sokrates' (in German) refers to [etc.] Plato's mentor.

Co-referential singular terms are freely intersubstitutable on the right.

17

What could be more evident, then, than that these expressions represent genuine word-world relations, that the 'Socrates' on the right in (6) is neither mentioned nor exhibited but rather genuinely *used*? Amazingly, Sellars disagrees.

18

In fact, Sellars proceeds to make what many commentators consider a truly outrageous suggestion: the referential transparency of (6) is the sign, not of a tighter word-world connection, but of a looser one. The right side of a 'refers', etc. statement, on his view is still dot-quoted, but it is dot-quoted at one remove. His strategy is to define a relation of 'material equivalence' among dot-quoted nominal expressions (names or singular descriptions) according to the scheme of Russell-Leibniz identity:

$$\cdot a \cdot ME \cdot b \cdot = df (f) (fa \equiv fb)$$

Letting 'INSENSE' be a variable which takes such dot-quoted nominals as substituends, Sellars proceeds to parse (6) as

    (8) (∃INSENSE) [(*Sokrates* are INSENSE's) & (INSENSE *ME* ·Socrates·)]

Since it is true that

    ·Socrates· *ME* ·Plato's mentor·

and that *Sokrates*s are ·Socrates·s.

on this parsing we can indeed correctly infer (7), which becomes

    (9) (∃INSENSE) [(*Sokrates*s are INSENSE's) & INSENSE *ME* ·Plato's mentor·)]

19

In spite of the lack of overt syntactic or inferential clues, then, on Sellars' view the right side of a 'refers', 'names', 'designates' or 'denotes' statement is thus as metalinguistic as that of a 'means', 'stands for', or 'expresses' statement. The initial oddness of this view may be mitigated somewhat by the observation that

    'Pegasus' refers to Pegasus
  and 'Santa Claus' denotes Santa Claus

for example, are not *obviously* absurd, but, of course, many theorists of reference, holding to the relational line, are perfectly prepared to deny all such claims (and 'Pegasus = Pegasus' as well).

20

I now have enough raw materials at hand (at last!) to develop the question which will be my central concern. If referential semantic discourse incorporating proper names is thus to be interpreted as metalinguistic, classificatory, and functional, we need to understand the linguistic role of proper names. How does the apparatus of dot-quotation interface with proper names? If to be a ·Socrates· is to play the role or do the job played or done by our *Socrates*s, how shall we characterize that role? What *is* the job done by our *Socrates*s?

21

The problem is that, on the face of it, Sellars' strategy of language entries, intra-linguistic moves, and language exits won't work for proper names. I have already noted the centrality to the functional individuation and sorting of descriptive predicates of inferential relationships among claims. But while it may be plausible to so identify the sense of one of our predicate expressions with a family of term-term relationships representable as material inference moves in which the relevant expressions occur non-vacuously, this is not true of proper names. For there do not appear to *be* any material inferences in which proper names occur non-vacuously.

22

A formal analogue to the material principles illustrated earlier for compass directions would be something like this:

(10) that Socrates is f implies that Plato's mentor is f.

A moment's reflection reveals, however, that the analogy goes no further than the formalism. (10), for example, is not a candidate for non-contingent modal status. It does not support the full range of appropriate counterfactuals. While 'If x had been east of y, y would have been west of x' is true for arbitrary singular substituends for 'x' and 'y',

(11) If Socrates had been f, Plato's mentor would have been f

is *not* true given an arbitrary, grammatically allowable, substitution for 'f'. For there are many substitutions in the antecedent of (11) which imply instead that Socrates *would not have been Plato's mentor*. Nor does the conditional counterpart of (10) enjoy analogous epistemological privilege. Indeed,

(10*) (f) (If Socrates is f, then Plato's mentor is f)

is epistemologically no more secure than

(12) Socrates was Plato's mentor.

(10*), in fact, is confirmed by whatever confirms (12), disconfirmable by whatever would disconfirm (12), and necessary only to the extent that (12) is necessary. Since (12) is at best contingently true, supported by specific documentary evidences, and potentially defeasible by the unearthing of new evidences of the same sort, it follows that the same holds for (10*). The troublesome fact of the matter is that we could comfortably abandon (12) tomorrow—and with it (10*) and (10) as well—without imperiling in the least our ability to talk about Socrates. The inference principle (10), then (and, by implication any formally analogous principle), is simply not constitutive of the proper name 'Socrates' (and, by implication, any other proper name) as our earlier family of principles proved constitutive of the system of direction terms containing 'east' and 'west'.

23

What I have just been recapitulating is, with a Sellarsian slant, what has become a standard criticism of Descriptivism. The basic thesis of Descriptivism is that proper names, like descriptive predicates, have senses; the sense of a proper name is a uniquely individuating singular description or a cluster of such descriptions. As with descriptive predicates, the sense determines the reference (denotation, extension). Reference is a relation between words and the world. The reference of a proper name is the unique object satisfying the singular description (or a weighted majority of descriptions in the cluster).

24

As a relational theory of reference, Descriptivism has been criticized by Kripke in terms paralleling those just mobilized against its inferential (non-relational) variant. (See NN, especially pp. 291–6.) What Kripke offers in its place (NN, 302–3) is what has come to be called the Causal Theory of Reference. The Causal Theory is also presented as relational. On Kripke's view, a proper name enters our language through an 'initial baptism' or reference-fixing event. Such an event consists of an original using or usings of the name in a context *causally* implicating some specific object as an eliciting stimulus (and consequent candidate target of demonstrative ostension). The name is then transmitted and disseminated from speaker to speaker through a series of *causal* links, in which a suitable using of the name produces an appropriate uptake in the audience who becomes, in turn, a potential source of further causal transmissions. On this view, the reference of a proper name will be whatever object lies at the origin of such a causal chain.

25

Now this model has considerable initial appeal and, indeed, manages to avoid many of the pitfalls of Descriptivist theories of reference. But while there is surely something right about it (later I shall attempt to locate what this is), the model is not without difficulties of its own. Perhaps the major problem is the specification of a *suitable* causal chain and *appropriate* audience uptake. Kripke offers us comparatively little help here. He suggests that the possession of appropriate intentions to refer by speaker and audience may be necessary conditions for completion of a reference transmitting link in such a chain, but he goes on to admit that this piece of the story presupposes the notion of reference and, consequently, to that extent, cannot elucidate it.[8]

26

Looked at Sellarswise, the most striking feature of the Causal Theory may be its suggestion of a spurious epistemology for reference. The implicit picture has us

---

[8] Not to mention the fact that intentions to refer are themselves rather mysterious beasts.

answering questions about the references of singular terms by skipping happily down a causal chain from link to link until we *encounter* the object in an initial baptismal setting, rather like traveling upstream from Egypt to locate the source of the Nile. But, apart from the fact that in a typical case there probably wasn't any unique reference-fixing event of the sort Kripke posits, it is clear that this picture just won't do. Even supposing the existence of an appropriate causal chain linking a here/now using of a proper name to a there/then baptismal event causally implicating the object of reference, such a causal chain cannot be here and now given. If it existed at all, its existence must be inferred from and confirmed by what is here and now epistemically available to us.

27

Yet setting aside these difficulties with Kripke's views (and many others[9]), we are still left with an overriding problem. The Causal Theory offers no advance at all on the question of linguistic roles. What we are looking for is a way of making sense of the notion of the *sense* of a proper name. The gist of the Causal theory is that proper names don't have senses. The Causal Theory is essentially relational. The job of proper names (and rigid designators generally) is to provide a set of anchorage points for the web of belief, tethering the linguistic order to the non-linguistic by causal chains. What a proper name has is a referent, not a sense, and its link with that referent is not semantic, proceeding indirectly through a sense (in the form of a descriptive content) by some truth-move, but is rather intended to be a direct, naturalistic, causal hookup. Our names don't get at things by being stuck on them like labels, to be sure. But they still don't connect up via senses or descriptive contents either. Instead they're tied to things by (causal) strings.

28

An approach more promising for Sellarsian ends is provided by Chastain.[10] While his theory is still relational *au fond*, at least some of the relations have gone intra-linguistic. Chastain's strategy is to pair the notion of reference with what he calls *contexts*. The simplest example of a context is provided by a story:

> A man was sitting under a tree. Along came a squirrel. The man offered it a peanut. The squirrel took it from him and climbed the tree. He watched it go.

---

[9] I have explored a variety of Kripkean failings in N&C.

[10] In his R&C. This is an important paper, I think, and would well repay careful study.

Within such a context, Chastain notes, we find reference controlled by *anaphoric chains*. The specific linguistic machinery of anaphora is used to render reference contextually definite. In this little story, there are four anaphoric chains:

> A man . . . . The man . . . . him . . . . he
> A tree . . . . the tree
> A squirrel . . . . it$_1$ . . . . the squirrel . . . . it$_3$
> A peanut . . . . it$_2$

At any point in such a story, information accumulated along the anaphoric chain to which a given term, *t*, belongs will supply a contextually definite answer to the *identification-question*, "What (who) is being referred to by *t*?", asked of that term. Thus, for example, the answer to "Who is being referred to by the term 'him' in the fourth sentence?" is "The man, sitting under the tree, who offered the peanut to the squirrel." For later members of anaphoric chains, in other words, the claims made earlier in which their anaphoric antecedents were used supply the materials for assembling what Strawson calls (I, 18) a 'story-relative' identification. But for the first member of an anaphoric chain this will not do. To answer identification-questions about the referent of such a term, it will be necessary to go outside the given context.

29

If the context is marked as purely fictional (i.e., having fictional characters and, perhaps, setting, as well as fictional events—cf. historical novels), there will be nowhere else outside of it to which it is appropriate to go for the answers. Story-relative identifications will be the end of the matter. But if, as it is traditionally put, the purported reference is to something in the world, we need a further account. Now one place we might go to answer identification-questions is to *another* context. Thus, for example, in the narrative:

> I just heard about a fellow who owns two cats. He got them as kittens. One of them is black and the other is grey. He claims that the black one weighs over twenty-five pounds. He feeds them raw meat.

the anaphoric chain

> a fellow . . . . He$_1$ . . . . He$_2$ . . . . He$_3$

begins with a term, 'a fellow' which, *for the speaker*, is linked to certain singular expressions which he encountered in another context—the conversation in which he heard about the cat fancier. Such trans-context linkages produce what Chastain calls 'referential chains'. We may note that a referential chain between contexts could be thought of simply as an anaphoric chain on the condition that the two distinct contexts could be joined to form, so to speak, a single larger context. (Presently I shall want to look at what this means.)

30

While inter-context referential chains can thus be longer than intra-context anaphoric chains, they are essentially the same sort of animal. The same problem then arises for the first members of referential chains: What supplies the answer to identification-questions for such terms? A natural move at this point is indoors—to thoughts or intentions—and, indeed, that is where Chastain next goes. But he goes Sellarswise. Thoughts, intentions, and similar mental paraphernalia are merely *covert contexts*. Chastain, of course, does not treat this notion with full Sellarsian subtlety. He offers nothing like Sellars' theory of functional classification and analogical concept formation but simply takes as his model the covert *discourse* of a person thinking his thoughts 'in the words of the language he speaks'.[11] But his explicit views are at least not incompatible with Sellars' on these points, and so there is nothing to prevent us from treating Chastain's notion of a covert context completely along Sellarsian lines. When we do so, however, we find that the move to the mental has again yielded only more of the same. Referential chains now wind in and out of both overt and covert contexts, but the same problem returns again to haunt us: How do they get started?

31

One way they get started, Chastain proposes, is with *perceptual contexts* (and things like them—more on this in a minute). When someone conscious-ly perceives something, Chastain points out, that person is at least having an experience with a particular content, a content which determines what sort of thing he *seems* to see, hear, feel, and so on. Such an experience is a perceptual context. In addition, according to Chastain, there will be a causal connection between a person's perceptual context and the thing (if there is one) which he perceives. Like other contexts, perceptual contexts con-tain singular elements which may or may not refer to objects in the world. The experience qualifies as a perceiving just in case its singular elements do refer:

A person perceives something if and only if he possesses a perceptual context with a singular element which refers to that thing. (R&C, 248)

Either side of this biconditional will be true if and only if there is a certain sort of causal connection between the thing perceived (= the referent) and the perceptual context. *Exactly* what sort of connection? As things stand at present with the theory of perception, one cannot say. (R&C, 248)

---

[11] No criticism is intended here, by the way. A theory of the mental is not what Chastain is up to.

32

So far this sounds fairly Kripkesque, the main difference being that referential chains have been substituted for Kripke's causal chains following an initial causal transaction. But Chastain actually intends something different. Perceiving an object is only one way of *having knowledge of it*. It is on this more general notion that Chastain comes finally to rest:

A singular element E in a context C possessed or produced by a person P refers to an object O if and only if either (i) E in C is referentially linked with an element E' in an antecedent context C' and E' in C' refers to O, or (ii) P has *knowledge of* O via E in C. (R&C, 251)

Perceiving something, detecting or observing it, introspecting it, precognizing it, remembering it—these experiences (and others) all count as having knowledge of a thing. The resulting theory of reference is not, then, as was Kripke's, *essentially* a causal theory:

If it must be pigeonholed it would be more accurate to call it an 'epistemic' theory; what gives it a 'causal' flavor is the incidental fact that the processes of inter-contextual translation and the formation of referential chains are intelligible to most people only on a causal analysis, as are perception and memory; but that is not essential to the theory. (R&C, 256)

Chastain's theory of reference is causal, in other words, only to the extent that an adequate theory of knowledge must posit a causal connection between the knower and the known. And, parenthetically, I would observe (as promised earlier) that this surely locates just what it was about Kripke's more restricted view which felt so appealing and correct.

33

Alas, Chastain's theory still gives us no handle on the question of the *senses* of proper names. We still have no suggestion as to what it is for some token to be a ˙Socrates˙. Our problem basically is that the dot-quote apparatus itself is characterized in terms of an *inferential* semantics. What we need, then, is some elucidation of reference in terms of inference. Like Kripke, however, Chastain focuses his account on reference as an ostensible word-world connection. While not essentially causal, Chastain's theory is essentially relational, and thus he fails to provide the required elucidation. Unlike Kripke, however, Chastain has given us a place to look. He relates singular reference not directly to the (metaphysical) notion of causality but, if to causality at all, only indirectly through a primary hookup between reference and the (epistemological) notion of knowledge. This suggests that a fruitful procedure may be to interface Chastain's views about contexts, anaphora, and referential chains with the *Sellarsian* epistemology, in the hope that the intimate connections between Sellars' epistemological views and his theory of material inference may yield the desired elucidations.

34

At the heart of Sellars' epistemology is the rejection of the given. The world is not given to us; rather it acts on us. Our representations are responses elicited by a world to which our only cognitive access is provided by those representations themselves. The world is thus not an object of comparison against which such representations can be severally measured but a constraint to which they must be progressively and collectively attuned. The fundamental unit of knowledge is the whole system of representations, and an individual belief gains epistemic warrant from the fact and to the degree that it contributes to the collective adequacy of this systematic whole. The measure of such systemic adequacy, however, cannot be the degree of isomorphic fit between our representations and a represented world antecedently given but is rather the internal coherence of the system of representations as a whole and its stability in the face of the continued experiential impact of the represented world on us, the representers.

35

I shall assume a general familiarity with the manner in which Sellars fleshes out these skeletal commitments. Specifically, I shall take for granted his view of an ostensible perceiving as a conceptual representing—'Lo! a red triangle', for example—elicited by a sensing which is itself a non-conceptual state of the perceiver. A perceptual taking is a judgment with which we *find* ourselves, and its defeasibility or endorsement as veridical perceptual experience is essentially a matter of tracing its inferential connections among prior beliefs, collectively constituting our picture of the world, in an effort to afford its occurrence in us an explanatory accommodation. It is a rogue star, encroaching on an initially stable galactic configuration, and it finds a permanent place in the new and larger whole by a mutual readjustment of the forces between and among the multitudinous parts into a new coherent equilibrium. An ostensible perceiving viewed in this light is one example of what Sellars calls a language entry. It mobilizes a representational system already fully constituted by inferential principles, and it is by *using* such (material) principles of inference that we accommodate—or discover that we cannot accommodate—the perceptual taking as a veridical component of our world-picture drawn through the medium of that system. It follows that, while language entries are indeed indispensible to the existence of such a representational system, their indispensibility is of an entirely different order from that already noted for intra-linguistic moves. Intra-linguistic moves are *constitutionally* indispensible. They determine the representational system entered or exited as a system. Entries, I have argued (§§12–13), cannot be thus constitutive of a system of representations—a remark functionally equivalent to the rejection of a given. They provide instead its *raison d'être*. They are the locus of what such a representational system is *for*. A language entry is precisely the point at which the world to which our representations are to be adequate impinges and exercises its contraint on our representational activity. The adequacy of the representational system to that world consists precisely in its ability to explanatorily accommodate those points of entry at which we *in fact* find ourselves.

36

It is in this way that the coherentist Sellarsian epistemology escapes the charge of arbitrariness leveled against traditional coherence theories of truth. Having rejected a correspondence with the given as the measure of the adequacy of our representational system to the represented world, the challenge then becomes that of avoiding a collapse into objective idealism. If representation cannot be adequate to the world by virtue of a discoverable correspondence with it, the argument runs, then it cannot be adequate *to* the world at all—and we are left with a merely aesthetic choice among a, possibly infinite, number of equally coherent representational schemes. The solution is to ground the adequacy of a representational system *to* something in its adequacy *for* something. What a representational system must be adequate for is the coherent explanatory accommodation of the very language entries which it makes possible. And if it is adequate *for* such accommodation, then it will be adequate *to* the represented world as well, for the simple reason that, in the absence of a given, such language entries constitute the whole locus of that world's impingement on us as representers.[12]

37

It is time to return to reference. The intra-linguistic machinery of anaphora, recall, was sufficient to allow us to assemble contextually definite answers to identification-questions by accumulating information along an anaphoric chain. The sticking point for all classical theories of reference has been that such identification is merely 'story-relative', and while that will do for works of pure fiction, it cannot do when reference to something in the world is at issue. What my recent Sellarsian epistemological ruminations show, I want to argue, is that

---

[12] I have offered my own detailed elaboration and defense of this picture in LR. Ch. 8 is particularly apposite.

(A) *All* identification is 'story-relative',

but that

(B) Story-relative identification is enough for *objective* reference.

The quick way to say it is this: The word-picture is a story, but it is not a *mere* story. It is not an arbitrary story. It is an objectively adequate story (or aims at being one) and its objective adequacy is subject to non-arbitrary constraints. That's the quick way. Now let me say it slowly—and more elaborately.

38

I want to introduce a notion for which there isn't currently any convenient title. Every context is associated with a method for arriving at answers to questions about the things mentioned in it. If the context is a work of pure fiction, for example, the method consists of consulting the relevant canonical text. The question 'What did the Tin Woodsman want from the Wizard of Oz?', for example, is answered by looking it up in the book.[13] Nothing else is necessary and nothing else is relevant. Of course, on some questions—"What was Dorothy's blood type?", for example—the text stands mute. This is the locus of the notorious 'indeterminacy of fictional entities', which turns out to thus be an epistemological rather than an ontological phenomenon. And, of course, the question of whether a given text *is* canonical is not answered by consulting the text itself but by investigating what one might call its editorial history. In this way—and in some others—fact is necessarily prior to fiction. For historical novels and comparable genres, the method is more complicated. Different questions may require different sorts of investigations—a distinction we sometimes signal by appending the tags 'in the story' and 'in real life' to our queries.

39

I shall call such a method for settling questions arising within a context the *epistemics* of the context. Every context has an epistemics. But the logical order is, in fact, inverted: *A context is defined by its epistemics.* I remarked earlier (§29) that what Chastain calls a referential chain between contexts could be thought of simply as an anaphoric chain on the condition that the two distinct contexts could be joined to form a single extended context. I propose now that such ligature is possible just in case the two original contexts have the same epistemics. In literature and drama, we often achieve this consilience of epistemics by fiat. Among the expressions which signal such epistemic legislation are 'The Further Adventures of ...', 'Son of ...', 'Return to ...', and 'The Continuing Story of ...'. But, crucially, the *primary*

---

[13] It was a heart. See Baum (WO), p. 39.

representational means not only for indicating but indeed for accomplishing such contextual ligature is precisely *the re-use of the same proper names*.

40

I'll return to this observation in a moment. First, however, we must combine this notion of contextual epistemics with our earlier epistemological discussion. The method of testing a projected, inferentially constituted, system of representations by the explanatory accommodations of the language entries which it makes possible is nothing but abductive theory confirmation writ large, the testing of a postulational theory by its adequacy to explain the phenomena conceived under redescriptions which the theory itself provides. It is the method of science. One of Sellars' fundamental epistemological commitments is that the method of science thus understood is the *only* method yielding matter-of-factual knowledge, objectively warranted beliefs about the world. (This, after all, is just the rejection of a given again.) In accord with this view, I shall speak of the method of science as the empirical epistemics. The Sellarsian commitment can then be cast as a definition framed in the new terminology: The *world-story* is the context whose epistemics is the empirical epistemics.

41

And now, I think, I am at last in a position to say something about the sense of proper names. The issue of individual senses has been dominated by the model of the uniquely individuating description. *If* one regards reference as a word-world relation, and *if* reference is to be channeled through sense by something like a truth-move, then the demand that reference provide *objective* world anchorages for our language requires that the sense of a given name be potentially *invariant* across all the diverse members of the relevant discourse community. To guarantee such objective adequacy and potential invariance, nothing less than a uniquely individuating description would do. Our having abandoned the relational picture and letting the determination of objectivity rest on the contextual epistemics, however, opens the door to rejecting this dominant tacit supposition of *shared* individual senses. What I propose instead is that we think of the sense of a proper name as something which varies from speaker to speaker and, for a given speaker, from time to time. Individual senses are time-bound and idiolectic. They are not shared. But they *are* shareable, in virtue of something which is shared—a shared epistemics. On my view, Russell was closer to getting it right than most philosophers have been prepared to grant:

When one person uses a word, he does not mean by it the same thing as another person means by it. It have often heard it said that that is a misfortune. That is a mistake. It would be absolutely fatal if people meant the same things by their words. It would make all intercourse impossible, and language the most hopeless and useless thing imaginable. ... We should have to talk only about logic—a not wholly undesirable result. (PLA, 195)

42

A proper name is an accumulation point for claims.[14] In each speaker's individual world-picture, a proper name is a planet about which orbits a family of endorsed satellite claims—roughly, those of his beliefs in the expression of which that name would be used. The idiolectic sense of the name for a speaker at a time consists simply of whatever information he has accumulated along the extended anaphoric chain of his encounters with that name up to that time. Such an idiolectic sense could happen to be *de facto* uniquely individuating, but it could also be as thin as, to take Kripke's example, "Feynmann is a physicist". Most importantly, however, what orbits one speaker's planet may be quite different from what orbits another's.

43

How, then, do we achieve objectivity of reference? Well, what exactly is wanted? Fundamentally, what we need is some non-arbitrary way of arriving at intersubjective agreements—but this we already have. Just that is provided by the common epistemics which, by dictating the ligature of two contexts into a single extended context, allows the fusion of two idiolectic senses into a shared individual sense.

44

Briskly put, sameness of name is a *prima facie* signal of consilience of epistemics. When two speakers agree that they're 'talking about the same person/place/thing', they contract for a mutual exchange of satellites. Each speaker is licensed to add to the satellites orbiting his planet those claims made by the other in which the name is used. The current discourse context is anaphorically joined to the already-fused prior contexts of encounter for that name. Each speaker's idiolectic sense alters and evolves as the conversation proceeds. In the limit, given an idealized 'complete exchange of information', they would match. By their common usings of the same proper name, the two speakers commit themselves to a shared epistemics and thereby to the collective endorsement of whatever that epistemics has individually yielded. And if the two families of satellite claims constituting the two idiolectic senses are not initially collectively coherent, it is to the shared

---

[14] Compare Ziff: "A name is a fixed point in a turning world" (SA, 104). Much of what Ziff has to say about proper name—pp. 85–105 of (SA)—is extremely helpful.

epistemics and the methods of inquiry which it prescribes which they must appeal to settle the controversy and reequilibrate the enlarged collective sense.

45

It is through the medium of this agreement in epistemics that the question of whether two speakers *are* 'talking about the same thing' is settled if it arises. If one speaker turns to the shelf labeled 'contemporary fiction' and the other to 'medieval history', for example, the question is settled in the negative.[15] But if the question is whether John Smith your neighbor is John Smith my uncle's foreman, then the ligature of contexts is granted. We must turn to the method of science and run the question to ground. And what this amounts to is, roughly speaking, seeing whether the claim that your neighbor is my uncle's foreman or the claim that he is not better coheres with and is afforded a better explanatory accommodation within the whole of each of our separate world-pictures.

46

There is no *a priori* guarantee, of course, that any two given speakers will be able to reach such a referential agreement in some finite stretch of time. Much of my idiosyncratic world-picture may initially be substantially askew from much of yours. But when the shared epistemics is the empirical epistemics (as ultimately it must be, given the priority of fact over fiction remarked on in §38 above), there is an *a priori* guarantee that any such disagreement is resolvable *in the limit*. Indeed, we can say something even stronger. Consider the fusion of idiolectic senses for a given proper name controlled by the empirical epistemics over all the members of the discourse community consisting of rational beings generally carried to its temporal limit. Call this the *Peircean sense* of the name. The stronger result is this: Peircean senses are uniquely individuating.

47

What guarantees both the weaker and stronger claims are certain features of the controlling epistemics, the method of science. It is, to begin with, a *convergent* epistemics. There is, in the limit, only one world-story and it is, in a specifiable sense, a picture of the world. Given that we're proceeding Sellarswise here, it isn't necessary to argue that case or provide the specifications. Sellars has quite eloquently done that for us.[16] More significantly for our present inquiry,

---

[15] Maybe not. If the first speaker pulls out an historical novel with a medieval setting, they may keep going.

[16] I argue it myself in LR, from different starting points and with different emphases—and I provide a few more specifications along the way.

however, the method of science is an *indexical* epistemics. The world whose story we're telling has us *in* it. Thereby hangs a tale.

48

The requirement that the represented world hang together as an objective unity is the same as the requirement that the objects of that world be represented as independent in their existence of our representings and as occupying a common space and time in which we and our conceptual activities also have location. That these requirements are the same, and that one's so representing the world is a condition of the possibility of any unitary consciousness, are the central burdens of Kant's transcendental deduction. And this argument, in turn, is itself the most generic instance of the abductive form of legitimization constitutive of the very empirical epistemics which we have been discussing. I have secured and developed these points elsewhere[17] and will not pause to do so here. For our present purposes, what I need to stress is that this location which the empirical epistemics most broadly conceived requires that we assign ourselves in the represented world is exactly the locus of that world's constraint on our representational activities. This is a point already secured in the discussion of the indispensibility of language entries (§§34–6): The explanatory accommodation of the language entries it makes possible is what a representational system is *for*.

49

Recall the form of a Sellarsian perceptual taking: 'Lo! a red triangle' was our example. Regarding this as a paradigm language entry, one may be struck by how little it resembles the full-fledged claims which, through their inferential interconnections, are to constitute the balance of the representational system thus entered. As an episode it is undeniably *conceptual*, but it seems insufficiently *judgmental*. Its ultimate defeasibility or endorsement as veridical perception is to be a matter of tracing inferential connections among the prior beliefs constituting a world-picture, but it seems structurally ill-suited to play the *premissory* role thus made mandatory. The moral which I draw from these observations is that there's more to Sellars' 'Lo!' than meets the eye. I propose, in fact, that it is properly interpreted as containing a demonstrative element, a *this-here-now*. (Not only that, of course. It also has the dialectical role of signaling the receptivity of sensibility—the fact that we *find* ourselves with such representings.) What we have then is

---

17 In TAR, RFOS, SSSN, and GHTI.

something more like an ur-judgement: 'This-here-now, a red triangle'. Following Sellars, we might think of this on the model of a Kantian intuition
"synthesized by the productive imagination" (S&M, 4–5). From such a representation it is only a short step to the full-fledged claim 'This-here-now *is*
a red triangle' which can straightforwardly serve the appropriate premissory
role.[18]

50

The point of these observations is that the language entries which are the
raison d'être of our representational system already mobilize the apparatus of
spatio-temporal individuation. The 'here-now' is a *representer's* here-now and it
carries with it a full commitment to there's and then's in a common space and
time, occupied by both representer and representeds, already transcendentally
demanded as a condition of any unitary consciousness. The inferential elaboration
of a perceptual taking must then proceed, so to speak, not only through the
question "What is this?" but through the questions "Where is here?" and "When
is now?" as well. A uniquely individuating indexical (perspectival) sense is thereby
assured *in the limit* for any individual representer.

51

The ultimate resolvability of referential disagreements between speakers turns on
this result. Their shared epistemics is responsible for the explanatory accommodation of *all* their language entries—including the thises in the here-now which,
as potential communicants in a speech situation, they have in common. The
existence of some such common origin is guaranteed since every communicant
is also at least an object of representation for any other and in consequence
is assigned a determinate location in the unitary space and time as indexically
coordinatized by that other. It follows that every two such idiosyncratic limit
perspectives necessarily admit of consistent pairwise fusion into a common third.
To return to my astronomical metaphor, the two planets whose identity or
non-identity must be adjudicated through the medium of a shared empirical
epistemics float in a single representational space the coordinatizability of which
from a shared origin is guaranteed *a priori*. This is roughly Strawson's point
concerning the possibility of a regress to what he calls "demonstrative identification" (I, 19), but Strawson advances the thesis as an *a priori* constraint on the
possibility of communication while the burden of my present argument has been

---

[18] This interpretation, incidentally, makes Kant's claim that the contribution of the understanding is the *forms of judgment* less of a half-truth than it has often seemed.

to endorse the deeper Kantian insight that it is a transcendental condition of the possibility of objective representation *überhaupt*.

52

The fact that a language entry presupposes a fully constituted language system entered implies, however, that the synchronic representational role of such demonstrative expressions must ultimately be understood in terms of the diachronic claim-collecting function of full-fledged proper names. Rather than being, as Russell would have it, the only "logically proper names", demonstrative elements turn out to have a function logically derivative from that of genuine proper names. Roughly, a ·this· is a *temporary* proper name. Unlike genuine proper names, demonstrative elements have no diachronic role and do not represent *in absentia*. Their job is precisely to provide a momentary center for the collection of entry claims, and descriptive content accumulates about a given 'this' only so long as what it represents is represented *as* there and then present to the representer. A demonstrative introduces a new context under the auspices of the method of science and thus *as* a candidate for ligature with that single evolving context whose epistemics is that method. But the representational method for *achieving* such contextual ligature is precisely the introduction of re-usable proper names to serve as the fixed points about which an intersubjective and diachronic world-story can evolve.

53

The notion of a Peircean sense (or a *complete* individual concept) controls the empirical epistemics as a regulative ideal. It is a notion which involves two iterated limit concepts. It not only sums diachronically over the representations of a single representer to arrive at the notion of a uniquely individuating *indexical* limit sense but also socially over successive pairwise fusions of such individual indexical limit perspectives to arrive at the idea of a *non-indexical* representational scheme, equally *instantiable* to any of these (potentially infinitely many) individual limit senses through an identification move of the form 'This = a'.[19] A Peircean sense thus abstracts from idiosyncratic indexical perspectives by positing a limit representation which is wholly aperspectival but which *includes* all individual perspectives by containing a representation of each individual representer as an object having location and duration within the represented world.[20] It is

---

[19] This two dimensional structure—diachronic and communal—is a necessary feature of rational processes generally. I have argued the case concerning the semantic or epistemic appraisal of acts of characterizing, classifying, describing, and attributing in detail in my CLC.

[20] Thus allowing for instantiations of the form 'here = x', 'now = t', and crucially, 'I = p', as well as 'This = a'.

because Peircean senses in this way include all individual perspectival encounters between representers and represented objects that they are, although themselves aperspectival, necessarily uniquely individuating, for they embody the consistent fusion of all individual uniquely individuating *indexical* limit senses.

54

The trench in which I have been digging was labeled 'Kant and Peirce' but, of course, it should be obvious that we have just struck a vein of pure Leibniz. On the present conception, each representer is indeed a monad—windowless, in the absence of a given, and mirroring all others (as represented objects) from its own perspective. It is the constraint of the empirical epistemics controlling the representational activities of these monads which establishes the 'pre-established harmony' embodied in the necessary possibility of consistent pairwise fusions of their individual indexical limit senses. And the Peircean senses which emerge from carrying this process to its ideal limit are nothing less than God's proper names, representing the world *sub specie aeternitatis* and rendering every truth infinitely analytic, for any true claim in which a proper name occurs belongs to its Peircean sense.

55

But as much as all this is Kant and Peirce and Leibniz, it is also very much Sellars. I remarked at the very beginning that, on some topics, what Sellars has to say he has said largely by implication. I have now run on at considerable length about proper names, idiolectic senses, contextual epistemics, demonstrative elements, and spatio-temporal frameworks, and one may fairly wonder if, even by implication, Sellars has said all *that*. Well, in fact he did—but he said it very quickly. Here is how a piece of it went:

The job of referring expressions cannot be explained without taking into account the job of characterizing expressions, and, in particular, those characterizing expressions which stand for spatial and temporal relations; nor can the job of these, in their turn, be explained without taking into account the responsive role of linguistic expressions (language entry transitions) which is the key to the analysis of 'here' and 'now' and the consequence rules which give the 'axiomatics' of spatio-temporal discourse. ... (S&M, 126)

56

As is so often the case, then, where the action is, Sellars is too. As usual, he gets there first. What I have been doing more-or-less is writing a night-letter press dispatch to follow up one of Sellars' frequent telegraphed news items from the philosophical front lines. It is a position in which I often find myself, but I am always delighted to be there. If one wants to master the difficult art of philosophical reportage, I have found, there really isn't any better way to go about it.

REFERENCES

Baum, L. Frank, (WO), *The Wizard of Oz* (Bobbs-Merrill Co., Indianapolis, 1899).

Chastain, Charles, (R&C), 'Reference and Context', in *Language, Mind, and Knowledge*, ed. Gunderson, Minnesota Studies in the Philosophy of Science. vol. VII (University of Minnesota Press. Minneapolis, 1975). 194–269.

Kripke, Saul, (NN), 'Naming and Necessity', in *Semantics of Natural Language*, ed. Harman and Davidson, (D. Reidel Publishing Co., Dordrecht, Holland, 1972), 253–355.

Rosenberg, Jay F., (CLC), 'The Concept of Linguistic Correctness', *Philosophical Studies*, **30** (1976), 171–84.

—— (GHTI), 'The 'Given' and How To Take It—Some Reflections on Phenomenal Ontology', *Metaphilosophy*, 6/3–4 (1975), 303–37.

—— (LR), *Linguistic Representation* (D. Reidel Publishing Co., Dordrecht, Holland, 1974).

—— (N&C), 'Naming and Contingency: Reflections on the New Modality', unpublished Xerox typescript.

—— (RFOS), 'Russell and the Form of Outer Sense', forthcoming in *Bertrand Russell—A Memorial Symposium*, ed. George W. Roberts (George Allen & Unwin, Ltd).

—— (SSSN), 'On Strawson: Sounds, Skepticism, and Necessity', *Philosophia*, 8/1–2 (1978).

—— (TAR), 'Transcendental Arguments Revisited', *Journal of Philosophy*, 72/18 (1975), 611–24.

Russell, Bertrand, (PLA), 'The Philosophy of Logical Atomism', in Russell, *Logic and Knowledge* (Macmillan Company, 1956), ed. R.C. Marsh, 175–282.

Sellars, Wilfrid, (EPH), *Essays in Philosophy and Its History* (D. Reidel Publishing Co., Dordrecht, Holland, 1975).

—— (PP), *Philosophical Perspectives* (Charles C. Thomas, Springfield, Illinois, 1967).

—— (S&M), *Science and Metaphysics* (Routledge & Kegan Paul, London, 1968).

—— (SPR), *Science, Perception and Reality* (Routledge & Kegan Paul, London, 1963).

Strawson, P. F., (I), *Individuals* (Methuen & Co., Ltd., London, 1959).

Ziff, Paul, (SA), *Semantic Analysis* (Cornell University Press, 1960).

7

Wilfrid Sellars' Philosophy of Mind

Nowhere within philosophy is it more difficult to draw lines of demarcation than in an attempt to isolate the philosophy of mind as a coherent subregion of the total philosophical terrain. The philosophy of mind grades off smoothly into questions of epistemology (the structure of sensory awareness and perceptual cognition), of ontology (the nature and multiplicity of substances), of the theory of action, of the philosophy of language and representation, of moral and social and political philosophy, and nowadays even into questions centered in the philosophy of science, in the theory of theories. In the case of Wilfrid Sellars, these difficulties are especially acute, for Sellars' philosophy of mind is intricately and inextricably woven into the fabric of a systematic philosophical vision of classical scope.

Such considerations collaborate to render near hopeless the task of a sympathetic expositor. Particularly in a survey as limited in scope as the present effort, something important must necessarily be sacrificed. The expositor is faced with an unpleasant choice. He can attempt to secure a limited range of his subject's key insights by tracing their interconnections with, anchorage in, and argumentative buttressing by collateral theses more properly belonging to other, although related, areas of philosophical thought; or he can attempt to communicate a sense of the overall sweep, structure, and design of his subject's philosophical tapestry, at the risk of leaving his audience with the feeling that this whole pattern of thought is arbitrary, dogmatic, and inadequately grounded by cogent argumentation.

Despite the magnitude of the risk, I have elected to pursue the latter course. I shall attempt, in other words, to sketch *what* stands Sellars takes within the philosophy of mind, while saying relatively little about *why* Sellars takes the stands he does. What will emerge, if I am successful, will be a coherent, intricate, and powerful systematic vision of "the mind and its place in nature". What will be lost will be a family of insightfully reasoned considerations which conduce to render that vision as compelling as it is powerful. From the perspective of what is philosophically ideal, this remains an unsatisfying compromise, but circumstances permit no better. To the task, then.

Sellars' philosophical orientation in general may usefully be characterized as a sophisticated Kantianism tempered by the insights of an indigenous, especially Peircean, American pragmatism. In the philosophy of mind, in particular, these broad tendencies manifest themselves, negatively, in Sellars' firm rejection of the Cartesian picture of mind as *res cogitans*, and, positively, in his continuing commitment to the project of integrating the distinctive mentality of persons into the framework of that concept of the world which is being increasingly sharply delineated by the advances of a maturing natural science. The negative moment here forms an essential prolegomena to the positive. It secures, indeed, the possibility of the integration which Sellars' positive programme aims, at least in principle, at actualizing.

Sellars follows Kant in bringing critical pressure to bear against both elements of the *res cogitans* formula—returning from the bare, substratal Cartesian *res* to a more Aristotelian view of persons as natured, unitary "first substances", and dismantling Descartes' overarching "*cogitatione*" (the "ideas" of the British Empiricists) by enforcing a sharp distinction between sensation ("raw feels") and cognition (thought).

On Sellars' view, the Cartesian picture of mind as *res* is part and parcel of the enterprise which seeks to erect upon the foundation of the *cogito*—correctly viewed as capturing "the basic and irreducible form of self-awareness with respect to distinctively human states of one's person" ([1]: 236)—a *science* of Rational Psychology with ontological import. Like Kant, Sellars denies the *possibility* of such a science.

Traditional metaphysicians had argued that the subject of representations ... is a simple, non-composite substance which is "strictly" ... identical through time. ... Kant argues, *per contra*, that for all we know the subject or representer might be:

(a) an attribute of something more basic
(b) a system (composite)
(c) a series.

([1]: 236)

Sellars endorses Kant's account of the classical arguments to the contrary as fallacious or "paralogistic". On Sellars' reconstruction, these arguments share a common form:

The representation of the I is not the representation of

(a) an aspect of something more basic,
(b) a composite of parts,
[(c) a series]:

Therefore, *the I* is not

(a) an aspect of something more basic,
(b) a composite of parts,
[(c) a series].

([2]: 69–71; cf. [1]: 236–239)

These arguments would not be fallacious "if we could add the premise that our concept of the 'I' is the concept of a determinate kind of object" ([1]: 236–237) and, indeed, "Descartes takes it for granted that '*res cogitans*' is a proper sortal concept ... " ([2]: 67).

But the concept of the "I" is the concept of that which thinks..., and concepts pertaining to mental acts are "functional" in a way which leaves open the question as to the "qualitative" or ... contentual character of the items that function in such a way as to be the kinds of mental acts they are. ([1]: 237; cf. [2]: 67–68)

It is, in fact, "in the literal sense a category mistake to construe 'substance' ... as an object-language sortal word that differs from ordinary empirical predicates by being a *summum genus*" ([3]: 53).

Instead, Sellars endorses the thesis of the mediaeval terminist logicians, itself extended and deepened by Kant, "that certain statements (thus 'Man is a species') which seem to be about queer entities in the world are actually statements that classify constituents of conceptual acts" ([3]: 53). The categorial apparatus of classical metaphysics, in short, is to be understood as encoding a taxonomy of the "most generic logical powers" of conceptual representings. It is thus in itself devoid of any ontological import (vide [4–6]). This is the understanding which opens the way for Sellars' complete delegation of the *positive* ontological task to natural science in his much-remarked "*scientia mensura*":

... that in the dimension of describing and explaining the world, science is the measure of all things, of what is that it is, and of what is not that it is not. ([7]: 173)

From this metaphysical perspective, it follows straightforwardly that the fundamental concept of a person is not that of a Cartesian *res cogitans* but that of a *living organism* which both moves and thinks, feels and acts—an Aristotelian "first substance" which is the subject of both "physical" and "mental" predications. This ur-conception admits of an initial refinement, then, in terms of the picture of the world yielded by an emerging science, which produces a *trivial* version of what is typically called "the Identity Theory", to which Sellars, as a first step, unproblematically subscribes:

... There is a sense in which it is perfectly legitimate to suppose that [mental states] *are identical with* certain states of the empirical brain. This, for the simple reason that it makes sense to suppose that they *are* states of the empirical brain. Imagine a person who has been defleshed and deboned, but whose nervous system is alive, intact, and in functioning order. Imagine its sensory nerves hooked up with input devices and its motor nerves hooked up with an electronic system which enables it to communicate. Without expanding on this familiar science fiction, let me simply suggest that we think of what we ordinarily call a person as a nervous system clothed in flesh and bones. In view of what we know, it makes perfectly good sense to introduce the term "core person" for the empirical nervous system, and to introduce a way of talking according to which [mental states] are in the first instance states of "core persons" and only derivatively of the clothed person. ([8]: 380)

While this version of the Identity Theory is "almost undoubtedly true", it is also, as Sellars remarks, "relatively non-controversial and unexciting. ... All of the important philosophical problems pertaining to the relation of mental states to physical states remain" ([8]: 381).

On Sellars' view, a (perhaps, the) significant challenge for contemporary philosophy is the enterprise of uniting what he calls two "images" of man-in-the-world into a single "stereoscopic" synoptic understanding.

[The] philosopher is confronted not by one complex many-dimensional picture, the unity of which, such as it is, he must come to appreciate, but by *two* pictures of essentially the same order of complexity, each of which purports to be a complete picture of man-in-the-world, and which ... he must fuse into one vision. ([9]: 4)

These competing perspectives Sellars refers to as the *manifest* and the *scientific* images of man-in-the-world.

The manifest image is "the framework in terms of which, to use an existentialist turn of phrase, man first encountered himself ... " ([9]: 6). It is that image of man-in-the-world which is both endorsed and refined by the so-called "perennial philosophy", a tradition—spanning the centuries from Plato and Aristotle to G.E. Moore and P.F. Strawson—whose defining characteristic, indeed, is "an acceptance of the manifest image as the *real*" ([9]: 19). At the same time, the manifest image is constitutive of that which it depicts, for "man is that being which conceives of itself in terms of the manifest image" ([9]: 18).

The scientific image—even more of an idealization than the manifest image, since it is still in the process of coming to be—is that conception of man-in-the-world which emerges from the fruits of postulational theory construction. Like the manifest image, the scientific image purports to offer (the schematism of) a *complete* picture of man-in-the-world, but one radically different from—and at first sight in many ways incommensurable with—the picture embodied in the manifest image. From the metaphysical perspective of Sellars' scientific realism, the picture embodied in the manifest image is viewed (*sub specie* the scientific image) as codifying a system of "*appearances*" to human persons of a reality which is *constituted* of, e.g., systems of imperceptible particles. It is the fact that the human organism (which, within the manifest image, *is*—*qua* Aristotelian "first substance"—the person) is, within the scientific image, represented as one such "system of imperceptible particles" among others, which sets the philosophical problematic of mind and body.

For if the human body is a system of particles, the body cannot be the subject of thinking and feeling, *unless thinking and feeling are capable of interpretation as complex interactions of physical particles*; unless, that is to say, the manifest framework of man as *one* being, a *person* capable of doing radically different kinds of things, can be replaced without loss of descriptive and explanatory power by a postulational image in which he is a complex of physical particles, and all his activities a matter of the particles changing in state and relationship. ([9]: 29)

Securing the possibility of such a replacement would constitute a defense of an "Identity Theory" in a non-trivial sense, and it is, indeed, to such a *significant* Identity Theory of mind and body that Sellars himself is philosophically committed.

The Cartesian concept of self (mind) as *res cogitans* unites under the rubric '*cogitatione*' a variety of classically separate capacities. Cognitions (thoughts), sensations ("raw feels"), and volitions ("acts of will") are all *cogitatione*. The guiding thread of Descartes' ontological unification here is essentially the *epistemological* fact of "privileged access". As Sellars reconstructs the epistemology of the mental, however, the first-person reporting role of the language of the mental constitutes a "dimension of the use of these concepts which is *built on* and *presupposes* [an] intersubjective status" ([7]: 189). The ability to report, using the language of the mental, one's own mental states is an *acquired* ability—for the language of the mental, like all languages, must be learned.

In his seminal "Empiricism and the Philosophy of Mind" [7], Sellars sketches the learning process—in essence, that of operant conditioning—by which what *begins* as a language with a purely theoretical use can *gain* a (first-person, self-descriptive) reporting role. His account shows

> ... that the fact that language is essentially an *intersubjective* achievement, and is learned in inter-subjective contexts ... is compatible with the 'privacy' of 'inner episodes'. It also makes clear that this privacy is not an 'absolute privacy'. For if it recognizes that these concepts have a reporting use in which one is not drawing inferences from behavioural evidence, it nevertheless insists that the fact that overt behavior *is* evidence for these episodes *is built into the very logic of these concepts*, just as the fact that the observable behaviour of gases is evidence for molecular episodes is built into the very logic of molecule talk. ([7]: 189)

Seeing the epistemological fact of "privileged access" in this way not as constitutive of the concept of the mental but as a derivative status accruing to the concepts of certain "inner episodes" and thus as devoid of ontological consequences, Sellars is free to uncouple what Descartes brings together as "*cogitatione*". Thoughts, sensations, and volitions, on Sellars' view, pose *different*, if related, challenges to the fusion of the manifest and scientific images, and Sellars proceeds to offer different, if related, discussions of these diverse dimensions of the mental.

Sellars distinguishes in [10] among the "logical (semantic)", "action", and "causal" sense of "the expression of thoughts". An utterance by some person can be said to express *the* thought that-p, a remark which *classifies* the utterance according to its place in the "logical space" of inference and argumentation; to express *his* thought that-p, a remark which classifies the occurrent speech episode as a speech *act* (an intentional action caught up in an economy of means and ends); or simply to be the expression of *a* thought, a remark which identifies the overt episode as the culmination of a causal process which beings with an "inner episode", an occurrent thinking. Only the last of these engages the *ontology* of thoughts. While thoughts *qua* occurrent thinkings are prior to meaningful utterances in the causal order, the *intentionality* of speech, on Sellars' view, is not derivative from the intentionality of thought. Rather, he sees the language of intentionality in general as functional and classificatory, employed for sorting episodes according to their roles in structuring the total behavioral economy of the speaking and thinking organism. (See, e.g., [11], [12].)

In [7], Sellars began what has become a continuing project of understanding the *epistemic* status of the concept of occurrent thought-episodes after the pattern of theoretical postulations. The *model* for his mythological "theory of thoughts" (mythological in Plato's sense—enlightening through its plausibilities) are the candid utterances ("thinkings-out-loud") of a hypothetical sophisticated "Rylean community"—"Rylean" in lacking the concept of covert "inner episodes", but sophisticated in having a command of the full repertoire of logical and semantic notions (validity, inference, meaning, truth) in their application to *sayings* and proximate *dispositions to say*. Sellars' myth introduces the concept of thoughts into this community in two stages. In the first stage, "Verbal Behaviorism", the (ur-)concept of a thought just *is* the concept of a proximate, although perhaps unactualized, disposition to think-out-loud (i.e., to *say*). In the second stage, thoughts are explicitly postulated (by one "Jones") as occurrent thinkings, covert ("inner") episodes (N.B.: not entities) which have, in effect, the *semantic place* of certain thinkings-out-loud—that is, which play an equivalent role in a system of responses to non-cognitive stimuli ("language entries"), inferential passages from cognitive item to cognitive item ("intra-linguistic moves"), and the triggerings of overt behavior ("language exits"). (See [13]; [14]: ch. IV.)

The key to this account of thoughts lies in the recognition that, while the items of the *model* for Jones's theory have, *qua* acoustical disturbances, a determinate intrinsic character, the episodes (hypothetically) *postulated* by his theory as covert (mediating) states of persons—initially to explain the appropriateness and intelligence of conduct in contexts where no thinking-out-loud is occurring—are introduced by a purely *functional* analogy. The concept of a thought (occurrent thinking) is not the concept of something encountered *propria persona* but that of a causally mediating *logico-semantic role-player*, the ontological instantiation of which is, so far, left open. It is thus possible to discover, in the order of being, that these role-players intrinsically *are*, for example, determinate states of the central nervous system. (This would, parenthetically, supply part of an explanatory account of why it *is* possible to train people to have "privileged access" to some of their thoughts—i.e., to respond directly and non-inferentially to the occurrence of an "inner episode" with the (meta-)thought that one is thinking a determinate thought; to respond, that is, with *another* "inner episode".) The manifest image conception of persons as thinkers, then, can fuse smoothly with the concept of organisms of determinate neurological structure, which, from the standpoint of the scientific image, those persons *are*. On Sellars' account, the concept of a thought is at ground the concept of a *functional* kind, and so no ontological tensions are introduced by the scientific image's identification of items of that functional kind as *being*, structurally, states and episodes of the central nervous system.

In the case of sensations, however, the fusion of the two images cannot be achieved with an analogous unproblematic smoothness. Few aspects of Sellars' philosophy have provoked as much comment and resistance as his theory of sensations. (See, e.g., Cornman [15], Delaney [16], Hooker [17].) Here it becomes necessary to supply considerably more detail.

For a time, Sellars' account of sensations does run parallel to his account of thoughts. Sellars, however, sharply separates the "of-ness" of sensations from the "of-ness" of thoughts. The "of-ness" of thought is the "aboutness" of intentionality. To think of, for example, Socrates is to think *something* of Socrates, i.e., to think *that* ... Socrates ... , where the open context is filled by the remaining elements of a complete sentence. Thinking-of is thus, on Sellars' view, an elliptical thinking-that, and the "propositional" idiom of 'that'-clauses, in turn, is once again a functional classificatory idiom which abstracts from specific material embodiments to sort logico-semantic role-players (overt or covert) *according to* their logico-semantic roles.

Like thoughts, sensations are merely "nominal objects". The hypothetical explanatory postulation of Jones's mythological "theory of sensations" within Sellars' account is a postulation of *states* of persons rather than of entities. And, as in the case of thoughts, talk of "of-ness" is again fundamentally classificatory. Here, however, the *sort* of classification is not logical or semantic.

The "rawness" of "raw feels" is their non-conceptual character. The sense in which "raw feels" are "of something" is not to be assimilated to the intentionality of thoughts. ([8]: 376)

Sellars illustrates his understanding of the place of sensations *within the manifest image* through a series of grammatical transforms from the customary "nominal" style of sensation-attributions, e.g.,

(a) S has a sensation of a red triangle,

to an ontologically-more-perspicuous, contrived "adverbial" style. 'Of a red triangle' is first represented as a classificatory modifier of 'sensation', thus:

(b) S has an of-a-red-triangle sensation.

The contrived adjective 'of-a-red-triangle' is, second, itself represented as a form of *analogical* predication, the fundamentum of which is the attribution of sensory qualities to manifest (physical) objects, thus:

(c) S has a red$_S$ triangular$_S$ sensation,

where the subscripts signal the invocation of the analogical transposition. Finally, viewing the "verbal noun" 'sensation' as a nominalization of the verb 'to sense', Sellars transforms the noun-adjective construction of (c) into a verb plus adverbs, roughly:

(d) S senses red$_S$ly and triangular$_S$ly

(paralleling the understanding of, e.g., "S wore a wry seductive smile" as "S smiled wryly and seductively"). The *person*, S, then emerges explicitly revealed as the only ultimate *ontological* subject of attributions of sensation. (See [7], [18], [19].)

The *analogy* underlying the categorial transposition of redness and triangularity from qualities of manifest objects to modes of sensing is, as in the case of thoughts, mediated by viewing sensations, *qua* sensory states, as having the epistemic status of postulates of a mythological explanatory theory. Here, too, "privileged access" is treated as an added and derivative dimension of use of concepts essentially intersubjective in character. But where thoughts were (hypothetically) postulated as causally mediating logico-semantic role-players to explain the intelligence and appropriateness of conduct in certain contexts, sensory states are introduced as elements of an explanatory account of the appropriateness of certain *cognitions* ("propositional attitudes") themselves, whether covert (thinkings, believings) or overt (sayings, thinkings-out-loud). In particular, the state adverted to in (d) above is invoked to explain the occurrence of *thoughts* ("perceptual takings") of red triangles, both in instances in which a person's eyes are directed toward a red triangular object in good light and, more importantly, in cases of "non-veridical perceptual takings", where no red triangular objects are suitably positioned in the proximate environment of the perceiving subject at all.

In the *first* instance, then, the concept of a state of sensing red$_S$ly (dropping 'triangular$_S$ly' for compactness) is introduced by an *extrinsic causal* analogy: It is that sort of state which is brought about in normal perceivers in standard conditions by the action of red objects upon the eyes.

The temptation is to stop at this—that is, to hold that the concept of sensory states within the manifest image is the concept of causal role-players in the same way that the concept of occurrent thinkings within the manifest image amounts to the concept of certain causally mediating logico-semantic role-players. It is precisely here, however, that Sellars' treatment of sensations parts company from the account which he has offered of cognitions.

The key to this departure is a recognition of the different *explanatory* role which sensory states are being (hypothetically) posited to fill. Grasping the important of this difference, however, requires a metaphysical excursis.

The fundamental *concept* of color in the manifest image is the concept of a *content* (what Kant called "an intensive magnitude" and, more revealingly, "the real in space"). The conceptual space of colors as the qualities of natured substances (wood, ice, metal, pigment, etc.) rests upon a more basic conceptual framework in which colors are themselves the *stuffs* of which objects consist. The natures of natured substances are clusters of transformational, interactive, and causal powers, propensities, and dispositions. While such powers and propensities are implicitly adverted to in the perceptual *judgment* that, to take a favorite Sellarsian example, there is a pink ice cube before one, they are properly no part of the correlative perceptual *taking*. We do not *see* the natures of what we see, but *see* only what is conceived as thus natured. The concept of a pink ice cube, then, is in the first instance the concept of a *cube of pink* with determinate causal powers and transformational propensities—e.g., the power to cool tea and the propensity to melt in the process. Sellars insists, in other words, that we take seriously Berkeley's argument that there can be no primary qualities (form) in the absence of secondary qualities (contents) and thereby reverses Descartes' conclusions vis-à-vis "the real wax". Colors are not modes of appearing of bare *res extensa* but rather fundamentally to be conceived as *themselves* the extended (space-filling) continua in which empirical natures inhere. And the *basic* logical grammar of color space, in turn, is not at ground adjectival but rather is analogous to the familiar grammar of mass terms. It is *this* family of observations and considerations which Sellars summarily expresses by saying that the concepts of colors are concepts of "*ultimately homogeneous* (henceforth 'UH') qualities" ([9], [20]).

The fundamental explanatory job which must be done by the posited sensory states of persons is to account for the appropriateness of certain cognitions. We can now flesh out this bare constraint in greater detail. The crucial point is that the cognitions at issue *include* the concepts of color-contents—that is, the concepts of UH qualities—*as* UH. What the postulated sensory states must explanatorily do, in other words, is in part to supply an account which renders intelligible the occurrence of *concepts of UH qualities* as a response to irritations of the sensory surface of the human organism. But they can satisfy this specific explanatory demand, Sellars argues, only if these states themselves are posited as having a determinate *intrinsic* character. They must, in fact, be conceived of as themselves *instantiating* a logical space formally analogous to the logical space which color-contents are conceived as occupying—as preserving, within the logical space of states of a person *qua* perceiver, the resemblances, differences, orderings, exclusions, and the UH (in short, the "topology") of the logical space of color-contents which is the fundamentum of the *analogy* in terms of which these sensory states are (hypothetically) originally introduced. The concept of a state of sensing red$_S$ly, in other words, cannot be *simply* the concept of a state which is brought about in a certain fashion. Rather, it must be the richer concept of a state of a perceiver which resembles and differs from states of, e.g., sensing blue$_S$ly, pink$_S$ly, green$_S$ly, etc. in a manner formally analogous to the way in which red, blue, pink, green, etc. contents are conceived to resemble and differ from one another—and which *is* (*qua* state) itself UH.

The reason that characterizing such states as sensing red$_S$ly only extrinsically, according to their paradigmatic causes, cannot do the relevant explanatory job here is that, already in the manifest image, *there are no color-contents*. Since the fundamental conceptual/experiential sense of 'red' is that *of* a red content, this seems puzzling, but the point is relatively straightforward: Considerations of the sorts mobilized in the classical (skeptical) Argument from Illusion already suffice to establish the conclusion that the basic *ontological* locus of color-contents must lie on the side of the subject, that is, must be somehow "within" the perceiving organism. It is crucial here to separate the order of understanding from the order of being. In the order of understanding, the basic *concept* of color is that of UH space-filling contents, and the concept of such states of perceivers as sensing red$\underset{5}{}$ly is a concept formed by an analogical transposition into the category of *states* of those fundamental concepts belonging to the category of *stuffs*. This view, however, is compatible with the conclusion that, in the order of being, there are no such stuffs. It is the states which alone *instantiate* the logical space which colors-*qua*-contents are conceived of as instantiating—and both our experiences of color-contents-in-space and our *having* concepts of such contents are properly to be (explanatorily) accounted for in terms of our being in such states. To postulate states to explain such experiences and the possession of such concepts *when there are no color-contents*, and then to characterize these states *only* "extrinsically", in a manner which makes essential *ontological use* (as posited *causes*) of the notion of such color-contents, is clearly self-defeating. We must consequently think of our mythological theory as postulating a family of states which themselves instantiate the topology of the logical space which colors are conceived of, *qua* contents, as occupying. Unlike the extrinsic (causal) characterization, this *intrinsic* characterization makes sense even if there are no color-contents, since such contents do not enter into this account ontologically, as the causes of sensory states, but only via their *concepts*, as paradigms for analogical concept formation. The upshot is that, within the manifest image, the concept of a sensory state, unlike the concept of an occurrent thinking, is not the functional concept of a role-player but the contentual concept of something with a determinate intrinsic character. It is sensory states *thus* conceived, then, which must be accommodated within the scientific image if the two images are to be fused, and this accommodation *cannot* be simply a matter of leaving it entirely to the scientific image to supply structural, ontological (intrinsic) specifications for items conceived within the manifest image purely functionally (extrinsically).

When we now turn to the emerging scientific image with which this purified manifest-image conception of sensations is to be fused, what we note first and foremost is that the *persons*, who within the manifest image are the single, basic logical subjects of sensory states, come themselves to be reconceived as *systems* of more basic logical subjects (cells, neurons, molecules, atoms, etc.). Such a system of logical subjects is the *counterpart* within the scientific image of the single logical subject which is a perceiver within the manifest image. Let us write "perceiver-ctpt".

Such an ontological reconceptualization of the subjects of sensory states demands an analogous reconceptualization of the states themselves, since "sensing red$\underset{5}{}$ly", for example, is *analytically* the state of a single logical subject. Let us put "senses-red$\underset{5}{}$ly-ctpt" for the state of a system, within the scientific image, which "corresponds" to the state of sensing red$\underset{5}{}$ly attributed within the manifest image to the unitary person which, as conceived within the manifest image, that system *is*. In Sellars' account, then, colors have so far gone through *two* ontological relocations and also through *two* categorial transpositions, from:

	(i) is (made of) red	a content "in the world"
to	(ii) senses red$_S$ly	a state of a person-*qua*-perceiver
		(= single logical subject)
to	(iii) senses-red$_S$ly-ctpt	a state of a perceiver-ctpt
		(= system of logical subjects).

In this process, analogical concept formation has been invoked twice as well: once *within* the manifest image to form a "transcategorial" analogy between the concept of a family of contents (the *basic* color concept) and the concept of a family of states; and once *between* the manifest and the scientific images to form a "trans-framework" analogy between the concept of a family of states of a single logical subject and the concept of a family of counterpart states which are states of the system of logical subjects which is the theoretical counterpart of that pre-theoretically unitary single subject.

Just as the logical topology (formal properties) of colors conceived as contents is carried over from (i) to (ii) in order that the appeal to the states (ii) be able to explain our possession of the concepts of contents (i), so, too, the logical topology of colors conceived as contents should be carried over *again* from (ii) to (iii) in order that these states, now theoretically reconceived, of persons, also theoretically reconceived, can explain *both* the states (ii) of persons pre-theoretically conceived *and* the success of our appeals to those states (ii) in explaining what they were introduced to explain, namely, our possession of the concepts of the contents (i). *But*, Sellars argues, we *cannot* carry over the logical topology of color-contents from (ii) to (iii) in this way *on metaphysical grounds*. No state of a system or multiplicity of basic logical subjects *could* instantiate the logical topology of color-contents. In particular, no state of a system of basic logical subjects could *be* ultimately homogeneous. Position (iii) must therefore be rejected. It is metaphysically incoherent. Counterparts to those sensory states of persons which, within the manifest image, are the ultimate ontological locus of, e.g., colors must be introduced into the scientific image by a different route.

Sellars' ground for his rejection of position (iii) is what he calls a "principle of pure *a priori* metaphysics", the "Strong Principle of Reducibility" (SPR):

If an object is *in a strict sense* a system of objects, then every property of the object must consist in the fact that its constituents have such and such qualities and stand in such and such relations. ([9]: 27)

The argument then runs as follows: Since a perceiver-ctpt *is* "in the strict sense" a system of objects, the SPR implies, with repect to the supposed property (state) of sensing-red$_S$ly-ctpt

(e)   some or all of the constituents of the perceiver-ctpt (the neurons, atoms, etc.) *themselves* have the property (or are in the state) of sensing-red$_S$ly-ctpt,

or   (f)   the perceiver-ctpt's being in that state (having that property) is "analyzable" ("without residue") into the atoms, etc. having *other* properties and standing in certain relations.

Since "sensing-red$_S$ly-ctpt" was to be the scientific image analogue of the state "sensing red$_S$ly" of manifest image *persons*, (e) is ruled out. But, since "sensing-red$_S$ly-ctpt" was to *instantiate* the logical topology of colors-conceived-as-contents, (f) is ruled out as well—for the *ultimate homogeneity* of a state or property of a system *logically* cannot be a matter of the objects composing that system having, separately, certain properties and standing in certain relations. Position (iii) is thus incompatible with the Strong Principle of Reducibility.

Nor can it be argued that the UH of colors-*qua*-contents is a mere *appearance*. For, to put it briefly, what our hypothetical postulations have been designed from the outset to *explain* is just *the appearance of UH*. The explanations here operate in a "transcendental mode". What was to be accounted for was the fact that we possess the *concepts* of "features" or "aspects" of experience or the world which are UH. Position (iii) proposes to supply such an explanation against the background of a set of ontological posits which imply that *literally nothing* actually *instantiates* the (formal, topological) property of UH. But, argues Sellars, if nothing actually *is*, in some sense, an UH continuum, then nothing can be *mistaken* for such a continuum either, for to mistake something for a continuum requires that we already possess the concept of such a continuum. While our possession of the very concept of a multiplicity of discrete entities *can* ultimately be explained by appeal to actualities which *are* continuua (locally qualitatively differentiated, for example), our possession of the very concept of an ultimately homogeneous continuum itself *cannot* in the last analysis analogously be explained by appeal to actualities which are *not* (or do not include) such homogeneous continuua.

The upshot, Sellars concludes, is that the fusion of the manifest and scientific images at the point of sensations will require the postulation of a further family of *basic entities* which themselves actually *do* individually ontologically instantiate the logical topology of colors-*qua*-contents, i.e., which themselves actually *are* UH. For reasons external to the philosophy of mind (deriving, instead, from the metaphysical problematic of constancy and change), Sellars foresees here another categorial transposition as well. Such "sensa", as he calls them, will need, on his view, to be postulated, not in the category of substances or states of substances but rather as "absolute processes", as, for example, "reddings". A perceiver-ctpt within the scientific image will thus ultimately emerge as conceived as a "harmony" or system of diverse such "absolute processes" ("reddings", "electronings", etc.), only *some* of which are "sensa". The final ontological locus of sensation (and color) within the scientific image will thus be not (iii) but

(iv)   is a redding   a *constituent* (not: state) of a perceiver-ctpt
                                    (= system or "harmony" of diverse such
                                    "absolute processes").

The scientific image as we have it today, in other words, is arguably *incomplete*. Fusing the manifest image fact of sensory consciousness with the scientific image, on Sellars' view, will turn out to demand *more science*—that is, the postulation of further basic constitutive entities, parallel to the postulations of, e.g., electrons required to integrate the pre-theoretical appearances of what turned out to be electromagnetic phenomena into the mechanical world-picture of Newtonian physics. Sensa, thus understood, will be what Sellars calls physical$_1$ (belonging in the space-time network) but not physical$_2$ ("definable in terms of theoretical primitives adequate to describe completely the actual states ... of the universe before the appearance of life") ([21]: 252; cf. [7], [18], [9], [8]). They would need to be appealed to only in explanatory accounts of the behavioral competences (cognitive and non-cognitive) of those systems of basic entities which are sentient organisms. This, however, would be no more mysterious—and would no more support a *Cartesian* dualism—than the fact that electrical charge must be appealed to in explanatory accounts of lightning bolts but not of the motions of the planets.

There remains only the question of accommodating volitions, intentions, and the like—in short, of accommodating *practical* cognitions, "reason in its practical employment"—within the synoptic stereoscopic vision of the fused images. This is, in effect, the most crucial moment of Sellars' three-part story, for it amounts, in the end, to the question of whether it is possible to put *persons* into the scientific image, to

the task of showing that categories pertaining to man as a *person* who finds himself confronted by standards (ethical, logical, etc.) which often conflict with his desires and impulses, and to which he may or may not conform, can be reconciled with the idea that man is what science says he is. ([9]: 38)

The reason is that

to think of a featherless biped as a person is to construe its behaviour in terms of actual or potential membership in an embracing group each member of which thinks of itself as a member of the group. Let us call such a group a 'community'. ([9]: 39)

Now, the fundamental principles of a community, which define what is 'correct' or 'incorrect', 'right' or 'wrong', 'done' or 'not done', are the most general common *intentions* of that community with respect to the behaviour of members of the group. It follows that to recognize a featherless biped or dolphin or Martian as a person requires that one think thoughts of the form, 'We (one) shall do (or abstain from doing) actions of kind A in circumstances of kind C'. To think thoughts of this kind is not to *classify* or *explain*, but to *rehearse an intention*.

Thus the conceptual framework of persons is the framework in which we think of one another as sharing the community intentions which provide the ambience of principles and standards ... within which we live our own individual lives. A person can almost be defined as a being that has intentions. ([9]: 39–40)

The challenge that this last accommodation poses to the fusion of the two images is radically different in kind from those already discussed. It is not, so to speak, an *ontological* challenge. Ontologically, indeed, intentions and volitions just *are* thoughts (occurrent thinkings)—although they are thoughts of a special (functional) kind. They are *practical* thinkings, which is to say that their unique functional role within the total cognitive-*cum*-behavioral economy of a person is to be understood in terms of their special relationship to *conduct*. (Analogous to the way in which the unique functional role of those cognitions which are perceptual takings or judgments is understood in terms of their special relationships to *sensations*, i.e., their status as non-inferential *responses*.) Sellars signals this unique conduct-structuring role by a contrived use of the auxiliary 'shall' as an operator on logico-semantically classified thinkings. (Categorical) intendings are time-determinate future-tensed shall-thinkings:

(g) Shall (I will do X at t),

and volitions ("acts of will") are those special cases of intendings in which the time-determination is the immediate present:

(h) Shall (I will *now* do X).

Such practical thinkings mediate between reasoning and conduct. They are related to the former by a single principle which unites practical and theoretical reasonings:

If p implies q then Shall(p) implies Shall(q).

And they are related to the latter by being caught up in a network of (acquired) causal propensities which guarantee, roughly, that intentions of the form (g) regularly give rise *at t* to volitions of the form (h), which, in turn, (barring paralysis and the like) regularly give rise then and there to those bodily movements which (further circumstances being suitable) *are* the initial stages of a doing of X. (For detailed accounts of these interfaces, see [22]; [23]; and [24]: ch. VII.)

The manifest image concept of an intention or a volition—of a practical thinking—is thus again the concept of a causally mediating logico-semantic role-player, and thus again not the concept of something with a determinate intrinsic character, given *propria persona*. The *ontological* accommodation of practical thinkings within the scientific image consequently proceeds as does the accommodation of thinkings in general—an emerging scientific understanding progressively supplying structural (e.g., neurophysiological) ontological cash to back the purely functional promissory-note conceptions of the manifest image.

But here, Sellars insists, such an accommodation cannot be the end of the story. Taking seriously the idea that the scientific image purports to be a *complete* image of man-in-the-world and presents itself as (potentially) an *alternative* to the manifest image requires that the categories pertaining to persons reappear within the scientific image *as such*. To be authentically a candidate to *replace* the manifest image—"the framework in terms of which ... man first encounters himself"—the scientific image must itself become a framework within which man can continue to encounter himself *as man*. Thus, Sellars concludes,

> to complete the scientific image we need to enrich it *not* with more ways of saying what is the case, but with the language of community and individual intentions, so that by construing the actions we intend to do and the circumstances in which we intend to do them in scientific terms, we *directly* relate the world as conceived by scientific theory to our purposes, and make it *our* world and no longer an alien appendage to the world in which we do our living. ([9]: 40)

Unlike the framework of thoughts and sensations, "the conceptual framework of persons [*as such*] is not something that needs to be *reconciled with* the scientific image, but rather something to be *joined* to it" ([9]: 40). Such a "direct incorporation of the scientific image into our way of life" is something which, from our present perspective, we can only speculatively imagine. But, with the possibility of *ontologically* accommodating within the scientific image the thoughts and feelings of the organisms which *are* thinking and feeling persons now argumentatively secure, no irreducible dualism remains to stand as an in-principle obstacle to our imagining it. And *that* possibility, in the end, stands as the strength and culmination of the systematic synoptic vision which is Wilfrid Sellars' philosophy of mind.[1]

REFERENCES

By Wilfrid Sellars

[1] "Metaphysics and the Concept of a Person", In K. Lambert (ed.), *The Logical Way of Doing Things*, 219–252 (New Haven, Conn.: Yale University Press, 1969), repr. in [25]. Page citations to [25].

[2] " ... this I or we or it (the thing) which thinks ... ." *Proceedings of the American Philosophical Association*, 44 (1970–1), 5–31; repr. in [25]. Page citations to [25].

[3] "Some Remarks on Kant's Theory of Experience", *Journal of Philosophy*, 64 (1967), 633–647, repr. in [25]. Page citations to [25].

[4] "Abstract Entities", *Review of Metaphysics*, 16 (1962–1963), 627–671; repr. in [26].

[5] "Towards a Theory of the Categories", in L. Foster and J.W. Swanson (Eds.), *Experience and Theory*, 55–78 (Amherst: University of Massachusetts Press, 1970); repr. in [25].

---

[1] Sellars extends and clarifies his account of (intentional) thinking in "Mental Events", *Philosophical Studies*, 39 (1981), 325–345. His Carus Lectures ("Is Consciousness Physical?", "Naturalism and Process", and "The Lever of Archimedes"—published in *Monist*, 64 (1981), 3–90) offer a detailed elaboration and supplementary argumentative support of his complex theory of sensation. The same issue of the *Monist* contains preliminary responses, by, *inter alia*, Daniel Dennett and Roderick Firth, to the issues raised in these lectures. A subsequent issue—*Monist*, 65 (1982)—is devoted entirely to the philosophy of Wilfrid Sellars. For a further discussion of Sellars' views on sensation, see "The Place of Color in the Scheme of Things", ch. 9 in this volume.

[6] "Empiricism and Abstract Entities", in P.A. Schilpp (ed.), *The Philosophy of Rudolf Carnap*, 431–68 (LaSalle, Ill.: Open Court, 1963); repr. in [25].

[7] "Empiricism and the Philosophy of Mind", *Minnesota Studies in the Philosophy of Science*, vide [21], 253–329.

[8] "The Identity Approach to the Mind-Body Problem", *Review of Metaphysics*, 18 (1964–1966), 430–451; repr. in [26]. Page citations to [26].

[9] "Philosophy and the Scientific Image of Man", in R. Colodny (ed.), *Frontiers of Science and Philosophy*, 35–78 (Pittsburgh: University of Pittsburgh Press, 1962); repr. in [27]. Page citations to [27].

10] "Language as Thought and Communication", *Philosophy and Phenomenological Research*, 29 (1968–1969), 506–527; repr. in [25].

11] "Notes on Intentionality", *Journal of Philosophy*, 61 (1964), 655–665; repr. in [26].

12] "Meaning as Functional Classification", *Synthese*, 27 (1974), 417–437.

13] "Some Reflections on Language Games". *Philosophy of Science*, 21 (1954), 204–228; repr. in revised form in [27].

14] *Naturalism and Ontology* (Reseda, Calif.: Ridgeview Publishing Company, 1979).

18] "Phenomenalism", in H.N. Castañeda (ed.), *Intentionality, Minds, and Perception*, 215–274, (Detroit: Wayne State University Press, 1967); originally printed in [27].

19] "The Adverbial Theory of the Objects of Sensation". *Metaphilosophy*, 6 (1975), 144–160.

20] "Seeing, Sense Impressions, and Sensa: A Reply to Cornman", *Review of Metaphysics*, 24 (1970–1), 391–447.

21] "The Concept of Emergence" (with Paul Meehl), in H. Feigl and M. Scriven (eds.), *Minnesota Studies in the Philosophy of Science*, vol. 1, pp. 239–253 (Minneapolis: University of Minnesota Press, 1956).

22] "Imperatives, Intentions, and the Logic of 'Ought'", *Methodos*, 8 (1956), 228–268.

23] "Actions and Events". *Noûs*, 7 (1973), 179–202; repr. in [25].

24] *Science and Metaphysics: Variations on Kantian Themes* (London: Routledge and Kegan Paul, 1967).

25] *Essays in Philosophy and its History* (Dordrecht: Reidel, 1975).

26] *Philosophical Perspectives* (Springfield, Ill.: Charles Thomas, 1967).

27] *Science, Perception, and Reality* (London: Routledge and Kegan Paul, 1963).

About Wilfrid Sellars
Essays cited

15] Cornman, J. "W. Sellars, Scientific Realism, and Sensa", *Review of Metaphysics*, 23 (1969–70), 417–451.

16] Delaney, C.F., "Sellars' Grain Argument", *Australasian Journal of Philosophy*, 50 (1972), 14–16.

17] Hooker, C.A. "Sellars' Argument for the Inevitability of the Secondary Qualities", *Philosophical Studies*, 32 (1977), 335–348.

Books

Castañeda, H.-N. (ed.), *Action, Knowledge, and Reality: Studies in Honor of Wilfrid Sellars* (Indianapolis: Bobbs-Merrill, 1975).

Delaney, C.F., *et al.*, *The Synoptic Vision* (Notre Dame, Ind.: University of Notre Dame Press, 1977). Contains an exhaustive primary and secondary bibliography through 1975.

Pitt, J.C. (ed.), *The Philosophy of Wilfrid Sellars: Queries and Extensions* (Dordrecht: Reidel, 1978).

8

Ryleans and Outlookers: Wilfrid Sellars on "Mental States"

Wilfrid Sellars' well-known "Myth of Jones", in his classic essay "Empiricism and the Philosophy of Mind",[1] is almost universally cited as the original source of the proposal that such "mental states" as beliefs, desires, intentions, and other "propositional attitudes" should be conceived of on the model of posited theoretical entities.[2] That proposal, in turn, is the keystone of something often called the *"theory" theory* (henceforth, for simplicity, "the T-theory"), although it is frequently not terribly clear just what the commitments of that theory are supposed to be.[3] According to what we might call the *minimal* T-theory, our everyday third-person ascriptions of propositional attitudes involve (implicit) theoretical reasoning in the form of explanatory or predictive inferences from observable public behavior, and, correlatively, our everyday *explanations* of the observable behavior of other persons involve the (implicit) *application* of such a theory. We ascribe (unobservable) mental states on the basis of behavior; we explain and predict behavior by appealing to (posited) mental states, paradigmatically beliefs and desires. A more robust T-theory extends the implicit theoretical stance to first-person self-ascriptions as well. Thus, for example, Ian Ravenscroft writes that

To weaken the grip of the myth of the given [Sellars] presented an alternative myth in which our ancestors, initially limited to a purely behavioristic understanding of action, learned a new theory of action that posits inner episodes as the causes of overt behavior. At first our ancestors only applied the new theory to others, but then they learned to "read" their own mental states off their behavior. In the final stages of the myth they became

---

[1] Reprinted in *Science, Perception and Reality* (Atascadero, CA: Ridgeview Publishing Co., 1963 & 1991), 127–96. Citations, henceforth as "EPM", are to this appearance.

[2] The quotation marks ("scare-quotes") are intended to signal that, in the present context, neither the concept of a mental state nor that of a propositional attitude should be regarded as philosophically unproblematic. The received concepts are loaded with (philosophical) theory in ways that I intend here to thematize and assess rather than simply take for granted.

[3] Nevertheless Sellars is also credited with having originally formulated it. Thus Alvin Goldman: "It is noteworthy that the first statement of the TT ['theory' theory] was in Wilfrid Sellars's paper 'Empiricism and the Philosophy of Mind'", in "Folk Psychology and Mental Concepts", *ProtoSociology*, 14 (2000), 7 n.

adept at mental state self-attribution without theorizing from their behavior; nevertheless the self-attributed states remain the posits of an introduced theory of mind.[4]

On this account, our ability to ascribe beliefs and desires to ourselves is epistemically dependent on our ability to ascribe beliefs and desires to others. Like our other-ascriptions, our self-ascriptions of mental states also apply what remain essentially theoretical concepts, concepts whose *sense* depends on their inferential connections with propositions describing public behavior and behavioral dispositions, but now without our having to infer them (either explicitly or implicitly) from observations of (our own) behavior.[5]

In "Sellars's Ryleans Revisited",[6] Robert Gordon especially takes issue with this last thesis. Our self-reports, he argues, can neither be directly theory-based nor a product of theory-based training. Our (non-evidential) first-person ascriptions of mental states are not, so to speak, "introjected" third-person theoretical descriptions, but rather are directly correlated with their "outward-looking" verbal expressions. One can consequently

answer a question about oneself, and specifically about one's mental states, by answering a question that is not about oneself, nor about mental states at all: an outward-looking question. ... The general idea is, roughly, that to ascribe a belief, desire, intention, or other mental state to ourselves in a reasonably reliable way, all we need is the ability to *express* the belief, desire, intention, and so forth. (SRR, 111)

Thus to determine, for example, whether I *believe* that it is raining outside, I simply ask myself whether it *is* raining outside. My readiness to assert that I do or don't believe that it is raining tracks with my inclination to give various answers to this "outward-looking" *meteorological* question. Gordon calls this procedure using an "ascent routine", since it answers "a question about a mental state that is about *x* by answering another question pitched at a lower semantic level, a question directly about *x*" (SRR, 111).

Our ascriptions of mental states to others, Gordon proposes, are accomplished in essentially the same way. They are, so to speak, "third-person self-ascriptions", in which we *simulate* another subject, taking into account all the available nonverbal evidence, and then "self-ascribe, using an ascent routine that connects *only*

---

[4] "Folk psychology, as a theory", in *Stanford Encyclopedia of Philosophy*, http://plato.stanford.edu/entries/folkpsych-theory/.

[5] Louise Röska-Hardy's characterization of the T-theory in "Self-Ascription and Simulation Theory" (*ProtoSociology*, 14 (2000), 115–44), includes the much stronger thesis that "we ascribe mental states both to ourselves and to others by means of theory-mediated *inference*" (114; my emphasis), that is, that self-ascriptions "deploy" or "apply" the theory in question by ("tacitly"?) *drawing theoretical conclusions*—presumably from evidence supplied by some sort of (implicit?) "self-observations". It may be that some putative T-theorists have been sufficiently confused to endorse some such thesis, although I'm hard-pressed to think of any plausible candidates. In any case, the thesis does not seem to be any part of what is ostensibly at issue in the criticisms of Sellars' views that I propose to engage here.

[6] In *ProtoSociology*, 14 (2000), 102–14. Cited henceforth as "SRR".

with verbal expression" (SRR, 112). Gordon thus rejects the T-theory in favor of a version of the so-called "simulation theory" (S-theory). He agrees with Sellars that "even the first person use of mental predicates is essentially an intersubjective achievement," but argues that

Sellars locates the intersubjectivity in the wrong place. We don't need other people to tell us what we think. ... Self-reports borrow from the intersubjectivity of the public language itself, the language of "public properties of public objects". ... To regulate our first person reports, we do not require any *new* intersubjective training—none, that is, beyond training in the appropriate ascent routines which teach us how to piggyback on the public language. (SRR, 113)

In what follows, I shall argue that Gordon's dispute with Sellars is ultimately a *Scheinstreit*. As is so often the case in philosophy, what is fundamentally needed is much more careful attention to a variety of important and interrelated *distinctions*: between reason-explanations and causal-explanations; between events or episodes and states or dispositions; and between expressing and reporting. These, I suggest, are distinctions that Gordon either ignores or blurs—in particular, his unexplicated notion of a "mental state" contributes a great deal of fog—but Sellars explicitly attends to all of them, and they are crucial to a proper understanding of both his *and Gordon's* views. Once we properly appreciate the sophistication and complexity of Sellars' philosophical views, that is, we will see that they supply more than enough resources both to respect Gordon's positive insights and to elucidate the linguistic and epistemological phenomena to which Gordon appeals in support of his ostensible alternative. I shall consequently proceed by first offering a detailed account of the relevant bits of Sellars' story, and only then return to Gordon's criticisms and the specific examples and arguments intended to illustrate and support them.

THE MYTH OF JONES IS A THEORY OF THOUGHTS

Despite a widespread conviction to the contrary, Sellars never suggested that beliefs and desires were theoretical entities, and his mythical Jones never postulated any propositional attitudes. What Sellars' Myth of Jones aimed at understanding was not propositional attitudes but *inner episodes*, specifically *thoughts*—"inner episodes which are neither overt behavior nor verbal imagery and which are properly referred to in terms of the vocabulary of intentionality" (EPM §50, 180).

While there is, of course, an idiomatic use of "S thinks that ... " roughly synonymous with "S believes that ... " (and, correlatively, an unfortunate contrived expression "occurrent beliefs" roughly synonymous with "thoughts"), the concepts of thoughts and beliefs come apart so clearly in most contexts that it is often quite surprising to find philosophers failing to differentiate them. The question of what a person believes is a question regarding her opinions, commitments, or convictions. When we wonder, for example, whether a person believes what she has just said, what we want to know is whether she was lying or merely speculating or speaking hypothetically or the like, or whether she is prepared to stand behind her claim, to endorse it and defend or support it. The stand in question is a normative one. Like assertions, beliefs can be warranted or unwarranted, justified or unjustified, and so one can inquire into the cogency of a person's reasons or grounds for believing this or that, and arrive at independent judgments regarding whether the claims to which she is in fact committed are claims to which she is also epistemically entitled. None of this fits the notions of thoughts and thinking.

Thoughts, in contrast, are essentially episodic. Like other episodes, they can have a mode of occurrence: sometimes, for instance, one is struck by a thought; it spontaneously pops into one's mind. One can also try to think of something—the name of one's 9th grade algebra teacher, for example, or a perspicuous new illustration of extensional equivalence—and if one succeeds, one's success is a dateable event. Chaining together sequences of thought-events issues in mental *activities* which are clockable processes, reportable using the continuous tenses: "I was just thinking about Paris (deliberating about whether to order dessert, wondering what will become of Monica, etc.)." None of this fits the notions of beliefs and believing.

In the Cartesian tradition, thoughts are not merely introspectible; they are also, so to speak, "self-disclosing". They present themselves *propria persona*. When a person is thinking this or that, in other words, she knows immediately and non-inferentially *that* she is thinking and *what* she is thinking, and her knowledge of her thoughts is a Rationalist paradigm of knowledge properly so-called, that is, certain, indubitable, and incorrigible knowledge. Any thinking thing, any *res cogitans*, can consequently reliably report her own thoughts. And crucially, as Sellars points out, "the classical scheme includes the idea that semantical discourse about overt verbal performances is to be analyzed in terms of talk about the intentionality of the mental episodes which are 'expressed' by these overt performances" (EPM §50, 180).

Sellars' project with respect to this traditional picture of thoughts in EPM is threefold. The *first* part of the project is to disengage the theme of "privileged access" from the Cartesian dialectic of certainty and incorrigibility, that is, as he puts it, to purge the classical tradition of the confused idea that thought-episodes cannot occur without being known to occur, an idea which he traces to the mistaken assimilation of thoughts to the category of *immediate experiences*, "the same general category as sensations, images, tickles, itches, etc." (EPM §47, 177). What remains of the traditional picture after this step has been taken is

the idea that to each of us belongs a stream of episodes, not themselves immediate experiences, to which we have privileged, but by no means either invariable or infallible, access. These episodes can occur without being "expressed" by overt verbal behavior, although verbal behavior is—in an important sense—their natural fruition. (EPM §47, 178)

And such thought-episodes are also distinct from the verbal imagery which may sometimes accompany them and so enable us to "hear ourselves think". Our "privileged access" to our thoughts, that is, our ability to know what we are thinking, should not be construed as any special sort of perceptual or quasi-perceptual capacity.

The *second* part of Sellars' project is to suggest an alternative to the classical view that "both overt verbal behavior and verbal imagery owe their meaningfulness to the fact that they stand to ... *thoughts* in the unique relation of 'expressing' them" (EPM §47, 177), and so, *inter alia*, to reject the essentially Cartesian thesis, explicitly articulated and advanced by Brentano, that intentionality is the defining characteristic of the mental.[7] On this point, Sellars is plainly committed to a sort of "Copernican revolution". Rather than analyzing semantic discourse about public linguistic episodes in terms of the intentionality of the mental, he advocates "the idea that the categories of intentionality are, at bottom, semantical categories pertaining to overt verbal performances" (EPM §50, 180). Thus he equips "our Rylean ancestors", who lack all mentalistic idioms, that is, the resources to "recognize each other as animals that *think, observe*, and have *feelings* and *sensations*, as we use those terms" (EPM §49, 179), not only with full mastery of subjunctive conditional discourse but also with "the fundamental resources of semantical discourse", for example, the ability to say of verbal productions that "they *mean* thus and so, that they say *that* such and such, that they are true, false, etc." (*loc. cit.*).

As he would later confess, at this point in his philosophical development, Sellars did not have a well worked-out *positive* account of the semantic idioms. The best he could do in EPM was to propose that

the rubric "' ... ' means—" is a linguistic device for conveying the information that a *mentioned* word, [for example,] the word "*rot*", plays the same role in a certain linguistic economy, in this case the linguistic economy of German-speaking peoples, as does the word "red", which [in the assertion "(in German) '*rot*' means *red*"] is not *mentioned* but *used*—used in a unique way; *exhibited*, so to speak—and which occurs "on the right-hand side" of the semantical statement. (EPM §31, 163)

It was only later that Sellars arrived at his mature view, probably best articulated in "Meaning as Functional Classification",[8] that the term occurring "on the right-hand side" of a meaning statement is, in its own way, also being mentioned,[9]

---

[7] As is always the case with Sellars, matters are never quite so simple. For there is *another* traditional Cartesian dialectic, namely, the misguided assimilation of sensations and feelings to thoughts (*cogitationes*), in connection with which Sellars was prepared to distinguish the *mind*-body problem from the *sensorium*-body problem, and, correlatively, to treat intentionality as the mark of inner episodes which are in *this* sense "mental".

[8] "Meaning as Functional Classification (A Perspective on the Relation of Syntax to Semantics)", in *Intentionality, Language and Translation*, J. G. Troyer and S. C. Wheeler, III, eds. (Dordrecht, Holland: D. Reidel Publishing Co., 1974) = *Synthese*, 27 (1974), 417–37, with replies to Daniel Dennett and Hilary Putnam = "Reply", *Synthese*, 27 (1974), 457–66. Cited henceforth as "MFC".

[9] Not that this is so different from the account vaguely glimpsed and sketched in EPM. When the chips are down, after all, mentioning a term *is* just a special way of using it.

along with his notational apparatus of dot- and star-quotes, his analysis of "means" as a specialized form of the copula, his correlative conception of normative-inferential functional roles, his distinction between pattern-governed and rule-governed conduct, and all the other bits of his complex and sophisticated "Verbal Behaviorism," some of which we will need to have a look at later. The rest of what we find in EPM on the topic of "the logic of 'means'", in contrast, is largely negative, rejecting, for example, the classical notion that "means" expresses a relation between a word and a nonverbal entity and the Carnapian notion that the fundamental resources of semantic discourse can be constructed out of purely formal logical primitives.

The Myth of Jones *per se* explicitly enters into Sellars' story in EPM only in connection with the *third* part of his project vis-à-vis the traditional picture of thoughts. For, having rejected both Cartesian self-presentingness for thoughts and classical perceptual or quasi-perceptual models of our knowledge of what we are thinking, Sellars then undertakes to offer an alternative positive account of how the idea of thoughts as "inner episodes which are neither overt behavior nor verbal imagery and which are properly referred to in terms of the vocabulary of intentionality" (EPM §50, 180) could have been *introduced* into such a hypothetical "Rylean" community, and how its members could then *come to have* the sort of (variable and fallible) non-inferential "privileged access" to such inner episodes that we properly take ourselves to have to our own thoughts.

It is specifically to this end that Sellars offers his memorable picture of *thought-episodes* as theoretical posits.

Jones develops a *theory* according to which overt utterances are but the culmination of a process which begins with certain inner episodes. (EPM §56, 186)

The associated *model* for these posited episodes, we are to suppose, is that of the sort of candid spontaneous utterances that our Rylean ancestors understand and characterize in intentional, that is, semantic terms, instances of what Sellars would later call "thinking-out-loud".

In other words, using the language of the model, the theory is to the effect that overt verbal behavior is the culmination of a process which begins with "inner speech". (*loc. cit.*)

The point of this model is that it allows Jones to carry over to the posited episodes, which he elects to call "thoughts", all the semantic-intentional categories applicable to public linguistic performances. The point of its being a *model* is that it leaves the intrinsic character of those episodes indeterminate. In particular, although thought-episodes are not introduced as (neuro-)physiological items, their *being* such items is not ruled out by Jones' theory. Episodes of "inner speech" need not occur in a "mental" substance, separate from the human organism, nor do they require an "inner tongue" or the production of "inner sounds".

After a number of such cautionary remarks regarding Jones' theorizing, Sellars proceeds to the promised dénouement, the re-institution of "privileged access".

[When] Tom, watching Dick, has behavioral evidence which warrants the use of the sentence ... "Dick is thinking 'p'" (or "Dick is thinking that p"), Dick, using the same behavioral evidence, can say in the language of the theory, "I am thinking 'p'" (or "I am thinking that p"). And it now turns out—need it have?—that Dick can be trained to give reasonably reliable self-descriptions, using the language of the theory, without having to observe his overt behavior. Jones brings this about, roughly, by applauding utterances by Dick of "I am thinking that p" when the behavioral evidence strongly supports the theoretical statement "Dick is thinking that p"; and by frowning on utterances of "I am thinking that p", when the evidence does not support this theoretical statement. Our ancestors begin to speak of the privileged access each of us has to our own thoughts. *What began as a language with purely theoretical use has gained a reporting role.* (EPM §59, 189)

What is characteristic of such a reporting role is its immediacy, that is, its non-inferential nature. Thus when Dick reports that he is thinking that p, he is not himself drawing an inference from behavioral evidence, nor is he, so to speak, drawing an inference from "phenomenological" evidence, that is, premises recording an immediate experience or quasi-perceptual awareness of verbal imagery or the like. He is not *inferring* at all. He is, as Sellars five years later stressed in correspondence with Hector-Neri Castañeda,[10] *responding* to a *stimulus* that consists of the mere occurrence of his thought that-*p* itself. Dick's training, in fact, is precisely a case of Skinnerian operant conditioning.

What more is needed to transform such a stimulus–response connection into non-inferential self-knowledge is precisely analogous to what is needed to transform linguistic responses conditioned to sensory stimuli into non-inferential perceptual knowledge, namely, its being a point of entry into a network of normative-inferential connections, that is, into the logical space of having and giving reasons. As Sellars goes on to point out, Dick, having mastered Jones' theory, "is already using 'I have the thought that-*p*' as an expression in a theoretical language which in its turn rests on a rich conceptual structure" (Corr., April 3, 1961, §14).

An essential element of that conceptual structure, Sellars points out, is that "the fact that overt behavior *is* evidence for [thought] episodes *is built into the very logic of these concepts*" (EPM §59, 189). This is the Sellarsian cash-value for Wittgenstein's maxim that inner states stand in need of outer criteria. But the account also supplies a clear sense for the notion that one has *privileged access* to one's own thoughts, "for ... only the person who has a thought that-p can respond to it (in the manner discussed ...) with the thought that he has the thought that-p" (Corr., April 3, 1961, §15).

---

[10] "Correspondence between Hector Castañeda and Wilfrid Sellars on Philosophy of Mind" (henceforth: "Corr."), ed. Andrew Chrucky, letter of April 3, 1961, Sellars to Castañeda, §10–11. Available at the Sellars website: http://www.ditext.com/sellars/.

In a clear sense, then, the topic of the propositional attitudes—belief, desire, and the like—does not figure in the Myth of Jones at all. The attitudes are not what Jones's theory posits, and they are not what he is theorizing about. Indeed, except *per accidens*, the topic of the propositional attitudes as such does not even make it onto the dialectical agenda of EPM in the first place. What is true, however, is that, on Sellars' view, the thought-episodes that Jones's theory is about do play a crucial role in *explaining* and so in *understanding* the attitudes. Indeed, precisely because his account explicitly allows for episodic thoughts, Sellars is able to give subtler and more sophisticated analyses of specific propositional attitudes than almost all his peers.[11] To fully appreciate this, however, we need to take a careful look, in particular, at the attitudes that enter crucially into reason-explanations of human behavior, namely, *belief* and *desire*.

BELIEVING IS BEING DISPOSED TO THINK

There is obviously a close connection between *beliefs* and the thought-episodes posited by Jones's theory. As we have noted, one ordinary idiom effectively *equates* "S thinks that ... " with "S believes that ... ", and, while "What are you thinking?" may be a request for a non-inferential report of an inner episode, the question "What do you think?" normally aims at eliciting a person's opinions or convictions, that is, her beliefs. One traditional view suggests that beliefs stand to thoughts as dispositions to their actualizations, but while Sellars indeed endorses the fundamental insight here, the interconnections between the notions of thought and belief are in fact multidimensional and complex, and, not surprisingly, no one has offered a better mapping of them than Sellars himself. The *locus classicus* is his 1969 essay "Language as Thought and Communication".[12]

The first part of LTC is concerned with the idea that linguistic behavior is a form of rule-governed behavior, a theme that will become increasingly salient when we turn to the relationships between thoughts and action. It is in the second part of the essay, however, that Sellars takes on the topic of belief *per se*, and he opens his discussion (LTC, 102) by offering a first characterization of "the state of believing something" along the lines of the traditional view:

Jones believes that-p = Jones has a settled disposition to think that-p.

Correlatively, the more complicated concept of the *expression* of belief yields, in first approximation, the schema

---

[11] Although it is subtle and sophisticated in rather different ways, Anscombe's extensive exploration of the notion of intention is perhaps a notable exception.

[12] First published in *Philosophy and Phenomenological Research*, 29 (1969), 506–27. repr. as ch. 5, pp. 93–117, of Wilfrid Sellars, *Essays in Philosophy and Its History* (Dordrecht, Holland: D. Reidel Publishing Co., 1974). Citations, as "LTC", are to the latter appearance.

x expresses Jones' belief that-*p* = *x* is a manifestation of Jones' settled disposition to think that-*p*.

As Sellars notes, however, these accounts imply that the primary manifestations of someone's belief that-*p* will be episodes of thinking that-*p*, and it is puzzling to regard the inner episodes of Jones's Myth—it is, by the way, not necessarily the *same* Jones—as making anything *manifest*, that is, observable, perceptible, or overt.

Sellars' strategy at this point is to shift into a self-consciously behavioristic *expository framework* ("Verbal Behaviorism", as he came to call it) and introduce the notion of "thinking-out-loud that-*p*", according to which

> in first approximation, "thinking that-*p*" is, in its most episodic sense, to be equated with "candidly and spontaneously uttering '*p*'", where the person ... who utters "*p*" is doing so *as one who knows the language to which "p" belongs*.[13] (LTC, 104)

Such thinkings-out-loud are not audience-directed social acts, and not everything that, broadly speaking, can be *said* can be thought-out-loud. Indeed, the fact that some *sayings*, for example, explicit performatives, are essentially doings of another sort (i.e., linguistic *actions* such as tellings, promisings, baptizings, and the like) precisely precludes their being thinkings-out-loud. Thinkings-out-loud, are indeed linguistic acts—both in the sense of being actualities and in the sense of being actualizations of dispositions—but they are not themselves actions.[14]

Sellars notes, too, that dispositions are normally actualized only in certain conditions. Litmus paper, for example, has the disposition to turn red, *if put in acid* (LTC, 107). It makes sense to inquire, then, what might analogously condition the actualizations of Jones' settled disposition to think-out-loud that-*p*. The upshot of these two lines of reflection is that the initial rough accounts of belief and its expression evolve into more elaborate methodologically behavioristic versions (LTC, 112):

> Jones believes that-*p* = Jones has a settled disposition to think that-*p*, if the question occurs to him whether-*p*, and, indeed, to think-out-loud that-*p*, unless he is in a keeping-his-thoughts-to-himself frame of mind.

---

[13] The point of the italicized restriction is simply to rule out the "linguistic" dispositions of, for example, parrots and programmed automata.

[14] A slightly more full-dress version of this lynchpin of Sellars' Verbal Behaviorism (VB) occurs in "Meaning as Functional Classification":

According to VB, thinking "that-*p*," where this means "having the thought occur to one that-*p*," has as its *primary* sense *saying* "*p*"; and a *secondary* sense in which it stands for a short term proximate propensity to say "*p*". Propensities tend to be actualized ...; when they are not, we speak of them as, for example, "blocked". The VB I am constructing sees the relevant inhibiting factor which blocks a saying that-*p* as that of not being in a thinking-out-loud frame of mind. (MFC, 418–19)

Here, too, Sellars goes on to stress that the candid spontaneous utterances that qualify as episodes of thinking-out-loud "must not be thought of as linguistic *actions*. More accurately, they must not be construed as *other*-directed or social actions" (MFC, 420).

x is a primary *actualization* of Jones' belief that-*p* → *x* is a thinking that-*p* (and, indeed, a thinking-out-loud that-*p*, unless he is in a keeping-his-thoughts-to-himself frame of mind).

x is a primary *expression* of Jones' belief that-*p* → *x* is a thinking-out-loud that *p*.

The connection between someone's candid spontaneous utterances and her epistemic and justificatory commitments is already implicit in the practice of understanding such instances of "thinking-out-loud" as *context-dependent* actualizations of dispositions to the thought-episodes that they thereby "causally" express. Sellars does not emphasize this dimension of the thought-belief nexus in LTC, but that is largely because other concerns dominate his agenda. In a footnote, he explains that the clause "if the question occurs to him whether-*p*" in the analysis of "Jones believes that-*p*"

can be taken to cover all cases in which, where the alternatives "*p*" and "not *p*" are relevant to his course of thought, he thinks that-*p*, even if the question whether-*p* is not actually raised (LTC, 117 n. 9)

but Sellars does not pause to explore the question of whether all such cases have anything in common. The suggestion seems plausible enough, however, that circumstances in which a choice between the alternatives "*p*" and "not-*p*" become relevant to Jones' line of thought are, in the first instance, typically connected to contexts in which he needs or wants to *take a stand* on the matter, and those are precisely the contexts that elicit Jones' epistemic commitments.

The implications of this account are well worth exploring; however, before doing so, I want to take a quick look at Sellars' interlocking stories regarding two other attitudes, intention and desire.

Sellars is one of the few philosophers who have undertaken to say something useful about, so to speak, the logical form of desire. The *locus classicus* for that discussion is his 1966 essay "Thought and Action".[15] As we might expect, the basic account of desire parallels that of belief. But where belief-states were initially characterized as settled dispositions to "assertoric" thought-episodes, desires are in first approximation characterized as "relatively long-term dispositional intentions" (TA, 117), which in turn, also in first approximation, are themselves identified with *practical* thinkings that something shall be the case, schematized in Sellars' exposition by sentences of the form "Shall[*p*]". This analytic strategy establishes a conceptual connection between desires and *action*, since

intentions imply ... other intentions, and indeed, on those occasions in which practical reasoning reaches its proper conclusion, intentions pertaining to action, and hence, where the time of action is *hic et nunc*, volitions. (TA, 117–18)

Intentions imply other intentions because, although an intention is *more than* a thinking that something will be the case, it *includes* a thinking that something will

---

[15] In Keith Lehrer, ed., *Freedom and Determinism* (New York: Random House, 1966), 105–39. Cited henceforth as "TA".

be the case (TA, 128). Practical inference consequently tracks with theoretical reasoning according to the schema

If p implies q, then Shall[p] implies Shall[q].

A volition, in turn, is a thought-episode of the form "Shall[I will *now* do A]", which functions as what Sellars elsewhere calls a "language exit transition", directly coupling thought and conduct. That is, in normal circumstances (absent paralysis, posthypnotic suggestion, drugs, shackles, and the like), such a volitional thinking is the last "inner" stage of a causal process whose first "outer" stages are the initial stages of one's actually doing A.[16]

EXPRESSING ONE'S BELIEFS IS A FORM OF RULE-GOVERNED BEHAVIOR

There is more to Sellars' accounts of both desires and intentions—we shall see some of it later[17] —but these brief sketches already give us enough to return fruitfully to the central and paradigmatic case of belief. What we have seen is

---

[16] We shall have more to say about these themes later, but this is a good point at which to collate some additional references: Sellars' "Imperatives, Intentions, and the Logic of 'Ought' ", *Methodos*, 8 (1956), 228–68; "Actions and Events", *Noûs*, 7 (1973), 179–202, repr. as ch. 10, pp. 189–213 of *Essays in Philosophy and Its History* (cf. n. 10, above; later citations as "A&E" to this appearance); and "Volitions Reaffirmed", in M. Brand and D. Walton, eds., *Action Theory* (Dordrecht, Holland: D. Reidel Publishing Co., 1976), 47–66.

[17] Well, more about intention, volition, and action. The balance of his story about desires will have to fit into this note.

What complicates the case of desires, Sellars suggests, is "the fact that, in addition to having something to do with action, desires also have something to do with pleasure or satisfaction" (TA, 118). It is tempting, for that reason, to propose something analogous to a bodily need, in particular, an explication of "X desires that-p" along the lines of "X needs to believe that-p", but adopting this strategy threatens to sever the connection already envisioned between desire and action. What is wanted, then, is a way to give an account of desire as a dispositional intention that has a conceptual connection both with satisfaction and with conduct. Sellars' subsequent discussion of the implications of these desiderata is detailed and complex, but we do not need to survey the full range of dialectical subtleties to appreciate that while his final proposal again has the general form of a disposition, it is no longer directly a disposition to thought-episodes as such. Instead he suggests (not yet, in 1966, in the thinking-out-loud idioms of his later more fully developed Verbal Behaviorism) that X desires that-p be understood along the lines of

X is disposed (*ceteris paribus*) to *enjoy* thinking "it shall be the case that-p".

The fact that

X is disposed to enjoy thinking "it shall be the case that-p" implies that X is disposed (*ceteris paribus*) to *think* "it shall be the case that-p",

(i.e., implies that X is disposed to intend that-p), then reestablishes the conceptual connection with action (TA, 123 ff.). And in fact, even this is not *exactly* Sellars' account. He actually identifies "X desires that-p" with "X is disposed to enjoy thinking 'it *is* the case that-p' ", which connects less directly to "X is disposed to think 'it shall be the case that-p' " (i.e., "X is disposed to intend that-p") via "X is disposed to enjoy thinking 'it *will be* the case that-p' " and then "X is disposed to enjoy thinking 'it *shall be* the case that-p' ". But that is rather more nuance than we need today.

that, on Sellars' account, the notions of belief and thought interact along three different dimensions: cause, content, and (contexts of) commitment. To have a belief is, roughly, to be causally disposed to have (episodic) thoughts with a certain content in contexts that elicit one's epistemic (justificatory) commitments. These three dimensions correspond neatly to the threefold ambiguity that Sellars argues attaches to the notion of "*expressing thoughts*". Thus he distinguishes (LTC, 109) an "action" sense of "express", for example,

(1)   Jones expressed *his* thought that-*p* by saying ... ,

in which expressing is something a *person* does, from a "causal" sense of "express",

(2)   Jones' utterance of "*p*" expressed *a* thought that-p,

which in essence reports the fact that Jones' overt behavior is the culmination of a process which began with the occurrence of a particular sort of "inner" thought-episode, and both of these from a "logical" or "semantical" sense of "express", illustrated by

(3)   Jones' utterance of "*p*" expressed *the* thought that-*p*,

where "thought" is used as Frege uses *Gedanke*, that is, as roughly synonymous with "proposition", (1) explicitly concerns commitments; (2), causes; and (3), content.

When a person makes public one of her *beliefs* by "expressing a thought" in sense (1), then, she conveys her epistemic commitment, roughly, to support the presented propositional content by appropriate justificatory appeals when confronted with various sorts of legitimate cognitive challenges. That commitment is characteristically *instantiated* in a suitable conditional disposition to the occurrence of "thoughts" in sense (2), that is, thought-*episodes* (paradigmatically thinkings-out-loud), which, in sense (3), "express" its (propositional) content.

As we have already remarked, Sellars' strategy with respect to the propositional content of thought-episodes (and so of beliefs and desires) has always been to relocate its discussion to a separate theory of meaning. This is not the occasion to explore that theory in detail, but we do need to recall a couple of its major points. Its leading idea is that "to say *what* a person says, or, more generally, to say *what* a kind of utterance says, is to give a functional classification of that utterance" (MFC, 421).

Some of the functions with respect to which utterances are classified are purely intra-linguistic (syntactical). ... Others concern language as a response to sensory stimulation by environmental objects. ... Still others concern the connection of practical thinking with behavior. (MFC, 421)

In the familiar Sellarsian idiom, we have "Language Entry Transitions" (roughly, perceptions), "Intra-linguistic Moves" (that is, inferences, both formal and material), and "Language Exit Transitions" (willed actions) (MFC, 422–4).

All these dimensions of functioning recur at the metalinguistic level in the language in which we respond to verbal behavior, draw inferences about verbal behavior and engage in practical thinking about verbal behavior—i.e., practical thinking-out-loud (or propensities to think-out-loud) about thinking-out-loud (or propensities to think-out-loud). (MFC, 421)

Central to Sellars' story is the thesis that these are all instances of *pattern governed* activity, that is,

behavior which exhibits a pattern, not because it is brought about by the intention that it exhibit this pattern, but because the propensity to emit behavior of the pattern has been selectively reinforced, and the propensity to emit behavior which does not conform to this pattern selectively extinguished. (MFC, 423)

Two points are crucial to understanding this notion. First, "a piece of pattern governed behavior is *as such* not an action (though actions can consist of sequences of pattern governed behavior)", and, second, there can be correctness and incorrectness with respect to it (*loc. cit.*). Pattern governed behavior can thus be a topic of norms, that is, subject to "ought"s, but precisely because an instance of such behavior is not as such an action, these cannot, in the first instance, be norms which specify how someone ought to act, that is, *ought-to-do* norms.

In LTC, therefore, Sellars stresses that a proper understanding of the way in which linguistic behavior is rule-governed turns on an appreciation of the role of rules which specify not what someone ought to do in specific circumstances but how something *ought-to-be*, for example,

X's ought to be in state j, whenever such and such is the case. (LTC, 95)

What is significant about such *rules of criticism* (in contrast to rules of action) is that the "subject-matter subjects" to which the rule applies, the X's, need not themselves be agents, capable of obeying ought-to-do rules, and hence they need not themselves be capable of having the concept of being in state φ or of what it is for this or that to be the case.[18]

The rules governing language entry transitions, language exit transitions, and intra-linguistic moves are in the first instance rules of criticism. Thus the "subject-matter subjects" to which they apply can include merely *potential* language users, that is, language *learners* for whom linguistic ought-to-be's become translated through training (paradigmatically, operant conditioning) into behavioral uniformities. And while

---

[18] Sellars' own useful example is: "Westminster clocks ought to chime on the quarter-hour." Nevertheless, he argues, ought-to-be rules do have an essential connection with rules of action. They imply them. Roughly that X's ought to be in state φ whenever C implies that, *ceteris paribus* and where possible, one ought to bring it about that X's *are* in state φ whenever C, where the latter is an ought-to-do rule which requires that the items to which *it* applies, persons, do have the relevant concepts and recognitional capacities (LTC, 96). Thus the ought-to-be rule regarding Westminster clocks, for instance, implies various ought-to-do rules for agents who *make* or *repair* them.

one isn't a full-fledged member of the linguistic community until one not only *conforms* to linguistic ought-to-be's (and may-be's) by exhibiting the required uniformities, but grasps these ought-to-be's and may-be's themselves (i.e., knows the rules of the language),

having the requisite conception of oneself as an agent subject to rules (both ought-to-be and ought-to-do rules) is nothing different in kind, but rather consists in one's own pattern-governed propensities—themselves originally shaped by learning subject to rules of criticism—to connect linguistic responses to *linguistic* stimuli and to conform to the uniformities pertaining to the use of *practical* language (LTC, 100–1).

REASONED ACTION IS BEHAVIOR CAUSED BY APPROPRIATE THOUGHTS

This account enables Sellars to pass beyond the epiphenomenalist worries that haunt the T-theory's imputations of causal efficacy to intentionally characterized mental states, that is, to give an acceptable account of the way in which specifying a person's *reasons for* an action in terms of beliefs and desires also identifies *causes of* that action. The central point is that the thought-episodes constituting a person's intentions and volitions would not have the intentional content that they do *qua* representations unless they had acquired the causal potencies that they have *qua* events.

Consider the child who is learning to use sentences which, as we say, formulate intentions. ... From the standpoint of non-functional description, it is a matter of learning how to use sentences involving [we shall suppose for simplicity] the *sound* "shall":
>   I shall *now* raise my hand.
Clearly the child has not learned how to use this sound unless he acquires the propensity to raise his hand, *ceteris paribus*, upon uttering (or being disposed to utter) the sound "I shall *now* raise my hand." Given that this propensity has been acquired, a necessary condition has been met for *redescribing* his utterances of the *sound* "____ shall____ " as *saying* of "____ shall____ ." (A& E, 203)

From the expository standpoint of Verbal Behaviorism, the salient modus of saying "I shall ... " is thinking-out-loud "I shall ... " (or having a short-term propensity to do so), and an episodic thought of "I shall *now* raise my hand" (whether out-loud or kept-to-oneself), functionally regarded, thus becomes a *volition*, a willing to raise one's hand.

[The] utterance of the *sound* "I shall now raise my hand" has become, in the relevant circumstances, "the" cause of his raising his hand. Thus described, the connection is conceptually contingent. When redescribed, however, as a *saying* of "I shall now raise my hand," the connection becomes a conceptual one, for it is a conceptual truth that *ceteris paribus* a saying or proximate propensity to say "I shall *now* raise my hand" is followed by a raising of one's hand. (A& E, 204)

The conceptual connection between the volition ["I shall now raise my hand"] and the raising of the hand *pertains to* causality, yet it is not itself the causal connection; for what is conceptually true is *that there is* a causal connection between the volition non-functionally described and the raising of the hand; [analogous to that,] between the presence of [a] red book to one's senses and the saying "Lo, here is a red book" *non-functionally described.* (A&E, 205)

The causal relevance of *beliefs* (dispositions to "is-the-case" thoughts) to action, in turn, is secured through their collaborating, along with practical intentions (dispositions to "shall-be-the-case" thoughts), in supplying additional premises in those series of intra-linguistic moves constituting stretches of practical reasoning that culminate in "shall-now" volitions. The crucial point vis-à-vis epiphenomenalist worries is that the sequentiality of such *inferential* moves is *causal* in precisely the same way, and for precisely the same reasons, that the sequentiality of a volition and the onset of action or an environmental stimulus and an appropriate perceptual response is causal, for rules of inference (both formal and material) are *also* rules of criticism.

[Statements] of the form:

    that-*p* implies that-*q*

are *normative* statements to the effect that, from a logical point of view, thinkings that-*p* ought not to be accompanied by thinkings that-not-*q* and that if a thinking that-*p* is epistemically sound, then it is properly accompanied by a thinking that-*q*. These ought-to-be statements are essential to the practical thinking which shapes the language learning of the young. ... (A& E, 199)

What it significant here is the observation that, where that-*p* implies that-*q*, an epistemically sound thinking that-*p* is properly accompanied by a thinking that-*q*, for this entails that, if a person's inferential behavior has been successfully shaped in accordance with the norm, his thinkings-out-loud that-*p* will have become *ceteris paribus* occasions of subsequent thinkings-out-loud that-*q*. He will have acquired, that is, a standing propensity to think-out-loud that-*q* whenever he thinks-out-loud that-*p*. Thus when he in fact

utters or is disposed to utter the sequence: "*p*", "*q*", where we would not classify his utterances as "*p*" and "*q*" unless the relevant functioning of these utterances was in his repertoire, we could say that *ceteris paribus* the former caused the latter and also that the fact that the former is followed by the latter is an instance of a uniformity *for which the entailment is responsible*—in the sense that persons who accept the entailment statement[19] have followed the norm it formulates in teaching him the language. (A& E, 199)

---

[19] The implication statement "that-*p* implies that-*q*" is clearly what Sellars here intends. His point regarding the causal character of inferential moves is the same in any event, whether the relevant normative principle be a purely formal entailment or a contentive material rule of inference.

The fact that a ceteris paribus causal relationship between (manifested or covert) thinkings of one sort (e.g., that-*p*) and thinkings of another (e.g., that-*q*) exists *because* language-users subscribe to the ought-to-be norms formulated by the relevant (formal or material) principles of implication is what separates such inferential thought-sequences from mere associations. And, in the last analysis, Sellars concludes, it is because inferential relationships are in this way *per se* causal, that is, "because practical premises can be the *causes* of practical conclusions, that reasons can be *causes* of actions" (A& E, 205).

GORDON VISITS THE OUTLOOKERS—AND MEETS RYLEANS AFTER ALL

With this rather telegraphic survey of relevant aspects of Sellars' philosophy in hand, we are finally in a position fruitfully to explore Gordon's essay. After his own (basically accurate) short summary of Sellars' Myth of Jones, Gordon proceeds to offer a what he calls a brief myth of his own, a description of his visit to the "Outlookers", so called "because they are always looking outward to the world, never inward to the mind of the agent" (SRR, 105).

> We are tracking across the savanna, lots of excited talk. After ten minutes, the leader makes a sharp turn, and we all follow. I ask one of them, *Why did she turn this way?* My Rylean does not seem puzzled by the question. He replies: *This is the way to the mounds.* Testing further, I ask, *But why is she leading you to the mounds?* The answer: *They are the termite mounds!* I persist: *What is special about the termite mounds?* A few others overhear me. They turn around in surprise. *That is where we can get termites! For you, our honored guest!* Rudely I ask: *What is so special about termites?* They look at one another and break out in general laughter. The leader walks over to me with a solicitous smile and says, *It is the way they taste, of course. Nothing else in the whole wide world ... nothing has a more pleasant taste! That is why we are laughing.* (SRR, 104–5)

"Ryleans they were not," Gordon concludes. "Although they never referred to mental states or episodes, they gave appropriate explanations of action—causal explanations, it would seem, in terms of the reasons for which the actions were performed—though strictly in terms of public properties of public objects ... " (SRR, 105).

This passage gives us quite a bit to discuss. Gordon, for instance, speaks of "testing" the Outlookers. *What* he is testing, he tells us, is their ability to "explain human behavior" (SRR, 104), and his proximate conclusion is that they are able to explain it quite well—indeed, to explain it causally. But what bits of Outlooker behavior does Gordon have in mind, and how are the causal explanations supposed to run? It seems clear, for example, that the Outlookers offer no explanations at all of their *verbal* behavior. The leader does make an explanatory remark regarding the group's *laughter*, but it is difficult to understand what her explanation is supposed to be. Taken at face value, what she *says* is that her companions are laughing because termites taste good, but, on the face of it, that can hardly be a *causal* explanation. Perhaps the pleasant taste of termites *per se* does, on occasion, causally evoke episodes of laughter, but on this occasion no termites are actually being eaten. Of course, the Outlookers' *anticipation* of the delectable taste of termites might also causally evoke a bout of laughter, but that is precisely the sort of explanation that, by stipulation, they are *not* in a position to give. The proximate *public* occasion of the group's laughter, in fact, is evidently Gordon's *question*, "What is so special about termites?" but, absent a good deal of additional information, it is hard to see how the question explains the laughter.

The most salient instance of human behavior in Gordon's scenario, however, is clearly the leader's making a sharp turn, and Gordon apparently does "test" the Outlookers' ability to explain that bit of behavior by asking "Why did she turn this way?" In this case, there does not seem to be any problem in understanding his informant's reply, "This is the way to the mounds," as an *explanation*, specifically, as giving the leader's *reason* for turning in the direction she did. What remains difficult to understand, however, is how (and why) to interpret the reply as a *causal* explanation.

Gordon insists that the primary form of a *reason* explanation locates the *explanans* "out in the world".

> Not only the direction of the mounds, but also the taste of termites, and the pleasantness of that taste, resides in the world, unless one must for some special reason locate the cause in the agent. (SSR, 106)

We revert to a "mentalistic" idiom, he suggests, for example, "She turned this way because she thinks it is the way to the mounds," only

> under special conditions, for example, if we ourselves don't agree that it is the way. ... [Where] there is a choice between "because p" and "because she thinks (or: believes) that p," it is the former, the factive form, that is the *standard* or *default* form of explanation. It is the form that is used unless one has some reason not to use it. The relatively noncommittal "because she thinks" form accordingly caries a conversational implicature to the effect that one does have some reason not to make the stronger commitment implicit in the factive form. (SRR, 105)

But if that is right, then what properly count as reasons are plainly ontologically ill-suited to function as causes. On the face of it, *that this is the way to the mounds* and *that termites have a pleasant taste* are facts (or states of affairs), but what is wanted as a proximate cause of a particular bit of behavior must surely itself be a dateable event or occurrence that precedes it.

This observation relates directly to the ambivalence in Gordon's text regarding whether or not his Outlookers are also Sellarsian Ryleans, that is, to the fact that he both explicitly refers to one of his informants as "my Rylean" and also explicitly concludes that "Ryleans they were not." But why not? Like

Sellars' Ryleans, the Outlookers *ex hypothesi* have "a vocabulary limited to public properties of public objects and … no conception of an inner mental life" (SRR, 104), and although Gordon makes no determinate representations regarding their command of logical operations, subjunctive conditionals, and dispositional concepts, he also gives us no reason to suppose that they are deficient in these and other relevant respects. Why, then, does Gordon conclude that his Outlookers are *not* Sellarsian Ryleans?

The answer is that, as Gordon sees it, Sellars' Ryleans "carry a much heavier burden than the restriction to a public language".

They are restricted to a much more austere idiom, which eschews not only causal explanations of human action in terms of mental states and episodes, but also causal explanations of human action in terms of reasons like, "it is the way to the mounds," which make no mention of mental states and events. (SRR, 105–6)

That is why, "unlike Sellars' Rylean ancestors, [the Outlookers] seemed in no need of a Jones to teach them how to explain behavior" (SRR, 105). But if, as I have just suggested, paradigmatic explanations of human actions in terms of reasons "out in the world" are not causal explanations to begin with, and if, as Gordon's own exegesis of Sellars has it, what the Ryleans needed was "someone to teach them how human speech and action could be *causally* explained" (SRR, 104; my emphasis), then there is no reason to suppose *either* that Sellars' Ryleans are not *ab initio* in a position to offer *reason* explanations *or* that Gordon's Outlookers don't also need someone to teach them precisely what the Ryleans needed to learn.

In fact, Sellars' account of acting for reasons gives us precisely the distinctions and theses that we need to sort this out. There is, to begin with, no reason to suppose that Sellars' original Ryleans could not have passed Gordon's test just as well as his own Outlookers did and, indeed, in exactly the same way. For what Gordon was testing was plainly his informants' ability to give *reason explanations* of human behavior, and his method, in essence, was to inquire into their own reasons for their own behavior, that is, to ask them to *express* their relevant beliefs and desires. But to express, for example, the belief that *that is the way to the termite mounds* or the desire *to eat some termites*, all that a Rylean needs to be able to do is to *think-out-loud* "That is the way to the termite mounds" or "Shall[I will eat some termites]," and, since thinking-out-loud is a bit of public verbal behavior, such reason-giving clearly falls within their competences.

Sellars, in fact, arguably envisions his Ryleans as typically *not* being in a keeping-one's-thoughts-to-oneself frame of mind, and so as characteristically accompanying most of their intelligent behavior by the appropriate public practical-reasoning-out-loud:

Shall [We will eat some tasty termites]
One can eat termites only at the termite mounds
That is the way to the termite mounds
Ergo: Shall [We will *now* go that way]

Jones develops his theory of thoughts precisely to deal with those occasions on which his peers *are* in a keeping-one's-thoughts-to-oneself frame of mind, that is,

to account for the fact that his fellow men behave intelligently not only when their conduct is threaded on a string of overt verbal episodes—that is to say, as *we* would put it, when they "think out loud"—but also when no detectable verbal output is present. (EPM §56, 186)

What Gordon sees correctly is that the ability to give reasons requires only the ability to *express* beliefs and desires, and that expressing beliefs or desires no more requires *mentioning* beliefs or desires than drawing conclusions requires mentioning rules of inference. But what he crucially fails to see is that, *absent a mediating theory of thought-episodes*, there is nothing either *mental* or *causal* about such reason explanations. Thus, since their cognitive repertoire includes a suitable semantic meta-language, nothing precludes Sellars' Ryleans' having an active command not only of a concept of someone's thinking-out-loud that *p*, but also of a correlative proto-concept of someone's believing that *p* (call it "R-believing") as his having a settled disposition to think-out-loud that *p* in situations (including contexts of practical reasoning) where his epistemic commitments are relevant—although, of course, not yet having the concept of a *thought*, they couldn't and wouldn't *call* it "thinking-out-loud".

Gordon concedes that the success of the Outlookers in understanding and explaining each other's behavior "is bound to be fragile".

[If] one is privy to information another lacks, the two may find one another's behavior beyond explanation. That is why we, at least, find it useful to speak *also*, when the need arises, of the mental causes of action. (SRR, 106)

And he cites approvingly Jane Heal's thesis that

the capacity to think about the thoughts of others is just an extension of the capacity to think about the objects of these thoughts, their subject matter, "together with some extra sophistication." That is, "the capacity to think about thoughts must be seen as an extension of the capacity to think about their objects."[20] (SRR, 106)

Quite right—but there is surely no disagreement here with Sellars. On his account, "the capacity to think about thought", that is, about thought-*episodes*, is an extension of "the capacity to think about their objects" in precisely the same sense that the capacity to talk about *utterances* is an extension of the capacity to *produce* them, that is, of the capacity to *say things*. What comes first in the order of *understanding* are episodes of "candidly and spontaneously uttering '*p*'", that is, what Sellars calls instances of *thinking-out-loud about the world*. Then

---

[20] Gordon gives no source for these *prima facie* citations, but there are contextual reasons to conclude that they derive from Jane Heal, "Understanding Other Minds from the Inside", *Proto Sociology*, 14 (2000). [Also in A. O'Hear, ed., *Current Issues in the Philosophy of Mind* (Cambridge: Cambridge University Press, 1998), 83–99.]

comes the ability to mention and semantically classify such utterance-events as instances of *saying that-p* and to treat them as actualizations of an R-belief, that is, a correlative standing disposition that causally instantiates one of the speaker's epistemic commitments. All of this falls explicitly within the competence of our Rylean ancestors. Only then is Jones in a position to apply such semantic categories *analogically* in elucidating the *model* for the thought-episodes posited by his explanatory theory, that is, in the (contrived, theoretical) context "*thought that-p*". Finally, only after Jones' theory is in hand, can *anyone* be in the position to introduce the notion of someone's being in a "keeping-his-thoughts-to-himself" frame of mind, to *redescribe* the original candid and spontaneous utterances *as* "thinkings-out-loud", and to generalize the proto-concept of an R-belief to that of a belief as a standing disposition to *think*, either out-loud or to-oneself.

But none of this is incompatible with the Sellarsian thesis that thought-episodes are prior in the order of *explanation*, and so in the order of *being*. If Jones' theory is a *good* one, that is, it gives us a good reason to conclude that people in general—including Ryleans and Outlookers—are and always have been thinking, and that *all* their intelligent behavior—including in particular their verbal behavior—is and always has been *causally* occasioned by the occurrence of appropriate thought-episodes.[21] And if Jones' theory is a good one, it also gives us a good reason to speak of the propositional attitudes (e.g., belief and desire) as "mental states", since they are then, in the (ontologically) first instance, conditional dispositions to have various sorts of *thoughts* ("is"-thoughts or "shall"-thoughts).

MOORE'S PARADOX REFLECTS ONLY THE DIFFERENCE BETWEEN EXPRESSING AND REPORTING

Gordon, however, is convinced that Jones' theory cannot be a good one. While he expresses sympathy with Sellars' thesis that privileged access to the truth about one's own thoughts does not require that one be (quasi-)perceptually aware either of them or of one's own behavior, he argues that "Sellars' account will not do".

If something like it were true, then we would not talk the way we do about our own mental states. The problem is easily illustrated for the ascription of beliefs and thoughts. (SSR, 109)

What immediately follows in Gordon's text are two examples of *Moore's paradox*—"It is raining, but I don't believe it is"; "I believe it is raining, but it is

---

[21] This, of course, is an expression of Sellars' well-known "scientific realism". I subscribe to such scientific realism myself and have explicitly defended it on other occasions, but since it is not a thesis that Gordon either criticizes or denies, I will here simply take it for granted.

not"—and then, a bit later (SRR, 111), parallel examples for other "mental states", for example, fear, delight, and enjoyment. What is paradoxical about such conjunctions is that, despite the fact that neither is formally inconsistent, to *assert* either "would be self-stultifying, as the asserting it conversationally defeats what is being asserted" (SRR, 109). But Sellars' account of how we could come to be in a position to report our own mental states, argues Gordon, cannot account for this pervasive feature of our discourse about them.

Now suppose you have received Jones's theory-based training in the use of "I believe" in self-reports. Now, you use the "I believe that p" form only when the behavioral evidence strongly supports the theoretical statement that you have the belief in question. Consider, "It is raining, but I don't believe it is." The first clause is a *weather* report, the second clause is a *self*-report. If we accept Sellars's account, there should be no reason to expect the two always to correspond.[22] The weather report requires only training in the public language. The self-report, however, is guided by the special theory-based training you received for giving such reports. Such training is based on your behavior, both verbal and non-verbal. Part of the behavioral evidence … may be outweighed by other behavioral evidence. … So there are liable to be occasions on which you might justifiably and without inconsistency say, for example, "It is raining, but I don't believe it is." Likewise, there should be no appearance of inconsistency if you say, "I believe it is raining, but it is not." For the two clauses concern two quite different topics. (SRR, 110)

By now it should be obvious that the *first* thing we need to say about this argument is that it simply gets the Myth of Jones *wrong*. Jones never trains his peers to report their *beliefs*. Jones' theory doesn't say anything at all about beliefs. Jones trains his peers to report their episodic *thoughts*, that is, to respond to the occurrence of a thought that-*p* with the meta-thought *that* one is thinking that-*p*, a meta-thought which, if one is not in a keeping-one's-thoughts-to-oneself frame of mind, takes the form of a meta-thought-*out-loud*, viz., a candid and spontaneous utterance of "I am thinking that-*p*".[23]
Now Gordon in fact argues that

the same problem occurs with reports that one is *currently thinking that p*, as distinguished from reports of a standing belief that p; thus, with reports of … episodes rather than states. Consider, "It is raining, but I am not thinking it is," and "I am thinking that it is raining, but it is not." Unless "thinking" is merely *entertaining* a thought, you will hear these as pragmatically inconsistent. (SSR, 109–10)

---

[22] Gordon's exposition here has gone awry. What he presumably has in mind is the correspondence that we expect to find between a person's reports that it is raining and her reports that she *does* believe that it is. The Moore-paradoxical conjunction that he mentions precisely puts together a weather report and a self-report that we *don't* expect to be correlated.

[23] There is arguably a small problem about *simultaneity* here. Since the meta-thought in question is causally occasioned by the thought that-*p*, it must presumably, however briefly, succeed the thought that-*p*, and so, strictly speaking, have something like the form "I *was just now* thinking that-*p*." Apart from this note, however, I shall continue to ignore such nuances.

I rather suspect that these examples are actually too odd to evoke any coherent linguistic intuitions, but let us nevertheless try our hand at analyzing them. One way to begin is by making both the content of the thought-episodes ostensibly being reported and their putative episodic character more explicit, thus: "It is raining, but I am not (here and now) thinking that it is raining"; "I am (here and now) thinking that it is raining, but it is not raining". On Sellars' mature Verbal Behaviorist account, such reports, candidly and spontaneously uttered, are themselves instances of thinking-out-loud, that is, *public* thought-episodes. The first example conjoins an instance of thinking-out-loud that it is raining with an instance of thinking-out-loud that the subject is not (then and there) thinking that it is raining. Since an instance of thinking-out-loud that it is raining is an instance of thinking that it is raining, the first conjunct straightforwardly falsifies the second, and thus the conjunction as a whole is "self-stultifying" and false.

The second example conjoins an instance of thinking-out-loud that the subject is (then and there) thinking that it is raining with an instance of thinking-out-loud that it is not raining. The first conjunct is a meta-thought, attributing to the subject a thought with the content *it is raining*, and so not itself an instance of thinking that it is raining. The second conjunct is an instance of thinking that it is *not* raining, and so also not an instance of thinking that it is raining. But the first and second conjuncts together exhaust everything that the subject is then and there thinking. Since neither conjunct is a thought with the content *it is raining*, the first conjunct is false, and thus the conjunction as a whole is "self-stultifying" and false.

Now what theoretically justifies treating candid spontaneous *saying* as instances of public *thinking* in this way, in the interest of philosophical expository clarity, is precisely the Jonesean thesis that *all* intelligent behavior is causally occasioned by the occurrence of appropriate thoughts, and so, in particular, that all such instances of significant public *verbal* behavior are proximately caused by the occurrence of content-corresponding "inner" thought-episodes. In other words, Sellars' account is not just *compatible* with acknowledging the "pragmatic inconsistency" of "paradoxical" conjunctions which include continuous-present-tensed reports of current thought-episodes. Taking Sellars' account seriously actually enables us to *locate* and *explain* the "self-stultifying" character of such claims: They are, as we have just seen, instances of *self-referential self-falsification*.

But, perhaps surprisingly, none of this has any direct application to Moore-paradoxical conjunctions formulated in terms of *propositional attitudes*, for example, believing. What is operative there is fundamentally the distinction between *expressing* an epistemic commitment and *reporting* an epistemic commitment, and here Gordon's own "ascent routines" turn out to be very much to the point. In the first instance, one's epistemic commitments are expressed by what one is disposed to *affirm*, and so one straightforward way of discovering whether one is (oneself) epistemically committed to *p* is by, as it were, asking oneself *whether p*, and noting what one is inclined to answer. But that is precisely what we should expect given *Sellars'* account of belief. On that account, one's epistemic commitments are causally instantiated in certain *contextual dispositions to think*, and one way for a person to discover whether she has a standing disposition to think that *p* in contexts in which her epistemic commitments are relevant is to *put herself* into such a context and observe what disposition is *actualized*, that is, see whether she then and there in fact *does* think that *p*.

But this obviously requires that the subject has *access* to her episodic thoughts, that is, that she is able on such occasions to *know* what she is then and there thinking. The very possibility of Gordon's ascent routines for *propositional attitudes*, in other words, depends upon a person's having precisely to sort of "privileged access" to at least some of her own *thoughts* whose (non-Cartesian) possibility Sellars' Myth of Jones aims to secure. In short, if Jones' theory is a good one, it also explains why and how Gordon's ascent routines *work*. It is precisely because they *actualize* and *manifest* the dispositions to think that causally instantiate my pertinent epistemic commitments, that we expect my candid weather reports, for example, "It is raining", to correspond to my self-reports regarding my meteorological convictions, for example, "I believe that it is raining".

As we have seen, Gordon observes that we employ explicit "mentalistic" idioms, that is, mention propositional attitudes, in our third-person reason-explanations of behavior only when there is some reason to depart from the standard or default factive form. We say "because she believes that *p*" when we ourselves are not fully convinced that *p*, that is, when we would be reluctant to express our own epistemic commitments by straightforwardly and unconditionally affirming or asserting that *p*. What we now need to notice is that essentially the same situation holds with respect to *first-person* uses of "mentalistic" idioms. I employ the expression "I believe that *p*" primarily in circumstances in which, although I am indeed *inclined* to endorse the proposition that *p*, I am not prepared to do so straightforwardly and unconditionally. I have at least some reason to suspect that I may be mistaken about *p*, and so my degree of conviction falls short of complete certitude. Rather than *expressing* an unqualified disposition to think that *p* by simply affirming that *p*, then, I *report* my more tentative disposition to think that *p* in an idiom that allows me, if I wish, to communicate my degree of conviction in more detail, for example, "I firmly believe … ," "I believe … , but not very strongly," and so on.[24] Unqualified assertions, not embedded in the matrix "I believe that … ," can then be reserved for expressing unqualified conviction or certitude.[25]

---

[24] At some point along the spectrum between certitude and doubt, even "I believe … " conveys too strong an epistemic conviction and, correlatively, too strong an inclination to think. Then we revert to propositional-attitude idioms specially tailored for such situations, for example, "I surmise … ", "I suspect … ", "I conjecture … ", etc.

[25] Parenthetically, we also have a propositional-attitude idiom for *reporting* the sort of epistemic confidence or certitude that is expressed by bare unqualified assertions. That's one of the fundamental jobs of "know".

This difference between *expressing* and *reporting* is what explains the "pragmatic inconsistency" of Moore-paradoxical sentences. My asserting "*p*, but I don't believe that *p*" would be "self-stultifying" because my asserting the first conjunct would express my unqualified epistemic commitment to the proposition that *p*, while the second conjunct disclaims any degree of epistemic commitment to that same proposition, and thus my asserting it would express the absence of such a commitment. The conjunction as a whole is thus "*expressively* inconsistent". Although it can be true—in the sense that it can both be true that *p* and true *of me* that I don't believe that *p*—the proposition is not one that I can coherently assert. The point stands out even more clearly in connection with other propositional attitudes, for example, "I intend to do A, but I won't do it". The first conjunct reports, and my asserting it would thereby express, my intention to do A, while my asserting the second conjunct would express my intention *not* to perform the same action.

The upshot, however, is that Moore's paradox has no critical implications at all with respect to either the (quasi-)theoretical conception of thought-episodes embodied in the Myth of Jones or Sellars' account of the propositional attitudes in terms of dispositions to think. For *this* distinction between expressing and reporting already applies to the R-beliefs of Ryleans. "It is raining, but I don't (R-)believe it" is just as "self-stultifying" when uttered by one of our Rylean ancestors as it is when uttered by one of us, and for just the same reasons. For the contrast between expressing and reporting an *epistemic conviction* is independent of the distinction between the respective Rylean and Jonesean conceptions of the way in which such a conviction is causally instantiated, viz., as a contextual disposition to *candid and spontaneous utterances* or as a contextual disposition to *thought-episodes*.

DÉNOUEMENT: THEORY AND SIMULATION REVISITED

I conclude, then, that none of the considerations adduced by Gordon gives us any reason at all to call into question any aspect of Sellars' account of "mental states", that is, of episodic thoughts and dispositional propositional attitudes. Indeed, Sellars' nuanced and sophisticated story supplies the conceptual and theoretical resources needed to elucidate and explain what is "mental" about reason-explanations, in what way such explanations identify the causes of behavior, how and why Gordon's own "ascent routines" for self-ascriptions of propositional attitudes work, and just what is paradoxical about various forms of Moore's paradox.

There remains only the matter of other-ascriptions. The T-theory and the S-theory are supposed to give different and competing accounts of the epistemology of such ascriptions, but once the conceptual and ontological issues have been sorted out along Sellarsian lines, it becomes surprisingly difficult to find and articulate either the substance of the ostensible dispute or the difference between the putative competitors. If, ontologically speaking, ascribing propositional attitudes to other people ultimately amounts to attributing to them particular dispositions to think, then there is clearly no alternative to relying on behavioral evidence, that is, on what they can be observed to *say* and *do*. The epistemic relationship between such observations and the propositional attitudes that we ascribe to a person on their evidence is basically no different from that between, for example, observations of the behavior of iron filings and the magnetic properties that we ascribe to an object on their evidence. In both cases, we in effect make a fallible explanatory inference that rests on a theoretically secured conceptual connection. For both the fact that overt behavior is evidence for the occurrence of thought-episodes and the fact that the behavior of iron filings is evidence for the presence of magnetic forces are "built into the very logic of these concepts" (EPM §59, 189) by the relevant theories.

On the face of it, however, all this is compatible with the thesis that the *way* in which we "in effect" make such a fallible explanatory inference is by, first, "simulating" the person in question and, then, using a (first-person) "ascent routine". But just what does this mean? How does one "simulate" another person?

Gordon, we noted earlier, characterizes such an other-ascription as a "third-person self-ascription," and, on *one* way of interpreting this notion, there is nothing problematic about it. Suppose, for example, that I notice someone carrying an umbrella. Then one strategy for arriving at an explanation of her behavior is for me to ask myself why *I* might carry an umbrella. In this case, especially if I knew that recent weather reports had been pessimistic and the skies were threatening, the simplest and most plausible answer would be that I would likely do so if I both believed that it was shortly going to rain and wanted to stay dry—and it is then a straightforward procedure to base my (other-)ascriptions of beliefs and desires to the observed umbrella-carrier on those hypothetical self-ascriptions.[26] If that is all there is to "simulation", then the S-theory is basically just a matter of conjectural role-playing and analogical inference and is clearly entirely compatible with the commitments of the T-theory.

But that does not appear to be the way in which *Gordon* thinks about "simulating" another person. In various writings, he speaks of "recentering one's egocentric (or: cognitive) map", of "identifying oneself with", "transforming oneself into", or "becoming" the other individual,[27] and what is supposedly characteristic of such a "simulation" is that, after a successful "recentering",

---

[26] Of course, other less simple and less plausible answers are (always) also possible—for example, I might believe that I was in danger of being possessed by a malicious demon and that carrying an umbrella would protect me from that unpleasant and undesirable fate—but, absent further evidence or very special reasons, it would be frivolous to ascribe such idiosyncratic beliefs to any other umbrella-carrier.

[27] Louise Röska-Hardy surveys Gordon's "simulation" idioms in "Self-Ascription and the Simulation Theory", cited in n. 5, above. See p. 133.

"identification", or "transformation," the referent of one's *first-person* pronoun "I" is no longer oneself but rather the person being "simulated".

[Once] a personal *transformation* has been accomplished, there is no remaining task of mentally *transferring* a state from one person to another, no question of *comparing* [the other] to myself. For insofar as I have recentered my egocentric map on [the other], I am not considering what [*I*] *RMG* would do, think, want and feel in the situation. Within the context of the simulation, RMG is out of the picture altogether.[28]

Perhaps this sort of "S-theory" would also be compatible with the basic commitments of the T-theory, and perhaps not—but I submit that Gordon's story does not put us in a position to make any reasonable judgment about the matter. For, as far as I can tell, what we have here is a charming collection of dramatic metaphors, and *only* that. What we unfortunately do not yet have, however, is an intelligible *thesis*. For, however vivid my imagination, when I imagine, for instance, how things look *to her*—wearing rose-colored glasses and facing the other way, over there across the room—I am still *not* her, and things still don't look that way *to me*.

Nor can I understand how such a "simulation" could be an indispensable *first* step in a process culminating in an other-ascription of, for example, beliefs and desires. For if "recentering my cognitive map" on another person requires that I imaginatively "become" her—and, specifically, that I imaginatively "become" someone who believes and desires what *she* believes and desires—then surely I must *first* arrive at some conclusion regarding what it *is* that she believes and desires. For how else could I know *how* and *where* to "recenter my cognitive map"? And if I have already reached a conclusion regarding her beliefs and desires, then any further "recentering" exercise is entirely superfluous.

I conclude, then, that, while there is indeed something to the idea that we ascribe propositional attitudes to others by "simulating" them—for we normally ascribe to others, on the basis of their speech and action, beliefs and desires that would move *us* to speak and act in similar ways—there is nothing useful to be made of Gordon's *fanciful* notion of "simulation" as "recentering", "transformation", or "identification." That, however, is not in the least troublesome. For, once we have learned what Sellars has to teach us about "mental states", it is abundantly clear that we have absolutely no need for it.

---

[28] Robert M. Gordon (RMG), "How to Think about Thinking", in M. Davies and T. Stone, eds., *Mental Simulation* (Oxford: Blackwell, 1995), 56. Cited on p. 133 of Louise Röska-Hardy, *op. cit.*

9

The Place of Color in the Scheme of Things: A Roadmap to Sellars' Carus Lectures

Sellars' views on the Myth of the Given and the ontological status of secondary qualities, one would have thought, are well-known, even if not always well-understood. One would not have expected his Carus Lectures, then, to offer anything radically new and exciting. The ground that they cover is, after all, familiar—from "Empiricism and the Philosophy of Mind" (1956), from "Philosophy and the Scientific Image of Man" (1962), from "The Identity Approach to the Mind-Body Problem" (1965), and from the ensuing debates with Cornman ("Science, Sense Impressions, and Sensa: A Reply to Cornman", 1971) and with Firth ("Givenness and Explanatory Coherence", 1973). One would not really have anticipated many surprises. But one would have been wrong.

Sellars' Carus Lectures, in fact, engender a sense of shock. What has become of "ultimate homogeneity" and the notorious "Grain Argument" over which so much ink has been spilled? Where is the "Strong Principle of Reducibility" which played such a central role in Sellars' reply to Cornman? What are we to make of the new distinction between the mind-body problem and the *sensorium-body problem*? And why has an ontology of "absolute processes"—hitherto always merely mentioned, more or less as a postscript—suddenly assumed such extraordinary prominence, becoming, indeed, the centerpiece of Sellars' lectures and evidently the linchpin upon which their story turns? Is it possible that, after more than twenty years, we had not *yet* quite understood what Sellars was up to all along? ("What have you done with the *real* Wilfrid Sellars?" asked a participant in a symposium at which Sellars presented portions of the Carus Lecture materials.)

Yes, curiously enough, it is possible. It is even possible that *Sellars* has only recently fully understood just what he has been up to for more than twenty years. For while the story Sellars tells in the Carus Lectures is *not*, I think, radically new and different from that told in his earlier works, it is *in* those earlier works, I am tempted to say (Sellarsianly) only as the mature oak tree is in the acorn. One thing which it would be useful to have, then, would be some tools for seeing the acorn in the oak, and that, in fact, is what I intend to provide here. I do not, that is, propose here to engage Sellars' story critically, argumentatively, or evaluatively, but rather to attempt to command a clear view of what his project and his story in fact *are* (and, in the sense indicated, indeed always have been)—a clear view which is a prolegomenon to the sort of critical, argumentative, and evaluative engagement that is the stuff of which fruitful philosophical dialectics are made. I intend, in short, to construct a kind of "road map" to Sellars' Carus Lectures, for I think we *need* a road map—if for nothing else, at least to show us clearly just what and just where the *questions* are with which philosophical encounters with Sellars' story ought now to begin.

The first thing which needs to be said is that we needn't brood overlong on the seemingly-new distinction between the *mind*-body problem and the *sensorium*-body problem. This is just old Sellarsian wine in new terminological bottles. Sellars, that is, has always insisted that the *traditional* "mind-body problem" subdivides into two quite different families of questions corresponding to two kinds of "mental states"—*conceptual* states (e.g., thoughts, beliefs, desires, intentions) and *non*conceptual states (pains, sensations, or, generally, "raw feels"). To put it in Kantian terms, under the rubric "*the* mind-body problem" Sellars has always found two entries: the problem of the understanding and the problem of the sensibility. ("In this connection it should be noted that even if... such things as seeing a color and having an image are not bodily states, the resulting dualism would not as such be a *mind*-body dualism, even though in one sense of 'consciousness' it would be a *consciousness*-body dualism." Thus Sellars in "A Semantical Solution of the Mind-Body Problem", 1953!)

What has happened recently is that a large segment of the philosophical community has caught up with Sellars or, more accurately, with Kant. But they phrase it differently. They speak, for example, of the "deconstruction" of "the Cartesian concept of mind", (Rorty, *Philosophy and the Mirror of Nature*, 1979). In this new idiom, in other words, cognitive states of persons and sensory states of persons are no longer bundled together under the heading "mental states". The heading "mental states", indeed, is simply abandoned—or, more accurately, discarded as fallacious and archaic.

Sellars, however, is a conservationist, and so he meets his colleagues halfway. While he joins them in the "deconstruction of the *Cartesian* concept of mind", he retains, in his own philosophical idiom, *a* concept of mind, now limited, however, to talk about those cognitive or conceptual states of persons the characteristic mark of which is (semantic) *intentionality*. The new Sellarsian "mind-body problem", then, is nothing but the classical project of giving a philosophical account of thoughts, beliefs, intentions, desires, and the like, and the new Sellarsian *sensorium*-body problem is nothing but the complex of puzzles and inquiries left over once this project has been subtracted from the *old* ("deconstructed") "mind-body problem"—a complex of puzzles and inquiries which, as usual, becomes *thematized* in a single question:

(1) What is the place of *color(s)* in the scheme of things?

I have written "a complex of puzzles and inquiries" because, by Sellars' lights, question (1) immediately unpacks into a multiplicity of questions. There are, to begin with, *two* "schemes of things" according to Sellars, one of ancient lineage and the other a relative newcomer which offers itself as a replacement for it, and so (1) subdivides accordingly into

(1A) What is the place of color in the Manifest Image?

and

(1B) What is the place of color in the Scientific Image?

But, second, there are also many ways of *structuring* or *describing* some "image" or "scheme of things", and, accordingly, there will be many sorts of "places" which color might have within such an "image". Sellars is concerned with two of these many. Consequently (1A) again subdivides, into

(1A1) What is the "conceptual place" of color in the Manifest Image (its place in the order of *thinking*)?

(1A2) What is the "ontological place" of color in the Manifest Image (its place in the order of *being*)?

(1B), of course, subdivides in principle analogously as well, but here the story becomes more complicated, for, on Sellars' view, questions of "ontological place" are, in an important way, *methodologically* dependent upon questions of "conceptual place". The "ontological place" of some entity, of course, is specified by indicating the *category* to which that entity belongs. Sellars has argued, however, that a system of categories is not a family of (meta-)empirical *summa genera* but rather a family of generic *meta-conceptual* classifications. A categorial apparatus, on Sellars' view, encodes a taxonomy of the "most generic logical powers" of *conceptual representings*. Roughly, then, to specify an entity's category will be to adumbrate certain logico-semantic features of *representations* which are, as one says, *of* that entity. The ability to answer questions about the "ontological place" of some entity within a given "image" thus presupposes that the "image" itself contains representational resources which *instantiate* those "generic logical powers" which are *indicated* by a correct categorial assignment. To put it crudely, what a correct answer to the question of the "ontological place" of some entity within a given "image" tells us is the "conceptual place" occupied by certain *correct* representings (true representings, if you prefer) within that "image". The ability to *give* a correct answer to the question of "ontological place" thus presupposes that the "image" in view contains the "conceptual place" which *would* be occupied by such correct representings.

What is unique about Sellars' account of the place of color in the Scientific Image is his claim that this Image does *not yet* contain the resources which would be required for such correct representings of color. We can *correctly* answer the question of the "ontological place" of color in the Scientific Image, then, only if we simultaneously (speculatively) envision the introduction of *new* representational resources—and thus of new "conceptual places"—within that Image. And this, indeed, is exactly what Sellars proceeds to do. That is why the second lecture is the linchpin upon which Sellars's story turns. For the "conceptual place" which is needed within the Scientific Image to make possible correct representings of color is precisely the "conceptual place" which would be occupied by *representations of "absolute processes"*. Sellars' second lecture is dedicated precisely to specifying, albeit provisionally and schematically, just what the "most generic logical powers" of representations of "absolute processes" *are*.

Against the background of this understanding of the structure of questions into which Sellars' "sensorium-body problem" unfolds, we can now anticipate the answers which he proposes for his first two leading questions, (1A1) and (1A2), as well. They are, indeed, it turns out, the same answers to these questions which Sellars has, admittedly sometimes obscurely, always given. The basic *concept* of, for example, the color red, "the only available determinate concept in terms of which to grasp the redness which is *somehow* present in ... experience" (I-93),[1] the concept which "must serve as the *fundamentum* from which analogical thinking can form a proto-concept of red which has a *new categorial structure*" (I-93), is the concept of a *stuff*, "a physical stuff, the redness of physical objects in the spatial-temporal-causal order" (I-92). But what colors in the Manifest Image turn out to *be*—that is, what colors are *correctly* represented within the Manifest Image as being—is not stuffs but *states*, specifically, certain sensory states of persons-qua-perceivers. Our task now is to attempt to understand all three of Sellars' answers, and the reasoning by which he arrives at them, in greater detail. I turn next to that task.

What *might* the conceptual place of color—e.g., of red—in the Manifest Image be? That is, what might we take to be the basic concept pertaining to red within the Manifest Image? As Sellars sees it, there are two fundamental alternatives. The basic concept pertaining to red might be, as I shall put it, the concept of an "entity-in-the-world" or that of a "modification of the mind". Call the first sort of view "ontic" and the second sort "noetic". Sellars' view is ontic: "I shall argue that the phenomena are saved by supposing our basic concept pertaining to red to have the form of a mass term, the predicative concept *is red* having the form *is an expanse of red*" (I-46). Sellars does not, however, argue for this ontic view directly. Instead, he develops it in contrast to a noetic alternative which he attributes to Firth and, later, Chisholm: the thesis that our basic concept pertaining to red is the concept of an *experience*—of a kind of experience or (in an adverbialist version) of a manner of experiencing (e.g., "redly").

What is to dictate a choice between ontic and noetic views? What are "the phenomena" which must be "saved"? I think we can focus on three

---

[1] Sellars' Carus Lectures, "Foundations for a Metaphysics of Pure Process" [FMPP], consist of three essays, each composed of numbered paragraphs. Citations here are by lecture number (I, II, or III) and paragraph number.

such "phenomena" within Sellars' discussion, that is, three *desiderata* for a (philosophical) theory of the "conceptual place" of red:

(a) The account must, first, respect the "basic phenomenological fact" that "when an object looks red to S, and S is, so to speak, 'taken in' ... S has an experience which is intrinsically like that of seeing that object *to be* red" (I-69). That is, the account must provide for an epistemic concept of *seeming to see* (ostensibly seeing) which is prior to the contrastive concepts I *(really) see* and *I (merely) seem to see* [cf. I-158, I-162/3].

(b) Second, the account must respect the epistemically-fundamental distinction between cognitive and non-cognitive states of a perceiving subject, the distinction between "being experienced in the mode of sensing" and "being experienced in the mode of conceptualization" (I-114). That is, the account must provide for a distinction between the manner in which red is involved in a sensation of red and the manner in which red is involved in the perceptual awareness of something (red) *as* (being) red [cf. I-158, I-162/3].

(c) And, third, the account must respect the (phenomenological) "seamlessness" of ostensible physical objects, "i.e., of what there seems to be or what we seem to see". That is, the account must "imply that the perceptual object is not a mixture in which *some* items are experienced in the mode of sensing and *others* in the mode of conceptualization" (I-118).

Sellars' fundamental thesis with respect to the question of the conceptual place of color in the Manifest Image (1A1) is that no *noetic* view can simultaneously satisfy these three desiderata.

The number of possible noetic views, of course, is indefinitely large, and Sellars makes no attempt to canvas them all. But each of the three desiderata serves as a "choice point", a nexus of decision, from which a noetic account may proceed in one of several directions, and, in Lecture I, Sellars does undertake to explore the dialectical structures generated by certain key choices made at such "forks in the road". His method is to supply, and then criticize, a series of interpretations of the noetic accounts offered by Firth and, later, Chisholm which represent the various dialectical choices those philosophers *might* have made at such nexes of decision—"*might* have made", since, on Sellars' view, no such noetic account *can* consistently satisfy the three desiderata and, consequently, any proffered noetic account can maintain the appearance of doing so only by leaving certain important matters significantly blurry and ambiguous.

Here, however, I want to abstract from such expository encounter with specific noetic accounts. Let us, instead, simply consider the primary dialectical structure which is generated by the desiderata themselves. Every noetic answer to question (1A1) departs from the thesis that our *basic* concept pertaining to, say, red is the concept of an experience, an "experience of red". But 'experience of red' is ambiguous. It can be interpreted on the model of '*sensation* of red'—adverting to a nonepistemic, noncognitive "experience"—or on the model of '*thought* of red'—adverting to an epistemic, cognitive "experience". Our second desideratum requires, however, that we come down on one side or another of this dichotomy.

> A taking reveals its distinctive character ... by always being a taking there to be something, a taking something to be somehow, and hence to involve propositional form. The taking expressed by 'this cube of ice' takes something to be a cube of ice. The sensing which accompanies this taking may be *of a cube of pink*, but it is not an awareness of something *as* a cube of pink. (I-158)

On the former model, an "experience of red" will be in *some* sense (if only an adverbial one, cf. I-152/6) an actual *case* of red, whereas on the latter model, *red* will be present in an "experience of red" only as "believed in", the sort of "intentional inexistence" which does not imply the existence of *any* actual cases of red, any more than thoughts of centaurs imply the actuality of centaurs (cf. I-162/3).

Now, according to our first desideratum, central to the phenomenology of perception is an "experience" which *is* epistemic or cognitive— "seeming to see" or "ostensibly seeing" an object *to be* red. There are, in other words, ostensible perceptual *takings*, and such takings are ostensibly *of* (perceptual) objects *as*, e.g., variously colored *and* variously shaped. Any noetic account must therefore provide for "experiences" which can found such ostensible *perceptual* acts as, e.g., seeming to see (there to be) a blue triangle. And these "experiences", in turn, cannot be bare "experiences of blue" somehow adjoined to bare "experiences of triangles" but must rather be experiences of *blue triangles* in which "the blue and the triangle are seamlessly joined and in the same ontological boat" (I-164).

Our third desideratum, that is, now comes into play. Viewed in the light of the dichotomous choice imposed by the second desideratum, we see that a noetic account must hold *either* that when one has an "experience of a blue triangle" there is an actual case of a blue triangle—and, what is more, that the fundamental concept pertaining to *triangles* is, like that pertaining to blue, the concept of a kind of experience or manner of experiencing—*or* that blue and triangularity are both present in an "experience of a blue triangle" only as "believed in"—and thus that there may not be any *actual* cases of blue or triangularity at all (I-167). Neither choice, argues Sellars, is philosophically stable.

The former ("ontological") alternative requires the paradoxical conclusion that some experiences are not only *actually* triangular (which does not trouble Sellars, provided that 'triangular' be understood as predicated derivatively and analogically—cf. I-165), but indeed *literally* triangular—and even Descartes was clear that a "modification of the mind" could not in any *literal* sense have a shape. For if the first and most fundamental concept pertaining to triangles is the concept of an *experience*, of a triangular "modification of the mind", then the concept of a triangular object *in space* must be derived from *it*. It will, in consequence, be "modifications of mind" which literally and primarily answer to the axiomatics of a spatial geometry, and objects conceived as actually *being* in space must be thought as answering to this axiomatics only secondarily and by analogy. This conclusion Sellars regards as prima facie absurd.

The alternative, we have seen, is to hold that triangularity is present in an "experience of a blue triangle" only as "believed in"—in a traditional terminology, that space (and *a fortiori* any object experienced as in space) is "transcendentally ideal". But this ("intentional") alternative does not fare any better than the first ("ontological") gambit. For our third desideratum (of "seamlessness") requires then the conclusion that blue, too, is "transcendentally ideal", that is, that blue, too, exists in an "experience of a blue triangle" only as "believed in", and thus that there might not be any *actual* cases of blue at all. And not only does this conclusion lead fairly directly to "the 'coal pit' of skepticism" (I-110), but an analogous reasoning seems to generate the consequence that there might even be "experiences of *pain*" in the absence of any actual cases of pain (I-167). That is again, however, a prima facie absurdity.

What Sellars concludes from this line of reasoning is, as we have already remarked, that *no* noetic alternative can simultaneously satisfy the three philosophical desiderata for an account of the conceptual place of color in the Manifest Image. His own account, accordingly, is not noetic but ontic. The basic concept pertaining to red—our "ur-concept" of red—has "the form of a mass term, the predicative concept *is red* having the form *is an expanse of red*" (I-46). More generally, the ur-concept of red is, on Sellars' view, the concept of a *quantum* of red (an expanse or volume *consisting of* red), and this is not—as he is anxious to stress—the concept of an experience but rather, from the beginning, the concept of a (possible) *object* of experiences.

This ur-concept of red is, indeed, prior to our mature concept of the redness of a physical object. What allows for this priority, however, is not any refinement or sophistication of the ur-concept of red itself but a sophistication or refinement of the concept of a physical object. The *ur*-concept of a physical object, according to Sellars, precisely *is* the concept of such a quantum of color-stuff, thought of as "having properties which individuate *it* and make *it* belong to some thing-kind or other" (I-56, my emphases). Ur-physical objects are Aristotelian "materiate individual substances". "In the child's proto-theory of the world, it is volumes of color stuff which are *objects* by virtue of interacting with *other objects* in specific ways and by so impinging on him that they are responsible for the fact that he comes to see them" (I-57). Our mature concept of an object's being red "in the adjectival sense in which we think of an apple as red although white inside" evolves from this ur-concept by a complication of the concept of an *object* which allows quanta of different colors to be *constituents* of one and the same object, a development fueled by perspectival encounters with opaque objects motivating a distinction between the object one sees and *what one sees of* the object. (Sellars thus regards adjectival predications of color as having, roughly, the logical form of statements to the effect that one simple particular (a color quantum) is an *ingredient* of some complex particular (which, by virtue of its being caught up in a spatio-temporal causal system, *is* a physical object). He has, in fact, always so regarded adjectival predications—although for quite a few years he has scarcely mentioned that fact. (See, however, his "Particulars", 1952, and "On the Logic of Complex Particulars", 1949.)

Our mature concept of a physical object's (really) being red, then, is ontic through and through. It has no *experiential* component at all, but instead is the concept of an individuated quantum of red behaving in "generically stuffy ways" or, more accurately, of such a quantum's belonging as a constituent to an individuated complex of such quanta.

The fundamental *noetic* concept pertaining to redness, on the other hand, is, according to Sellars, the concept of *seeing* such a quantum of red, more precisely, of an awareness of a quantum of red *as* an expanse or volume of red—a concept which, he emphasizes, is "*ab initio* cognitive" (I-49). This ur-concept of seeing an *ur*-physical object then admits of being refined along *two* dimensions. The first of these retains the concept of *seeing* in its basic ("veridical") form—i.e., as a "success word"—while responding to the increasing complexity of the ur-concept of a physical object. Thus, from thinking of himself as (ur-) seeing a quantum of red which *is* a physical object, a maturing perceiver can come to think of himself as (ur-) seeing a quantum of red which is a *constituent of* (e.g., the surface of) a physical object. He thus comes to be equipped with a distinction between (ur-) seeing a physical object (e.g., an uncut watermelon) which *is* red (inside)—i.e., which has a quantum of red as one of its constituents—and (ur-) seeing, as Sellars puts it, "the very redness" of the object (e.g., of a sliced watermelon)—i.e., of an epistemic encounter with that constituent quantum of redness.

On Sellars's view, the family of concepts pertaining to *looking* red is built upon *this* (epistemic) fundamentum by *disconnecting* from the ur-concept of seeing a red object its original implication of veridicality or success. What serves in Sellars' account for

    (1) O (at t) looks red to S,

is

    (2) S (at t) *ostensibly* sees (*seems* to see) O to be red,

where seeing an object *to be* red is understood as entailing seeing "the very redness" of the object, thus, more fully,

    (2′) S (at t) ostensibly sees O to be red and, indeed, *ostensibly* sees (*seems* to see) its very redness.

The concept of ostensibly seeing an object to be red differs from the concept of *seeing* an object to be red not by being the concept of a "more primitive" "awareness of red" into which both veridical seeings and *mere* lookings are to be analyzed, but by being *noncommittal* about whether an experience which *would* be a (veridical) seeing if certain additional conditions were realized (e.g., the object is in fact red and appropriately responsible for the experience) *is* a (veridical) seeing. The constrastive concept "*merely* seems to see" (the converse of "*merely* looks") is then related to this noncommittal concept of ostensibly seeing precisely by entailing the *denial* of the very veridicality or success which the noncommittal concept suspends and which the *fundamental* concept of seeing implies. (And this, too, has been a perennial feature of Sellars' epistemology of perception. See, for example, section 22 of "Empiricism and the Philosophy of Mind".)

What is significant about Sellars's account here is that—in contrast to all noetic options—it puts even the most minimal *experiential* concept pertaining to red, the noncontrastive concept 'looks red', not on the level of 'is red'—as a fundamentum in terms of which ontological concepts pertaining to red are noetically to be analyzed—but on the *epistemic* level of 'is seen to be red'. The concept 'looks red' is thus

... *ab initio* a *cognitive* concept and, indeed, an *epistemic* concept in that broad sense in which a mental state is epistemic or cognitive, even if it is not as such a *knowing* or *cognizing*, provided that the concept of that state is to be analyzed in terms of propositional form and the concepts of truth and falsity. (I-71 n. 5)

The ontic ur-concept of quanta of red (materiate individual substances *consisting* of red) is *basic* in the sense that there is "no ... *determinate* category prior to the concept of red as a physical stuff, as a matter for individuated physical things" (I-84). Although we are free phenomenologically to "bracket" the concept of a quantum of red and thereby to abstract from the specific implications of its being the concept of something physical (its being caught up in a spatio-temporal system of causally interacting entities),

... by so abstracting we do not acquire a concept of red which belongs to a more basic *determinate* category—we simply abstract from such determinate categorial status it has, and construe it merely as a *particular* having *some determinate categorial status or other*. (I-84)

When the dialectical pressures which call for a distinction between *seeing* and *ostensibly seeing* in the first place (cf. I-77) then ultimately lead us to worries about the ontological status of the redness which one (ostensibly) sees when it is *not* the very redness of a physical object—to ask what we are to say about quanta of color stuffs which are *not* constituents of physical objects—we must not suppose that we *already have* some category other than that of the physical to fall back on—and still less that such an alternative categorization can simply be "read off" a phenomenological scrutiny of such quanta in an ontological frame of mind.

All that is available is such transcendentals as *actual, something* and *somehow*. The red is something actual which is *somehow* a portion of red stuff, *somehow* the sort of item which is suited to be part of the content of a physical object, but which, though *somehow* that sort of item, is not, in point of fact, a portion of physical stuff. (I-90)

To suppose otherwise, indeed, is to embrace the "Myth of the Given" in what Sellars calls perhaps its "most basic form", as a principle to the effect that

If a person is directly aware of an item which has categorial status C, then the person is aware of it *as* having categorial status C.

The challenge of accounting for the (categorial) ontological status of quanta of red which are *merely* ostensibly seen, then, can be met only by constructing *new forms of concept* pertaining to color.

Phenomenology nears the end of its descriptive tether when it points out that when we ostensibly see the very redness of an apple, we see an *actually existing* expanse of red which, if circumstances were normal, would be part of the surface of a physical object, and, indeed, part of its very redness.

We acquire new forms of concepts pertaining to colors, then, neither by "reading them off" our phenomenological scrutinizings nor by "throwing away concepts of the colors of physical objects," but by "transposing our concepts into a new key" (I-86). It is the job of "*analogical* thinking" to depart from the fundamentum of our determinate categorial concept of *physical* redness and "form a proto-concept of red which has a *new categorial structure*".

It does this by forming a proto-theory in which items which satisfy an axiomatics of shape and color play roles which promise to account for the fact in question. (I-93)

We have now, of course, arrived at question (1A2): "What is the *ontological* place of color in the Manifest Image?" Consonant with Sellars' "scientific realism", this question of "positive" ontology is to be answered by locating the "conceptual place" of color within the *best explanatory theory* internal to the "image" within which the ontological question is raised. In the present case, the explanatory theory which does the job is the evolved, mature form of the "proto-theory" of perception and perceptual error which we have just mentioned.

This "proto-theory", in fact, is precisely the theory constructed by the mythic genius Jones twenty-five years ago in Sellars' "Empiricism and the Philosophy of Mind". It posits a family of items—Sellars here speaks of them as "quasi-expanses of color stuff" or "quasi-stuffs"—which it proceeds to *characterize* as

... *states of the perceiver* which satisfy an axiomatics of shape and color and which are brought about in standard conditions by physical objects which actually consist of volumes of color stuff and, in nonstandard conditions, by physical objects of other colors, or by bodily states with no external cause. (I-94, my emphasis)

This theory *evolves* under the pressures of

... a tension ... between the idea that the quasi-stuffs are functionally dependent upon the perceiver, among other things, for their determinate character as, for example, a quasi cube of pink stuff, and the idea that in veridical perception what one is directly aware of is, for example, the very pinkness of a pink ice cube. (I-96)

into a mature form which ultimately *abandons* the notion of color quanta as (ontological) constituents of physical objects. While the fundamental concept pertaining to color remains that of such physical color quanta, in other words, ontological status is ultimately granted by the theory only to items characterized in terms of concepts which are *analogical derivatives* of this basic concept. The mature form of the Jonesean proto-theory, as Sellars reconstructs it, holds roughly

... that in perception items which are in point of fact, for example, quasi cubes of pink stuff (of-a-cube-of-pink-stuff states of a perceiver) are conceptualized (i.e., responded to perceptually) as cubes of pink stuff *simpliciter* having the causal properties of ice. (I-97)

The *ontological* place of color in the Manifest Image thus emerges as that of *quasi-stuffs*, i.e., states of a perceiver. What colors, within the Manifest Image, then *are*, in the final analysis, are conscious states of perceivers—states which, however, are systematically *taken* by those perceivers to be "independent existences," color quanta that are constituent ingredients of causally interactive spatio-temporal physical objects. (Cf. III-10/15.)

The evolution of the Jonesean proto-theory into its mature form is simultaneously driven as well, of course, by the complex of explanatory demands and theoretical challenges which lead to the emergence of the Scientific Image as a *global* competitor to the Manifest Image. For, to compress a familiar story, it is a consequence of the ontological authority of successful explanatory theories that what we pre-scientifically conceive of as a pink ice cube *in fact* "consists of molecules of H_2O, along with some molecules of dye stuff" (III-16)—and these, in turn, successively of atoms, of protons, neutrons, and electrons, of quarks, and of ... What we pre-scientifically think of as a pink ice cube, in short, we come to recognize as being ultimately composed of constituents *none* of which is (indeed, none of which *can be*) colored "in the occurrent sense of the term" (III-20).

Given that "scientific realism" is not itself here to be brought into question, Sellars discerns two main lines of reply to this clash of images. He calls them the "Reconciliationist" and the "Cartesian" strategies. The essential difference between reconciliationism and Cartesianism is that between a line of reply which *affirms* the existence of an actual case of *occurrent* pinkness "over there where the ice cube [i.e., the system of molecules] is" and one which *denies* the existence of any *such* case of occurrent color in the spatial world.

Reconciliationist views, in turn, may be either reductive, emergentist, or supervenient. The reductive reconciliationist *identifies* his actual case of occurrent pinkness with a family of (physical) attributes and relations holding among the molecular (or sub-molecular) elements of the system which *is* the (pink) ice cube (III-22, 24). The emergentist reconciliationist, in contrast, views occurrent pinkness as an indefinable "holistic" attribute of this same system, one which, however, is (lawfully) *correlated* with a reducible "complex" attribute definable in terms of the (physical) properties and relations of individual systemic elements (III-22, 26). Finally, the supervenient reconciliationist treats occurrent pinkness as an independent *object* (a cubical volume of pink) occupying the region of space *also* occupied by the ice cube (i.e., the system of molecules) and, once again, a (lawful) *consequence* of the obtaining of (physical) properties and relations among the systemic elements constituting that ice cube (III-29/33).

The fundamental role of Sellars' erstwhile "Strong Principle of Reducibility" was to dislodge the would-be reconciliationist from reductionism and drive him in the direction of emergentism or supervenience. In the Carus Lectures, Sellars simply takes it for granted:

How, we would surely expostulate, can an object's having occurrent pinkness consist in facts about its parts, none of which facts involves occurrent color?! (III-25)

We should not, however, suppose on this account that Sellars has opted for dogmatism where once he attempted to give principled arguments. It is rather that his target is now a different one. Sellars is now after bigger game. He now proposes to offer a *global* critique of reconciliationism *per se*.

What reconciliationist views have in common is their commitment to an actual case of occurrent pinkness—whether *conceived* as a reducible attribute, an emergent attribute, or a supervenient object—*in space*, where the ice cube (system of molecules) is. And what, according to Sellars, is ultimately mistaken about any such view is that—given the explanatory, and thus ontological, triumph of the Jonesean theory—*already in the Manifest Image* there is no actual case of occurrent color in space where the ice cube is, *nor could there be*. To suppose otherwise is to fail to appreciate what *sort* of theory our mythical Jones has (successfully) devised.

For Sellars now proposes to distinguish sharply and explicitly between *two kinds* of explanatory theories (III-36/47). Let us call them "postulational" and "interpretive". The leading feature of a postulational explanatory theory is that it introduces *new domains of entities*. The leading feature of an interpretive explanatory theory, in contrast, is that it does *not*. An interpretive theory instead supplies a family of *new forms of concepts* by means of which what we may refer to in a category-neutral (transcendental) vocabulary as actual *items* or *entities* are re-represented in terms of a new categorial structure.

The key point that is overlooked by the would-be reconciliationist is that the *Jonesean* theory is not postulational but interpretive.

[The] theory of sense impressions does not *introduce*, for example, cubical volumes of pink. It reinterprets the *categorial status* of the cubical volumes of pink of which we are perceptually aware. Conceived in the manifest image as, in standard cases, *constituents* of physical objects and in abnormal cases, as somehow 'unreal' or 'illustory', they are *recategorized* as sensory states of the perceiver and assigned various explanatory roles in the theory of perception. (III-44)

The pinkness of a pink sensation (i.e., of a "quasi-stuff" or state of the perceiver), in consequence,

... is 'analogous' to the pinkness of a manifest pink ice cube, not by being *a different quality* which is in some respects analogous to pinkness ... , but by being the same 'content' in a different categorial 'form'. (III-47)

This is the point which Sellars used to try to make by talking about "ultimate homogeneity"! The "ultimate homogeneity" of a quantum of color (-stuff) is precisely the paradigm of an aspect of the 'content' of an ur-conceptualized color quantum which must be invariantly *carried over* in successive theoretical *transpositions* of that item or entity (to speak in neutral, transcendental terms) from one categorial 'form' to another.

All this looks dramatically new, but what is new here is really only the clarity with which a family of Sellars' views of long standing are now being put. Once sensitized to them, in fact, we can recognize them as having occurred in various guises even in Sellars's very early writings on perception. To cite two examples: Sellars' original strong emphasis (e.g., in §61 of "Empiricism and the Philosophy of Mind") on the fact that Jones's theory does *not* introduce "a class of particulars" was surely *intended* to capture the present distinction between postulational and interpretive theories. And Sellars' lifelong conviction (see, for instance, ch. VI, §59 of *Science and Metaphysics*, 1968) that, as sense-datum theorists have always insisted, it is ultimately impossible to explain perceptual *beliefs* (or thoughts) to the effect that something is or appears to be, say, red without acknowledging the actual existence of something (somehow!) *actually red* (the so-called "Sense-Datum Inference") precisely reflects his standing commitment to an invariant 'content' which must—on pain of explanatory inadequacy—be preserved in various 'forms' across diverse categorial embodiments in diverse theories of perception.

Once we appreciate, then, that the point of *any* form of reconciliationist maneuvering is to find an ontological place for occurrent color *in space*, Sellars argues, we can also appreciate that the reconciliationist enterprise as a whole is fundamentally misguided. For the nerve of the (explanatorily triumphant) Jonesean theory lies in its assertion that the color quanta of which we are perceptually aware *as* in space *are actually* states of persons-qua-perceivers. And so, to the reconciliationist suggestion that "manifest cubes of pink might exist both as objects in physical space *and* as sensory states of perceivers",

the Cartesian need only reply that if the cube of pink of which we are perceptually aware is a *state* of ourselves as perceivers, then neither it nor anything resembling it could be an object in physical space. (III-65)

That is, the "sensory states" of which Jonesean theory speaks are not (postulated) *new* entities—the being-pink of which *needs* to be ontologically reconciled with the actual pinkness of color quanta in space—but rather *those very entities* which we pre-theoretically *took* to be (conceptualized as) spatial volumes of pink, now re-interpreted as items *actually* belonging to an entirely different ontological category, items of which it now no longer *makes sense* to suppose that they might actually be located in physical space.

Sellars, then, is (*mirabile dictu!*) in this sense a Cartesian. Like Descartes, that is, he holds that

the *esse* of cubes of pink is *percipi* or, to use a less ambiguous term, *sentiri*. Of course, ... we are not perceptually aware of cubes of pink *as* states of ourselves, though that is in point of fact what they are. (III-66)

But this position, too, is finally unstable in the context of a global Scientific Realism. The difficulty is that this form of Cartesianism presupposes the *unity* of the person-qua-perceiver as the logical subject of sensory states, and this unity, too, is ultimately challenged and denied by the explanatory march of the Scientific Image. Sooner or later, in short, "we are ... confronted with the idea that persons have actual parts—microphysical particles" (III-74). We are thus compelled to seek yet another categorial re-interpretation for those actual entities which we originally conceived (so long ago, dialectically speaking) as color quanta in space. And this brings us to the final act in Sellars's drama.

In his final lecture, Sellars considers a range of alternative strategies for reconciling the (ontological) complexity of persons within the Scientific Image with their (conceived) unity as perceivers. One of these, "Reductive Materialism", fails on the same grounds as our earlier reconciliationisms. According to reductive materialism,

a person is a complex system of micro-physical particles, and what really goes on when a person senses a-cube-of-pinkly consists in this system of micro-physical particles being in a complex physical-2 state. (III-79)

But, argues Sellars, what we are being offered here "is no longer a recategorization of the original entity, an unproblematic cube of pink, but a recategorization of a supposedly *postulated* entity, a sense impression of a cube of pink" (III-80). And since we are *ab initio* committed to the idea that cubes of pink in *some* categorial guise or other are *actual* items belonging to "the furniture of the world", we have no alternative at this juncture but to dismiss the suggestion of the *reductive* materialist as, in Sellars' word, "absurd".

The difficulty with reductive materialism can be pinpointed by contrasting it with three further alternatives: Cartesian or *Substantial* Dualism, Emergent or *Wholistic* Materialism, and Epiphenomenalism. Unlike reductive materialism, each of these positions does hold that a (Jonesean-theoretical) state, σ, of sensing a-cube-of-pinkly is *itself* something actual. Substantial dualism takes it to be a state of a distinct, noncomposite, non-physical *substance*—"the mind", in the Cartesian idiom, or "the sensorium" in a "deconstructed" (neo-Aristotelian) idiom (III-75/78). Wholistic materialism takes it to be an *emergent* state of the complex physical system which is the person, a state correlated with but *not* reducible to a complex (purely) physical state of that system (III-84/87).

And epiphenomenalism, finally, takes it to be a *"sensum"*, that is, *not* a state of anything at all but a nonphysical, nonmaterial *particular*—an item belonging to a posited second category of *objects*, standing alongside the micro-physical particulars acknowledged by the neuro-physiology of the current Scientific Image (III-88/94).

Like wholistic materialism, reductive materialism aims at being an *object-monism*. That is, it subscribes to the thesis that the only *objects* having ultimate ontological status are "atoms in the void", and thus rejects both substantial "sensoria" and epiphenomenal "sensa". But reductive materialism attempts to go further in proposing that the only actual *items* or *entities* having ultimate ontological status are these "atoms in the void", and thus rejects as well the idea that there can be states of a person which are *not* complex motions of such atoms (although, of course, "lawfully correlated" with such motions). Like epiphenomenalism, that is, reductive materialism also aims at being a *state-monism*. But to thus combine object-monism and state-monism is to deny the ultimate actuality of color quanta in *any* categorial guise—and that ultimate *actuality*, Sellars insists, is a *sine qua non* of any *explanatorily adequate* account of the sensuous content of perceptual experience.

The three alternatives which survive this criticism, Sellars claims, differ "only ontologically", that is, in terms of the *category* into which they reinterpret Jonesean-theoretically-actual sensory states. Viewed epistemologically, however, they all share a fatal flaw: none of them allows sensory items to play an essential *causal* role in the behavior of the bodies of sentient beings. Each of these three philosophical positions, that is, is an instance of "what might be called the epiphenomenalist form":

$$\psi_i \qquad \psi_i \qquad \psi_i$$
$$\uparrow \qquad \uparrow \qquad \uparrow$$
$$\Rightarrow \phi_i \quad \Rightarrow \phi_i \quad \Rightarrow \phi_i$$

For the substantial dualist, the 'ϕ's would represent states of the CNS [central nervous system], the 'ψ's would represent states of the sensorium. For the wholistic materialist, the 'ϕ's would represent physical-2 states of the CNS; the 'ψ's proper sensible states (physical, but not physical-2) of the CNS. The diagram is the same; only the ontology is different. (III-110)

The key feature of the "epiphenomenalist form" is that

... from the standpoint of *explanation*, the basic role is being played by the ϕ-states. For, (a) the ϕ-state laws are autonomous, i.e., stand on their own feet; (b) the ψ-object sequences are themselves explained in terms of ϕ-state laws and ϕ-ψ laws of supervenience. (III-99)

The idea is that the occurrence of a ϕ-state is adequately explained by the occurrence of another, preceding ϕ-state, no reference to the associated ψ-object being necessary.

Thus the only nomologicals to which (in principle) appeal need be made are laws formulated in terms of ϕ-states. (III-97)

These observations bring us, finally, to what *is* in some respects new and exciting in Sellars' Carus Lectures. The "epiphenomenalist form", Sellars proposes, is the historical product of a "scientific ideology"—"the autonomy of the mechanical". The sufficiency of mechanistic variables and an impact paradigm of causation for explanation in the *inorganic* realm "made it difficult to conceive of a mode of causation in which the development of a system of material particles might be influenced by nonmaterial items … ", and this difficulty, in turn, "made it only too tempting to extend the autonomy of mechanical explanation to the bodies of sentient beings".

That the proper sensibles—e.g., shades of color—could function alongside of mechanistic variables in psycho-physical laws in such a way that the mechanical variables by themselves did not constitute a closed system with respect to necessary and sufficient conditions … made no more scientific sense, given the paradigms of the day, than would a Compatibilist attempt to involve the proper sensibles in the laws of motion. (III-102/4)

But while "the autonomy of the mechanical" is thus an historically-understandable idea with a de facto empirical basis, viewed philosophically, it is, in the end, nothing but a metaphysical prejudice. *The point of proposing an ontology of absolute processes is to pass beyond this prejudice.*

Sellars' proposal, in fact, has two steps. The first is that we distinguish sharply between *object-bound* processes—items which are, in a sense explored by Sellars in Lecture II, "logical constructions" out of changes in *things*—and "absolute processes"—which rather would be the ontologically *basic* items of a world that would be "an ongoing tissue of goings on" (II-103). Second, however, we must take seriously the idea that everything which we have heretofore *conceived of* as a things is *itself* a "logical construction" out of such "absolute processes"—including the central nervous system and the items (neurons, molecules, atoms, quarks, …) of which it consists.

Taking the first step alone yields only another variant on the "epiphenomenalist form". The 'ϕ's of our diagram become reinterpreted as standing for *object-bound* physical-2 processes in the CNS (which itself, however, still consists of *things*), and the 'ψ's as standing for sensuous "reddings", "C#-ings", and the like (σ-ings) which, although conceived of as irreducible and ontologically basic "absolute processes", are still thought of as only epiphenomenally *correlated* with the autonomous changes in (equally ontologically basic) *objects*.

But if we take the second step as well and entertain the idea of a *monistic* ontology whose *sole* basic category is that of "absolute processes," we can integrate the σ-ings of sensory consciousness and the (physical-2) ϕ_2-ings of organic (and inorganic) matter into a unitary "image" which is explanatory through and through.

If the particles of micro-physics are patterns of actual and counterfactual ϕ_2-ings, then the categorial (indeed, transcendental) dualism which gives aid and comfort to epiphenomenalism simply *vanishes*. (III-119)

For current well-confirmed psycho-physical theory,

... does not require ... that these ϕ_2-ings be nomologically autonomous.

Nor does it require that neuro-physiological objects which have ϕ_2-ings as constituents have *only* ϕ-ings as constituents. σ-ings could in a legitimate sense be constituents of neuro-physiological objects. (III-122/3)

And "sensings" (σ-ings) would thus be *physical*,

not only in the weak sense of not being mental (i.e., conceptual), for they lack intentionality, but in the richer sense of playing a genuine causal role in the behavior of sentient organisms. They would, as I have used the terms, be physical-1 but not physical-2. Not being epiphenomenal, they would conform to a basic metaphysical intuition: to be is to make a difference. (III-126)

Over twenty-five years ago, Sellars asked, (in §61 of "Empiricism and the Philosophy of Mind"), "What would correspond in a *micro*-theory of sentient organisms to *molar* concepts pertaining to [sense-] impressions?" And he proceeded to speak speculatively about an ideal-scientific world-picture in which

... the theoretical counterparts of sentient organisms are Space-Time worms characterized by two kinds of variables: (a) variables which also characterize the theoretical counterparts of *merely* material objects; (b) variables peculiar to sentient things; and ... these latter variables are the counterparts in this new framework of the perceptible qualities of physical objects of the common sense framework.

And more than twenty years ago (in "Phenomenalism"), Sellars spoke of constructing "a framework alternative to the framework of interacting things" in which "changing things become genidentical patterns of 'events'". And he wrote that

... epiphenomenalism, with its disparate categories of *things* ... and 'phantasms', is a half-way house; ... a unified picture requires a translation of the physiological context in which epiphenomena occur into the framework of 'events'.

It would be, he claimed,

... a category mistake to suppose that sensa can be construed as a dimension of neural process as long as one is working within a framework of thing-like particulars, whether nerve cells, organic compounds, or micro-physical particles ...

However provisionally, in other words, "absolute processes" have been an element of Sellars' account of sensory consciousness from the very beginning.

That the (ideal) Scientific Image locates the ultimate ontological place of color in the category of "absolute processes", then, is not something excitingly new. What *is* new—and, I think, exciting—is Sellars' answer in the Carus Lectures to the inevitable question, "Why?". *Why* can we not solve the sensorium-body problem short of speculatively envisioning in this way a radical interpretive-theoretic recategorization of *all* the items and entities acknowledged by our evolving physics as actual? At last we have Sellars' answer: There is another myth to be broken—the Myth of the Autonomy of the Mechanical, as pernicious in its way as the Myth of the Given.

The point is that the sensorium-body problem will be *solved* just in case we can, in principle, find a place for colors (or, more generally, for "raw feels") among the *actual* items of a Scientific Image which is both *categorially monistic* and *globally explanatorily closed.* As with the question, (1A1), of the conceptual place of color in the Manifest Image, then, there are again *three* criteria against which the adequacy of a proposed solution must be measured—categorial monism, global explanatory closure, and actuality. Substantial dualism and epiphenomenalism both "solve" the sensorium-body problem only by sacrificing the first desideratum to the third. Wholistic materialism achieves a categorial monism, but only at the epistemological price of denying global explanatory closure. And reductive materialism can pretend to both ontological and epistemological adequacy only by flying in the face of the third, phenomenological, desideratum, by denying that sensuous contents in the end have *any* place among those actual items which, for the Scientific Realist (*sub specie Peircii*, as it were), must *be* the ultimate ontological furniture of the world.

A thoroughgoing ontology of absolute processes can in principle pass all three tests. That is Sellars' point. Such a transformed Scientific Image would be categorially monistic—for "absolute process" would be its sole *basic* category. By including sensuous σ-ings among its ultimate actualities, it would respect the demands of an adequate sensory phenomenology. And by insisting that what we pre-theoretically conceive of as sensory consciousness *can* only be accounted for if σ-ings as well as ϕ_2-ings enter *essentially*—as the subjects of genuinely explanatory nomologicals—into the Peircean-theoretical account of those patterns of absolute processes which in the last analysis *are* individual perceivers, it would satisfy the epistemological demand that explanatory closure be global as well—precisely *by* rejecting the myth of the (explanatory) autonomy of the mechanical. Nothing short of such a radically-reconceived, categorially-reinterpreted ontology for psycho-physics could simultaneously satisfy these three requisites of an adequate *solution* to the philosophical problem posed by the challenge of reconciling the phenomenology of sensory consciousness with that "image" which a Scientific Realist must hold is the final arbiter of what is, in the last analysis, *real.* That, at any rate, is Sellars' claim—and has always been his conviction.

It was over *thirty* years ago (in section IX of "Realism and the New Way of Words" (1948), that Sellars first publicly considered—and rejected—what he would *now* call "reductive materialism". He concluded then that what was needed was "some form of dualism"—"either of minds and bodies as *interacting things*, or of different kinds of events taking place in the *same* thing (the emergence form of the identity approach)". And he went on to write,

May I express my (inherited?) predilection for the latter approach, while insisting that emergence has nothing to do with indeterminism or Bergsonian *élan*? Emergence is one form taken by a negative answer to the question: "Could a world which includes minds be described with the same primitive predicates (and laws) as a mindless universe?".

Today, in the Carus Lectures, the answer is still the same, still negative. While sensuous σ-ings would play a genuine *causal* role in the behavior of sentient organisms (i.e., would be physical-1), the nomologicals pertaining to their occurrence would need to specify that they occur *only* "in the context of ϕ_2-ings which belong to patterns of absolute processes which constitute specific kinds of neuro-physiological process" (III-121). They would not, on this account, be required for an adequate explanatory account of a world devoid of sentient organisms (i.e., not be physical-2). The idiom, of course, is much changed. "Different kinds of events in the same thing" have given way to different kinds of "absolute processes"—σ-ings and ϕ_2-ings—and to no "*things*" at all. This, however, I have tried to show, is not because Sellars is now up to anything new. It is rather because even Sellars has only recently fully understood what he has been up to for more than twenty years. Yet what is especially valuable about Sellars' Carus Lectures is not that they finally do make clear *what* he has been up to all along. What is especially valuable, indeed exciting, is that they finally also let us see more clearly *why*.

10

Still Mythic After All Those Years: On Alston's Latest Defense of the Given

It was almost fifty years ago, in his modern classic *Empiricism and the Philosophy of Mind* (EPM),[1] that Wilfrid Sellars declared the Given a Myth and proposed definitively to exorcise "the entire framework of givenness". As is typically the case in philosophy, there is no consensus as to whether he succeeded, but, surprisingly, the alleged mythic status of the Given is still being actively disputed. One of the reasons, as it has become almost mandatory to remark, is that, as William Alston puts it, "it is not easy to pin down the target to which Sellars applies that title" (SMG, 69).[2] "One of the stranger features of Sellars's discussion of the myth," observes Michael Williams, "is that, although he introduces many forms that the myth has taken, he never pauses to characterize the myth in general terms" (ATG1, 97-8).

Citing Sellars' well-known "logical space of reasons" passage (EPM §37, 169):

The essential point is that in characterizing an episode or a state as that of knowing, we are not giving an empirical description of that episode or state; we are placing it in the logical space of reasons, of justifying and being able to justify what one says,

Williams proceeds to identify the "central motif" of the myth as the idea that non-epistemic facts can entail epistemic facts, and the core of Sellars' critique as the contention

that 'epistemic' facts are essentially normative: they concern what a person *may or ought* to accept in her particular circumstances. And normative facts cannot be entailed by purely 'naturalistic' considerations. (ATG1, 98)

This essay was completed during the author's tenure as a Fulbright Senior Research Fellow in Bielefeld, Germany, in 1995–1996. Thanks are gratefully extended to the Fulbright Foundation for their support. A version of the essay was presented at a Conference on the Philosophy of Wilfrid Sellars held in Dunabogdany, Hungary, in the Fall of 1996.

[1] Originally published in 1956, in volume 1 of the *Minnesota Studies in the Philosophy of Science*, Sellars' monograph has been variously reprinted. Citations to EPM here, by numbered section and page, will be to the canonical version appearing in his *Science, Perception and Reality*.

[2] Subsequent citations from Alston by page number alone will all be to SMG.

As Sellars' equally well-known "naturalistic fallacy" passage confirms, that is indeed unquestionably *one* central theme of his critical discussion.[3]

[The] idea that epistemic facts can be analyzed without remainder—even 'in principle'—into non-epistemic facts, whether phenomenal or behavioral, public or private, with no matter how lavish a sprinkling of subjunctives and hypotheticals is ... a radical mistake—a mistake of a piece with the so-called 'naturalistic fallacy'. (EPM §5, 131)

From this perspective, then, we might expect to find friends of the Given employing two different strategies for neutralizing Sellars' critique:

(1) They might quarrel with the "naturalistic fallacy" passage, attempting to argue that at least some epistemic 'oughts' can indeed be analyzed in terms of non-epistemic 'is's.

(2) They might quarrel with the "logical space of reasons" passage, attempting to argue that, for at least some episodes or states, characterizing them in epistemic terms is just giving an empirical description of them.

What we often find, however, are proposals that cannot straightforwardly be subsumed under either of these characterizations. Alston's most recent disagreement with Sellars and defense of a form of givenness offers a useful case study.

Alston proposes to interpret commitment to the Given, as

taking non-inferential knowledge to be based on (or to be) an immediate awareness of something—that something's being given to one's awareness—in contrast to other conceivable bases of immediate knowledge. ... (70)

And he adds that he will "confine attention to the idea that certain things are given to experience, particularly sensory experience, in contrast to, e.g., rational intuition" (70). Alston takes some pains to exclude other candidate forms of givenness, e.g., sense-datum theory or "the idea that there is an immediate, non-conceptual awareness of facts" (70). The question that exercises him, he says, is

whether we have a direct (nonconceptual) awareness of particulars, one that constitutes a kind of *cognition* of a nonconceptual, nonpropositional sort. (71)

It is reasonably clear, he adds, that Sellars "reserves the term 'cognition' for mental states or activities that are conceptually, indeed propositionally structured" (71) and Alston's disagreement is ultimately with *that* restriction. In order to avoid an empty dispute over the *word* 'cognition', however, he proposes to "put more flesh on the dispute by adding the claim that our direct awareness of X's ... provides a basis (justification, warrant ...) for beliefs about those X's"

---

[3] Another is indicated by his remark that the principle "If a person is directly aware of an item which has categorial status C, then the person is aware of it *as* having categorial status C" is "perhaps the most basic form of what I have castigated as 'The Myth of the Given' " (LA, 11).

(71). "My thesis", he declares, "is that there is a cognitive component of perception that is non-conceptual" (73).

One serious and unfortunate consequence of almost fifty years of debates about the Given is that pretty much all of the relevant vocabulary has by now become hopelessly philosophically corrupt. Any discourse framed in terms of, e.g., 'immediacy', 'directness', 'cognition', 'consciousness', 'experience', 'awareness', 'perception', and 'sensation' runs a high risk of turning into a dialectical quagmire within which the words slip, slide, and ooze among a number of different senses.[4] Take, for instance, 'immediate'. As we have already seen, Alston speaks both of "immediate knowledge" and "immediate awareness". Immediate knowledge is evidently *non-inferential* knowledge. Since inference is a relationship among propositions, what we are concerned with here is presumably *propositional* knowledge, i.e., knowledge *that so-and-so*, none of which, Alston concedes, is "nonconceptual". But what then is immediate *awareness*? For, as we have also seen, what Alston wants to defend is "nonconceptual awareness of particulars", and in this case the further modifier 'immediate' (or 'direct') can hardly be intended to contrast with 'inferred'. But without any explanation of the intended contrast, classifying an awareness of something as 'immediate' or 'direct' is, at best, idle. At worst, it runs precisely the risk of blurring the distinction between propositional and nonconceptual states of affairs.

Or take 'awareness'. In the first sentence cited above, Alston apparently equates "an immediate awareness of something" with "that something's being given to one's awareness". *One's* awareness is thus evidently something like a faculty, presumably the power or ability to be aware of something, and *an* awareness is the result of exercising that faculty, an instance of being aware of something. Alston also speaks of things being given to "experience", to "sensory experience", to "rational intuition", and to "consciousness" (72). But what does it mean for a particular to be *given to* one's awareness? The natural suggestion is that X is given to one's awareness just in case one is aware of X, but until we have a better understanding of what Alston means by *that*, it is not clear where he and Sellars part company, for Sellars would hardly deny that we are normally aware, indeed perceptually aware, of all sorts of things.

Indeed there is arguably *a* sense in which Sellars would agree that we have an "immediate (direct) nonconceptual, nonpropositional awareness of particulars", namely, insofar as objects *causally affect* our sensory systems, resulting in *sensations* or *sense impressions*, nonconceptual states of perceivers which, along with propositional contents, are essentially implicated in perceptual episodes. Alston, of course, is cognizant of this aspect of Sellars' story, but, since Sellars restricts *cognitions* to conceptually or propositionally structured states, his

---

[4] Not that Sellars himself is entirely innocent on this front. Particularly troublesome is his conflation of "sense-impressions" or "sensations" and "immediate experiences". See, for instance, EPM §45, 175, and §60, 190.

sensations or sense impressions clearly do not answer to Alston's description of what is given in perception.

Fortunately, Alston does not conduct his argument entirely in such contentious terms as 'awareness' and 'experience', but rather proposes to articulate the "view of perception" in the context of which he is "committed to the givenness of perceived objects" (71).

> On this view, the heart of sense perception of external objects consists of facts of "appearing", facts that some object or other looks, feels, sounds, smells, or tastes in a certain way to a perceiver. These appearings are nonconceptual in character. ... In order for [a] tree to look green to S it is only necessary that S visually discriminate the tree from its surroundings by its color (not necessarily only by its color). (71-2)

This last claim can't be right as it stands, since S will presumably also "visually discriminate the tree from its surroundings by its color" *whatever* color it looks to her. And here we might well also pause to worry about "visually discriminate", but let us temporarily take the thought for the deed and instead let Alston continue to tell his story about 'appears'.

In normal perception, *what* appears thus-or-so to the perceiver is the external object perceived. Hence direct awareness

> though it is "intentional" in the intuitive sense of being *of* something, lacks some of the usual philosophical marks of an intentional relation. *X appears φ to S* entails *X exists*. No "intentional inexistence" here. And it is refreshingly transparent. If *X appears φ to S* and *X = Y*, it follows that *Y appears φ to S*.[5] (72-3)

The Theory of Appearing thus construes the "phenomenal character" of perceptual experience in terms of "an irreducible relation between the subject and the object perceived" (72). The obtaining of such a relation typically is not the whole of sense perception. "Adult human perception" is also "heavily concept laden" (73). But, Alston holds, an object's appearing so-and-so to a subject is a *non-conceptual cognitive component* of all perception, and, in fact, "it is this element that gives perception its distinctive character vis-à-vis other modes of cognition" (73).

From what we have already seen, it is clear that, on Alston's view, *looking* is just a species of *appearing*, viz., *visually* appearing, and so itself an "irreducible relation between the subject and the object perceived". One disagreement is thereby directly joined, for Sellars explicitly denies that *looks* is any kind of relation:

> 'x looks red to S' does not assert either an unanalyzable triadic relation to obtain between x, red, and S, nor an unanalyzable dyadic relation to obtain between x and S. Not,

---

[5] At this point, one might well be moved to ask about the cogency of yet another entailment: where φ is a simple sensible quality, from *X appears φ to S* to *Something is φ*. As we will see, Alston rejects this implication. Sellars, it turns out, accepts a very carefully qualified version of it.

however, because it asserts an *analyzable* relation to obtain, but because *looks* is not a relation at all. (EPM §13, 142)

By this, Sellars adds, he does not mean to deny that 'x looks red to S' has a *prima facie* relational syntax, but rather to insist that *looks*-sentences also have "certain other features which make them very unlike ordinary relation sentences". To bring out these features, beginning with his well-known story of young John in the necktie shop, Sellars proceeds to offer his own, non-relational, account of 'x looks φ to S', the upshot of which is that

to say [for instance] that 'X looks green to S at t' is, in effect, to say that S has that kind of experience which, if one were prepared to endorse the propositional claim it involves [namely, that X is green] one would characterize as *seeing x to be green at t*.[6] (EPM §17, 146)

As Alston observes, Sellars' account of the "endorsement-withholding" function of 'looks'

brings out another opposition between Sellars and the Theory of Appearing. He asserts, and it denies, that perceptual experiences essentially involve "propositional claims", or, as it might better be put, "propositional content". (74)

Alston, of course, concedes that "typical human perceptual experience, as a whole, involves such content" (74), but he takes Sellars' view to be that propositional content is "*essential* to perception, part of what makes a perceptual experience *perceptual*" (74), and that is something which his version of the Theory of Appearing denies.

Alston's last imputation here is seriously misleading. Sellars does indeed hold that, insofar as perception is a mode of *cognition*, propositional content is essential to perception. But what makes perceptual experiences *perceptual*, i.e., as Alston puts it, what "distinguishes perception from memory, (mere) judgment, reasoning, wondering, hypothesizing, and other forms of abstract thought" (73), is not propositional content but what Sellars calls *descriptive* content. (Cf. EPM §22, 151-2.) Later we shall have occasion to return to this element of Sellars' account. In any case, however, we now have two clear and significant points of disagreement:

(1) Sellars denies and Alston asserts that *looks* is a relation, and
(2) Sellars asserts and Alston denies that all *cognition* is conceptual, i.e., has a propositional content.

Our only hope of adjudicating such disagreements lies in a detailed examination of what each of our disputants does or would say about the other's contentions.

---

[6] Cf. EPM §22, 151: " 'x looks red to S' has the sense of 'S has an experience which involves in a unique way the idea *that x is red* and involves it in such a way that if this idea were true [and if S knew that the circumstances were normal], the experience would correctly be characterized as a seeing that x is red'."

Since "does say" is easier than "would say", I shall begin with Alston's specific criticism of Sellars' account of 'looks'.

Alston's primary allegation is that "Sellars ignores the diversity of looks-concepts" (74). In particular, Sellars fails properly to distinguish a "comparative" sense of 'looks', according to which 'X looks red to S' "means something like 'X looks to S the way red things normally look' ", from a "noncomparative" sense which 'X looks red to S' "reports ... the *qualitative distinctiveness* of this appearance, the intrinsic character of this presentation of X to S" and has "no logical connection [with] any statement about how what *is* red normally appears" (74). Alston calls the second of these a *phenomenal* looks-concept, and proceeds to distinguish it from *doxastic*[7] and *epistemic*[8] looks-concepts. As Alston sees it, the phenomenal concept is fundamental. The comparative, doxastic, and epistemic looks-concepts are all "indirect ways of identifying what is directly identified by the phenomenal concept" (75).

When S sees a red object in standard conditions, all four concepts can be used to say, truly, how the object looks to him. Only one of the concepts, the phenomenal one, can be used to specify the intrinsic character of that look; the others identify it by its relations to other things. But it is the same look that is identified, now intrinsically and now relationally. (76)

What is wrong with Sellars' account of 'looks', Alston contends, is that "it fails to recognize the fundamental place of the intrinsic character of looks that is brought out by the phenomenal looks-concepts, since it ignores (or rejects on principle) such phenomenal concepts altogether" (77). Like the comparative, doxastic, and epistemic looks-concepts, on Sellars' account 'X looks red to S' supplies, at best, only an *indirect* characterization of the intrinsic or phenomenal character of the look that X presents to S. It "fails to bring out *what it is like* for an object to look a certain way to someone" (76). In Alston's most paradoxical formulation, "as [Sellars] understands 'X looks red to S', this is not a way of saying how X looks to S" (75).

Well, what *is* it like for something to look, e.g., red to someone? Is it perhaps, as Locke's blind man suggested, like the sound of trumpets? Here's as close as Alston comes to an answer:

If someone doesn't know what it is *like* for something to look red, what qualitative distinctiveness attaches to that way of looking, we must use one of the other concepts to initiate him into the language game. We must present some red objects to him under standard conditions (having ascertained that his optical system is functioning normally, if necessary) and tell him that looking red is looking like that. (76)

---

[7] 'X looks red to S' means 'X looks to S in a way that would naturally lead S, in the absence of sufficient indications to the contrary, to believe that X is red'. (74-5)

[8] 'X looks red to S' means 'X looks to S in a way that would prima facie justify S in taking X to be red'. (75)

Now there's quite a lot to discuss here, but the immediately salient question is what Alston would say about the claim that

> (R) To a perceiver with a normally-functioning optical system, red objects viewed under standard conditions *look red*.

The most plausible expectation is surely that, like almost everyone who has thought about the question, including Sellars, Alston will regard (R) as some species of *necessary* truth.[9] But that does not seem to be what Alston actually does, since on his view, as we have already seen, for the "noncomparative" or "phenomenal" sense of 'looks', "there is no logical connection between 'X looks red to S' and any statement about how what *is* red normally appears" (74).

The only alternative is to hold that (R) is only contingently or generally true, but that view confronts some serious problems. It implies, for instance, that there might then be perceivers with normally-functioning optical systems to whom red objects viewed under standard conditions look blue or yellow or green, and that conclusion *should*, I submit, strike us as simply absurd. The notion that a red object viewed under standard conditions might look, say, green to some perceivers is, of course, a staple of familiar "inverted spectrum" scenarios, but in those scenarios such perceivers are precisely supposed *not* to have "normally-functioning optical systems", i.e., visual sensory systems that are structured as most perceivers' normally are and non-defectively function as most perceivers' normally do. In any case, it is difficult to see how the view can be reconciled with Alston's conviction that "we have effective intersubjective tests for when an object presents the same simple sensory qualities to different perceivers" (72 n. 7). If (R) is merely contingently and generally true, what could those tests possibly be?[10]

In fact the question of the relationship between Alston's "phenomenal looks" and the visual sensible qualities of objects is attended by even more difficulties. For Alston also tells us that the appearing-concepts for which the phenomenal looks-concept is fundamental—i.e., the concepts mobilized in comparative, doxastic, and epistemic 'looks'-claims—do not use 'red' in 'X looks red' in the same sense it bears in 'X is red'. This is so, he suggests, because

'looks red' is treated as a single semantic unit, rather than being constructed out of combining 'looks' with a predicate 'red' that could occur in other phrases. (81)

---

[9] Sellars' formulation of (R) is: "x is red .≡. x looks red to standard observers in standard conditions", which, he argues, "is a necessary truth *not* because the right-hand side is the definition of 'x is red', but because 'standard conditions' means conditions in which things look what they are." (EPM §18, 147).

[10] Alston's view evidently admits, for instance, the hypothesis that there are two sorts of sufferers from red-green colorblindness: some to whom red things look green and others to whom green things look red. But what could be an "effective intersubjective test" for distinguishing between them?

"Sellars gives this suggestion the back of his hand", remarks Alston in a footnote (81, n. 10), without seeing fit to say *why*, but the reason is not far to seek. If 'looks red' is a "single semantic unit", then it is hard to see how it has *anything at all* to do with the redness of physical objects. The gambit of treating *looking-red* as an "insoluble unity" derives its (spurious) plausibility, writes Sellars, from the fact that "the minute one gives 'red' ... an independent status, it becomes what it obviously is, namely 'red' as a predicate of physical objects" (EPM §12, 142), and one is once again immediately confronted with the *prima facie* necessity of (R).

Notice that, in the passage cited above, what we are ostensibly doing when we tell our subject that "looking red is looking like that" is initiating him into a *language game*, presumably the language game of reporting a "phenomenal look" by using a term that picks out a "simple sensory quality" (76). Since "in normal perception the ... awareness involved is awareness of the external object perceived" (72), it is natural to suppose that the "simple sensory quality" in question is *red*, and that one could truly say that X, which *looks* red, might also *be* red *without equivocating on the term 'red'*. But if 'looks red' is a "single semantic unit", this reading must be mistaken. The logical form of 'X looks ϕ to S' will not be 'L(X, ϕ, S)', but 'R(X, S)', and 'X, which looks ϕ to S, is indeed ϕ' will thus be a conjunction of the form 'R(X, S) & ϕ(X)'. It is consequently at best misleading—indeed, I would argue, it is strictly speaking false—to say (as Alston does) that objects present simple sensory qualities to perceivers.

Imagine a philosopher, call him 'Walston', who subscribes to something quite like Alston's version of the Theory of Appearing, but for whom objects literally *do* "present simple sensory qualities to perceivers". On Walston's view, in other words, 'X looks red to S' picks out an unanalyzable *triadic* relation between a perceiver, an object, and a property. In his story, 'red' is used *univocally* in 'X looks red to S' and 'X is red', and his counterpart to (R), namely,

> (RW) An object, X, is red *if and only if* X would look red to normal perceivers with non-defective vision when viewed under standard conditions,

has the status of a *necessary* truth.

It is, in effect, against Walston that Sellars originally presses the issue of conceptual priority. The crucial question is how we are to understand the necessity of (RW). The answer Sellars imputes to Walston is that (RW) presents an *analysis* of being red in terms of an autonomous prior phenomenal concept of looking red. But the idea that the connective 'if and only if' in (RW) expresses something tantamount to a definition is *prima facie* incompatible with the idea, also endorsed by Walston, that 'red' is used univocally on both sides of the biconditional, which implies that "*being red* is logically prior, is a logically simpler notion, than *looking red*" (EPM §12, 142). "One begins to see the plausibility of the gambit that *looking-red* is an insoluble unity," Sellars writes, for the minute one gives 'red' (on the right hand side) an independent status, it becomes what it obviously is, namely 'red' as a predicate of physical objects, and the supposed definition becomes an obvious circle. (EPM §12, 142)

Since he himself maintains both the conceptual priority of *being red* to *looking red* and the necessity of (RW), Sellars must explain that necessity differently, and so he does. On his view, it is a reflection of the fact that "'standard conditions' means conditions in which things look what they are" (EPM §18, 147).

From this perspective, we can see that, figuratively speaking, Alston has taken out two insurance policies against Sellars' EPM critique of the Theory of Appearing: His version of that theory rejects the necessity thesis—unlike Walston's (RW), Alston's (R) is not a necessary truth—and it rejects the univocity thesis—'looks red' is a "single semantic unit", not an expression "constructed out of combining 'looks' with a predicate 'red' that could occur in other phrases" (81). In the process, however, I shall argue, Alston has also rendered the ostensible *cognitive* character claimed for his nonconceptual relations of appearing simply unintelligible.

In what is that cognitive character supposed to consist? Since Alston is evidently willing to accept Sellars' identification of conceptual content with propositional content—"I agree that there is no nonconceptual knowledge that so-and-so" (70)—the answer can only be that it consists in the *epistemic effectiveness* claimed for such relations, i.e., in the alleged fact "that our direct awareness of X's … provides a basis (justification, warrant …) for beliefs about those X's" (71). To assert that relations of appearing are cognitive, in other words, is just to maintain "that how things appear is a reliable, though fallible, guide to how they are" (73). Call this "Alston's reliability claim".

Now one's first reaction to this claim is likely to be that it is *of course* reasonable to suppose that how things appear is a reliable guide to how they are, and, when all the chips are down, that is undeniably Sellars' view as well. In particular, in his later writings,[11] Sellars explicitly endorses the *epistemic principle* (adapted from Chisholm) that

> (EPP) If a person ostensibly perceives (without ground for doubt) some-
> thing to be ϕ (for appropriate values of ϕ) then it is likely to be true
> that he perceives something to be ϕ (MGEC, 177)

for ostensible perceptions, as well as corresponding principles regarding the *prima facie* veridicality of ostensible introspections and ostensible memories. When we recall that Sellars consistently treats 'perceives' as a success word—i.e., 'S perceives

---

[11] Besides EPM, the issues discussed by Alston figure centrally in at least three later Sellarsian works: GEC, MGEC, and the first of his Carus Lectures, LA. Although all three later essays contain significant amounts of material directly relevant to Alston's criticisms of theses first articulated in EPM, there is no evidence in SMG that he is even aware of them, much less familiar with their contents.

X to be ϕ' implies 'X is ϕ'—and further observe that, as he explained in his Carus Lectures (LA, 17), his account of 'looks' equates

    (1) X (at t) looks red to S

with

    (2) S (at t) ostensibly sees X to be red,[12]

it is clear that Sellars endorsement of (EPP) effectively amounts to an endorsement of Alston's reliability claim *as Sellars would interpret it*.

Consequently, when Alston later wonders "what Sellars would say to my contention that I can be prima facie justified in believing that what I perceive is my computer because it looks to me like my computer" (83), the correct answer is *not*, as Alston claims,

> that he would have the same objection to this as to the claim that the belief is justified by my awareness of a computer-shaped sense datum

but rather that Sellars would say something like,

> Quite right. That is simply an instance of (EPP) and it is arguably reasonable to accept (EPP), and, indeed, arguably reasonable to accept the more general principle that our ostensible introspections, perceptions, and memories (IPM judgments) are likely to be true. (see MGEC, 175–81)

Later we shall have a look at some of the details, but first there is some unfinished business that needs our attention. For we still need to ask why Alston thinks that it is reasonable to accept his reliability claim *as he himself interprets it*. And in light of what we have already noticed in connection with his version of the Theory of Appearing, that is not an easy question to answer. Indeed, the only explicit answer that we find in Alston's text is deeply unsatisfying.

> [The] principle that things are generally what they look to be, and hence that if X looks P it can be presumed to be P until it is shown otherwise is one that commends itself to reason. Therefore, if, as I have been arguing, looking P is in itself a nonconceptual mode of experience ... beliefs about what is perceived can be justified by a nonconceptual experience from which they spring. (83)

There is a certain nostalgic charm to the contention that a principle "commends itself to reason". It reminds one of Descartes' appeals to what is "obvious according to the true light of nature". But, in the last analysis, that a principle commends itself to reason means only that it is intuitively plausible, that one is initially inclined to accept it, and that alone is hardly a sufficient reason for one to accept it all things considered.

What is fundamentally wrong with Alston's answer, however, is that the epistemic principle

---

[12] More precisely, with "S (at t) ostensibly sees X to be red and, indeed, ostensibly sees its very redness" (LA, 18).

(LP) If X looks P, it can be presumed to be P until it is shown otherwise

commends itself to reason *only if both occurrences of 'P' have the same sense*, and, as we have seen, when 'P' picks out a simple sensory quality, that is something that Alston explicitly denies. This is perhaps why none of his "intuition-pumping" illustrative examples take that form. That something "looks like a computer", "looks like a meadow", and "looks rabbity" are all *comparative* looks-constructions involving, not simple sensible qualities, but *kinds of objects*. Since the comparative claim

> X looks like a K to S

can plausibly be taken to imply

> The way X looks to S (in the present conditions) is the way that Ks look to normal perceivers (in standard conditions),[13]

the corresponding epistemic principle would not be (LP) but rather

> (LK) If the way X looks to S is the way that Ks looks to normal perceivers, then S can [legitimately] presume that X is a K until it is shown otherwise.

in which 'K' occurs univocally in both the antecedent and consequent.

In contrast, when 'P' picks out a simple sensory quality, the logical form of (LP), for a given perceiver S, on Alston's account will be, roughly,

> (LP*) If R(X,S) then S can [legitimately] presume that $\phi(X)$ until it is shown otherwise,

and, if there is *no* logical or even conditionally necessary connection between 'R(X,S)' and '$\phi(X)$', nothing about *that* principle "commends it to reason" in the least. On the face of it, the fact that an object, X, stands in an unanalyzable nonconceptual *looks-red* relation to a person, S, gives her no more of a reason to presume that X is *red* than would the fact that X stands to S in the nonconceptual relation *weighs-more-than* or *contains-less-cadmium-than* or, for that matter, *feels-cold* or *tastes-sweet*.

What might further mislead one into supposing otherwise is the tendency, to which Alston himself here conspicuously succumbs, to mistake (LP) for "the principle that things are generally what they look to be" (83). By Alston's own lights, however, the claim 'X looks *to be* red' does invoke "an appearance concept in which when something appears red, it is in just the sense in which a physical object would be red", although it is also an appearance concept which falls "outside the group of look concepts for which the phenomenal concept is

---

[13] Notice that this much of an account of *comparative* looks-claims is noncommittal about, and so compatible with, various different accounts of *non-comparative* looks-claims, including Alston's. The *prima facie* equally plausible claim that "X looks like a K to S" implies "S is inclined to take X to be a K", in contrast, is not one that Alston can consistently accept.

fundamental" (81). As he interprets it, in other words, the principle "that things are generally what they look *to be*" would not be (LP) but rather

> (LB) A If X looks *to be* P it can be presumed to be P until it is shown otherwise,

where 'P' is used *univocally* to pick out a possible sensible property of physical objects. Since Alston holds that 'That looks to be red' "means something like 'So far as I can tell, that is red' " (81), the principle (LB) is *au fond* epistemic and conceptual. As Alston remarks, 'So far as I can tell, that is red' "is close kin to Sellars' understanding of 'X looks red to S' " (81). That the principle (LB) arguably *does* commend itself to reason, however, lends no plausibility to Alston's principle (LP), where 'looks P' is supposed to pick out an inherently nonconceptual relation between objects and persons.

I conclude that Alston has given us no reason at all to accept the principle (LP) *as he himself interprets it*. Only his failure to distinguish (LP) from the principles (LK) and (LB) leads him to think otherwise, i.e., to suppose that (LP) as he interprets it "commends itself to reason". Sellars, in contrast, takes it upon himself to confirm the initial appeal of (LP) as *he* would interpret it, that is, the intuitive plausibility of (EPP)—and of parallel principles regarding ostensible introspection and ostensible memory—by an independent supporting argument. His strategy, he tells us,

> might well be called 'Epistemic Evaluation as Vindication'. Its central theme would be that achieving a certain end or goal can be (deductively) shown to require a certain integrated system of means. [For present purposes] the end can be characterized as that of being in a *general* position … to *act*, i.e., to bring about changes in ourselves and our environment in order to realize *specific* purposes or intentions. (MGEC, 179)

There is, in other words, "a necessary connection between being in the framework of epistemic evaluation and being agents" (MGEC, 181). In particular,

> since agency, to be effective, involves having reliable cognitive maps of ourselves and our environment, the concept of effective agency involves that of our IPM [introspection, perception, memory] judgments being likely to be true, i.e., to be correct mappings of ourselves and our circumstances. … [It is thus] reasonable to accept
>
> > [EE] IPM judgments are likely to be true,
>
> simply on the ground that unless they *are* likely to be true, the concept of effective agency has no application. (MGEC, 180)

It is crucial, Sellars adds, to recognize that this reason for accepting (EE) *as* correct—a sort of transcendental deduction of the reliability of ostensible introspection, perception, and memory—is not an explanation of why (EE) *is* correct, i.e., of *why* IPM judgments are likely to be true. *That* explanation involves "finding inductive support for hypotheses concerning the [e.g., neuro-physiological] mechanisms involved and how they evolved in response to evolutionary pressures" (MGEC, 180) and so can be given only within a framework which presupposes the *general* reasonableness of relying on introspection, memory, and perception. It is this justificatory interplay between the general epistemic principle (EE) and particular IPM judgments, Sellars explains, that he had in mind when he wrote in EPM that

There is clearly *some* point to the picture of knowledge as resting on a level of propositions—observation reports—which do not rest on other propositions in the same way as other propositions rest on them. On the other hand, I do wish to insist that the metaphor of 'foundation' is misleading in that it keeps us from seeing that if there is a logical dimension in which other empirical propositions rest on observation reports, there is another logical dimension in which the latter rest on the former. (EPM §38, 170)

An essential component of this second, "contra-foundational", logical dimension will be an elucidation of the concept-eliciting *causal* role of the non-conceptual sensations or sense-impressions in the complex episode that is a perceptual taking, i.e., of its "descriptive content". As we have already remarked, Alston acknowledges this aspect of Sellars' story, but emphasizes that it is also an essential part of that story that

although nonpropositional experience (or the objects thereof ...) may *cause* beliefs about perceived objects, it cannot function as a justification of perceptual beliefs. (82)

His own contrary thesis is that "beliefs about perceived objects can be justified by springing from nonconceptual cognitions of those objects" (82). Why, he asks, should we suppose that the causal role assigned by explanatory theory to the nonconceptual element in perception rules out its epistemic efficacy? Indeed, he continues,

in initially presenting the intuitive case for my position, I said that the belief that what I am looking at is my computer is prima facie justified by the fact that it (the belief) *springs from* its looking to me like my computer. So far from the casual role being incompatible with the epistemic role, the latter presupposes the former. If the belief were not engendered by the looking, it would not be nearly so plausible to suppose that the looking justifies the belief. (84)

In the case of Alston's "computer" example, I have argued, the operative epistemic principle is (LK), and the relevant belief is consequently justified by that *comparative* looking just to the extent that the subject is justified in believing his perceptual circumstances and himself *qua* perceiver to be normal. But we have also seen that, when ϕ' is a simple sensible quality, then, *as Alston interprets* 'looks ϕ' and the corresponding principle (LP), it is *not at all* plausible to suppose that "the looking justifies the belief". The current citation from his text allows us a useful diagnosis of why Alston might think otherwise. For, although he here misrepresents what he actually *said* in initially presenting the intuitive case for his position, he perhaps accurately represents what he *had in mind*, and that, as it turns out, is something correct. *The fact that* a perceptual belief has been caused by a particular nonconceptual state of affairs can indeed function as a justifier for that belief, i.e., as a reason for the perceiver to accept or endorse it—but it can do so only if that fact is, so to speak, *available* to the perceiver.[14] Here's a relevant citation from Sellars:

[Surely,] we are inclined to say, to believe something *because* it is reasonable (to believe it) involves not only that there *be* a reason but that, in a relevant sense, one *has* or is *in possession of* the reason. (SK iii, §16, 337)[15]

That a belief has been caused in such-and-such a way is, of course, a *propositional* reason, i.e., it has a logical shape which makes it suitable to serve as the premise or conclusion of an argument, i.e., a piece of reason*ing*. Sellars' thought is that epistemic justification is a matter of being suitably situated "in the logical space of reasons" in the sense of being able to support by adequate justificatory reasoning a belief that has been appropriately challenged, i.e., itself called into question *for reasons*. Alston himself cites a pertinent sentence from "The Structure of Knowledge": "Presumably, to be justified in believing something is to have good reasons for believing it, as contrasted with its contradictory" (SK, 332).

Alston finds Sellars' concentration on reasons "parochial", and suggests (not for the first time) that it results from "a conflation of being justified in a belief and the activity of justifying a belief". "One can be justified in believing many things," he writes, "that one has not justified and, indeed, is not able to justify" (85). This is familiar territory, and I have had a good deal to say about it elsewhere,[16] for instance, that it is important to distinguish (as Alston does not) between non-inferential *reasonableness*, which Sellars admits, and non-inferential *justification*, which he rejects. On this occasion, however, I will limit myself to the observation that Alston himself is arguably guilty of a serious conflation. For it is one thing to say that *the fact that* S's belief that X is P has been caused by ("springs from", "is engendered by", "stems from") X's appearing P to S—or, for that matter, *the fact that* X appears P to S—can function as a justifier for that belief and quite another to say that *X's appearing P to S* ("the looking"), as Alston interprets it, can do so.

The crucial point is that, when all the chips are down, 'justify' is first and foremost a *verb*. The *state* of "being justified in a belief" must therefore ultimately be elucidated in terms of the *activity* of justifying a belief, and, as Sellars recognizes, the latter can only consist in adducing supporting reasons for it. The conclusion that justifiers must have propositional form is then an immediate consequence of the observation that a *reason* is in the first instance essentially something that can function as a premise in *reasoning*.

---

[14] For a detailed exploration of this point in connection with a similar attempt to sustain a form of givenness, see my RTSH.

[15] That is, §16 of Part iii, "Epistemic Principles", in SK.

[16] In ch. 3, "Immediate Knowledge", of TAK.

Alas, there remains a final opportunity for confusion. For there is a familiar idiom which *labels as* 'a reason' (or 'the reason') something significant that is *mentioned in* a (propositional) reason. That an illness is caused by a bacterial infection, for instance, is a reason for administering antibiotics. A common and convenient shorthand cites the infection itself as the reason. The bacterial infection, one says, *justifies* administering antibiotics. Obviously a bacterial infection does not have propositional form, but, equally obviously, its role as a "reason" is essentially derivative from justifiers which do. In this *derivative* sense, one could also say, as Alston does, that *X's appearing P to S* is a reason for (or prima facie justifies) S's belief that X is P, for, as Sellars acknowledges, *that* X appears P to S is indeed a reason for S to believe that X is P. The confusion arises when such derivative constructions are treated as fundamental and interpreted as reports of non-logical (non-inferential) justificatory relationships between nonconceptual (nonpropositional) items and beliefs. It is, alas, a confusion to which Alston also succumbs.

Alston's latest defense of the Given thus fails on all fronts. His own version of the Theory of Appearing cannot perform the epistemic tasks for which he invokes it, and his criticisms of Sellars rest on an incomplete and inaccurate understanding of the latter's complex and sophisticated views. What is perhaps most disturbing in a philosopher of Alston's caliber, however, is the manifest lack of precision of expression and argumentative rigor in his latest engagement with Sellars. Early on, I lamented the corruption of most of the relevant philosophical vocabulary and implicitly congratulated Alston for not conducting his argument entirely in such contentious terms as 'awareness' and 'experience'. Unfortunately, such congratulations proved to be both premature and unwarranted. For Alston straightaway proceeded to do further damage to that vocabulary by blurring and then ignoring the differences among 'looks P', 'looks like a K', and 'looks to be P', and his putative "argument" for his central positive thesis turned out to be merely an appeal to the initial intuitive plausibility of what critical scrutiny then revealed to be a different thesis entirely. Despite Alston's most recent efforts, then, I conclude that his thesis that "there is a cognitive component of perception that is non-conceptual" (73), remains where Sellars left it long ago, still mythic after all those years.

REFERENCES

Alston, William P. (SMG), "Sellars and the 'Myth of the Given' ", *Philosophy and Phenomenological Research*, 65 (2002), 69–86.
Rosenberg, Jay F. (TAK), *Thinking About Knowing* (Oxford University Press; Oxford: 2002), esp. 101–122.
——— (RTSH), "Red Triangles and Speckled Hens: Critical Notice of BonJour and Sosa on Epistemic Justification", *International Journal of Philosophical Studies*, 12 (2004), 463–77.

Sellars, Wilfrid (EPM), "Empiricism and the Philosophy of Mind", in *Science, Perception and Reality* (Ridgeview Publishing Co.; Atascadero, CA: 1963, 1991), 127–96.

____ (GEC), "Givenness and Explanatory Coherence", *Journal of Philosophy*, 70 (1973), 612–24.

____ (LA), "The Lever of Archimedes", Lecture I of "Foundations for a Metaphysics of Pure Process", *Monist*, 64 (1981), 3–36.

____ (MGEC), "More on Givenness and Explanatory Coherence", in George S. Pappas (ed.), *Justification and Knowledge* (D. Reidel Publishing Co.; Dordrecht, Holland: 1979), 169–82.

____ (SK), "The Structure of Knowledge", in Hector-Neri Castañeda (ed.), *Action, Knowledge, and Reality* (Bobbs-Merrill; Indianapolis, IN: 1975), 295–346.

Williams, Michael, (ATG1), "Mythology of the Given: Sosa, Sellars and the Task of Epistemology", Part I of "Are There Two Grades of Knowledge?", in *Proceedings of the Aristotelian Society*, supp. 77 (2003), 91–112.

11

Perception *vs.* Inner Sense: A Problem about Direct Awareness

In the final movement of Sellars' story of the mythical genius Jones, "Jones develops, in crude and sketchy form, of course, a theory of sense perception" (EPM, 191).[1] The *model* for Jones' theory, Sellars tells us, consists of particulars, "a domain of 'inner replicas', which, when brought about in standard conditions, share the perceptible characteristics of their physical source" (EPM, 191). The theory itself, however, does not introduce any new particulars, but rather postulates a family of *non-cognitive states of perceiving subjects*, "episodes, which he calls, say, *impressions*, and which are the end results of the impingement of physical objects and processes on various parts of the body ...". (There is a bit of temporal slippage here between states and episodes, but we will assume that it can be relatively easily tidied up.)

Sellars goes on to make a number of points about Jones' theory of sense impressions: that their status as theoretical entities enables us to understand how they can be *intrinsically* characterized, and that the relevant intrinsic characterization is effected by means of an *analogy*, controlled by the model and its accompanying commentary "which qualifies, restricts, and interprets the analogy between the familiar entities of the model and the theoretical entities which are being introduced" (EPM, 192). Finally, after some speculative remarks about the ultimate fate of Jonesean impressions in the Scientific Image (as we later learned to put it), Sellars proceeds to discharge the philosophical obligation to explain the Cartesian appearances by casting Jones in a double pedagogical role. First, Jones teaches his fellows to "[use] the language of impressions to draw theoretical conclusions from appropriate premises" (EPM, 194). Finally, however,

he succeeds in training them to make a *reporting* use of this language. He trains them, that is, to say 'I have the impression of a red triangle' when, and only when, according to the theory, they are indeed having the impression of a red triangle. (EPM, 194–195)

This essay was completed during the author's tenure as a Fulbright Senior Research Fellow in Bielefeld, Germany, in 1995–1996. Thanks are gratefully extended to the Fulbright Foundation for their support. A version of the essay was presented at a Conference on the Philosophy of Wilfrid Sellars held in Dunabogdany, Hungary, in the Fall of 1996.

[1] "Empiricism and the Philosophy of Mind", reprinted as ch. 5, pp. 127–196 of *Science, Perception and Reality* (Ridgeview Publishing Co.; Atascadero, CA: 1963, 1991). Cited here as "EPM".

This account has the philosophical virtues, Sellars reminds us, of understanding how the concept of sense impressions, although pertaining to inner episodes,

> can be primarily and essentially *inter-subjective*, without being resolvable into overt behavioural symptoms, and that the reporting role of these concepts, their role in introspection, the fact that each of us has a privileged access to his impressions, constitutes a dimension of these concepts which is *built on* and *presupposes* their role in intersubjective discourse. (EPM, 195)

He goes on to stress that the explanatory role of the (theoretical) language of impressions *vis-à-vis* facts about how something looks to someone or how it looks to someone to be makes it more than a mere notational alternative to such claims. Finally, Sellars reminds us that, although it is correct both to say that our Jonesean ancestors thereby came to *notice* impressions and that the language of impressions embodies a *discovery*, the discovery did not, so to speak, consist in the noticing. Rather, in accordance with the principle that

> instead of coming to have a concept of something because we have noticed that sort of thing, to have the ability to notice a sort of thing is already to have the concept of that sort of thing, and cannot account for it (EPM, 176),

it is more accurate to say that, having *discovered* that his theory of impressions does the explanatory work necessary to qualify it as an account of what is real, Jones brings it about that his fellows are *able to notice* the real entities, i.e., the states or episodes, to which the theory first gives cognitive-epistemic access.

So much, for the moment, for sense impressions in their ur-theoretical form. Let us turn now to some specifics about their role in the analysis and explanation of perception. The key points are quickly made. If we take our initial cue from EPM, §22, a perceptual experience—construed broadly enough to encompass qualitative and existential appearings as well as perception proper—can be characterized in terms of its *propositional content*, the *degree of endorsement* of that content, and a residual *descriptive content*. Jones' theoretical sense impressions are introduced precisely as the locus of descriptive content. Having abandoned the abstractive theory of concept formation, Sellars tells us in "Phenomenalism",[2] the remaining crucial steps toward an "adequately critical" direct realist account of perception consist in a proper appreciation of the relationship between propositional and descriptive content:

> [Step two] consists in the recognition that the direct perception of physical objects is mediated by the occurrence of sense impressions which latter are, in themselves, thoroughly non-cognitive. Step *three*: this mediation is causal rather than epistemic. Sense impressions do not mediate by virtue of being known. (P, 91)

The propositional content of a perceptual experience is thus a cognitive episode—taking the dimension of endorsement for granted, we can speak

---

[2] Published as ch. 3, pp. 60–105, of *Science, Perception and Reality*. Cited here as "P".

here of a *perceptual judgment* —causally evoked by a non-cognitive sensory state, in short, a *conceptual response* to a Jonesean impression. The concepts in terms of which such perceptual judgments are framed are, in the first instance, our rich common sense concepts of physical objects.

In the second instance, Sellars reminds us, we can draw on distinctions available within the framework of common sense to distinguish an object which one perceives from what one perceives *of* the object. Proceeding along these lines, we can isolate an "ur-concept" of a physical object which brackets, for instance, its causal and dispositional properties and takes into account the fact that, typically, not all parts and aspects of an object can be simultaneously perceived. In "The Lever of Archimedes",[3] he characterizes such an ur-concept in terms of the Aristotelian notion of a materiate individual substance, e.g., an expanse or volume of color, conceived as a (space-filling) stuff. The "ur-concept" of a red physical object, in other words,

is simply that of an individuated volume of red stuff which behaves in generically stuffy ways; and, specifically, in the manner characteristic of a determinate thing kind. (FMPP, 15)

On this view, the concept of an object which is red "in the *adjectival* sense in which we think of an apple as red although white inside" (FMPP, 14) becomes the more complicated notion of a complex object which contains expanses and volumes of different colors as constituents. What is crucial to this picture, emphasizes Sellars, is that the "ur-concept" of *red* is not that of an aspect or element of an *experience* but "the concept of a redness which, along with other colors, is the very stuff of which physical objects are made" (FMPP, 15).

What I especially want to notice is that, on Sellars' view, the qualitative concepts with which one responds to sense impressions in perceptual experiences are never analogical. The phenomenological attitude brackets causal and dispositional properties and the like but does not shift the sense of sensory quality predicates. One of the clearest statements of the point occurs in "Scientific Realism or Irenic Instrumentalism":[4]

[The] rejection of given-ness is compatible with a distinction between the attributes which physical objects and processes can *strictu sensu* be perceived to have and those which they can be perceived to have in less stringent senses. Thus, I can perceive that this is a pad of writing paper—indeed perceive it *as* a pad of writing paper—but *strictu sensu* I perceive that it is, for example, a physical object which, on the facing side, is rectangular, yellow, and lined with parallel blue lines. ...

---

[3] Lecture I, pp. 3–36, of "Foundations for a Metaphysics of Pure Process", *Monist*, 64 (1981), 3–90. Cited here as "FMPP".

[4] Reprinted as ch. 8, pp. 157–189 of *Philosophical Perspectives: Metaphysics and Epistemology* (Ridgeview Publishing Co.; Atascadero, CA: 1959, 1967). Cited here as "SRII".

If the framework of common sense physical objects is analyzed along [these] lines it is easy to see that, while the fundamental concepts of the framework are not concepts of sense impressions, they are concepts which, so to speak, project or transpose the attributes of sense impressions into the categorial framework of physical things and processes. But, although the conceptual framework of physical color is in this sense ontologically grounded in visual impressions, the conceptual framework in terms of which common sense conceives these impressions is itself an analogical offshoot from the conceptual framework of physical color and shape. (SRII, 176–177)[5]

Finally, here is a useful quotation from "Is Consciousness Physical?", the third Carus Lecture:

I have been writing as though we could take for granted that persons have such sensory states as, shall I say, sensing bluely, ...

On the other hand, ... if there are such sensory states, the idea of such a state is not to be confused with that of an awareness of a sensing bluely *as* a sensing bluely.

If there are states of sensing bluely, they obviously do not present themselves *as such*—otherwise the very existence of a controversy about their existence would be inexplicable.

If we are aware of states of sensing bluely, we are, at best, aware of them as *blue items*—*cases* of blue—and not as states of ourselves. An the awareness of a sensing as a case of blue is ... logically distinct from the sensing itself. (FMPP, 67)

What I want to ask is whether Sellars' story allows for *any* awarenesses of sense impressions *as* sense impressions, and I want to suggest that there are some reasons to doubt that is does. What my brief survey of some highlights of that story suggests is that Sellars evidently acknowledges two paradigms of "direct awareness", that is, two distinct ways in which someone, say Susanna, might non-inferentially respond to one of her sense impressions, e.g., a sense impression of a red rectangle. She can, in the first instance, respond *in the mode of perception*, that is, with a perceptual judgment, for instance, "This thick red book is cluttering up the table". The subject term of such a judgment signals a perceptual *taking*. Here Susanna takes something, deictically indicated by the demonstrative 'this', to be (the facing surface of) a thick red book; she is aware of it *as* a thick red book.

As we have noted, such a perceptual response can also occur, so to speak, "phenomenologically bracketed", a form sometimes represented by the Sellarsian idiom, "Lo! a red rectangle." Here Susanna is operating conceptually *strictu sensu*. She is aware of something as an "ur-object", a red rectangle *qua* "individuated volume of red stuff". But it is important to be clear that there is also perceptual *taking* in this case, i.e., a deictic dimension—indicated here by the interjection "Lo!"—according to which Susanna is responding to something *present to her*

---

[5] In *Science and Metaphysics: Variations on Kantian Themes*, (Routledge & Kegan Paul; London: 1967), henceforth "SM". Sellars formulates the relevant thesis as the claim that "sense impressions [are] properly described by a special use of a minimal physical vocabulary" (SM, 15).

with the concept of a red rectangle. Thus the conceptual (propositional) element here is perhaps more perspicuously given by: "Lo *and behold*! [*This is*] a red rectangle."

What Susanna is, in either case, responding *to* in this or that conceptual way, of course, is, on Sellars' view, her sense impression of a red rectangle, i.e., something which is *per se* a sensory state of a person. This is the notorious thesis that perception rests on a systematic categorial mistake. Susanna mis-takes a non-conceptual state of herself for a physical object, a thick red book cluttering up the table or, more conservatively, a rectangular expanse of red over there in space. Such a response in the mode of perception, in short, can correctly be described as an awareness of a sense impression, but, even phenomenologically "stripped down", it is not an awareness of a sense impression *as* a sense impression.

On the other hand, Susanna could presumably respond to her sense impression of a red rectangle, also directly and non-inferentially, *in the mode of a learned Jonesean report*, e.g., "I am having a sense impression of a red rectangle." Does this count as an awareness of a sense impression *as* a sense impression? I find myself reluctant to say that it counts as awareness of a sense impression *at all*. For when I ask after the *object* of Susanna's awareness, what she is aware *of*, the natural answer seems to be that she is aware of *herself*, more specifically, of herself *as* having a sense impression of a red rectangle. The key point, I think, is that this sort of learned Jonesean "self-awareness" is not, in Kant's sense, a *schematized intuition*. In the sense in which there is something present in Susanna's perceptual experience—namely, a sense impression of a red rectangle—of which she judges that *it* is a red rectangular physical object, there is nothing present in her "Jonesean self-awareness", as we might put it, of which she judges that *it* is a sense impression. The form of an episode of Jonesean self-awareness is not deictic, "*This* is a sense impression of a red rectangle" or "Lo! a sense impression of a red rectangle". The form of an episode of Jonesean self-awareness is self-ascriptive. "Sensing-of-a-red-rectangle-ly(I)". The adverbial form of sense-impression concepts, indeed, seems tailor made for their reporting use.

It is instructive in this connection to compare Susanna's *reporting* that she is having a sense impression of a red rectangle with her *concluding*, e.g., from the fact that it looks to her as though there is a red rectangular object over there, that she is having a sense impression of a red rectangle.

Notice that the evidence for theoretical statements in the language of impressions will include such introspectible inner episodes as *its looking to one as though there were a red and [rectangular] physical object over there*, as well as overt behavior. (EPM, 194)

The inner episode of its looking to one as though there were a red and rectangular object over there to which Sellars here adverts is *conceptual*,[6] and

---

[6] Given the earlier account of such episodes as having both a propositional and a descriptive content, this can't be quite right. Only the propositional content of such an episode, i.e., the

its being "introspectible" is thus a consequence of Jones' earlier pedagogical activities in connection with his theory of *thoughts*. In connection with that theory, Sellars takes special pains to emphasize both the distinction between Jones' model of "inner speech" and the notion of *verbal imagery* and the fact that Jones does not introduce thoughts as *immediate experiences*. Indeed, Sellars stresses that Jones and his compatriots do not at that point possess either *concept*, that of an image or that of an immediate experience. These restrictions on Jones' theory of thoughts surely suggest that cognitive episodes *as such* have *no* phenomenology. In a fashionable contemporary idiom, there is nothing that it is like to know what one is thinking. In contrast to perceptual awareness of objects, in other words, "introspective awareness" of one's own conceptual states seems not to be an *experience*. In any event, despite its (direct, non-inferential) immediacy, it is certainly not an *immediate experience*.

At this point in EPM, "the items which philosophers lump together under the heading 'immediate experiences'" include "such things as impressions, sensations, or feelings" (EPM, 190), but *not* thoughts. Crucially, composite sensory-cognitive episodes of perceiving (or seeming to perceive), although they *include* "immediate experiences", are not *themselves* "immediate experiences". This usage was introduced in §24:

Notice that the common descriptive component of the three experiences I am considering it itself often referred to ... as an *experience*—as, for example, an *immediate experience*. (EPM, 154)

The terminology, however, is highly unstable, and, as the *first* occurrence of 'experiences' in the quotation indicates, it is much more characteristic for Sellars to reject the distinctly non-Kantian idea that any episode lacking a cognitive dimension could be an *experience*.[7] Sellars thus makes an effort to sort out the accompanying ambiguities:

The notorious 'ing-ed' ambiguity of 'experience' must be kept in mind. For although *seeing that x, over there, is red* is an *experiencing*—indeed, a paradigm case of experiencing—it does not follow that the descriptive content of this experiencing is itself an experienc*ing*. Furthermore, because the fact that *x, over there, looks red to Jones* would be a *seeing*, on Jone's part, *that x, over there, is red*, if its propositional content were true, and because

---

perceptual judgment, can be introspectible in consequence of Jones' first theoretico-pedagogical initiative. As the discussion to follow will show, the terminological slippage here is potentially significant.

7 For example, earlier in EPM we find:

[To] say that a certain experience is a *seeing that* something is the case, is to do more than describe the experience. It is to characterize it as, so to speak, making an assertion or claim, ... I realize that by speaking of experiences as containing propositional claims, I may seem to be knocking at closed doors ... [but] the justification of this way of talking is one of my major aims. (EPM, 144)

if it *were* a seeing, it *would* be an experiencing, we must beware of concluding that the fact that *x, over there, looks red to Jones* is itself an *experiencing*. Certainly, the fact that something looks red to me can be *experienced*. But it is not itself an experiencing. (EPM, 154)

And while he ultimately rejects the idea that the common descriptive component of such episodes is an [epistemic] experien*cing*, he is prepared to say "that it is a component in states of affairs which are experien*ced*, and it does not seem unreasonable to say that it is itself experien*ced*" (EPM, 154).

One reasonably clear upshot of these distinctions, I think, is that, a sense impression is experien*ced* when it is responded to in the mode of perception. Sellars also seems to suggest that the complex "state of affairs" constituting the perceptual episode of which the sense impression is a constituent is also experienced. What is much less clear, however, is whether, for example, the propositional content of a perceptual episode is thereby experienced. And, as far as I can see, the distinctions drawn here shed no light at all on the question of whether either thoughts or sense impressions are experienced when they are responded to in the mode of Jonesean self-awareness. I think that there are good reasons for concluding that they are not, and, if this is right, then there are no awarenesses of sense impressions as sense impressions *inter alia* because sense impressions are never experienced as sense impressions, i.e., never experienced *as such*.

The problem to which I want to call attention, then, is how properly or best to distinguish these two ways of conceptually responding to sense impressions. And I want in particular to worry in this connection about the case of *pain*, since it seems to hover uncomfortably between these two paradigms of direct awareness. To put it crudely, although the *epistemology* of pain-avowals seems to answer to the paradigm of Jonesean *self*-awarenesses, the *phenomenology* of pain experience is essentially perceptual. One useful way of explaining what I have in mind here is by exploring a crucial difference between Sellars' account of perception and Kant's.

Sellars explicitly engages Kant's account of perception on two occasions—in his 1965–1966 John Locke Lectures, published as *Science and Metaphysics*, and in his 1977 Dotterer Lecture "The Role of Imagination in Kant's Theory of Experience".[8] The results of these two encounters are significantly different. In SM, Sellars is primarily concerned to support and sharpen Kant's distinction between conceptual and non-conceptual representations. One unavoidable subsidiary project is the sorting out of Kant's various uses of the technical term 'intuition'. In particular, Sellars finds textual support for a distinction between "intuitions which do and intuitions which do not involve something over and above sheer receptivity" (SM, 4). Kant, he concludes,

---

[8] Published in *Categories: A Colloquium*, ed. Henry W. Johnston, Jr. (Pennsylvanian State University; College Park, PA: 1978), 231–245. Cited hence-forth as "IKTE".

applies the term 'intuition' to both the representations which are formed by the synthesizing activity of the productive imagination and the purely passive representations of receptivity which are the 'matter' which the productive imagination takes into account. (SM, 7)

Let's call this second family of representations "the manifold of sense", taking care not to suppose that the items in question are representations of a manifold *as* a manifold. Kant is quite clear and, especially in A, quite explicit about the need to draw a distinction here:

Every intuition contains in itself a manifold which can be represented as a manifold only in so far as the mind distinguishes the time in the sequence of one impression upon another; for each representation, *in so far as it is contained in a single moment*, can never be anything but an absolute unity. In order that unity of intuition may arise out of this manifold (as is required in the representation of space) it must first be run through, and held together. This act I name the *synthesis of apprehension* ... (A99)[9]

Kant, in turn, ascribes synthesis in general, and so the synthesis of apprehension in particular, to the *imagination* (A78 = B103). One key exegetical question, then, is just what to make of this notion.

In SM, Sellars is relatively noncommittal about the imagination. He cites Kant's reference to "a blind but indispensable function of the soul" (A78 = B103), and, following the lead of (A79 = B104) according to which "the same function which gives unity to the various representations *in a judgment* also give unity to the mere synthesis of various representations *in an intuition* ..." concludes, correctly, that "this imagination, under the name 'productive imagination', is the understanding functioning in a special way" (SM, 4).[10]

When we then proceed to inquire in *what* "special way" the understanding functions *qua* imagination, the answer we find in SM is: to produce a special sub-class of *conceptual* representings (SM, 7), namely, *cognitive* representations of a *this-such* nexus, e.g., " 'this-cube', which, though not a judgment, is obviously closely connected with the judgment 'This is a cube' " (SM, 5). On this reading, the synthesis of apprehension in intuition (A98 ff.) differs from the synthesis of recognition in a concept (A103 ff.), not by being *non*-conceptual, but by making use of a (general) concept in a special, *non-predicative* way. (SM, 16) As Sellars sees it, then, a fully discerning and perspicuous Kant would be

clear about the radical difference between sense impressions proper and the intuitions synthesized by the productive imagination. Such a Kant would then have distinguished between:

[9] Citations in this form are to Kant's *Critique of Pure Reason*, tr. Norman Kemp Smith (Macmillan & Co., Ltd. & St. Martin's Press; New York: 1929 & 1965). In the interest of exegetical accuracy, I shall occasionally depart from Kemp Smith's translation.

[10] Sellars appropriately cites in this connection Kant's treatment of the imagination at B151 ff. He evidently overlooks, however, the explicit echo of A78 = B105 at B162 n. b: "It is one and the same spontaneity, which in the one case, under the title of imagination, and in the other case, under the title of understanding, brings combination into the manifold of intuition."

(a) the non-conceptual representations of outer sense proper which ... are strictly speaking non-spatial complexes of unextended and uncoloured impressions;

(b) the intuitive (but conceptual) representations of extended structures located in space. (SM, 28)

In IKTE, in contrast, Sellars acknowledges a second, distinct and important, job for the productive imagination, namely, the construction of what he there calls "sense-image models":

[Perceptual] consciousness involves the *constructing of sense-image models of external objects*. This construction is the work of the imagination responding to the stimulation of the retina. From this point on I shall speak of these models as image-models ... (IKTE, §26)

Sellars' argument for the conclusion that perception involves image-models is phenomenological: When we see an object, for instance, a cool juicy red apple, although we see it *as* having a juicy cool white interior and *as* red not only on the facing side but also on the opposite side as well,

we do not see *of* the apple its opposite side, or its inside, or its internal whiteness, or its coolness, or its juiciness. But while these features are not *seen*, they are not *merely* believed in. These features are present in the object of perception as actualities. (IKTE, §21)

Certain features of a perceived object, in other words, while they are not themselves *strictu sensu* perceived, are nevertheless not merely "intentionally inexistent" but actually "bodily present" in the perceptual experience. Sellars concludes that they are present as *imagined*.

Roughly imagining is an intimate blend of imaging and conceptualization, ... Thus, imagining a cool juicy red apple (*as* a cool juicy red apple) is a matter of (a) *imaging* a unified structure containing as aspects images of a volume of white, surrounded by red, and mutually pervading volumes of juiciness and coolth, (b) *conceptualizing* this unified image-structure as a cool juicy red apple. (IKTE, §23)

Perceiving simply adds sensing to this mix; it is a matter of *sensing-cum-imagining* such a unified structure and, here, conceptualizing it as an apple.

The thesis that imagination is an indispensable constituent of perception is thoroughly Kantian.

Psychologists have hitherto failed to realise that imagination is a necessary ingredient of perception itself. This is due partly to the fact that that faculty has been limited to reproduction, partly to the belief that the senses not only supply impressions but also combine them so as to generate images of objects. For that purpose something more than the mere receptivity of impressions is undoubtedly required, namely, a function for the synthesis of them. (A120 n. a)

Sellars' "sense-image models" are precisely such Kantian "images of objects" (*Bilder der Gegenstände*).[11] Such images embody the *perceptival* character of

---

[11] As Sellars of course recognizes (cf. IKTE, §§31–45), the story of such images and their perspectival character is part of the larger Kantian story regarding what he calls the *schematism* of

perceptual experience, i.e., the fact that we experience the world, and so objects in it, from a point of view:

When, for instance, by apprehension of the manifold of a house I make the empirical intuition of it into a perception, the *necessary unity* of space and of outer sensible intuition in general lies at the basis of my apprehension, and I draw as it were the outline of the house in conformity with this synthetic unity of the manifold in space. (B162)

As Sellars puts it:

The perspectival character of the image model is one of its most pervasive and distinctive features. It constitutes a compelling reason for the thesis of the transcendental ideality of the image-model world. Image-models are "phenomenal objects." Their *esse* is to be *representatives* or *proxies*. Their *being* is that of being complex patterns of sensory states constructed by the productive imagination. (IKTE, §28).

As Kant tells us, in short, "the transcendental synthesis of the imagination" is "an effect [*Wirkung*] of the understanding on the sensibility" (B 152).

The upshot of these reflections is that, in contrast to the purely conceptual work envisioned for it in SM, the productive imagination in IKTE is doing two different and complementary jobs. As "a unique blend of a capacity to form images *in accordance with* a recipe, and a capacity to conceive of objects in a way which *supplies* the relevant recipes" (IKTE, §31),

the productive imagination generates both the complex demonstrative conceptualization [e.g.]

>   This red pyramid facing me edgewise

and the simultaneous *image-model*, which is a point-of-viewish image of ... a red pyramid facing one edgewise. (IKTE, §36)

Thus where Sellars' account of perception in SM was, we might say, "two level", distinguishing only the (non-cognitive) deliverances of pure receptivity that we are calling the manifold of sense and a (cognitive) perceptual judgment, causally evoked by them:

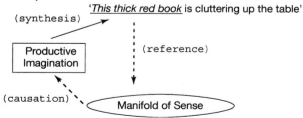

the pure concepts of understanding (A 137–147 = B176–187). I explore these connections in "Kantian Schemata and the Unity of Perception", in *Language and Thought*, Alex Burri, ed. (Walter de Gruyter Verlag; Berlin and New York: 1997), 179–87.

the account offered in IKTE is "three level", interposing an image-model, worked up by the productive imagination, between the materials supplied by the manifold of sense and their conceptualization in a perceptual taking:[12]

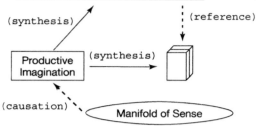

'*This thick red book facing me frontwise* is cluttering up the table'

Jonesean self-awareness resembles the first of these pictures in being "two-level", but the similarity ends there. The relevant judgment contains no demonstrative indexical, and the productive imagination simply isn't involved at all.

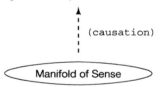

'I am having a sense impression of a red rectangle'

What convinces Sellars in SM that he can get along without image-models is his critique of Kant's failure to appreciate the possibility that the manifold of sense admits of *intrinsic* characterization in terms of "analogical counterparts of the perceptible qualities and relations of physical things and events" (SM, 30). A receptivity which is thus *in itself* both qualitied and relationally-structured, Sellars there concludes, is already capable of guiding " 'from without' the unique conceptual activity which is representing of *this-suches* as subjects of perceptual judgment" (SM, 16). While this is surely correct as far as it goes, the sensitive phenomenology of IKTE is one route to the realization that a complete theory of perception nevertheless requires a further mediating synthetic construction out of sensory materials *per se*.[13]

---

[12] The diagram tidily represents two aspects of Kant's "threefold synthesis": the synthesis of apprehension in an intuition, which issues in the *image-model*, and the synthesis of recognition in a concept, which issues in the *perceptual taking*, i.e., the indexical subject term of the perceptual judgment. The remaining aspect, the synthesis of reproduction in imagination, specifically concerns perception across time. It is implicit in all of these diagrams which, so to speak, represent instantaneous cross-sections of temporally extended processes and activities.

[13] A consideration of ambiguous figures, e.g., Jastrow's duck-rabbit or the familiar reversible cube, leads to the same conclusion. On the face of it, the intrinsic qualities and structural relationship of elements of the manifold of sense remain constant during a "Gestalt switch" from seeing one aspect of such a figure to seeing the other, but the *image* changes dramatically.

The *rough* outlines of a Sellarsian account of pain concepts are relatively straight-forward. Our genius Jones postulates a further family of states of sentient organisms—let us say "*algesic* states"—which (1) are characteristically brought about by damage or injury to some part of the organism and (2) typically result in the complex of observable phenomena that philosophers have become accustomed to referring to as "pain behavior" (perceptive behavioral phenome-nologists in the tradition of the later Wittgenstein properly include under this heading not only, so to speak, the explicit cries and twitches of the injured party, but also those subtler behaviors which characteristically evoke a variety of relevant *social* conducts, e.g., the tendency of other organisms to behave sympathetically, comfortingly, and even therapeutically toward the suffering organism). Unlike sense impressions and thoughts, however, which are intro-duced as states of the perceiving or thinking organism as a whole, algesic states are introduced as states of *bodily parts* of the organism. Paradigmatically, a feeling of pain is assigned a bodily location, L, corresponding to the locus of organic injury or damage which characteristically produces it. Finally, Jones once again engages in his patented two-step pedagogy, teaching his companions, first, to *conclude* that they feel pain in L when, in accordance with his theory, such a conclusion is in fact warranted, and second, to make a *reporting* use of the same theoretical language.

The account is so far so tidy that it may seem obsessively pedantic to ask what the *model* for Jones' theory of algesic states might be and whether the language in which his protégés report their feelings of pain is basic or analogically derived, but the questions strike me as unavoidable. For when we ask which of our three theoretical pictures most closely captures the phenomenology of pain, the answer must be that it is *something like* the second, full-blown Kantian, picture of perception, complete with image-models. When I feel a pain in my foot, there is surely something "bodily present" in my experience, present other than as merely believed in, which I *take to be* the pain in my foot. Feelings of pain are veritable paradigms of "immediate experiences". Unlike self-ascriptions of thoughts or sense impressions, the judgments characteristic of pain experience seem to be as intuitive and schematized as those characteristic of sensory perception, e.g., "*This throbbing pain in my left foot* makes it difficult to concentrate."

That we are dealing only with *something like* Kantian perception, however, is shown, for example, by the fact that, unlike expanses of red, pains are only indirectly located in space. The *immediate* locus of a pain is rather a region of the *sensible body*, and while the sensible body normally spatially coincides with the physical organism, such phenomena as phantom limb pain show that this is not inevitably or necessarily so. Like the sense-image models of perception proper, the sensible body is a transcendentally ideal *construct*. It is a "phenomenal object" whose *esse* is to represent or stand proxy for the spatially-articulated living organism. And it seems reasonable to conclude that here, too, we are dealing with complex patterns of sensory states worked up into a synthetic unity by the productive imagination.

The most common way of describing pains is in terms of their characteristic *causes*, e.g., as stabbing, shooting, or burning pains. A pain can be an ache or a twinge, dull or sharp, tingling, smarting, or throbbing.[14] These idioms suggest that Jones has available at least an *extrinsic*, "topic neutral", characterization of his postulated algesic states. But does the fact that such states are theoretical entities enable us, as it did in the case of sense impressions, to "understand how they can be *intrinsically* characterized—that is to say, characterized by something more than a *definite description*, such as 'entity of *the kind which* has [such and such] as its standard cause'" (EPM, 192)? It seems unlikely that it does. For where we could draw on the model of "inner replicas" to implicitly define "two families of predicates … applicable to sense impressions, one of which has a logical space analogous to that of colours, the other a logical space analogous to that of the spatial properties of physical things" (P, 94), the appeal to characteristic causal antecedents in the case of pains yields no appropriate analogously articulated model. Surely we do not want to say, for example, that shooting, stabbing, and burning pains resemble and differ from one another in a way which is formally analogous to that in which shootings, stabbings, and burnings resemble and differ.

Nor, I think, do we want to say, what may initially seem more plausible, that shooting, stabbing, and burning pains resemble and differ from one another in a way which is formally analogous to that in which being shot, being stabbed, and being burned, *qua* forms of bodily damage, resemble and differ. The relevant logical space here is perhaps available to forensic pathologists, but it hardly has either the salience or the pervasiveness of, for instance, the relationships of betweenness and exclusion fundamental to the logic of color-space. The unavoidable conclusion seems to me to be that there is in fact no suitable model for Jones' introduction of algesic states, i.e., no model with the inferential richness requisite to found a sufficiently comprehensive family of analogical predicates to intrinsically characterize such states. But if this is so, it is by no means obvious how to adapt Sellars' insightful account of the derivative character of our privileged access to our thoughts and sense impressions to the case of pains.[15]

---

[14] Pain also comes in *degrees*, from mild to excruciating, and, of course, the *temporal* structure of pain experience also enters significantly into our descriptions. Thus pains can be characterized as momentary, continuous, or intermittent; transient or recurring. Here, however, we will continue to bracket diachronic aspects of awareness.

[15] The alternative reporting idiom exemplified by "My left foot hurts" suggests the possibility of a hybrid position according to which one is intuitively (deictically) aware of a region of one's sensible body *as*, for instance, "throbbing painfully". the form of the correlative judgment, in other words, would be something like "This painfully throbbing left-foot-region-of-my-body makes it difficult to concentrate". The suggestion is certainly ingenious, but I am convinced that, unfortunately, it does not reflect the actual phenomenology of pain experience.

12

Sellarsian Seeing: In Search of Perceptual Authority

INTRODUCTION

In this essay, I propose to insert myself into an ongoing dispute between John McDowell and Robert Brandom regarding the relationship between perceptual experience and epistemic justification.[1] Each is reacting in his own way to a well-known account offered by Sellars in "Empiricism and the Philosophy of Mind" [EPM], and each offers a critical alternative to it. I want to suggest that neither Brandom's nor McDowell's alternative is ultimately satisfactory—Brandom's for some of the reasons that likely motivated Sellars to reject a reliabilist externalism, and McDowell's for some of the same reasons that Sellars brings critically to bear on classical foundationalist givenness. Sellars' own notoriously strong epistemic internalism, I shall argue, is preferable in its essentials to both Brandom's and McDowell's alternatives. I will close by suggesting that some of Brandom's ideas, while not sufficient to serve as a complete self-standing account of the matter, can nevertheless be useful in defusing the most problematic elements of Sellars' position, those which have repeatedly drawn critical fire.

McDOWELL

The original locus of the Sellarsian account of perceptual knowledge that frames the dispute in question here is Part VIII, §§32–38 of EPM. One thing that McDowell and Brandom do share is a commitment to the *normative* conception of the epistemic on which Sellars there insists:

---

[1] Although the dispute had doubtless already been under way at Pittsburgh for a while—I witnessed a version of it at a Chapel Hill Colloquium in the early 1990's—it first surfaced in print in 1995, in McDowell's [KI] and Brandom's response [KSA]. It reemerged in 1998 in a *Philosophy and Phenomenological Research* book symposium on McDowell's *Mind and World* in Brandom's [PRC] and McDowell's [RC], elements of which echoed a prior, less-accessible encounter—Brandom's [PRC0] and McDowell's [RB]—published in 1996 in the Proceedings of the 7th SOFIA conference, on Perception. Its most recent outcropping is McDowell's 2002 retrospective protest, [KIR], which is the immediate occasion of my present comments. (I have also engaged aspects of McDowell's views in [SU], appearing obscurely in 2001.)

In characterizing an episode or state as that of *knowing*, we are not giving an empirical description of that episode or state; we are placing it in the logical space of reasons, of justifying and being able to justify what one says. [EPM §36]

What they disagree about, to put it in McDowell's terms, is the shape and extent of the logical space of reasons.

That a satisfactory standing in the space of reasons is necessary for knowledge is not a matter of dispute. McDowell, however, presses the question of sufficiency. To highlight the issue, he asks us to consider one instance of an epistemically satisfactory standing within the space of reasons—*prima facie*, a paradigm of perceptual knowledge—namely, an instance of *seeing that things are thus and so*. When I see that things are thus and so, he writes,

I take it that things are thus and so on the basis of having it look to me as if things are thus and so. And it can look to me as if things are thus and so when they are not: appearances do not give me the resources to ensure that I take things to be thus and so on the basis of appearances only when things are indeed thus and so. If things are indeed thus and so when they seem to be, the world is doing me a favor. So if I want to restrict myself to standings in the space of reasons whose flawlessness I can ensure without external help, I must go no further than taking it that it looks to me as if things were thus and so. [KI, 877–8]

The classical sequel to this sort of Argument from Illusion is an attempt to tell a story designed to show that it is possible to begin with such an "interiorized" conception of the space of reasons, as McDowell calls it, and, availing myself of "anything else that the ground rules allow", to proceed to "a derivatively satisfactory standing in the space of reasons, with respect to the fact that things are as they look, which I achieved by myself without needing to be indebted to the world". The "dreary history of epistemology", he dryly remarks, shows that our hope of finding such a story is "rather faint" [KI, 878].

The problem, as he understands it, arises from the *factive* character of seeing that things are thus and so. It is, McDowell emphasizes, "a position that we cannot be in if things are not thus and so". But our epistemic project is

to reconstruct the epistemic satisfactoriness implicit in the idea of seeing that things are thus and so, using [only] the following materials: first, the fact that it looks to a subject as if things are that way; second, whatever further circumstances are relevant ...; third, the fact that the policy or habit of accepting appearances in such circumstances is endorsed by reason, in its critical function, as reliable. And now the trouble is this: unless reason can come up with policies or habits that will *never* lead us astray, there is not enough here to add up to what we were trying to reconstruct. [KI, 880]

Eschewing, on the one hand, skepticism and, on the other, the rationalist *hubris* of supposing human reason to be equipped with belief-forming dispositions or policies that are utterly immune to the possibility of error, what ostensibly remains is a "hybrid" account of knowledge according to which a satisfactory standing within the space of reasons is necessary but *not* sufficient.

Rather, knowledge is a status that one possesses by virtue of an appropriate standing in the space of reasons when—this is an extra condition, not ensured by one's standing in the space of reasons—the world does one the favor of being so arranged that what one takes to be so is so. [KI, 881]

It is now easy to recognize this hybrid conception as nothing different from the traditional account of knowledge as justified true belief. To have an appropriate standing in the space of reasons is to be rationally warranted or justified in believing what one does. What such "doxastic blamelessness", as McDowell sometimes puts it, cannot guarantee, and so what it remains for the world to provide, is the truth of what is believed. But one way to show the unsatisfactoriness of this sort of hybrid conception, McDowell proposes, is precisely to interrogate the classical distinction between knowledge and true belief. For the traditional role of a justification is precisely to distinguish knowledge from *accidentally* true belief, and while

it is admittedly not a complete accident, relative to someone's standing in the space of reasons, if things are as she takes them to be ... the reason why the extra stipulation that the belief is true—what is distinctive of the hybrid approach—is needed is that the likelihood of truth is the best that the space of reasons yields, on the interiorized conception of it: the closest we can come to factiveness. The extra that we need for knowledge ... is, relative to the knower's moves in the space of reasons, a stroke of good fortune, a favor that the world does her. [KI, 884]

The believer's having gotten hold of the truth, in other words, if not accidental, is at least *adventitious*, a piece of *epistemic luck*, and that is quite enough to render it problematic as a supposed instance of perceptual knowing.

The immediate moral that McDowell proposes to draw from these considerations is that "it is not a good idea to suppose that a satisfactory standing in the space of reasons might be part but not the whole of what knowledge is" [KI, 884]. We must either reject the relevance of a believer's standing in the space of reasons *tout court* and embrace an uncompromising radically externalist account of knowledge, or accept the conclusion that a satisfactory standing in the space of reasons is *both* necessary *and* sufficient for knowledge. Adopting the latter course, McDowell consequently proposes to abandon the *interiorized conception* of the space of reasons.

In *Mind and World*, this abandonment takes the form of an insistence that the space of reasons is not *bounded*.

Although reality is independent of our thinking, it is not to be pictured as outside an outer boundary that encloses the conceptual sphere. *That things are thus and so* is the conceptual content of an experience, but if the subject of the experience is not misled, that very same thing, *that things are thus and so*, is also a perceptible fact, an aspect of the perceptible world. [MW, 26]

On this conception, perceptual experience is a matter of "taking in how things are", of "openness to the layout of reality" itself [MW, 26]. There is no *distance* between a knower's standing in the space of reasons and what is known, "no ontological gap between ... the sort of thing one can think, and the sort of thing that can be the case".

When one thinks truly, what one thinks *is* what is the case. So since the world is everything that is the case ..., there is no gap between thought, as such, and the world. [MW, 27]

Only by recognizing that the space of reasons *subsumes* the experienced world, can we escape from an "interminable oscillation" [MW, 9] between the idea that in order to be genuinely empirical our thoughts must somehow be grounded by the world, i.e., from *outside* the conceptual realm, and the recognition that what lies completely outside the realm of understanding, although it might indeed *cause* our empirical thoughts, cannot function as a *reason* for holding them.

SELLARS

True to his normative conception of the epistemic, Sellars frames the issue of perceptual knowledge in terms of the epistemic authority of observation reports:

[If] some statements ... are to express *noninferential* knowledge, they must have a credibility which is not a matter of being supported by other statements. Now there does seem to be a class of statements which fill at least part of this bill, namely such statements as would be said to *report observations*, thus, 'This is red.' These statements, candidly made, have authority. Yet they are not expressions of inference. How, then, is this authority to be understood? (EPM §32)

How is authority in general to be understood?[2] On the one hand, the locus of authority evidently lies in the authoritative. Expertise resides in the expert. The educated palate, the trained ear, or the discerning eye inheres in the connoisseur. Authority, in other words, is conceived as already there, available to be recognized or acknowledged. But, on the other hand, like any normative status, authority also appears to be *constituted by* its recognition or acknowledgement. An ostensible divine right of kings is empty and impotent unless accepted by their subjects; a general whose commands the troops will not obey has lost his authority. As Kukla puts it,

making sense of something's authoritative status is not the same kind of project as making sense of, for example, its empirical properties. Something is authoritative only if it is binding, and makes a claim on the subject of its authority. Furthermore, for it to genuinely bind or make a claim, its authority must be legitimate. There can be no such thing as real yet illegitimate authority, since such 'authority' would not in fact bind us; the closest there could be to such a thing would be coercive force which makes no normative claims

---

[2] The question is brought into sharp relief by Rebecca Kukla in [MMM], a remarkable essay to which the present discussion is strongly indebted.

upon us. Thus, recognizing authority is inseparable from at least implicitly recognizing that this authority is *already legitimate* ... [MMM, 165]

Recognizing the legitimacy or bindingness of authority, that is, is a condition of recognizing *the very existence* of such authority. A knowledgeable individual is not yet an *expert*, a person capable of fine discriminations not yet a *connoisseur*, until and unless their relevant judgments are ones to which the less knowledgeable and less discriminating are prepared to *defer*.

Against this background, however, the two poles of McDowell's "interminable oscillation" take on the lineaments of paradox. As Sellars emphasizes, the epistemic authority of an observation report or noninferential perceptual judgment is *prima facie* correlative to the epistemic authority of the perceptual *experience* to which it gives expression.

[Two] tokens of a sentence ... can make the same *report* only if, made in all candor, they express the *presence*—in *some* sense of 'presence'—of the state of affairs that is being reported; if, that is, they stand in that relation to the state of affairs ... by virtue of which they can be said to formulate observations of it. ...
[Credibility may thus accrue to a sentence token] from the fact that it came to exist in a certain way in a certain set of circumstances, e.g., 'This is red.' [EPM §32]

But how, then, is the epistemic authority of a perceptual experience—of an instance of *seeing that things are thus and so*—to be understood? Sellars' first answer is this:

To say that a certain experience is a *seeing that* something is the case, is to do more than describe the experience. It is to characterize it as, so to speak, making an assertion or claim, and ... to *endorse* that claim. [EPM §16$_1$]

It is this endorsement which Ryle has in mind when he refers to *seeing that something is thus and so* as an *achievement*, and to 'sees' as an *achievement word*. I prefer to call it a 'so it is' or 'just so' word, for the root idea is that of *truth*. To characterize S's experience as a *seeing* is, in a suitably broad sense ... to apply the semantical concept of truth to that experience. [EPM §16$_2$]

On the face of it, then, the locus of epistemic authority lies in what is *perceived*, for it is by virtue of what is perceived that an ostensible perceiving is veridical or non-veridical. In perceptual experience, an assertion or claim is thus, "so to speak, evoked or wrung from the perceiver by the object perceived" (EPM §16$_2$)—an exercise of the epistemic authority inhering in it. If the correctness of an observation report is construed as the correctness of a rule-governed action, Sellars concludes, then

we are face to face with givenness in its most straightforward form. For these stipulations commit one to the idea that the authority of [observation reports] rests on nonverbal episodes of awareness—awareness *that* something is the case, e.g., *that this is green*—which nonverbal episodes have an intrinsic authority (they are, so to speak, 'self-authenticating') which the *verbal* performances ... 'express'. One is committed to a stratum of authoritative nonverbal episodes ('awarenesses'), the authority of which accrues to a superstructure of *verbal actions* ... [EPM §34]

In this way, McDowell's "oscillation" arrives at its first pole. Seeking an alternative, we may then be tempted by the reliabilist picture:

An overt or covert token of 'This is green' in the presence of a green item is an [observation report] and expresses observational knowledge if and only if it is a manifestation of a tendency to produce overt or covert tokens of 'This is green'—given a certain set—if and only if a green object is being looked at in standard conditions. [EPM §35]

But this clearly does not yet accommodate the *normativity* of the epistemic.

The first hurdle ... concerns the *authority* which, as I have emphasized, a sentence token must have in order that it may be said to express knowledge. Clearly, on this [reliabilist] account the only thing that can remotely be supposed to constitute such authority is the fact that one can infer the presence of a green object from the fact that someone makes this report. [EPM § 35]

Mere possibility, however, is not yet epistemic authority. Authority is constituted by its recognition or acknowledgement. And so there is a "decisive" second hurdle:

[To] be the expression of knowledge, a report must not only *have* authority, this authority must *in some sense* be recognized by the person whose report it is. And this is a steep hurdle indeed. For if the authority of the report 'This is green' lies in the fact that the existence of green items appropriately related to the perceiver can be inferred from the occurrence of such reports, it follows that only a person who is able to draw this inference, and therefore who has not only the concept *green*, but also the concept of uttering 'This is green'—indeed, the concept of certain conditions of perception, those which would correctly be called 'standard conditions'—could be in a position to token 'This is green' in recognition of its authority. In other words for [a tokening of] 'This is green' to 'express observational knowledge' not only must it be a *symptom* or *sign* of the presence of a green object in standard conditions, but the perceiver must know that tokens of 'This is green' *are* [such] symptoms ... [EPM §35]

This is Sellars' notorious *strong internalism*, and its *prima facie* paradoxical character was manifest even to its author:

Now it might be thought that there is something obviously absurd in the idea that before a token uttered by, say, Jones could be the expression of observational knowledge, Jones would have to know that overt verbal episodes of this kind are reliable indicators of the existence, suitably related to the speaker, of green objects. [EPM §36]

What Kukla's discussion of the nature of normative authority usefully brings out is how deep the ostensible paradoxicality lies:

Objects may *demand of us* that we make certain claims ... but they can do so only in virtue of our being already committed to recognizing these demands and taking them as binding. Sellars thus finds himself in a circle, wherein epistemic authority depends upon recognition of the authority of things, and recognition of the authority of things depends upon our already being negotiators of the space of reasons who are capable of this recognition. [MMM, 204]

BRANDOM

Turning now to Brandom, while it would be a distortion to describe him as embracing an "uncompromising radically externalist account of knowledge", he does explicitly endorse what he calls the 'Founding Insight' of reliabilist epistemologies, namely,

the claim that true beliefs can, at least in some cases, amount to genuine knowledge even where the justifcations condition is not met (in the sense that the candidate knower is unable to produce suitable justifcations), provided the beliefs resulted from the exercise of capacities that are *reliable* producers of true beliefs in the circumstances in which they were in fact exercised. [AR, 97]

Such reliabilism, Brandom insists, is an acceptable form of *moderate externalism*. At least sometimes, "knowledge can be diagnosed quite apart from any consideration of the space of reasons" [KSA, 896]. In contrast,

Extreme, or … *gonzo* externalists mistakenly infer from the fact that issues of justification and reason-giving can be treated as *locally* irrelevant to attributions of knowledge in such cases, that they can safely be treated as *globally* irrelevant. The problem with this form of externalism is not with its construal of the *justification* condition on knowledge, but with its construal of the *belief* condition on knowledge. [KSA, 899]

Like McDowell, then, Brandom adopts Sellars' metaphor of the "space of reasons", but, unlike McDowell, he insists that it

ought to be understood as an abstraction from concrete practices of giving and asking for reasons. The space of reasons is a normative space. It is articulated by proprieties that govern practices of citing one standing as committing or entitling one to another—that is, as a reason for another. What people actually *do* is adopt, assess, and attribute such standings—and if they did not, there would be no such standings. For in the absence of such normative attitudes of taking or treating people as committed or entitled, there are no commitments or entitlements. They are not part of the furniture of the prehuman world. [KSA, 898]

Brandom consequently insists that it is a mistake to "*individualize* the space of reasons". "The complaint I want to make about McDowell's discussion," he writes, "is that he makes nothing of the essential *social* articulation of that space" [KSA, 902]. The fundamental sort of standing in the space of reasons is "*staking a claim*, that is, undertaking a commitment of the sort that might be expressed by making a claim or assertion" [KSA, 898]. Claims or assertions paradigmatically express one's *beliefs*, and

Beliefs—indeed, anything that is propositionally contentful ... and so conceptually articulated—are essentially things that can serve as premises and conclusions of inferences. [AR, 108]

Only the *inferential articulation* of perceptual responses, Brandom concludes, i.e., only their role in the sort of discursive reasoning by which entitlements are challenged, commitments defended, and standings in the space of reasons thereby secured, makes them applications of concepts and expressions of beliefs in the first place. It follows that

nothing that can't move in the space of reasons—nothing that can't distinguish some claims or beliefs as *justifying* or being reasons for others—can even count as a concept user or believer, never mind a knower: it would be in another line of work altogether. [KSA, 897]

That is why extreme or gonzo externalism misconstrues the *belief* condition on knowledge.

What reconciles Brandom's moderate externalism with his conceptual inferentialism is what he calls the 'Implicit Insight' of epistemological reliabilism, the thesis that "concern with reliability should itself be understood as concern with the goodness of a distinctive kind of *inference*" [AR, 117].

The key point to understanding reliability as a warrantive standing in the space of reasons is that the notion of reliability itself is essentially an *inferential* notion: a matter precisely of what is a reason for what. ... [Reliability] is precisely a matter of a *socially* articulated inference. For me to take you to be a reliable reporter of [for instance] lighted candles in darkened rooms is just for me to endorse a particular pattern of reasoning; ... the inference that could be made explicit by saying:

> *If* in a darkened room S noninferentially acquires the belief that there is a lighted candle, *then* (probably) there is a lighted candle there.

... [This] is an inferential connection between a suitably noninferentially acquired commitment *attributed* to you and a corresponding commitment that I *undertake*. It is treating your commitment as a (defeasible) reason for my own. [KSA, 905–6]

Brandom thus "externalizes" Sellars' strong internalism. The authority of an observation report is indeed constituted by recognition of that authority, but it need not be recognition by the person who *issues* the report. *Pace* Sellars, in order for Jones' utterance of 'This is green' to be correctly judged to be an expression of observational knowledge, Jones himself does not need to know that verbal episodes of that kind are reliable indicators of suitably located green objects. Rather, one who *ascribes* observational knowledge to Jones must be willing to endorse the "reliability inference" from his having uttered 'This is green' in such-and-such circumstances to the existence of a green object suitably related to him.

Consider an expert on classical Central American pottery who over the years has acquired the ability to tell Toltec from Aztec—reliably though not infallibly—simply by looking at them. We may suppose that there are no separately distinguishing features of the fragments that she can cite in justifying her classifications. When looking closely at the pieces, she just finds herself believing that some of them are Toltec and others Aztec. Suppose further that she regards beliefs formed in this way with great suspicion ... Before reporting to colleagues, or publishing conclusions that rest on evidence as to whether particular bits are Toltec or Aztec, she always does microscopic and chemical analyses that give her solid inferential evidence for the classification. That is, she does not believe that she is a reliable noninferential reporter of Toltec and Aztec potsherds ... But suppose that her colleagues ... have noticed that she is in fact a reliable distinguisher of one sort of pottery from the other. ... It seems reasonable for them to say, in some case where she turned out to be right, that although she insisted on confirmatory evidence for her belief, in fact she already knew that the fragment in question was Toltec, even before bringing her microscope and reagents into play. [AR, 98–9]

Such epistemological reliabilism about perceptual beliefs, Brandom argues, "fully meets McDowell's demand for their rational criticizability" [PRC, 371]. It provides the proper normative component to the Sellarsian story that McDowell calls [MW, 34] the view "from sideways on". According to this story,

when we are properly wired up and trained, the perceptible facts wring from us perceptual judgments. In order to *explain* how this is possible—quite a different enterprise from *justifying* the resulting judgments—we postulate the existence of something like sense impressions ... But these sense impressions ... are not something we are aware of, and they do not themselves have conceptual content. They merely occasion contentful perceptual judgments. [PRC, 372]

Since such sense impressions play no *justificatory* role, this view sidesteps the Myth of the Given. A suitable story regarding the inferential engagement of such noninferentially elicited perceptual judgments with other judgments secures their standing in the logical space of reasons. And a socially normative externalism which keys our assessments of the perceiver's entitlement to such judgments of the reliability of the process which elicits them and identifies our acceptance of their correctness with our own undertaking of a commitment to them satisfies McDowell's central demand for "rational constraint by how things actually are". The story "from sideways on" is thus "precisely an account of how *in* experience (perception) the world exerts a rational (criticizable) influence on our thinking" [PRC, 372]. McDowell fails to appreciate this possibility "because he systematically underplays the significance of the *social* dimension of the practice of giving and asking for reasons ..." [PRC, 373].

McDowell insists that we cannot have perceptual knowledge unless,

... when we use our concepts in judgment, our freedom—our spontaneity in the exercise of our understanding—is constrained from outside thought, and constrained in a way that we can appeal to in displaying our judgments as justified. [MW, 8]

Here it is clear, Brandom argues, that McDowell implicitly accepts the individualist assumption that "the one whose judgment is justified must be the *same* one who can appeal to the external constraint in justifying it" [PRC, 373], and that assumption is gratuitous.

If we take the *we* seriously ..., the one who can see the constraint as justifying the application of the concept may be someone *else*, someone *other* than the one who is applying the concept. [PRC, 374]

Epistemological reliabilism, concludes Brandom, thus allows us consistently to sustain a "sideways on" view which distinguishes the *causes* of perceptual judgments from the *reasons* that justify them, and thereby to understand how there can be and is *more* to perceptual knowledge than a standing in the logical space of reasons *per se*.

CONTRA BRANDOM

Suppose there were a rare sort of brain injury, a "reflexive brain lesion", which had the curious effect of producing the *belief* the one was suffering from a reflexive brain lesion.[3] Finding himself with the persistently recurring spontaneous disturbing conviction that he has a reflexive brain lesion, Barney (let us call him) consults a knowledgeable neurologist. "I don't know what to make of it, Doctor. I just can't help thinking that I have a reflexive brain lesion." "That's because you *do* have a reflexive brain lesion," replies the neurologist. "It's an absolutely conclusive symptom. But don't worry about it. It's also the only effect of having one."

A person suffering from a reflexive brain lesion, in order words, is a reliable noninferential reporter of the fact that he is suffering from a reflexive brain lesion. The neurologist, who knows this, straightway concludes from Barney's spontaneous inclination to *believe* that he has such a brain injury that Barney *does* have such a brain injury. The neurologist thereby comes to know—by way of a reliability inference—that Barney has a reflexive brain lesion. But it is surely *not* reasonable to say that, before consulting the neurologist, Barney *himself* already knew that he had a reflexive brain lesion. Whatever its effects, his brain injury does not confer upon Barney a suitable standing in the logical space of reasons.

I want to suggest that the case of Brandom's expert on Central American Pottery—let's call her 'Meg'—resembles this one in significant ways. Of course there are differences as well, but I think that they are equally instructive. Confronted with a fragment of pottery, we are told, Meg finds herself spontaneously believing, correctly, that it is, say, Toltec. Like Barney's knowledgeable neurologist, Meg's colleagues know the evidentiary value of such spontaneous

---

[3] This is an adaptation of a scenario suggested by Ernest Sosa, in "Propositional Knowledge", *Philosophical Studies*, 20 (1969).

beliefs. Recalling Meg's track record of successful spontaneous identifications, they straightaway conclude, and thereby come to know—by way of a reliability inference—that the fragment *is* Toltec. But, unlike Barney's neurologist, Meg's colleagues go on to attribute such knowledge to *her* as well. Brandom insists that this is a reasonable thing for them to do. But the correlation between Barney's spontaneous neurological belief and *its* truth is just as reliable as the correlations between Meg's spontaneous classificatory beliefs and *their* truth. What might make it reasonable for a third party to attribute first-person knowledge in Meg's case, but not in Barney's?

One difference between the cases is that Meg has acquired her propensity to have reliable beliefs about the provenance of potsherds gradually, through repeated experience. Barney's propensity to have reliable beliefs about a specific sort of damage to his brain perhaps developed suddenly, when the damage occurred. Again, Meg knows what it *means* for a fragment of pottery to be Aztec or Toltec, and she knows what microscopic and chemical test results would confirm or disconfirm her spontaneous classificatory judgments. Those judgments have a rich sense for her, and one that is independent of her spontaneous inclinations to make them. Barney's spontaneous beliefs evidently have some independent sense for him as well—why else would he consult a *neurologist?*—but there's not much to it: A "reflexive brain lesion" must be some sort of damage to the brain. Neurologists are the people who know about such things.

But if all this is relevant, then, if Meg's colleagues *are* entitled to their ascription of first-person knowledge, what entitles them to it is much more than just a reliability inference. It includes as well the additional information that Meg has the training, experience, and expertise to be in a position to recognize Aztec fragments *as Aztec* and Toltec fragments *as Toltec*, and that she has in fact *learned* to do so. Each of Meg's spontaneous classificatory beliefs is then a position in the logical space of *her* reasons. She knows what justificatory considerations count for and against its truth, and she knows what it implies about the manufacture and history of the fragment in question.

But then Meg's own *attitude* toward her spontaneous classificatory judgments becomes deeply mysterious. Unlike her colleagues, Meg manifests a peculiar lack of awareness of the probative value of those judgments. Indeed, she actively distrusts them, viewing them, we are told, with "great suspicion". All those many successful spontaneous classifications that so instructively impressed her colleagues, classifications that she herself subsequently confirmed by her own microscopic and chemical tests, have evidently left no *epistemic* impression upon her at all. And these facts, I suggest, call her colleagues' knowledge ascriptions into question in another way. For *either* Meg's spontaneous reactions are too tentative and guarded to count as the sort of *beliefs* that might qualify as knowledge in the first place—an inclination to believe is not yet a belief—*or*, if Meg's spontaneous reactions are indeed full-fledged beliefs, marked by a suitable degree of conviction, then her insensibility to her *entitlement* to such convictions, by virtue of training, experience, and expertise, and to her own reliability manifests a degree of epistemic deviance sufficient to disqualify them as knowledge. They are then *for her* what Barney's spontaneous beliefs are *for him*, doxastic curiosities—epistemically disconnected from the results of her subsequent microscopic and chemical investigations of the fragments. One way or another, then, Meg does not *herself* have a suitable standing in the logical space of reasons.

CONTRA McDOWELL

McDowell agrees that Brandom's story fails to depict Meg as having the sort of standing in the logical space of reasons that is required for her spontaneous beliefs to qualify as perceptual knowledge, but his criticism rests on quite different grounds. The gravamen of his complaint against traditional accounts of knowledge is that they are committed to an *interiorized* conception of the space of reasons, and Brandom's social-perspectival account of knowledge, he argues, is equally committed to that conception.

I argue against views according to which knowledge is only partly constituted by standings in the space of reasons, with the requirement that what a knower takes to be so is indeed so [being] conceived as an extra condition ... Brandom purports to respect my point. In his account, an attributor of knowledge attributes a commitment and an entitlement, and herself undertakes a commitment corresponding to the commitment attributed. This third component of knowledge attributions is Brandom's counterpart to the traditional truth requirement for knowledge. Brandom purports to respect my argument by saying that the distinction of perspectives that matters for his account ... is "a distinction of perspectives *within* the space of reasons, not a distinction between what is within it and what is without it" [KSA, 906]. But this appearance of respecting my point is an illusion, generated by an equivocation on the phrase "space of reasons". [KIR, 101]

Brandom's social-perspectival conception of knowledge, insists McDowell, offers just another "view from sideways on".

What I object to is interiorizing *entitlements*, in the sense of refusing to let the connivance of the world enter into constituting them. Applied to the entitlements that perceptual, for instance visual, experience affords, the interiorizing move restricts them to appearances, conceived as a highest common factor between seeing that such-and-such is the case and having it merely look to one as if such-and-such is the case. ... Now Brandom's socially perspectival hybrid conception of knowledge has just that shape. It makes no difference that he can take over my phrase, "standing in the space of reasons," and define it so that it includes the satisfaction of the extra condition. The extra condition is still seen as extra to the knower's entitlement, and that is what ... precludes making sense of the status in question as one of knowledge. [KIR, 102]

Contra Brandom, McDowell insists that a standing in the space of reasons constituting "justification adequate to reveal a state of knowing must be incompatible with falsehood and can be had" [KIR, 98]. On his view, *seeing that such-and-such is the case* is just such a standing. Someone who can truly make a claim of the form "I see that ..."

> has an entitlement, incompatible with any possibility of falsehood, to a claim whose content is given by the embedded proposition. The entitlement consists in the visual availability to her of the fact she would affirm in making that claim. [KIR, 98]

Separating the third-person ascription of an entitlement from the first-person undertaking of the corresponding commitment, Brandom concludes that

> I may take you to have good reason for believing that there is a candle in front of you, and so take you to be entitled to your commitment, ... even if I know, as you do not, that there is a mirror five feet in front of you, and no candle behind it, so that I am not in a position to endorse or commit myself to what you are committed to. [KSA, 903]

This sort of entitlement, McDowell concedes, might suffice to make your judgment that there is a candle in front of you rational or "doxastically blameless", but "this is not the notion of entitlement or justification that should figure in a gloss on the Sellarsian thought that knowledge is a standing in the space of reasons" [KIR, 99].

> I insist that in the best case the subject can have an entitlement consisting in the fact that she *sees* that there is a candle in front of her. Or, to put it another way: for a subject in the best case, the appearance that there is a candle in front of her is the presence of the candle making itself apparent to her. This is not a mere seeming, which would be compatible with there being no candle there. The subject in the mirror case does not have an entitlement of this kind ... [KIR, 99]

Now one can hardly quarrel with McDowell's claim that someone who *sees that* such-and-such is the case is in a position to *know that* such-and-such is the case. And it is certainly also true that a person who *claims* to know that such-and-such is the case can sensibly respond to the request that he justify his claim, i.e., to the question "*How* do you know?", by *saying* that he sees that such-and-such is the case. Statements of the form "I see that ...", McDowell insists,

> are proper moves in the game of giving reasons, and their truth fully vindicates entitlement to the embedded proposition. [KIR, 98]

But I want to suggest that all this is so because "I see that such-and-such is the case" simply *means* "I *know by seeing* that such-and-such is the case". Seeing that such-and-such is the case is indeed a standing in the space of reasons and both necessary and sufficient for knowing because seeing that such-and-such is the case is an *instance* of knowing that such-and-such is the case. Knowing by seeing is a *species* of knowing. But it is not something *different from* an instance of knowing that is both somehow independently available to the knower and also able to vindicate or justify the knowing.[4]

"I see that things are thus and so" resembles in this way "I remember that things were thus and so". Like the former, the latter claim can sensibly be offered as an answer to the question "How do you know?", and the two claims are factive in just the same way. Each adverts to "a position that we cannot be in if things are not [respectively: were not] thus and so" [KI, 880]. But remembering is not something different from an instance of knowing that is somehow both available to the knower and able to justify or vindicate the knowing. Rather, to remember that things were thus and so is to know it now because one *has known* it and *still knows* it. It is *not*, to adapt McDowell's perceptual idioms, "the mnemonic availability of the fact that one would affirm in making that claim"[5] or "our being directly confronted by a past state of affairs"[6] or "a past state of affairs making itself mnemonically apparent to us".[7]

I confess that I do not know how to understand such idioms. They strike me as expressing yet another form of the Myth of the Given, one that seems to rest on a number of different confusions and misunderstandings. One of them is that "the world is everything that is the case",[8] i.e., the Tractarian thesis that the world *consists* of items that intrinsically possess propositional form, facts or states of affairs. What arguably makes this a confusion is its failure to distinguish a propertied object (e.g., a burning candle) or a group of related objects (e.g., a candle in front of me) from the truth that the object exemplifies the property (that the candle is burning) or that the objects stand in the relation (that the candle is in front of me). What the world *contains* are groups of variously related and variously propertied objects. What possesses propositional form are *truths about* those contents. The Tractarian thesis runs these together.[9]

In §22 of EPM, Sellars observes that the situations

---

[4] If 'I see that *p*' means 'I know by seeing that *p*', then, of course, on pain of ill-foundedness, "I know by seeing that *p* ..." cannot mean "I know that p because I see that *p*". Rather "I know by seeing ..." adverts precisely to an explanatory story in which *visual sensations* play an indispensable *causal* role in the genesis of my (authoritative perceptual) belief that *p*. Eike von Savigny impressed on me the importance of making this explicit.

[5] "The entitlement consists in the visual availability to her of the fact she would affirm in making that claim" [KIR, 98].

[6] "When we are not misled by experience, we are directly confronted by a worldly state of affairs itself, not waited on by an intermediary that happens to tell the truth" [MW, 143].

[7] "If one's justification for 'There's a candle in front of me' is that one sees that there is a candle in front of one (that the presence of a candle in front of one makes itself visually apparent to one), one's entitlement is ... not inherited from a commitment to 'I see that there's a candle in front of me' " [KIR, 100].

[8] "When one thinks truly, what one thinks *is* what is the case. So since the world is everything that is the case ..., there is no gap between thought, as such, and the world" [MW, 27].

[9] For more on this theme, see ch. 6 of my *Linguistic Representation* (D. Reidel Publishing Co.; Dordrecht, Holland: 1974).

(*a*) Seeing that x, over there, is red, and

(*b*) Its looking to one that x, over there, is red

plausibly share both what he calls a common *propositional content*—viz., that x, over there, is red—although the two descriptions differ in the extent to which that content is endorsed,[10] and what he calls a common *descriptive content*—'phenomenological content' would be more perspicuous—which differentiates such situations from, e.g., merely entertaining the thought that x, over there, is red. This clearly echoes Kant's thesis, also endorsed by McDowell, that empirical cognition results from a collaboration between the sensibility and the understanding, and so has both a matter and a form. A second of McDowell's apparent confusions is manifest in his refusal to accept any conceptual perspective "from sideways on" that *separates* propositional from phenomenological content in instances of seeing that such-and-such is the case.[11] What makes this a confusion is that such a perspective is simply unavoidable.[12] Indeed, it is already implicit in McDowell's own discussions, and this comes out when we attend carefully to the *qualifications* that McDowell builds into his claims, for instance:

I insist that *in the best case* the subject can have an entitlement consisting in the fact that she *sees* that there is a candle in front of her. [KIR, 99; first emphasis mine]

When we are not misled by experience, we are directly confronted by a worldly state of affairs itself, not waited on by an intermediary that happens to tell the truth. [MW, 143; my emphasis]

"The best case *of what*?", I want to ask. Well, the best case of visual (or: perceptual) *experience*, I suppose—no more plausible answer suggests itself—but, if there can be better and worse cases of it, then 'experience' must be understood here in the sense of the second citation above, namely, as something, presumably something phenomenological, that might or might not mislead us. Mislead us *about what*? Surely, about whether what we are inclined to *take* or *judge* or *believe* to be true actually *is* true. The best case is one in which we are *not* misled, one in which our experience is veridical, that is, things *are* as they *seem*.

McDowell insists that a case of seeing that there is a candle in front of one "is not a mere seeming, which would be compatible with there being no candle

---

[10] He actually considers three perceptual situations—the third being, (*c*), Its looking to one as though there were a red object over there—and relaxes his notion of the propositional content common to (*a*) and (*b*) to encompass such *existential* lookings as well, but the simpler and stricter notion is better for our purposes here.

[11] In *Mind and World*, this refusal is particularly explicit and uncompromising: "receptivity does not make an even notionally separable contribution to the co-operation [between receptivity and spontaneity]" [MW, 9] I've had a good bit more to say about this claim in [SU].

[12] Thus Sellars: "The very nature of 'looks talk' is such as to raise questions to which it gives no answer: What is the *intrinsic* character of the common descriptive content of these [two] experiences? and, How are they able to have it in spite of the fact that whereas in the case of (*a*) the perceiver must be in the presence of a red object over there, [while] in (*b*) the object over there need not be red ..." [EPM §22].

there" [KIR, 99], and this is correct. But the reason that it's correct is that to say that there *merely* seems to be a candle in front of one is not just compatible with there being no candle there; it *entails* that none is there. That's what 'merely' means. What seems to be true sometimes *is* true, but what *merely* seems to be true never is. But, although such a best case is consequently not a *mere* seeming, it can still be, for all that—and surely is—a *seeming*. That is, even a "best case" experience of seeing that there is a candle in front of one can be *noncommittally described* as its looking to one as if there is a candle in front of him. And then what distinguishes the "best case" of *seeing that* from the "worse case" of its *merely looking as if* is precisely what becomes salient only "from sideways on", namely, the relevant etiology.[13]

These two confusions can combine to create the notion of a *self-intimating* fact or state of affairs—something with the form of a proposition that "discloses itself" in a "best case" perceptual experience, something whose truth-guaranteeing epistemic authority is *inherent* and can thus be appropriated entirely "from within" the logical space of reasons, i.e., independently of any etiological considerations whatsoever "from sideways on". But that, as far as I can see, is just givenness come round again. For look again at Sellars' characterization of "givenness in its most straightforward form":

> ... the idea that the authority of [observation reports] rests on nonverbal episodes of awareness—awareness *that* something is the case, e.g., *that this is green*—which nonverbal episodes have an intrinsic authority (they are, so to speak, 'self-authenticating') which the *verbal* performances ... 'express'. [EPM §34]

McDowell's version is "exteriorized"—the putative intrinsic authority ostensibly ultimately resides in *what is seen*, a fact or state of affairs, rather than in a nonverbal perceptual awareness of it—but it is still the same picture for all that. For on McDowell's account, the authority of an observation *report* is still grounded in a nonverbal episode of perceptual awareness distinct from *it*, e.g., an instance of seeing that such-and-such is the case. His fundamental contention is rather that the content of such an episode is not distinct from the state of affairs reported. It is ostensibly *because* the authority of such an episode is thus, in that sense, "intrinsic" to it (because seeing that such-and-such is the case is, in that sense, a "self-authenticating" epistemic state) that it conveys a putative "entitlement, incompatible with the possibility of falsehood" to the corresponding claim.[14]

---

[13] Compare Sellars: "When I say 'X looks green to me now' I am *reporting* the fact that my experience is, so to speak, intrinsically, *as an experience*, indistinguishable from a veridical one of seeing that X is green. Involved in the report is the ascription to my experience of the claim 'x is green'; and the fact that I make this report rather than the simple report 'X is green' indicates that certain considerations have operated to raise ... the question 'to endorse or not to endorse'. I may have reason to think that x may not after all be green" [EPM §16₂].

[14] That is also is how Kukla reads McDowell: "McDowell is ... committed to claiming that authority needs no subject at all, and can be binding even if it is not taken as binding by anyone. The world makes claims even if those claims are not recognized ... For McDowell, ... things have

SELLARS REVISITED

I have argued that Brandom's resistance to "individualizing" the space of reasons results in incorrect third-person ascriptions of first-person knowledge, while McDowell's resistance to "interiorizing" it draws him into yet another version of the Myth of the Given. If this is right, then what we need is a conception of the logical space of reasons that is both "individual" and "interiorized"—and, amazingly, Sellars' original "strong internalism" satisfies precisely these constraints. On that view, Brandom reminds us,

> one is not justified unless one *knows* one is justified—in particular, ... noninferential reports should be accorded the status of knowledge only in cases where the knower can cite her own reliability as a reason, from which the correctness of the noninferential report could be inferred. [KSA, 905]

Brandom finds this view "excessive", objecting that

> once one is capable of achieving standings in the space of reasons—for instance, capable of committing oneself to the claim that there is a candle in the room—one can become entitled to such standings without being able to give reasons for them. [KSA, 905]

But, as I have argued, the correctness of a third-person judgment to the effect that a subject is entitled to some first-person commitment does not imply that the subject *herself* has a standing in the space of reasons sufficient to warrant ascription of knowledge.

McDowell, too, explicitly objects to Sellarsian strong internalism, but offers a different diagnosis of its ostensible shortcomings.

> Sellars claims that the authority of an observation report "must *in some sense* be recognized by the person whose report it is." And he cashes this out in terms of the idea that the reporter must be able to give evidence of her reliability in reporting the sort of state of affairs in question. This is certainly quite implausible. ... [The] mistake is in Sellars's proceeding as if the only available sense for the requirement were that the reporter can derive her reliability as the conclusion of an inference. Like most adults, I know that I can tell a green thing when I see one (in the right conditions of illumination) ... But I would be at a loss if pressed for premises for an argument that would have my reliability about greenness as a conclusion. [KIR, 100–1]

Now it is surely *not* implausible to suppose that someone like Meg could come to know that her spontaneous classificatory judgments regarding the provenance of Central American potsherds are reliable, and, indeed, come to know it in just the same way that her colleagues do, by noticing that her subsequent

authority whether or not we are polite enough to give it to them, and coming to be bound by this already-present authority involves coming to recognize the claims things already make" [MMM, 204].

definitive microscopic and chemical analyses regularly confirm those judgments. But what makes this plausible is surely the fact that, as we have already remarked, such judgments already have a rich sense for Meg, quite independently of her spontaneous inclinations to make them. Meg can learn to know *by seeing* that a given potsherd is Aztec or Toltec because she already knows what it means for a potsherd to *be* Aztec or Toltec and has a command of *other* ways of coming to know the provenance of particular fragments.

The problem, however, is that when it comes to such basic perceptual skills as the ability to know by seeing that something is red or green, that sort of story is *prima facie* not available. Sellars himself concedes that

it might be thought that there is an obvious regress in the view ... Does it not tell us that observational knowledge at time t presupposes knowledge of the form *X is a reliable symptom of Y*, which presupposes *prior* observational knowledge, which presupposes *other* knowledge of the form *X is a reliable symptom of Y*, which presupposes still other, and *prior*, observational knowledge, and so on? [EPM §36]

The crucial point is that Meg has available general premises that do not presuppose that she is *already* able to know *by seeing* that a fragment is Toltec or Aztec. She is consequently in a position to confirm inferentially her various spontaneous perceptual judgments regarding the provenance of particular potsherds, and thereby to assemble evidence for a non-question-begging first-person "inductive" justification of the belief that she *is* reliable. As Kukla stresses, however, our concern here is with the very *possibility* of observational knowledge, i.e., the epistemic authority of perceptual judgments *as such*. What we need to understand is how a person can come to be, as she puts it, a "negotiator of the space of reasons", *capable* of recognizing the epistemic authority of his perceptual experiences. In Ernest Sosa's words, we want to understand how one could

acquire the required knowledge about which conditions are standard, and the knowledge that those conditions are present, without *already* enjoying a lot of the observational knowledge the possibility of which is under explanation. [MG, 280]

Sellars' reply is to stress the *normative* nature of epistemic ascriptions. All that his strong internalist view requires, he writes,

is that no tokening by S *now* of 'This is green' is to count as "expressing observational knowledge" unless it is also correct to say of S that he *now* knows the appropriate fact of the form *X is a reliable symptom of Y*, namely that [his suitably spontaneous] utterances of 'This is green' are reliable indicators of the presence of green objects in standard conditions of perception. And while the correctness of this statement about Jones requires that Jones could *now* cite prior particular facts as evidence for the idea that these utterances *are* reliable indicators, it requires only that it is correct to say that Jones *now* knows, thus remembers, that these particular facts *did* obtain. It does not require that he *then knew* them to obtain. And the regress disappears. [EPM §37]

And he adds in a footnote that what he is proposing is

> that one can have direct (non-inferential) knowledge of a past fact which one did not or even (as in the case envisaged) *could* not conceptualize at the time it was present.

Now Sosa finds these proposals intensely problematic, and he is hardly alone in doing so. To begin with, he is deeply skeptical about the availability of pertinent memories, not to mention *enough* pertinent memories to constitute a reasonable "inductive" evidential basis for the requisite general reliability premise.

> Think, perhaps, of your knowledge that you are perceiving a rectangular sheet of paper with a certain pattern of marks on it. Is it realistic to suppose that, in believing perceptually that before you there lies such a sheet, you are relying on recollected incidents in which you successfully perceived thus? [MG, 281]

But even if we could find a way to make some such supposition plausible, we would still need to address the more troublesome objection that

> memory itself seems to require, no less than perception, some meta-awareness of its reliability when exercised in circumstances of the sort in which it is now exercised. And if there was a problem of regress attaching to the exercise of perception there would seem to be an equally disturbing problem of regress attaching to the exercise of memory. [MG, 281]

And although Sosa recognizes that Sellars might venture the same sort of response, i.e.,

> that *just as* earlier proto-perceptions can become data supportive of generalizations about our perceptual reliability ... that underlie later perceptual knowledge; *so, similarly,* earlier proto-memories can become data supportive of generalizations about our memorial reliability ... that underlie later memorial knowledge. [MG, 281]

he argues that this would only render the first, "paucity of data", objection more acute, for it is hardly plausible to suppose that anyone remembers sufficient (successful) earlier particular exercises of memory to constitute an adequate confirmation of the hypothesis that his memory is generally reliable.

What Kukla's discussion suggests is that the epistemological problematic here is arguably even graver than Sosa makes it out to be. For what *are* the "prior particular facts" or "past facts" regarding perception and memory that, on Sellars' view, Jones must *now* know *did* obtain? Presumably, if they are to be the sorts of facts that can properly be cited as "inductive" evidence of his present reliability, they must be facts about his past or prior *perceivings* or *rememberings*. As we have seen, Sellars concedes that Jones did not and, indeed, could not *conceptualize* his prior performances *as* such perceivings or rememberings at the time that they occurred. What Kukla reminds us is that, by Sellar's own lights, since Jones was not *then* in a position to satisfy the requisite internalist constraints, those performances could not literally have *been* perceivings or rememberings at the time that they occurred. Sellars, she concludes, is simultaneously committed to accepting two incommensurable stories about the origins of such modes of knowledge.

> On the one hand, Sellars is committed to making room for the fact that as far as literal, forward-looking history is concerned, we must come to be negotiators of normative space by evolving to display patterns of behavior of gradually increasing complexity. There cannot be an explicable single moment at which our induction into the space of reasons and our ability to make authoritative claims begin. For ... we can only do this once we recognize the way that things make authoritative claims on us, and unless we are already negotiators of normative space, such authority could never show up for us ... Yet it is the case that at the beginning of this story we were not authoritative knowers, and at the end of it we are doing things that count as making claims and wielding epistemic authority ... At the same time, when we tell the story of the origin of authority ... from our positions within the space of reasons, our induction into this space will always turn out to predate any moment that we try to place at the beginning of this induction. We must always understand ourselves retroactively as already in this space when we explain how we know what we know, in terms of our having made various mistakes, recognized various facts and the like in the past. In other words, once we are knowers, we must always remember ourselves as already members of the space of reasons, insofar as we use our memory to explain our epistemic status. [MMM, 182–3]

In short, "the facts that need to show up in memory could not have shown up in the past, which at first makes it seem impossible that they could be available to memory" [MMM, 188].

Kukla's own strategy at this point is to develop a theory of—and attribute to Sellars—a methodology of "constitutive misrecognition" and "constitutive misremembering", conceptual performances capable of *instituting* new normative facts and new normative standings for past empirical facts. On this account, Sellars' story of the *genesis* of the epistemic authority of perceptual and mnemonic takings is not intended as a literal or pseudo-literal history but rather as a retrospective *myth*, one of several myths that Sellars uses to "kill" the Myth of the Given [EPM §63].

> Our need to recognize and legitimize ourselves as authoritative knowers requires us to 'remember' our past responses *as if* we were always already bound by things. This memory is neither a true description nor a false description of the past, but an ongoing *project* of mythical legitimization carried out through insistently treating the past as necessitating certain demands and commitments. [MMM, 190]

This is not the occasion for an extended exploration of Kukla's provocative account of "mythical legitimization". But, as ingenious as her story turns out to be, we might still worry that it leaves the crux of McDowell's and Sosa's objections untouched. For it is one thing to argue that the epistemic role of a knowing subject's ostensible memories needs to be radically reconceived before an appeal to them could ground and explain his recognition of the normative authority of his present responsive dispositions, and quite another to argue that suitable ostensible memories appropriately conceived are even *available* to such a subject or that he is plausibly in a position to reason "inductively" *from* them *to* the requisite general conclusions regarding his own reliability as a perceiver. It is surely more likely that, if queried, a typical perceiver would respond that he knows that he can recognize green things when he sees them in suitable conditions, but have little inclination to support that conviction by anything resembling an inductive generalization from ostensibly remembered successful past perceptual judgments.

How *might* a typical perceiver respond to the question of how he knows that he can normally recognize green things when he sees them? Well, one likely response is surely to observe that it is a peculiar question. But what makes it peculiar? Here's a clue: If Meg were properly confident of *her* discriminative reliability, she might also find the question "But how do you know that you can recognize Aztec and Toltec fragments on sight?" peculiar, but she might instead find it insulting. "Are you suggesting that I *can't?*", she might indignantly respond—and then she could certainly go on to cite her experience, training, and expertise, and her outstanding track record of subsequent microscopic and chemical confirmations to rebut any such suggestion. But that, of course, shows the question is one that *can be* entirely warranted and entirely innocent. After all, an ability reliably to recognize Aztec and Toltec fragments on sight is hardly a part of most people's everyday epistemic equipment, and so anyone might reasonably simply be curious about the epistemic credentials of a person who purports to have such an ability.

What makes the corresponding question about a typical perceiver's normal ability reliably to recognize green things on sight peculiar is that such an ability *is* a part of most people's everyday epistemic equipment. Consequently, there's ordinarily no reason to ask how a person knows that he has that ability—unless there's some reason to suspect that he *doesn't* have it, i.e., that his confidence in his own perceptual reliability is misplaced. The queried perceiver finds the question peculiar, then, precisely when and because he knows of no reason to *call into question* his ability to recognize green things on sight. Exercising it almost never causes him any *difficulties*.

John, the sales clerk in Sellars' necktie shop [EPM §14], in contrast, ran into some difficulties. "Here is a handsome green one," he said to potential customer Jim. "But it *isn't* green," said Jim, and took John and the necktie out into the sunlight, where John, much to his surprise, then spontaneously judged that the tie was blue. "But we saw that it was green *in there*," he protested in his bewilderment. "No, we didn't …," Jim replied, "because it wasn't green and you can't see what isn't so!"

That's what difficulties look like—dissonance between one's own spontaneous responsive propensities and the judgments of others. Absent such difficulties, one is entitled to have confidence in one's own epistemic reliability. What I am suggesting, in other words, is that, rather than having concluded "inductively" that my spontaneous perceptual beliefs are generally reliable, my awareness that

they are reliable derives from the fact that other people *rely* on them. If Jim
wants to buy a green necktie and straightaway cheerfully purchases the one that
I confidently show him, then my confidence is not out of place. But if Jim says
to me, as he did to John, "But it *isn't* green"—and others appropriately sustain
his judgment—then I evidently *can't* recognize green things when I see them,
at least not always and especially not in *these* conditions. In short, I am able to
make out the contours of my own epistemic authority by registering when and
how others are prepared to treat me as epistemically authoritative.

   This, I think, is the proper locus of the social-perspectival relationship between
first-person entitlements and third-person commitments that Brandom mistakes
for an externalist-reliabilist insight about first-person knowledge. McDowell
suggests that my reliability about greenness has for me

the sort of status that Wittgenstein considers in *On Certainty*. It is held firm for me by
my whole conception of the world with myself in touch with it ... [KIR, 101]

What is right about this remark is that a normal perceiver's confidence in his
own most basic perceptual capacities is, so to speak, the "default condition".
The conviction that one can generally recognize green things when one sees
them is acquired in childhood right along with the ability reliably to do so. It
consequently does not *need* any subsequent "inductive" inferential backing, but
ordinarily "stands fast" for such a perceiver—that is, unless and until something
unsettles it. But, in the normal course of events, such confidence can "stand
fast" because something steadily *supports* it, and what supports it is not just a
personal "conception of the world", however comprehensive. What supports it,
as Brandom suggests, is something social, namely, the absence of difficulties, that
is, the general consonance between one's own spontaneous perceptual judgments
and the judgments of others.[15]

   This completes the agenda of tasks that I set for myself at the beginning of
this essay. I have argued that neither McDowell's ontological "exteriorization" of
the Sellarsian logical space of reasons nor Brandom's social-perspectival reliabilist
externalism offers a viable alternative to Sellars' own strong internalist conception
of perceptual knowledge. Brandom's account does not grant perceivers themselves
a suitable standing in the logical space of reasons, and McDowell's relapses into
a version of the Myth of the Given. Sellars' own strong internalism is also not
free of problems, but I have argued that the most salient objection to it, pressed
by both Sosa and McDowell, can be answered by properly relocating central

---

[15] Martin Carrier has stressed for me the importance of making it clear that I am *not* saying that
such general agreement regarding which things are green is what *makes it true* that those things are
green. The question which my appeal to social consensus is intended to answer is neither "By virtue
of what is it true that green things are green?" nor "How do I know that green things are green?"
but rather "How do I know that my spontaneous beliefs to the effect that something is green are
generally reliable?". And all of these are to be distinguished from the question: "What explains the
fact that people are generally able to agree about what things are green?"

features of Brandom's social-perspectival picture.[16] We have not, I suspect, seen the last of the ongoing dispute between Brandom and McDowell, but I hope that I have at least made it plausible that their views by no means exhaust the space of serious alternatives, and that Sellars' original stand on the issues is well worth our renewed careful consideration.[17]

REFERENCES

Brandom, Robert B., [PRC0], "Perception and Rational Constraint: McDowell's *Mind and World*", in Villanueva, PPI, 241–59.

_____ [PRC], "Perception and Rational Constraint", *Philosophy and Phenomenological Research*, 58 (1998), 369–74.

_____ [KSA], "Knowledge and the Social Articulation of the Space of Reasons", *Philosophy and Phenomenological Research*, 55 (1995), 895–908.

_____ [AR], *Articulating Reasons* (Cambridge, MA; Harvard: 2000).

_____ [MIE], *Making It Explicit: Reasoning, Representing, and Discursive Commitment* (Cambridge, MA; Harvard: 1994).

deVries, Willem A., and Triplett, Timm, [KMG], *Knowledge, Mind, and the Given* (Indianapolis, IN; Hackett: 2000).

Kukla, Rebecca, [MMM], "Myth, Memory and Misrecognition in Sellars' 'Empiricism and the Philosophy of Mind' ", *Philosophical Studies*, 101 (2000) 161–211.

McDowell, John, [MW], *Mind and World* (Cambridge, MA; Harvard: 1994, 1996).

_____ [KI], "Knowledge and the Internal", *Philosophy and Phenomenological Research*, 55 (1995), 877–893.

_____ [KIR], "Knowledge and the Internal Revisited", *Philosophy and Phenomenological Research*, 66 (2002), 97–105.

_____ [RB], Reply to Brandom, PRC0, in Villanueva, PPI, 290–8.

_____ [RC], Reply to Commentators, *Philosophy and Phenomenological Research*, 58 (1998), 403–9.

Rosenberg, Jay F, [SU], "Spontaneity Unchained: An Essay in Darwinian Epistemology", in *Idealismus als Theorie der Representation?*, Ralph Schumacher, ed. (Berlin; mentis: 2001), 181–209.

Sosa, Ernest, [MG], "Mythology of the Given", *History of Philosophy Quarterly*, 14 (1997), 275–87.

Villanueva, Enrique (ed.), [PPI], *Perception: Philosophical Issues, 7* (Atascadero, CA; Ridgeview: 1996).

[16] I am inclined to think that the worries which motivated Kukla to develop her intriguing story of Sellarsian "mythical legitimization" can also be at least partially defused along such Brandomian lines, but that is another project for another time.

[17] Special thanks to my friends and colleagues at the University of Bielefeld, whose excellent questions and insightful comments prompted a number of clarifications.

13

Divergent Intuitions: McDowell's Kant and Sellars' Kant

John McDowell's Woodbridge Lectures[1] constitute one of those remarkable documents that illustrate how serious philosophy draws on its own history. McDowell's primary aim is to contrast his own account of intentionality—of "how thought and language are directed toward the world" (HWV, 471)—with one that he finds more or less explicitly framed and defended by Wilfrid Sellars, originally and influentially in "Empiricism and the Philosophy of Mind".[2] This is not the first time that McDowell has attempted to articulate his differences with Sellars. A good bit of his challenging book *Mind and World*[3] was devoted to the project, but the issues are both deep and subtle, and there are indications that the earlier attempt was less than an unqualified success.[4] The Woodbridge Lectures consequently adopt an indirect strategy. His differences with Sellars will come properly into view, McDowell suggests, against the background of their divergent interpretations of Kant.

Now, I share this belief [with Sellars], that there is no better way for us to approach an understanding of intentionality than by working toward understanding Kant. ... I think a fully Kantian vision of intentionality is inaccessible to Sellars because of a deep structural feature of his philosophical outlook. I believe we can bring into clearer focus the way Kant actually thought about intentionality, and thereby ... how we ourselves ought to

---

[1] "Having the World in View: Sellars, Kant, and Intentionality", *Journal of Philosophy*, 95 (1998), 431–91. The published version is divided into three Lectures: I. "Sellars on Perceptual Experience", 431–50; II. "The Logical Form of an Intuition", 451–70; and III. "Intentionality as a Relation", 471–91. Citations here will take the form "HWV" followed by the page number.

[2] Originally published in 1956, in vol. I of the *Minnesota Studies in the Philosophy of Science*, Sellars' monograph has been variously reprinted. Citations here, as "EPM" followed by numbered section and page, will be to the canonical version appearing in his *Science, Perception and Reality* (Ridgeview Publishing Co.; Atascadero, CA: 1963, 1991), 127–196.

[3] (Harvard University Press; Cambridge, MA: 1994, 1996). Cited here as "MW".

[4] This is my own third attempt to appreciate and assess what is at issue between McDowell and Sellars. The first two appeared, somewhat infelicitously, in two relatively obscure German collections: "Spontaneity Unchained: An Essay in Darwinian Epistemology" in Ralph Schumacher (ed.), *Idealismus als Theorie der Representation?*, (mentis Verlag; Berlin: 2001), 181–209; and "Sellarsian Seeing: In Search of Perceptual Authority", Ch. 12 in this volume. McDowell finds aspects of these earlier interpretations of his views wanting and has informally criticized them in passing correspondence but not, as far as I know, in print.

think about intentionality, by reflecting on the difference between what Sellars knows Kant wrote and what Sellars thinks Kant should have written. (HWV, 432)

In what follows, I propose to take a careful critical look at McDowell's project and its outcome.

READING KANT: EXEGETICAL AND PHILOSOPHICAL DISAGREEMENTS

McDowell's principal proof text for "what Sellars thinks Kant should have written" is the latter's 1965–6 John Locke Lectures, published as *Science and Metaphysics: Variations on Kantian Themes*.[5] The specific thesis that McDowell claims is there "foisted on Kant by Sellars" is "the idea that perception involves a flow of conceptual representations guided by manifolds of 'sheer receptivity'" (HWV, 452). The focus of their disagreement is Kant's notion (or notions) of an *intuition*.

In S&M, Sellars is primarily concerned to support and sharpen Kant's distinction between conceptual and non-conceptual representations, and he claims to find textual support for a distinction between "intuitions which do and intuitions which do not involve something over and above sheer receptivity" (S&M, 4). Kant, he concludes,

applies the term 'intuition' to both the representations which are formed by the synthesizing activity of the productive imagination and the purely passive representations of receptivity which are the 'matter' which the productive imagination takes into account. (S&M, 7)

Now McDowell has no quarrel with the notion that Kant applies the term 'intuition' to "representations of individuals that already involve the understanding, the faculty associated with concepts". He characterizes as "very helpful" Sellars' suggestion that "an intuition on this interpretation of the term should be taken to represent an individual as a *this-such*" (HWV, 452), and adopts it himself as a working tool for elucidating central features of visual experience as he understands it. Intuitions in this sense, McDowell proposes, are usefully thought of as "shapings of sensory consciousness by the understanding" (HWV, 452), a characterization which he also (cf. HWV, 440) finds implicit in Sellars' conception of perceptual experiences as both containing propositional claims and being more than *merely* the occurrence of such claims. (EPM §15–16, 144–5). What McDowell denies is that, as Sellars contends, Kant also recognizes and applies the term 'intuition' to

a radically different kind of representation of an individual which belongs to sheer receptivity and is in no sense conceptual. (S&M, 7)

---

[5] (Routledge & Kegan Paul, Ltd.; London: 1967), reissued by (Ridgeview Publishing Co.; Atascadero, CA: 1992). Citations will be to "S&M" followed by the page number.

Sellars, as we have just seen, is convinced that Kant's use of 'intuition' is in fact ambiguous. In this connection, he cites a passage from the beginning of the Transcendental Deduction, in which Kant speaks of "the impressions of the senses" as providing

the first occasion for opening the entire power of cognition to [concepts] and for bringing about experience, which contains two very heterogeneous elements, namely a *matter* for cognition from the senses and a certain *form* for ordering it from the inner source of pure intuiting and thinking ... (A86/B118)

But to find *this* distinction he need not have ventured so far into Kant's text. The notion that the "raw material" of "sensible sensations" (A1) or "sensible impressions" (B1) is what gets "worked up" by the understanding into experience, a cognition of objects, is already present on the first page of the Introduction. And that, as Sellars contends, Kant applies the term 'impressions' to "representations of sensibility as such" is borne out by the remark near the beginning of the "Clue to the Discovery of all Pure Concepts of the Understanding" that

Concepts are ... grounded on the spontaneity of thinking, as sensible intuitions are grounded on the receptivity of impressions (A68/B93)

—a remark which also clearly indicates that there is at least one sense of 'intuition' in which "sensible intuitions" cannot be *identified* with such impressions. In Kant's official taxonomy of representations (A320/B376–7), a representation "with consciousness" (a "perception"[6]) is either a *sensation* or a *cognition*. The former "refers to the subject as a modification of its state"; the latter subdivides into *intuitions* and *concepts*. So I think it is clear enough that, although at least his *primary* use of the term 'intuitions' is to refer to a species of cognitions, Kant also acknowledges a species of representations—sensations or impressions of sense—which, in Sellars' terms, "belongs to sheer receptivity" and "is in no sense conceptual" (S&M, 7). To stabilize our terminology, let us call it the "manifold of sense" and its elements "sensations".

What is unfortunately less clear is whether, as Sellars contends, Kant acknowledges a species of representations *of individuals* "which belongs to sheer receptivity and is in no sense conceptual", representations to which he *also*, ambiguously, sometimes applies the term 'intuitions'. For, if that is so, the ambiguity will also infect the notion of a *form of intuition*, giving rise to the idea that, as McDowell puts it,

the "Transcendental Aesthetic" should have dealt with forms exemplified in manifolds of intuition on the second interpretation of the term—manifolds of sensory impressions that are prior to any operations of the understanding, and that transcendentally subserve intuition on the first interpretation of the term, according to which intuitions involve the understanding as well as sensibility. (HWV, 454–5)

---

[6] Here not the German '*Wahrnehmung*', but rather '*Perception*', directly from the Latin '*perceptio*'.

It is *this* idea that McDowell is fundamentally concerned to reject. Sellars explicitly accepts it. Kant notoriously held that space is the form of outer sense, but, on Sellars' view, Kant's own understanding of that thesis was at best deficient, at worst seriously confused.

> To reconcile the insights contained in Kant's treatment of 'sensibility' and 'intuition', the distinction we have been drawing ... must be paralleled by a corresponding distinction between two radically different senses of spatial terms, in one of which we can speak of *impressions* as having a spatial form, while in the other we can speak of *the objects of intuition* as having a spatial form. (S&M, 8)

McDowell's *exegetical* complaint is that, as Sellars himself apparently concedes, no such notion is in fact to be found in the relevant parts of Kant's text.

> It is perhaps implicit in the "Aesthetic" that Kant thinks of sensation as the matter of empirical intuition (A20/B34), and thereafter he occasionally speaks of sensation as the matter of perception or of empirical knowledge (for example, A42/B59–60, A167/B209). But he never suggests that this matter has its *own* form as the matter it is, independently of its being formed into intuitions, perceptions, and empirical knowledge in the understanding-involving way ... Sellars is convinced that a properly Kantian position requires forms of sense as such, forms of "sheer receptivity." Correctly in my view, he takes it that the "Aesthetic" does not consider such a topic. So something that should, he thinks, be fundamental to Kant's position is absent from the appropriate place in Kant's own presentation of it. (HWV, 456–7)

His *philosophical* complaint is that a satisfactory account of perceptual experience does not require attributing to non-cognitive impressions or sensations the specific (transcendental) role that Sellars assigns them, namely, "to guide the flow of conceptual representations in perception" (HWV, 453).

SELLARS' KANT: THE DETAILS

Sellars introduces the notion of "the 'guidedness' ... of the flow of conceptual representations proper" midway through the first chapter of S&M with the suggestion that something like it is at least implicit in the First Critique:

> Thus, when [Kant] speaks of the productive imagination as 'taking up' (A120) the manifold of outer sense into its activity (the synthesis of apprehension) the metaphor implies, of course, that the manifold is an independent factor which has a strong voice in the outcome. On the other hand, it is only if the manifold is mistakenly construed as belonging to the conceptual order that it *makes sense* to suppose that it, so to speak, bodily or literally becomes a part of the resulting intuitive representation. If it is, as I take it to be, non-conceptual, it can only guide 'from without' the unique conceptual activity which is representing of *this-suches* as subjects of perceptual judgment. (S&M, 16)

Now there is a lot going on in this passage, but the first point that needs to be made is that the bit of Kant's text at which Sellars gestures is rather more interesting and complicated than he here makes it out to be. Here's how it goes:

[Since] every appearance contains a manifold, thus different perceptions by themselves are encountered dispersed and separate in the mind, a combination of them, which they cannot have in sense itself, is therefore necessary. There is thus an active faculty of the synthesis of this manifold in us, which we call imagination, and whose action exercised immediately upon perceptions I call apprehension. For the imagination is to bring the manifold of intuition into an *image*; it must therefore antecedently take up the impressions into its activity, i.e., apprehend them. (A120)

Needless to say, this text hardly wears its interpretation on its sleeve. The place to begin is surely by noting that it introduces two new ideas, the idea of the *imagination* as an "active faculty" for the synthesis of "the manifold of intuition", and the idea of an *image* as the product of its activity. And so the second point that needs to be made is that, if we think of what Kant here calls "the manifold of intuition" as the thoroughly non-conceptual manifold of *sense*, it is no longer as clear as Sellars takes it to be that it cannot "bodily or literally" become a part of "the resulting intuitive representation", if that "intuitive representation" is in fact an *image*.

Now, as McDowell well knows, Sellars explicitly engages Kant's account of perception on *two* occasions—in *Science and Metaphysics* and again, a decade later, in his 1977 Dotterer Lecture "The Role of Imagination in Kant's Theory of Experience".[7] This second encounter receives only a passing mention in a footnote in the second Woodbridge Lecture:

Largely below the surface in *Science and Metaphysics* is a detailed picture of how the productive imagination generates intuitions out of (strictly) sensory material which helps account for the view of concept formation Sellars attributes to Kant. (HWV, 454 n. 2)

The footnote concludes with the citation to Sellars' IKTE and the laconic remark "I cannot go into this here," an unfortunate disclaimer, since the results of Sellars' second encounter with Kant are directly relevant to what is at issue between him and McDowell. This is a point which deserves a rather long excursis.[8]

In S&M Sellars is relatively noncommittal about the imagination. He cites Kant's reference to "a blind but indispensable function of the soul" (A78/B103), and, following the lead of the Clue at A79/B104 according to which "the same function which gives unity to the various representations *in a judgment* also gives unity to the mere synthesis of various representations *in an intuition*"

---

[7] In Henry W. Johnston, Jr., (ed.), *Categories: A Colloquium* (Pennsylvanian State University; College Park, PA: 1978), 231–45. Cited henceforth as "IKTE" followed by the paragraph number. There is also a roughly contemporaneous essay "Kant's Transcendental Idealism", published in *Collections of Philosophy*, 6 (1976), 165–81. The most accessible source nowadays is Andrew Chrucky's Sellars internet site *http:www.ditext.com/sellars/*. The phenomenological themes developed with reference to Kant in IKTE are recapitulated in "Some Reflections on Perceptual Consciousness", in R. Bruzina and B. Wilshire, eds. *Crosscurrents in Phenomenology* (Martinus Nijhoff; The Hague: 1978), 169–85.

[8] What follows recapitulates a discussion from my "Perception *vs.* Inner Sense: A Problem about Direct Awareness", Ch. 11 in this volume.

concludes that "this imagination, under the name 'productive imagination', is the understanding functioning in a special way" (S&M, 4).[9]

When we then proceed to inquire in *what* "special way" the understanding functions *qua* imagination, the answer we find in S&M is *not* "to bring the manifold of intuition into an *image*", but rather to produce a special sub-class of *conceptual* representings (S&M, 7), namely, representations of a *this-such* nexus, "a form illustrated by 'this-cube', which, though not a judgment, is obviously closely connected with the judgment 'This is a cube'" (S&M, 4–5). On this reading, the synthesis of apprehension in intuition (A98 ff.) differs from the synthesis of recognition in a concept (A103 ff.), not by being *pre-* or *non*-conceptual, but by making use of a (general) concept in a special *non-predicative* way. (See also S&M, 16.) As Sellars sees it, then, a fully discerning and perspicuous Kant would be

clear about the radical difference between sense impressions proper and the intuitions synthesized by the productive imagination. Such a Kant would then have distinguished between:

(a) the non-conceptual representations of outer sense proper which ... are strictly speaking non-spatial complexes of unextended and uncoloured impressions;
(b) the intuitive (but conceptual) representations of extended structures located in space. (S&M, 28)

At this point in Sellars' thinking, there is simply no mention of Kant's notion of an "image".

In IKTE, Sellars in essence offers an account of the *relationship* between (a) and (b), between sensations and the *this-suches* which are the subjects of perceptual takings. The thesis defended in IKTE is that the productive imagination produces representations of extended structures located in space by constructing "sense-image models":

[Perceptual] consciousness involves the *constructing of sense-image models of external objects*. This construction is the work of the imagination responding to the stimulation of the retina. From this point on I shall speak of these models as image-models ... (IKTE §26)

Image-models are plainly what Sellars takes Kant to have in mind when he speaks in A120 of "bringing the manifold of intuition into an *image*". Sellars' own argument for the conclusion that perception involves such image-models rests on a sophisticated bit of descriptive phenomenology, distinguishing among what we see (e.g., an apple), what we see it *as* (e.g., red on the outside; cool, juicy and white inside), and what we see *of* it (e.g., its red facing surface, but not its opposite side, its internal whiteness, its coolness, or its juiciness). "But

---

[9] Sellars appropriately cites in this connection Kant's treatment of the imagination at B151 ff. He evidently overlooks, however, the explicit echo of A78/B105 at B162 n. b: "It is one and the same spontaneity, which in the one case, under the title of imagination, and in the other case, under the title of understanding, brings combination into the manifold of intuition."

while these features are not *seen*", he maintains, "they are not *merely* believed in. These features are present in the object of perception as actualities" (IKTE §21): Certain sensory features of a perceived object, in other words, while they are not themselves *strictu sensu* perceived, are nevertheless not merely aspects of the way in which we *think of* what we perceive but somehow actually "bodily present" in the perceptual experience. Sellars proposes that they are present as *imagined*.[10]

> Roughly imagining is an intimate blend of imaging and conceptualization, ... Thus, imagining a cool juicy red apple (*as* a cool juicy red apple) is a matter of (a) *imaging* a unified structure containing as aspects images of a volume of white, surrounded by red, and of mutually pervading volumes of juiciness and coolth, (b) *conceptualizing* this unified image-structure as a cool juicy red apple. (IKTE §23)

Perceiving simply adds concurrent sensing to this mix; it is a matter of *sensing-cum-imagining* such a unified structure and, here, conceptualizing it as an apple. As Kant tells us, in short, "the transcendental synthesis of the imagination" is "an effect [*Wirkung*] of the understanding on sensibility" (B152).

The thesis that imagination is an indispensable constituent of perception is, of course, thoroughly Kantian.

> No psychologist has yet thought that the imagination is a necessary ingredient of perception itself. This is so partly because this faculty has been limited to reproduction, and partly because it has been believed that the senses do not merely afford us impressions but also put them together, and produce images of objects, for which without doubt something more than the receptivity of impressions is required, namely a function of the synthesis of them. (A120 n. a)

Sellars' "sense-image models" are precisely such Kantian "images of objects" (*Bilder der Gegenstände*).[11] Such images embody the *perspectival* character of perceptual experience, i.e., the fact that we experience the world, and so objects in it, from a spatial point of view,[12] a feature of experience also emphasized by McDowell.

> [In] an ostensible seeing whose content can be partly specified as that there is a red cube in front of one, the apparent red cube will be *placed* more determinately than just somewhere or other in front of one. From the standpoint of the subject of such an ostensible seeing, its content will be expressible by saying something like 'There is a red

---

[10] And he adds a cautionary note: That a sensory feature is *present* in a perceptual experience as imagined does not imply that it is *presented* in the experience as something (merely) imagined.

[11] As Sellars of course recognizes (cf. IKTE §§31–45), the story of such images and their perspectival character is part of the larger Kantian story regarding what he calls the *schematism* of the pure concepts of understanding (A137–47/B176–87). I explore these connections in "Kantian Schemata and the Unity of Perception", in Alex Burri, (ed.), *Language and Thought* (Walter de Gruyter Verlag; Berlin and New York: 1997), 175–90.

[12] Apposite here is, for instance, B162: "Thus if, e.g., I make the empirical intuition of a house into perception through apprehension of its manifold, my ground is the *necessary unity* of space and of outer sensible intuition in general, and I as it were draw its shape in agreement with this synthetic unity of the manifold in space."

cube there'. Here we have to imagine a use of 'there' that has a determinate significance by virtue of the subject's directing it in a specific way at the ostensible layout of the ostensibly seen environment. (HWV, 459)

As we shall see, Sellars takes this perspectivality of perceptual experience to have some important consequences.

SELLARS (AND McDOWELL) ON PERCEPTION

The present upshot of these observations, however, is that the productive imagination in Sellars' IKTE is doing two different and complementary jobs. As "a unique blend of a capacity to form images *in accordance with* a recipe, and a capacity to conceive of objects in a way which *supplies* the relevant recipes" (IKTE §31),

> the productive imagination generates both the complex demonstrative conceptualization [e.g.]
>
> > This red pyramid facing me edgewise
> > and the simultaneous *image-model*, which is a point-of-viewish image of … a red pyramid facing one edgewise. (IKTE §36)

In this account, the demonstrative conceptualization *is* the "relevant recipe", supplied by the productive imagination *qua* understanding (faculty of concepts). The point-of-viewish image is the representation of an object located in space that is worked up in accordance with that "recipe" by the understanding *qua* productive imagination (imaging faculty) *out of* the materials supplied by the manifold of sense. McDowell's own Kantian gloss on Sellars' EPM thesis that visual experiences "make" or "contain" claims in fact usefully elucidates the role of concepts whose "paradigmatic mode of actualization is in judgings" (HWV, 438) as "recipes" with respect to the "unified structure" of such an image-model.

Consider, say, judging that there is a red cube in front of one. There is a conceptual capacity that would be exercised both in making that judgment and in judging that there is a red pyramid in front of one, and another … that would be exercised both in judging that there is a red cube in front of one and in judging that there is a blue cube in front of one. In judging that there is a red cube in front of one, one would be exercising (at least) these two capacities together. What does 'together' mean here? Not just that one would be exercising the two capacities in a single act of judgment … In a judgment that there is a red cube in front of one, the two conceptual capacities … would have to be exercised with a specific mode of togetherness that is a counterpart to the "logical" or semantical togetherness of the words 'red' and 'cube' in the verbal expression of the judgment, 'There is a red cube in front of me'. (HWV, 438–9; cf. HWV, 457–8)

Now we can say that in an ostensible seeing that there is a red cube in front of one—an experience in which it looks to one as if there is a red cube in front of one—the *same* conceptual capacities would be actualized with the *same* mode of togetherness. … But this actualization of the relevant conceptual capacities, unlike the one that would be involved in the corresponding judgment, would be involuntary … (HWV, 439–40)

That the *same* conceptual capacities are exercised in an ostensible seeing of a red cube in front of one as in the corresponding judgment is McDowell's reading of Kant's Clue (A79/B104). As we have already seen, his favored metaphor for the *way* in which those conceptual capacities are exercised in such a visual experience is as *shaping sensory consciousness*:

> What makes it an ostensible seeing, as opposed to a conceptual episode of some other kind (for instance, a judgment), is that this actualization of conceptual capacities is a conceptual shaping of sensory (and in particular visual) consciousness. (HWV, 460)

This is, so to speak, a "top down" conception of the way in which "the flow of conceptual representations in perception" is "guided" (HWV, 453). Everything happens above the "line" that McDowell sees as the distinguishing feature of Sellars' account of perceptual experience.

> Above the line in a Sellarsian picture of a visual experience, there is a conceptual episode of a distinctive kind. Just by virtue of being a conceptual episode, such an episode "contains" a claim about the environment. But episodes of this kind are differentiated from conceptual episodes of other kinds in that they "contain" their claims in a distinctive way, as ostensibly required from or impressed on their subject by an ostensibly seen object.
> Below the line ... there is a complex or manifold of visual sensations, that is, non-concept-involving visual episodes or states. (HWV, 451)

McDowell's critical contention is that "the below-the-line element in Sellars' picture actually stands in the way of a useful conception of how perception and thought are directed toward objects" (HWV, 452), a conception that, he thinks, can also be found in a properly-interpreted Kant.

It may not have escaped notice, however, that we now apparently have *two* accounts of how ostensible seeings essentially differ from judgings, both of which McDowell endorses. According to one, what is determinative for a conceptual episode's being an ostensible seeing is that it is the actualization of the relevant conceptual capacities in an involuntary shaping of visual consciousness (HWV, 460); according to the other, that those conceptual capacities are "involuntarily drawn into operation under ostensible necessitation from an ostensibly seen object" (HWV, 458; cf. HWV, 440). On the face of it, however, both of these accounts are problematic.

The first of them carries the unacceptable suggestion that visual consciousness is some sort of *amorphous stuff*, which, under the influence of the appropriate concepts, could be worked up into red cubes, green pyramids, or blue spheres, much as a lump of bronze could be worked up into an ashtray, a flower vase, or a statue of Phidippides (cf. HWV, 457 n. 8). The second admits of a purely Humean reading, namely, that the claim "contained" in an ostensible seeing is regularly accompanied by an "impression of reflection" in the form of a *feeling* of necessitation, but that gives us at best a *de facto* and contingent difference between ostensible seeings and judgings where what we wanted was something essential and constitutive. There is, of course, another reading for the idea that ostensible seeings "contain" their claims "as ostensibly visually *imposed* or *impressed* on their subject" (HWV, 440)—roughly, that we *find ourselves* with perceptual beliefs which we properly treat as *prima facie* epistemically authoritative. But this addresses only the distinctive role of perceptual beliefs within "the logical space of reasons", and so, again, not the distinguishing features of perceptual experiences *per se*.[13]

It is at this point, I want to suggest, that the *explanatory* purpose discharged by Sellars' account of the manifold of sense—and thereby the transcendental "guiding" role of sensations—comes clearly into view. The primary purpose of the "sense impression inference", i.e., the conclusion that "receptivity culminates in a state which is neither 'purely physical' [i.e., is a state of consciousness] *nor* conceptual", Sellars tells us, "is to explain the occurrence of certain ["minimal"] *conceptual* representations in perceptual activity" (S&M, 17). McDowell parses the explanandum-question here as "How is it that sensory relatedness to the environment takes the form of conceptual episodes, episodes that ... 'contain' claims, at all?" (HWV, 444), but that is not exactly Sellars' question. His explananda are always concerned with *specific* conceptual episodes. In first approximation, they have the general form: "Why does the subject's visual experience 'contain' *this* claim in *these* circumstances?" And what is crucial is that the subject's visual experience "contains" the claim that it does, not as a thought or a judgment, but as an *image-model.*

The key point is that "sensory consciousness" is *not* an amorphous stuff that can be "shaped" by the understanding *qua* productive imagination "from above" into an image of *just anything*. In the case of spontaneous ostensible seeings, we *find ourselves* with visual experiences, e.g., of a red cube over there, each of which, in the sense we have been exploring, "contains" a particular claim. Sellars' leading thought is that there must be something that constrains and determines, so to speak, "from below" *which* conceptual capacities are involuntarily actualized in such a perceptual experience—and so can in principle be cited in explanations of why *just those* conceptual capacities were actualized on this occasion.

Thus the sense impression inference is an attempt to account for the fact that normal perceivers have *conceptual* representations of a red and rectangular object both

(a) when they are being affected in normal circumstances by a red and rectangular object; and

---

[13] Vindicating the *prima facie* epistemic authority of perceptual beliefs is one aspect of the second "logical dimension", gestured at in §38 of EPM (EPM, 170), within which observation reports depend on the world view that is grounded on them (cf. HWV, 435). Sellars' own most detailed elucidation of what he had in mind is presented in "More on Givenness and Explanatory Coherence", in George S. Pappas (ed.), *Justification and Knowledge* (D. Reidel Publishing Co.; Dordrecht, Holland: 1979), 169–82. For a relatively clear summary discussion, see my "Still Mythic After All Those Years: On Alston's Latest Defense of the Given", Ch. 10 in this volume.

(b) when they are being affected in abnormal circumstances by objects which have other, but systematically related characteristics. (S&M, 17)

Ambiguous figures provide a useful analogy. Consider Jastrow's duck-rabbit. Here it makes clear sense to think of what is seen (i.e., the aspect) as *explicitly* "guided" by concepts "from above". One can deliberately choose to see the figure as a duck or as a rabbit, and one does so precisely by invoking the *concept* of a duck or a rabbit in an appropriate thought. But, of course, one cannot choose to see the figure as *just anything*—an antelope, say, or a cantaloupe. The particular qualities and relationships of the ink marks on the page clearly constrain and determine, so to speak, "from below" the *specific set* of aspects that one might choose to see—and so can in principle be cited in explanations of why *just those* aspects are available to the deliberative subject on this occasion. In first approximation, that the figure can be seen as a rabbit is explained *inter alia* by the fact that the arrangement of those ink marks relevantly *resembles* arrangements which are, so to speak, canonical rabbit-images; that it can be seen as a duck, by the fact that it *also* relevantly resembles arrangements which are canonical duck-images.

This is precisely the form of explanation that Sellars envisages with respect to the occurrence of specific conceptualizations in spontaneous perceptual experiences:

> [Even] in normal cases there is the genuine question, 'Why does the perceiver *conceptually represent* a red (blue, etc.) rectangular (circular, etc.) object in the presence of an object having those qualities?' The answer would seem to require that all the possible ways in which *conceptual representations* of color and shape can resemble and differ correspond to ways in which their *immediate non-conceptual occasions*, which must surely be construed as states of the perceiver, can resemble and differ. (S&M, 18)

In other words, far from being an amorphous stuff, the manifold of sense consists of items (states of the perceiver) that admit of *intrinsic* characterization in terms of "analogical counterparts of the perceptible qualities and relations of physical things and events" (S&M, 30). Only a receptivity which is thus *in itself* qualitatively- and relationally-structured, Sellars concludes, can "guide 'from without' the unique conceptual activity which is representing of *this-suches* as subjects of perceptual judgment" (S&M, 16), i.e., selectively determine *which* conceptual capacities are to be actualized in the construction of the *image-model* contained in the perceptual experience. On Sellars' account, then, sensations have a dual function in perception: By virtue of their intrinsic qualities and relations, sensations *activate* the specific conceptual capacities which organize them into the image-models that they thereby *constitute*. The manifold of sense ("sensory consciousness") is "shaped" into representations of objects in space by the exercise of conceptual capacities whose actualization it (causally) *evokes*.

This account makes it clear why Sellars thinks of sensations not just as states of a perceiver but explicitly as *states of consciousness*, despite the fact that, on his view, they are never apperceived. He remarks that "the idea that there are broad classes of states of consciousness *none* of which are apperceived" is "startling, and to many absurd" (S&M, 10), and, indeed, Kant himself would seem to be among that "many":

The *I think* must *be able* to accompany all my representations ... That representation that can be given prior to all thinking is called *intuition*. Thus the manifold of intuition has a necessary relation to the *I think* in the same subject in which this manifold is to be encountered. (B131–2)

McDowell, in any case, appreciates that there is potentially a problem here:

Now it is hard to see how ... there could be a class of items in consciousness whose members were permanently and constitutionally incapable of being apperceived, incapable of being directly available for self-attribution. (HWV, 447)

After all, he reminds us, the point of the second Myth of Jones in EPM was precisely to secure a *reporting* role for the analogically-construed terms belonging to Jones' theory of sense impressions. McDowell consequently offers Sellars a solution:

The visual impressions or sensations in question are not apperceived *when they are playing their transcendental role*. That is not to say that they are not *apperceivable*. It is just to say that if they do get to be apperceived—if they do become objects for consciousness—they can no longer be playing their transcendental role of enabling episodes of "outer sense," episodes that "contain" claims about the environment. (HWV, 447)

Properly understood, McDowell's proposal is, I think, almost right on target. As I have argued elsewhere,[14] Sellars acknowledges two distinct ways in which a subject might non-inferentially respond to one of her sense impressions, e.g., to a sensation of a red rectangle. She can, in the first instance, respond *in the mode of perception*, i.e., by constructing an image-model of a red and rectangular object suitably disposed in space (of "that red rectangular object there", as McDowell might put it (cf. HWV, 459))—an object that she might conceive *as*, and thereby take *to be*, for instance, the facing cover of a red book. On the other hand, she could respond to the same sensation, also directly and non-inferentially, *in the mode of a learned Jonesean report*, e.g., with the self-attribution "I am having a sense impression of a red rectangle."

What corresponds to McDowell's suggestion that, in the second instance, the sensation is no longer playing its transcendental role is the fact that 'red' and 'rectangle' are there not used in their primary senses, to pick out properties of objects in space, but in their derived, Jonesean-theoretical senses to pick out "analogical counterparts of the perceptible qualities and relations of physical things and events" (S&M, 30). The qualitative concepts with which one responds to sense impressions in perceptual experiences, in contrast, are never analogical.

---

[14] In "Perception *vs*. Inner Sense: A Problem about Direct Awareness", Ch. 11, above.

Adopting a strict phenomenological attitude brackets causal and dispositional properties, but it does not shift the sense of sensory quality predicates.

Nevertheless, it would be a mistake, I think, to say, as McDowell suggests (HWV, 448), that, in the second instance, the sensation is apperceived by virtue of being an *object of consciousness*. In the sense in which, in perception, an intuition *qua* image-model is *present to* a subject as an object of consciousness, as something that she might judge *of it* that *it* is the cover of a red book,[15] there is nothing present to the subject of a "Jonesean self-awareness", nothing about which she might judge *of it* that *it* is the sense impression of a red rectangle. The form of an episode of Jonesean self-awareness is not demonstrative, "*This* is a sense impression of a red rectangle", but rather makes reference only to the self *qua* subject and predicates of it a characteristic mode of representational activity.[16]

Equally mistaken, I would argue, is McDowell's contention that

when a conceptual episode is apperceived as belonging to the kind, being under the visual impression that ... , what is apperceptively available, according to Sellars' picture, is *that* the flow of one's conceptual representations, of the sort involved in normal perceptual activity, is being guided into "containing" the relevant claim by the flow of one's impressions in the below-the-line sense. (HWV, 450)

On the interpretation of Sellars that I have been developing, "guiding" the construction of representations of objects in space "from below" is a (purely) *causal process*, whose occurrence can, of course, be *thought*, but which is not itself a representation and so not a viable candidate for apperceptive awareness in the first place.

In S&M, Sellars' central focus is on the role of sensations in *activating* the conceptual capacities operative in the synthesis of "intuitions proper". The *constitutive* role of those same sensations as the "matter" for that synthesis is less visible. The thesis that "the intuitive (but conceptual) representations of extended structures located in space" (S&M, 28) are *image-models*, as McDowell observes, remains "largely below the surface". In IKTE, in contrast, it occupies center stage. The fact that the *this-suches* represented in visual perception are necessarily represented from the perceiver's point of view—as determinately "placed", as McDowell puts it, "in the ostensible layout of the ostensibly seen environment" (HWV, 459)—is, for Sellars, convincing evidence that they are *actually* states of the perceiving subject.

The perspectival character of the image-model is one of its most pervasive and distinctive features. It constitutes a compelling reason for the thesis of the transcendental ideality of

---

[15] McDowell: intuitions are "conceptual occurrences in which objects are manifestly there for thinkers, immediately present to their conceptually shaped sensory consciousness" (HWV, 465).

[16] The adverbial form of sense-impression concepts, indeed, seems tailor made for their Jonesean reporting use, e.g., "Sensing-of-a-red-rectangle-ly(I)", i.e., "I am sensing of-a-red-rectangle-ly"; cf. "Moving-slow-and-deliberate-ly(I)" = "I am moving slowly and deliberately".

the image-model world.[17] Image-models are "phenomenal objects." Their *esse* is to be *representatives* or *proxies*. Their *being* is that of being complex patterns of sensory states constructed by the productive imagination. (IKTE §28)

The relative invisibility of the constitutive role of sensations in S&M carried with it some infelicitous terminological consequences. Sellars' talk of the manifold of sense guiding the representing of this-suches *"from without"* (S&M, 16) is unfortunate in much the same way that McDowell's reification of Sellars' references to "sheer receptivity" into a *"line"* is unfortunate. If the manifold of sense provides the *raw materials* for the construction of image-models (their "matter") which are, in their own way, *conceptual* (actualizations of conceptual capacities) then there can no more be a "line" between the guiding and the guided (receptivity and spontaneity, sensibility and understanding) than there can be a "line" between the matter and form of a bronze statue. The distinction between what is "above" and what is "below" Sellars' "line" is the product of a *theoretical* account of perception which, in the service of philosophical-explanatory ends, differentiates among elements or aspects of an experience which is, so to speak, in itself a "seamless unity". Like the distinction between a statue and the bronze that constitutes it, it is not a distinction *in re*, but what Hume called a "distinction of reason".[18]

Sensations belong to "sheer receptivity", "guide 'from without'", and are "below the line" only insofar as they are *non-conceptual* states of the perceiving subject, proximate causal outcomes of the impact of a sensory stimulus, which thereby provide "the 'brute fact' or constraining element of perceptual experience" (S&M, 9), i.e., insofar as they play the "guiding" *role* of selectively activating the relevant conceptual capacities. But they are also *contents* of sensory consciousness and so themselves "above the line" insofar as they are shaped by actualizations of those conceptual capacities into image-model representations of this-suches determinately located in space, i.e., insofar as they also play the *constitutive* role of being "the 'matter' which the productive imagination takes into account" (S&M, 7).

McDowell, I think, recognizes that something *like* this "multiple role" picture ought to be congenial to Sellars. On his own picture "guidance from without" is supplied by the "subject matter" of "the conceptual representations involved in perceptual experience", and he suggests that

Sellars' own imagery for expressing his sense of the need for external constraints—his talk of guidance and the like—actually fits this constraint by subject matter better than it fits Sellars' candidate, constraint by "sheer receptivity". (HWV, 467)

---

[17] The point, of course, is that space *as perceived* is subject-centered. Objects perceived *as in* space are perceived in their relationships to the subject, as near or far, to the left or right, above or below, or in front of or behind one another. *Physical* space, in contrast, is conceived aperspectivally, as unoriented and isotropic.

[18] See *A Treatise on Human Nature*, I, i, 7. Kant's "threefold synthesis", for instance, is similarly only a "distinction of reason".

What I have argued is that, on Sellars' account, "the conceptual representations involved in perceptual experience" are *image-models*, and there is consequently no *ontological* distance between them and the deliverances of "sheer receptivity", i.e., sensations. But that is not quite what McDowell has in mind, and, indeed, we might well wonder whether it even makes sense to speak of the "subject matter" of an image-model. The time has come, in short, to take a careful look at McDowell's own reading of the thesis, with which he explicitly agrees, that "the conceptual representations involved in perceptual experience must be guided from without". His view, to put it briskly, is that "the guidance is supplied by *objects* themselves ... becoming immediately present to the sensory consciousness of the subjects of these conceptual goings on". *Objects* are "the subject matter of those conceptual representations" (HWV, 467).

McDOWELL (AND SELLARS) ON PERCEPTION

McDowell invites us to imagine, from the subject's point of view,

an ostensible seeing whose content is (in part) that there is a red cube *there*. ... Now suppose this ostensible seeing is not a merely ostensible seeing, but a seeing. In that case, there *is* a red cube at the position the subject can mean by this kind of use of 'there' in an overt expression of the content of the experience in question,[19] or by its counterpart in the nonovert conceptual occurrence that the experience is. In the conceptual occurrence that the experience is, the red cube that there actually is, given that the experience is a seeing, is itself directly in the subject's view. It is in the subject's view as *that red cube*. (HWV, 459)

This is McDowell's paradigm of a Kantian intuition: a conceptual occurrence in which an object is "manifestly there" for a thinker, "immediately present to [her] conceptually shaped sensory consciousness" (HWV, 465). He agrees with Sellars that, unless perceptual experiences are constrained by something external to conceptual activity, we will not be entitled to think of that activity as directed toward an independent reality.

But ... once we understand how objects can be immediately present to conceptually shaped sensory consciousness in intuition, we can take this need for external constraint to be met by perceived objects themselves. (HWV, 473)

The specter of (empirical) idealism is laid by the fact that the actualizations of conceptual capacities in perception are "shapings of *sensory* consciousness".

That ensures that the objects we are entitling ourselves to see as present to subjects in intuition are genuinely independent of the subjects. (HWV, 473)

---

[19] This tortuous expression presumably reflects the subject-relativity of perspectival indexicals, i.e., that the location in *physical* space of an object perspectivally represented by a perceiving subject as being "there" will be a function not only of that representation but also of the subject's own location in physical space.

How are we to understand the notion of "conceptually shaped sensory consciousness"? McDowell, as we have seen, has a story to tell about "conceptual shaping", i.e., about the way in which the *same* conceptual capacities are exercised, "with the *same* togetherness" (HWV, 458), in an ostensible *seeing of* a red cube in front of one that would be exercised in *judging that* there is a red cube in front of one. Significantly, however, that is not exactly the way McDowell puts it. His idiom is not "an ostensible seeing *of* a red cube in front of one", but "an ostensible seeing *that there is* a red cube in front of one". On this way of thinking about ostensible seeings, what is ostensibly seen can be literally *identical* with what is judged, and that is surely what motivates McDowell's comment that

as actualizations of conceptual capacities with the appropriate togetherness, the judgment and the ostensible seeing would be alike. They would differ *only* in the way in which the relevant conceptual capacities are actualized. In the judgment, there would be a free responsible exercise of the conceptual capacities; in the ostensible seeing, they would be involuntarily drawn into operation under ostensible necessitation from an ostensibly seen object. (HWV, 458, my emphasis)

But this account so far neglects to mention that the "operation" of those conceptual capacities in an ostensible seeing is supposed to be an instance of "shaping" something, and that *what* is putatively being shaped is "sensory consciousness"—and about these notions McDowell has remarkably little to say.

Indeed, in light of McDowell's reading of Kant's idea that intuitions are "representations in which objects are immediately present to subjects" (HWV, 472), the metaphor of "shaping" seems particularly inept. If 'sensory consciousness' does not pick out something like the non-conceptual manifold of sense as Sellars conceives it, then there is nothing left in McDowell's picture to *be* "shaped". 'Consciousness' will then just be another name for the subject of experiences, and that an object is "present to sensory consciousness" will just mean that it is "sensorily present to consciousness", i.e., that it is ostensibly perceived rather than merely thought of or imagined. On this reading, the gravamen of McDowell's critique of Sellars' account of perception is that it does not reflect, and so does not respect, the fact that "Kant conceives intuitions as representations in which objects are immediately present to subjects" (HWV, 472).

"We debar ourselves from this notion of immediate presentness of objects to subjects," he writes,

if we let it seem that a seen object would have to figure in the content of a conceptual occurrence that is a seeing of it as, for instance, occupying a position at the outer end of a causal chain that generates the subject's current experiential situation in some suitably designated way. And Sellars' second thought suggests just that. It suggests that seeings that ... would need to "contain" not just claims about the environment but also claims to the effect that the subject's experience is "normally" related to the ostensibly seen environment (this being part of what the subject is supposed to know in enjoying an experience of the relevant kind). This introduces a mediation that would threaten our ability to take these same conceptual occurrences to be intuitions, immediately of objects … (HWV, 475)

What McDowell calls "Sellars' second thought" adverts to the "externalist" footnotes added by Sellars to §22, pp. 151–2 of EPM in 1963 to the effect that an ostensible seeing of something red over there will be a *seeing* that a thing over there is red only if the subject knows that the perceptual circumstances are normal. The idea that McDowell there finds in Sellars is that part of what differentiates actual from merely ostensible seeings is "extra conceptual content". Both an actual and a merely ostensible seeing of a red cube over there will "contain" the claim that *there is a red cube over there*, but the former will also "contain" an *additional claim*, embodying the subject's knowledge that her perceptual circumstances are normal.

As a reading of Sellars, this is, at best, uncharitable. There is nothing in EPM to suggest that the knowledge of perceptual circumstances that Sellars introduced in 1963 as a *condition* for an ostensible seeing to be a seeing must somehow be reflected in or incorporated into the *content* of the subject's experience. This is not to say that there is nothing problematic about Sellars' proposal. As McDowell points out,

one might have occasion to say: "I now realize I was seeing a red cube, although at the time—because I thought the circumstances were abnormal—I did not realize it." What is perfectly intelligibly claimed here is that the case was one of seeing, even though the subject did not know that the viewing circumstances were normal. What matters is that the circumstances should be normal, not that the subject should know they are. (HWV, 474)

The critical point is well taken. But it is one that Sellars can comfortably grant without conceding that the requisite normality of the circumstances must somehow be *represented* in the perceptual experience *per se*.[20]

If the crux of "immediacy" is, as McDowell suggests, the absence of "extra conceptual content", in other words, nothing prevents an instance of *seeing*, as Sellars understands it, from being an instance of the immediate presence of an object to a perceiver. But McDowell's thesis is a stronger one:

---

[20] Sellars misses the point in EPM, I suspect, by failing to distinguish the conditions in which it is *true of* S that she sees that x over there is red from the conditions in which S (herself) is *entitled to assert that* she sees that x over there is red. The "externalist" requirement added in the footnotes is arguably a necessary condition of the latter entitlement. In his first Carus Lecture, "The Lever of Archimedes" (*Monist*, 64 (1981), 3–36)—henceforth cited as 'LA' follows by numbered section and page—he gets it right:

[When] an object looks red to S, and S is, so to speak, "taken in" … S has an experience which is intrinsically like that of seeing the object *to be* red … in the sense that if certain additional conditions were realized the experience would in fact be one in which S *sees* an object to be red. Among these conditions are (a) that the object be in fact red; (b) that the object be appropriately responsible for the experience. Let me call such an experience *ostensibly seeing an object to be red*. (LA §§69–70, 16)

The actualizations of conceptual capacities that constitute ostensible seeings can amount to intuitions, cases of having objects immediately present to one, only if the ostensible seeings are seeings. (HWV, 475)

And this *is* incompatible with Sellars' interpretation of intuitions as image-models, for, on his account, an *image-model* of, e.g., a red cube over there is something that *actually* seeing a red cube over there and *merely ostensibly* seeing a red cube over there have in common, something that *inter alia* makes both of them instances of ostensible *seeing*. It is what he called in EPM (§22, 151–2) the common "descriptive content" of the two experiences.

McDowell agrees, of course, that merely ostensible seeings are ostensible *seeings*, but, since he limits the term 'intuition' to cases in which an *actual* object is *actually* present to a perceiver, he insists that such merely ostensible seeings only *ostensibly* contain intuitions. "[The] mere appearance of an intuition is just that; it is not an actual intuition" (HWV, 475). Using the term 'intuition' in McDowell's restrictive sense, the contrast between his view and Sellars' is, so to speak, a difference in the scope of a modifier. McDowell's view is that merely ostensible seeings (merely) *ostensibly contain* intuitions; Sellars' view is that merely ostensible seeings (actually) contain merely *ostensible intuitions*. Where Sellars' account posits an actual but merely *ostensibly veridical* content, McDowell's acknowledges only an *ostensible content*, i.e., no *actual* content at all, veridical or non-veridical.

If one is under the illusion of being perceptually confronted by an object, then one is liable to a counterpart illusion that there is available to one, for employment in conceptual activity, content expressible by a perceptual demonstrative reference to the supposed object—the content one might think one could express, in such a situation, by using a phrase such as 'that red cube'. (HWV, 475–6)

The idea is that for a conceptual episode to possess intuitional content just is for it to stand in a certain relation to an object; so if there is no object suitably related to a conceptual episode, then there is no such relation, and accordingly no such content. (Of course there is still a conceptual episode, an ostensible perceiving.) (HWV, 477)

On McDowell's account, then, the *only* thing that an ostensible seeing of a red cube over there and an actual seeing of a red cube over there appear to have in common is that they are actualizations of the same conceptual capacities, i.e., that both "contain" the *claim* that there is a red cube over there. "The content in question is the same as the content of a judgment the subject might express by saying 'There is a red cube *there*' " (HWV, 476). But, as we observed earlier, that is equally true of an episode of *thinking* that (or, we might now add, of wondering whether) there is a red cube over there. An actual and a merely ostensible seeing of a red cube over there indeed *seem* to have something more in common—something that we're surely inclined to call a *sensory* content that is not shared with a mere thinking that or wondering whether—but, on

McDowell's view, there cannot be any such additional *common* content, since the merely ostensible seeing has *no* additional content at all.

The relevant function—the "logical" togetherness with which the relevant conceptual capacities are actualized—certainly *seems* to give unity to a synthesis of representations in an intuition; that is to say that there *seems* to be a red cube immediately present to the subject. But ... this seeming intuitional unity is a mere semblance of an intuitional unity; that is to say, there *merely* seems to be a red cube immediately present to the subject. (HWV, 476)

Using 'intuition' in McDowell's restrictive sense, Sellars would parse a merely ostensible seeing as one in which the relevant conceptual functions *actually* give unity to a synthesis of representations (sense impressions) in a *seeming* intuition (an image-model). In the terminology of EPM, an actual and a merely ostensible seeing of a red cube over there have in common *both* a "propositional content" *and* a "descriptive content", i.e., they "contain" both the same claim and the same image-model. In either case, it is the latter which is *in fact* proximately indicated by what the subject could express by using a demonstrative phrase such as "that red cube over there".[21] And this account puts Sellars in a position to explain two things which, on McDowell's picture, necessarily remain utterly mysterious: first, why the *same* concepts—*red, cube,* and *there*—are *appropriately* called into play in both cases; and second, what those concepts—which, on McDowell's account, are "shaping sensory consciousness" in the case of an actual seeing—are *doing* in the case of the merely ostensible seeing.

McDowell does not seem to realize that explanations are *needed* here. I am consequently inclined to say of him what he says about Sellars, that he has a blind spot. *Sellars'* blind spot is supposed to be that he

cannot see how a determinate intentional directedness can be both a relation to an element in the real order and an intrinsic character of a conceptual occurrence. (HWV, 486)

He simply does not consider that someone might want to say a difference in what they are directed toward can itself be an intrinsic difference in intellectual acts. (HWV, 481)

Well, if that is a blind spot, then I have it too, for, not to put too fine a point on it, I simply cannot understand what McDowell is trying to say here. I do not know what he can possibly mean by *'intrinsic'*. In my idiolect, 'intrinsic' *contrasts with* 'relational'. A thing's intrinsic characters are the features that it has *independently* of its relationships to other things. On this understanding, the thought that McDowell charges "goes missing in Sellars' argument", namely, "that an unmediated relatedness to elements in the real order can be an intrinsic

---

[21] And precisely because it is thereby *conceived of as* and so *taken to be* a red cubical object in space, it is *not* conceived of as or taken to be what it in fact is, namely, a complex pattern of sensory states constructed by the productive imagination. (This is another way of putting the earlier observation that sensations are never apperceived *as such*.)

character of an intellectual act" (HWV, 482), is straightforwardly contradictory. But if that is not how we are to understand 'intrinsic', then my interpretive resources, at least, are nearing their limits.

The most charitable exegetical hypothesis that occurs to me is that what McDowell means by 'intrinsic' is 'essential', i.e., that it is an *essential* property of (genuine) intuitions that they are "representations in which objects are immediately present to subjects" (HWV, 472). In any event, that is plainly a thesis that McDowell advocates, and so the time has surely come to ask just what he has in mind. What does it mean for an object to be "immediately present" to a subject?

IMMEDIACY AND GIVENNESS

What *Sellars* would mean by it is clear and straightforward. From his earliest epistemological writings onward, his term of contrast for 'immediate' (or 'direct') has always been 'inferred'. "Immediate presence" in Sellars' sense consequently does not imply "unmediated presence", but only that the subject's awareness of the object is not *inferentially* mediated. *Causal* mediation, for instance, is obviously unavoidable. To put it brusquely, then, an object will be "immediately present" to a subject, in Sellars' sense, just in case it is *perceived*. Like the pig in J. L. Austin's example, which, on the basis of evidence (e.g., pig tracks or pig food), we may have *concluded* inhabits the barnyard, when the beast emerges from behind the shed into plain view, neither evidence nor inference remains in play. We can then *see* that there is a pig in the barnyard, i.e., the pig is "immediately present" to us. Cases of actually seeing some object, e.g., an apple, will then *trivially* be instances of the object's being "immediately present to sensory (visual) consciousness"; cases of merely ostensibly seeing an object will not. In other words, still using 'intuition' in McDowell's restrictive sense, Sellars can and does explicitly endorse the exegetical thesis that "Kant conceives intuitions as representations in which objects are immediately present to subjects" (HWV, 472). But *this* sense of "immediacy" is obviously independent of any particular *philosophical theory* of perception, and so cannot be what McDowell has in mind.

McDowell himself explicitly concedes at least one form of mediation. " 'Immediate' in a characterization of intuitions," he writes, "does not mean 'not involving the understanding' " (HWV, 460). That intuitions are *conceptually* mediated awarenesses of objects is a straightforward consequence of the idea that in a subject's representation of, e.g., *that red cube over there*, the same conceptual capacities are actualized as would be actualized in a judgment, from the subject's viewpoint, that there is a red cube over there.[22] And insofar as it is objects themselves that "guide" such perceptual experiences "from outside", the "immediacy"

---

[22] McDowell takes this concession to be sufficient to insulate him from the charge that his own account of perception embraces a version of the Myth of the Given. Shortly I shall argue that he is mistaken about this. Givenness is said in many ways.

of an intuition appears to require that it also be a *causal* consequence of an action of the object on the subject. But both of *these* theses are plainly compatible with Sellars' account of perception, and so, since McDowell reads Sellars as *denying* that objects are "immediately present" to subjects in perception, we have still not arrived at the crux of the matter.

We can perhaps come closer to bringing into focus what is ultimately at issue by exploring another exegetical charge that McDowell levels against Sellars, namely that, in light of his commitment to scientific realism, his picture

cannot accommodate Kant's insistence that the things in themselves that matter for his thinking about empirical knowledge are the very same things that make their appearance in intuition. (HWV, 469)

McDowell's proof text for this Kantian thesis comes from the B Preface, where Kant adverts to

the distinction between things as objects of experience and the very same things as things in themselves, which our critique has made necessary ... (Bxxvii)

to which McDowell adds, in a footnote, the gloss that

when we speak as philosophers, ... we speak of the same objects [that we experience] under a special mode of consideration in which we abstract from the way in which the objects figure in our world view. ... Considering things as things in themselves is considering the very things that figure in our knowledge, but in abstraction from how they figure in our knowledge. (HWV, 469 n. 23)

Since McDowell sees himself here as correcting the "two-worlds" picture of Kant which informed his discussions in *Mind and World*, I shall call the identity claim at issue the "Only-One-World" thesis.

Now it would be disingenuous to suggest that the thesis of transcendental idealism as Kant develops it through the two editions of the First Critique—for that, of course, is what is exegetically at issue here—is a paradigm of lucidity. In particular, his contention that objects are immediately present to subjects in intuition needs to be reconciled with his contention that the objects of sensible intuitions are *appearances*, and while it is understandable that McDowell emphasizes the first claim, is it not surprising that Sellars is interested in exploiting some of the implications of the second one.[23] In fact, both of these Kantian commitments are at work in McDowell's proof text, and there is consequently a reading of the Only-One-World thesis on which it expresses a claim that Sellars can comfortably accept. For that the "things in themselves that matter for [Kant's] thinking about empirical knowledge" are identical to the "things that make their appearance in intuition" is compatible with the idea that what those things appear

---

[23] Proof texts well-suited for that purpose are also available in Kant's text, e.g., "We have said above that appearances themselves are nothing but sensible representations, which must not be regarded in themselves, in the same way, as objects (outside the power of representation) (A104).

to *be* in sensible intuition may be very different from the best philosophical or scientific understanding of what those things actually *are*. Sellars, to be sure, is inclined to speak of the latter as delivering a conception of "what those things are *in themselves*" and to impute something like that view to Kant, but the commitments are separable.[24] In principle, there is nothing to prevent us from having good reasons for concluding that *when* things "make their appearance in intuition" *what* they then appear to be is not identical to what they *actually* are.

McDowell concludes that Sellars' scientific realism prevents him from accepting the Only-One-World thesis because he takes it to imply that "the red cubes and so forth that are, apparently, immediately present to us in intuitions do not really exist". We must consequently "suppose that our conceptual representations are guided by the items that the scientific image substitutes for these merely apparent objects—swarms of colorless particles or whatever" (HWV, 468). Now it cannot be denied that Sellars sometimes infelicitously expresses the implications of his scientific realism in the form of a claim to the effect that things of one kind or another—e.g., Newtonian masses or classical gases—"do not really exist". The idiom carries the unfortunate suggestion that such things are merely *illusory* or *imaginary*, but that, of course, is not what Sellars has in mind, and, indeed, Kant cautions us (at B69) against making precisely that error in understanding his own transcendental idealism. Rather, to say that Newtonian masses or classical gases "do not really exist" is only to say that there are good reasons to believe that nothing answers to the specifications for *being* a Newtonian mass or classical gas that are implicit in the corresponding *theories*, i.e., nothing actual strictly obeys the relevant laws. And the reasons for believing *that* are always reasons for accepting an alternative *and better* theory of what there is, e.g., theoretical accounts of relativistic masses or of particular sorts of ensembles of various kinds of molecules.

What complicates matters in the case of perception, however, is Sellars' explicit insistence that "the red cubes and so forth that are, apparently, immediately present to us in intuitions", i.e., the proper sensible features of experience, *clearly do* "really exist". His own favorite example is a pink ice cube, which, when we phenomenologically abstract from the causal and dispositional properties of ice, presents itself to us in an ostensible seeing as a cubical volume of pink determinately situated in space. "Obviously there are volumes of pink," Sellars writes. "No inventory of what there is can meaningfully deny that fact. What is at stake is their status and function in the scheme of things" (ICP §46, 73).[25] But

---

[24] McDowell criticizes the practice of reading "things in themselves" as "things as they are in themselves" (HWV, 469 n.23), but in fact both constructions can be found in Kant's text, e.g., "For we have to do only with our representations; how things in themselves may be (without regard to representations through which they affect us) is entirely beyond our cognitive sphere" (A190/B235). As we shall see, a case can be made that McDowell himself implicitly imposes a slightly aberrant reading on "things in themselves".

[25] "Is Consciousness Physical?", Sellars' third Carus Lecture (*Monist*, 64 (1981), 66–90). Cited as 'ICP' followed by numbered section and page. Compare: "The one thing we can say, with

we have already seen what Sellars concludes with respect to *that* question: What presents itself to a subject in an ostensible seeing, veridical or non-veridical, *as* a cubical volume of pink determinately situated in space actually *is* a complex pattern of sensations (sense impressions) constructed by the understanding *qua* productive imagination, i.e., an *image-model*.

[The] theory of sense impressions does not *introduce*, for example, cubical volumes of pink. It reinterprets the *categorial status* of the cubical volumes of pink of which we are perceptually aware. Conceived in the manifest image as, in standard cases, *constituents* of physical objects and in abnormal cases, as somehow 'unreal' or 'illusory', they are *recategorized* as sensory states of the perceiver and assigned various explanatory roles in the theory of perception. (ICP §44, 73)

For Sellars, then, in *both* seeing *and* merely ostensibly seeing, what presents itself *as* "that red cube over there", *actually is*, considered from the point of view of an adequate philosophical theory of perception, a complex sensory state of the experiencing subject. In contrast, the crux of McDowell's account of the difference between seeing and merely ostensibly seeing is that, in the former case, what presents itself to an experiencing subject (in a genuine intuition) *as* "that red cube over there" *actually is* a red cube over there, i.e., *actually is* a cubical volume of red determinately located in space. And in the latter case, the merely ostensible seeing, *nothing at all* presents itself to the subject as "that red cube over there", for there is only an *illusion* of (non-conceptual) content. When an object is "immediately present" to a subject in an intuition, in other words, it is present *in its actual categorial status*. In short, McDowell evidently subscribes to the principle that Sellars called "perhaps, the most basic form of ... 'The Myth of the Given', namely, that

if a person is directly aware of an item which has categorial status C, then the person is aware of it *as* having categorial status C. (LA §44, 11)

To reject the Myth of the Given is to reject the idea that the categorial structure of the world—if it has a categorial structure—imposes itself on the mind as a seal imposes an image on melted wax. (LA §45, 12)

Notwithstanding his disclaimers, then, I conclude that McDowell is still very much in the grip of the Myth. That is why he tends to interpret Kant's expression 'things in themselves' as if it were 'things themselves', and I suspect that it is why he is sometimes tempted by Heideggerian metaphors of truth as "disclosure". Thus, after criticizing Sellars' use of the term 'voice' as a trope for, roughly, 'influence' in his suggestion that, for Kant, the manifold of sense is "an independent factor which has a strong voice in the outcome" of the productive imagination's syntheses (S&M, 16), McDowell writes

phenomenological assurance, is that whatever its "true" *categorial* status, the expanse of red involved in an ostensible seeing of the very redness of an apple has *actual existence* as contrasted with the *intentional in-existence* of that which is believed in *as believed in*" (LA §88, 20–1).

But suppose we take it that the external constraint ... is exerted, in intuition, by objects themselves ... Now the image of voice fits more easily. A seen object, as it were, invites one to take it to be as it visibly is. It speaks to one; if it speaks to one's understanding, that is just what its speaking to one comes to. "See me as I am," it (so to speak) says to one; "namely, as characterized by *these* properties"—and it displays them. (HWV, 468)

That is, of course, a case of belaboring an innocent trope beyond necessity, but it is also, I submit, as clear an image of givenness as one could hope to find.

CONCLUDING REMARKS

McDowell's project in the Woodbridge Lectures was to articulate his substantial disagreements with Sellars by highlighting their interpretive disagreements about Kant. Since their purpose was in this way instrumental, exegetical questions have remained, in a sense, in the background. But I have nevertheless tried to show that Sellars' Kant is at least as true to the text of the First Critique as McDowell's Kant, and that there is in fact an acceptable Sellarsian reading for each of the key Kantian claims that McDowell suggests cannot be accommodated on Sellars' interpretation.[26]

The foreground of this discussion has been occupied by their two competing Kantianly-inspired philosophical theories of sensory perception. What I have argued here is that Sellars' account yields the better understanding—provided that, as I am tempted to put it, we have properly distinguished Sellars' Sellars from McDowell's Sellars. Giving a satisfactory account of *non-veridical* experience is a central project for any theory of perception, and just here McDowell's account leaves us empty-handed. For to say that, when a person merely ostensibly sees, e.g., a red cube over there, she is under the illusion that she is confronting an *object* because she is under the illusion that her experience has a corresponding *content* is an "explanation" in the grand tradition of opium's dormative powers.

In his own concluding remarks, McDowell offers us a summary of his fundamental disagreement with Sellars:

Suppose we agree with Sellars that it is an insight on Kant's part that the receptivity of sensibility must play a transcendental role. ... [The] conviction that Kant is right about the significance of sensibility presents us with a quite simple choice: either Sellars' picture of guidance by "sheer receptivity," or the idea I have recommended, that the guidance ... can be displayed, in the course of the transcendental project, as exercised by the immediate objects of perception themselves. (HWV, 491)

"I hope," he adds, "to have made it plausible that there is more to be said for the second option than Sellars allows". My own verdict is not encouraging. On

---

[26] As might be expected, the reading of the First Critique that I develop and present in *Accessing Kant: A Relaxed Introduction to the Critique of Pure Reason* (Clarendon Press; Oxford: 2005) is Sellarsian both by ancestry and design. My best case for the thesis that Kant's text supports that interpretation can consequently be found there.

the one hand, McDowell's "second option" arguably creates more philosophical mystery than it dispels. And on the other, now that we have passed beyond the *phrase* "sheer receptivity" and come to properly appreciate the way in which Sellars' "line" presents us with an ontologically innocent distinction of reason, I hope it has become plausible that there is more to be said for his option than McDowell allows.

APPENDIX

Sellars-Rosenberg Correspondence on Ontology: 1972–1973

SELLARS TO ROSENBERG: JULY 25, 1972

Dear Jay,

The idea of a symposium on the foundations approach to knowledge is an attractive one. The issue is lurking in many contemporary controversies, even when its presence is not immediately evident. I am tempted to volunteer, but would have to reassess my commitments before I give a definite response to your exploratory questions. Roderick Firth and a good Bergmannian would make an interesting "inconsistent triad", but there are many others whose names will occur to you.

Now for the seriousness of philosophy. Your question,

> How does one say perspicuously what "Facts are not objects (i.e., not particulars)" says unperspicuously?

calls for a commentary as well as an answer. And the answer itself needs to be given in stages.

The first step in the commentary is to counter with another question: Why should I want to say (perspicuously) that facts are *not* objects, when I clearly think that propositions *are* objects[1] and that facts are true propositions?[2]

Thus, from my point of view your question should be:

> How does one say perspicuously what "Facts are objects (i.e. particulars)" says unperspicuously?

or, to lay aside the dimension of truth (semantic assertibility),

> How does one say perspicuously what "States of affairs are objects (i.e. particulars)" says unperspicuously?

(where states of affairs are entities which may or may not 'obtain').

Consider, for example,

> (The state of affairs) that fa is an object (i.e. a particular).

Surely my view is that the expression 'that fa' has the form

> The [·f·]·a·

and is a DST which corresponds to the metalinguistic[3] sortal

> [·f·]·a·.

---

[1] *SPR*, 211 ff.

[2] However, see my concluding paragraphs for a sense in which propositions are *not* objects.

[3] For the purposes of your question I do not need to go into subtleties about 'speaking-out-loud' and 'inner thought episodes'.

which applies to any item in any language which does the job which is done in our language [in a PMese reconstruction] by an 'a' which has the property of being concatenated with a preceding 'f'.

Two comments:

(1) To be an [·f·]·a· is to be governed by semantical rules. In this respect, to be an [·f·]·a· is like being a pawn.

(2) Granted that something would not be an [·f·]·a· unless it were true (a fact) that it had empirical characteristics by virtue of which it was (in its language) an ·a· and was [f],[4] this does not mean that its being an [·f·]·a· is the same thing as this truth or fact. For clearly, unless it was true of a certain object, O, *that* it was of a certain empirical character, it would not be a pawn in our familiar game of chess; but this does not mean that pawns are facts and not objects.

The next step is to note that the phrase which follows the DST,

The [·f·]·a·

must be understood as a transformation of 'are particulars' which adopts it to the DST. Thus,

The pawn is a particular

becomes

Pawns are particulars

similarly,

The [·f·]·a· is a particular

becomes

[·f·]·a·s are particulars.[5]

The strategy should now be clear, but it should be rounded off with a discussion of categorizing statements. It is important to note that the latter are ambiguous in a way which calls for two "rational reconstructions".

(A) We can take (and improve) the way I took in "Empiricism and Abstract Entities". Here categorizing statements are construed as object language *showings* of how expressions belonging to different categories function. According to this "rational reconstruction"

1. a is a particular $=_{df} \bar{y}/y = y/a$[6]
2. f is a quality $=_{df} \bar{g}/(x)\ gx \sim gx/f$
3. p is a proposition $=_{df} \bar{q}/q \sim q/p$

where the forms which are illustrated on the right are introduced as follows:

---

[4] I neglect Jumblese languages which do not make use of auxiliary symbols to make the ·a· of a certain character by virtue of which it translates into our language by 'a's which have the character of being concatenated with a preceding 'f'.

[5] Notice that I am dealing with linguistic tokens on the inscriptional model. Things become far more complicated when we deal with linguistic tokens as pieces of verbal behavior or inner episodes. In what sense are events objects? That is a long story which calls for a *long* letter in its own right.

[6] Needless to say I use the Leibnitz-Russell definition of identity.

$\bar{y}/fy/x =^{df} (\exists g) : (y)gy \equiv fy \& gx^7$

where 'fy' represents any open (extensional) sentence with the variable 'y.'

$\bar{g}/F(g)/f =^{df} (\exists G) : (g) \, G(g) \equiv F(g) \& \, G(f)$

where 'F(g)' represents any open (extensional) sentence with the predicate variables 'g'. Again,

$\bar{q}/\phi(q)/p =^{df} (\exists \psi)\psi \, (q) \equiv \phi(q) \& \, \psi(p)$

where '$\phi(q)$' represents any open (extensional) sentence with the sentential variable 'q'.

Notice that as thus defined, expressions beginning with '$\bar{y}$', '$\bar{g}$', and '$\bar{q}$' are neither singular terms nor sortal predicates. They need not be predicative at all, save in the broad sense in which both

> Tall (Tom)

and

> Tom = Tom

are predicative with respect to Tom (roughly, say something about him), and in which

> $(\exists x)$ tall x

is predicative with respect to tall, for it says something about *tall* mainly that tall is how something is.

Thus, strictly, the above *definientia* should read, respectively,

> a is particular (*not* is a particular).
> f is qualitative (*not* f is a quality).
> p is propositional (*not* p is a proposition).

But once this is appreciated, one can allow the surface grammar of such categorizing statements to be that of ordinary classificatory statements.

In the above framework,

> The pawn is a particular

becomes

> $(x) \, x \in$ pawn $\supset \bar{y}/y = y/x.$

(B) We can take the line I took in "Towards a Theory of the Categories". According to that analysis

> _____ is a particular

was construed as the material mode for (in first approximation)

> . . . . . is a singular term

(where the subject of the former has been replaced by the corresponding explicitly metalinguistic expression). Thus

> Socrates is a particular

becomes

---

[7] Compare the *Principia* definition of '$x \in \hat{y}(fy)$', but remember that, as thus defined, ' $\in \hat{y}(fy)$' should not be read 'is a y such that fy', i.e. '$\hat{y}(fy)$' should not be construed as a sortal.

The ·Socrates· is a singular term

and hence

·Socrates·s are singular terms.

But how, on this account, are such general statements as

Men are particulars

to be construed? On the previous account there was available

$(x) x \in Man \supset \bar{y}/y = y/x.$

This time we need something like

For all expressions, e, if the result of concatenating e with ·is a man· is a wff, then e is a singular term.

I won't attempt to tidy this up so let's see where it gets us.

Applied to

The pawn is a particular

as reducible to

Pawns are particulars

we get

For all expressions, e, if the result of concatenating e with ·is a pawn· is a wff, then e is a singular term.

Applied to

(The state of affairs) that fa is a particular

we get

For all expressions, e, if the result of concatenating e with ·is an [·f·]·a·· is a wff, then e is a singular term.

For example, I shall write a token of [·f·]·a· and call it Tom

fa.

Now

Tom is an [·f·]·a·

is not only a wff, but true, and, indeed, 'Tom' is a singular term (as is the token on line 25 of p. 294). (i.e. fa)

I have already indicated some of the serious problems which must be disposed of before this strategy is home free. Let me add some more.

What of

(The state of affairs) that aRb is an object?

The first step is obvious:

The [·R·](·a·, ·b·) is an object.

The sortal corresponding to the DST applies to any inscription in any language which does the job done in our [PMese] language by 'a's and 'b's which (in that order) have an 'R' between them. This time, however, to be an [·R·](·a·, ·b·) an item must be a complex object, roughly a pair of objects which satisfy a certain relation; *which* relation depends of course on the language to which it belongs. Now it is not customary to call complex objects or, for that matter, pairs, particulars. Indeed, many ideal language philosophers so use the term 'particular' that to speak of complex particulars is *widersinnig*. I do not concur, yet it is useful to distinguish between within the broad domain of objects—which include distributive objects (e.g. the lion), average entities (the average man) and other interesting specimens—the domain of basic individuals and *composita* (of which, on one interpretation, pairs, triples, etc. are examples).

Now a cat-on-a-mat is an object, though not a simple object. It is a *compositum* which satisfies the on-relation in the direction cat to mat. (A cat-on-a-mat is to be distinguished from—though it is obviously related to—a cat which is on a mat.) Granted, the object would not exist unless it was true *that* a cat is on a mat. But this does not entail, as noted before, that a cat on a mat is the fact that a cat is on a mat.

Thus, given a satisfactory account of pairs and their identity

(The state of affairs) that aRb is a particular (albeit a complex one)

becomes

$$(x,y) : (x,y) \in [\cdot R \cdot](\cdot a \cdot, \cdot b \cdot) \supset (\bar{u}, \bar{v})/(u,v) = (u,v)/(x,y).$$

It is time, now, to drop the other shoe. You must remember that in "Abstract Entities" I explained how both of the following statements could be true:

(1) Triangularity is not an individual but an attribute.
(2) Triangularity is an individual.

The argument was that 'triangularity' is ambiguous. It can mean

The ·triangular·

or

The ·the ·triangular·· .

Thus (1) becomes

(1-1) The ·triangular· is not a ST, but a predicate

which reduces to

(1-2) ·Triangular·s are not STs, but predicates,

while (2) becomes

(2-1) The ·The ·triangular·· is a ST (i.e. a DST)

which reduces to

(2-2) ·The ·triangular··s are STs (i.e. DSTs).

Correspondingly, the following are both true

(3) That fa is not an object but a state of affairs
(4) That fa is an object.

The first of these, (3), becomes

(3-1) The [·f·]·a· is not a ST, but a proposition

which reduces to

(3-2) [·f·]·a·s are not STs but proposition tokens,

while (4) becomes

(4-1) The ·the [·f·]·a·· is a ST (i.e. a DST)

which reduces to

(4-2) ·The [·f·]·a··s are STs (i.e. DSTs).

How, you may ask, can I reconcile

(3) That fa is not an object but a state of affairs

with my opening claim that states of affairs, *are* objects? The answer is that although tokens of [·f·]·a· are objects, they are not objects which, *considered as linguistic role players*, are singular terms.

Thus we have

(5) (x) x ∈ [·f·]·a· ⊃ ȳ/y = y/x

and

(6) For all expressions, e, if the result of concatenating e with ·is an [·f·]·a·· is a wff, then e is a singular term

both of which tell us that [·f·]·a·s are particulars. On the other hand, we also have

(x) x ∈ [·f·]·a· ⊃∼ (x ∈ ST)

which is both true and consistent with each of the above.

It only remains to be noted that the sense of

That fa is an object

which is reconstructed by (4-2) above is to be carefully distinguished from both (5) and (6) above. It has as its chess parallel

The pawn is an object.

The ·The pawn· is a ST (i.e. a DST).

·The pawn·s are STs (i.e. DSTs).

In this context we should not say that the pawn is a particular, but rather that it is a funny kind of object, i.e. a distributive object.

I hope that you find the above remarks sufficiently intelligible to carry on the dialogue.

Cordially, Wilfrid Sellars

ROSENBERG TO SELLARS: AUGUST 29, 1972

Dear Wilfrid,

I see that you will be visiting with us at colloquium time. Great! My seminar on your work should be far enough along by then to have my students crying for a chance to ask you some questions. Me too, probably.

Thanks for the papers, which I am devouring, and the letter. I don't think that I've ever received a 12-page letter with footnotes before! I hope that my response (which follows immediately) will be intelligent enough to justify your obvious effort. To work:

I think that I understand now what you're trying to do, and I'd like to engage your views fairly far along, having no quarrel with most of your opening moves as such. Let me first, however, say a few things to let you decide whether I've, in fact, understood you.

1. I will need a token of [·f·]·a· to talk about. Let me produce one:

fa.

Since you've used 'Tom' for one of its relatives, we'll call this one 'Jim'.

2. Now, as I understand you, the first sentence of the last paragraph is, strictly speaking, ungrammatical. In particular, the expression "a token of [·f·]·a·" (which you also use, on p. 294) seems to have incoherent syntax. On your view,

(1) Jim is an [·f·]·a·

is a true wff, paralleling in grammar

(2) Fido is an orange dog.

Since it seems correct to say that

[·f·]·a·s are tokens,

employing the analogy with

Orange dogs are animals,

the expression "a token of [·f·]·a·" turns out to have the syntax of "an animal of orange dog", which won't do.

3. Of course there's no problem understanding what's intended:

a token which is an [·f·]·a·

(cf. "an animal which is an orange dog"). I go into the point only to let my misunderstandings about your grammar, if any, surface early.

4. Assuming that I'm OK so far, however, then, since the following transformations are permitted in the case of (2):

Fido is a dog which is orange,
Fido is a dog & Fido is orange,

I take (1) to entail:

Jim is an ·a· which is [·f·]

and, therefore

(3) Jim is an ·a· & Jim is [·f·].

5. This seems to mesh well with the schema in "Naming and Saying" that I was puzzling over in my long essay—your replacement for Wittgenstein's "Fact pictures fact":

Natural linguistic objects $O'_1, O'_2, \ldots O'_n$ make up a picture of objects $O_1, O_2, \ldots O_n$ by virtue of such and such facts about $O'_1, O'_2, \ldots O'_n$.

6. I take it that an instantiation of this schema in the present instance would be something like

The ·a· on line 3 of paragraph 1 (viz, Jim) is a picture of a by virtue of the fact that it (Jim) is [·f·].

Now we shall need to do something here about "by virtue of the fact that ...", but your strategy seems clear enough. It means, I would suppose, something like "since it is true that ...", yielding

Jim is a picture of a since it is true that Jim is [·f·].

And, moving down out of the metalanguage, we arrive at something like:

    (4) Jim is a picture of a because Jim is [·f·].

7. Thus my reading of your late syntax seems to fit the pattern of your early schema. But (4) really puzzles me. I would expect to find, not (4), but something like

    (5) Jim is a picture of a because Jim is an ·a· and since, in our linguistic community, ·a·s stand in certain C-H-L relations to a.

Let me drop this line of thought for the moment, however, and return to spelling out the implications of (3).

8. The first observation to make is that you are quite right to hold that Jim is a particular. For if we ask what *kind* of thing Jim is, the answer, by (3), has to be that Jim is an ·a· and, since ·a·s are, uncontroversially, particulars (natural linguistic *objects*), it follows that *Jim* is a particular.

9. But it also seems to follow that, since Jim is an ·a· and since ·a·s are singular terms, Jim is a *singular term*, and this seems wrong.

10. I have, of course, no quarrel with the conclusion that 'Jim' (note the quotes) is a singular term (cf. your conclusion on p. 294), but my conclusion that Jim (note the absence of quotes) is *also* a singular term is a different one, and more bothersome. The crucial point is that it seems to run directly counter to your claim that

    (3-2) [·f·]·a·s are not STs but proposition tokens,

for Jim is an [·f·]·a· and, as I've just argued, Jim *is* a ST.

11. Now there seem to be only two ways of meeting the argument in 9 above. The first is to deny that ·a·s are singular terms. This, I think, you would be reluctant to do. The second is to deny that Jim is an ·a·. He is rather, an [·f·]·a·, and, thus, that ·a·s are STs does not entail that Jim is a ST. But, unless I've radically misunderstood your syntax, this won't do either, for, as I read you, [·f·]·a·s *are* ·a·s, as orange dogs are dogs.

12. Now one thing I was looking for in my long essay was precisely a way of being *entitled* to your (3-2). I *would* be entitled to it, if, *à la* Wittgenstein, STs were natural linguistic objects and proposition "tokens" were natural linguistic facts, *and* there was a categorial ontological distinction between objects and facts, so that facts are *not* objects.

13. Like you, I am *now* convinced that Wittgenstein's strategy for defending (3-2) or its like won't work. But my reason is, I guess, not the same as yours. I presuppose *one* of Wittgenstein's moves (that facts are not objects) and use it to attack the other (that propositions are facts). I read "Facts are not objects", crudely, as "What can be stated cannot be named" and conclude that, if propositions *were* facts, a metalanguage would be impossible, since we must name (i.e., refer to) propositions in any metalanguage. It isn't completely clear in my mind why *you* reject Wittgenstein's view that propositions are facts, but it is clear that it can't be for *my* reason, for you reject also what I use as a premise, the claim that facts are not objects.

14. In any case, we are agreed that Wittgenstein's line of defense for your (3-2) won't work. Failing that, however, we need another line of defense, and what I've been suggesting is that *if* one adopts your view that facts *are* objects, there isn't going to be one. (Not, of course, that I have one to haul out of my pocket on my premises yet.)

15. I guess, recurring to your letter, what I really need to ask you for on this point is

(a) an elucidation of your claim on p. 296: "... Although tokens of [·f]·a· are objects, they are not objects which, *considered as linguistic role players*, are singular terms."

and

(b) an explanation of 'singular term' which shows how (as you claim on p. 296)

$$(x)\, x \in [\cdot f] \cdot a \cdot \supset \bar{y}/y = y/x$$

and

$$(x)\, x \in [\cdot f] \cdot a \cdot \supset \sim (x \in ST)$$

can be compatible with each other, for I would have thought that

$$(x)\, x \in ST \equiv \bar{y}/y = y/x.$$

(Hence it's Frege who haunts me in paragraph 33 of my long essay, since he finds 'p = q' well formed.)

16. I suspect that your reply to (a) and (b) is going to turn on precisely the matters I'm muddled about in 5 through 7 above, but, to return there for a minute, if one holds, as you do in N&S, that *what* pictures picture is *objects* and not, as Wittgenstein would have it, *facts* (implicitly enforcing some sort of object/fact distinction there, by the way), then that Jim is [·f] really seems to have nothing much to do with *what* it is that Jim pictures. I should like to say that that Jim is [·f] is relevant, not to what Jim pictures but to what Jim pictures it *as*. Thus Jim pictures a *as f* by being [·f]. But this looks suspiciously like the "Fact pictures fact" model which you reject:

that Jim is [·f] says (shows? pictures?) that fa.

I shall wait to be straightened out on all this.

Well, I think I've probably said more than enough to allow you to pinpoint major areas of confusion and conflict. Getting all this down on paper is certainly doing wonders for my thinking on these difficult matters, so I do hope that you'll find something here worth replying to. I'd like to carry on.

Hope your new academic year is a pleasant one. See you in October.

All my best, Jay Rosenberg

SELLARS TO ROSERBERG; SEPTEMBER 5, 1972

Dear Jay,

Many thanks for the long letter, the promise of which motivated my own effort. I reply at once in order to strike while the iron is hot, or, as I see it, the main question you now press can be answered by drawing a distinction which has always been implicit in my analysis, but to which I have failed until recently to give formal recognition. I first became aware of the shortcoming in question in the course of a seminar I was giving at UMass this spring. A student asked me: "How can you say that an [·f]·a· is an INDCON, when it is a PROP? Surely propositions are radically different from names!" To which I answered, of course, that [·f]·a·s are INDCONs, but not *mere* INDCONs, such as occur in a list, for they are INDCONs which, in addition to playing an INDCON role, and, in so doing, refer to a, are also, by virtue of being concatenated an ·f, playing the (atomic) propositional role of picturing a as f. And, indeed, the distinction which is needed to answer your question is exactly that between being a *mere* INDCON (as in a list) and being an INDCON which is also a PROP, e.g. an [·f·]·a·.

But let me get down to cases. I shall comment on your letter, paragraph by paragraph as you have numbered them:

Ad 1. Hello Jim.

Ad 2. As you yourself go on to point out, the context in which I am interested is not

Jim is a token of [·f·]·a·

but

Jim is an [·f·]·a·.

I do speak informally of tokens of [·f·]·a·, however, and have not exclusively commented on the grammar of 'token.' Now that you press me, I suggest that

… is a token of _____

is a special case of

… is a member of _____

Thus,

Jim is a token of [·f·]·a·

stands to

Jim is an [·f·]·a·

as

Socrates is a member of mankind

stands to

Socrates is a man.

In other words, token-talk, like member-talk, is one level up the semantic hierarchy from ordinary subject-predicate talk. Using it causes no trouble until we look *at* it instead of *through* it. From my point of view,

Jim is a token of [·f·]·a·

has the form

Jim is a token of [·f·]·a·-kind

and, made fully explicit, has the form

The INDCON ^·is an [·f·]·a·· is true of ·Jim·

which entails

The ·Jim is an [·f·]·a·· is true

and carries us, via the truth move, to

Jim is an [·f·]·a·

which is the way to talk about Jim in the context of our problem.

Ad 4. No comment.

Ad 5. No comment.

Ad 6. No comment.

Ad 7. We must distinguish between the C-H-L relations by virtue of which Jim refers to a, and the C-H-L relations between [·f·] INDCONs and f objects by virtue of which Jim, as an [·f·] INDCON, pictures a as f. Your (5) runs these together, i.e. runs together that which makes ·a·s the linguistic *representatives* of a, and that which makes relevantly configured as *pictures* of a. [See my Russell paper, [OPM]]

Ad 8. No comment.

Ad 9. Here comes the crunch. I am indeed committed to the following: ·a·s are STs and Jim, being an [·f·]·a·, and hence an ·a·, is a ST.

Ad 10. My introductory paragraph should have prepared you for what is coming. I abandon my claim on p. 295 in favor of the revised claim that

(3-2)-R [·f·]·a·s are not *mere* STs but PROPs

(I drop the word 'tokens' for reasons indicated in *Ad* 2. above).

Ad 11. I have, I believe, escaped between the horns of your dilemma.

Ad 12. No comment.

Ad 13. No comment.

Ad 14. No comment.

Ad 15(a). The sentence on p. 296 of my previous letter, which you quote, should be modified to accord with (3-2)-R as follows:

Although tokens of [·f·]·a· are objects, they are not objects which, *considered as linguistic role players*, are *mere* singular terms.

Ad 15(b). Correspondingly,

$$(x) \ x \in [·f·]·a· \ \supset \sim (x \in \ ST)$$

should read

$$(x) \ x \in [·f·]·a· \ \supset \sim (x \in \ mere \ ST).$$

I am puzzled by your

$$(x) \ x \in ST \equiv \bar{y}/y = \ y/x$$

for obviously it is false that

$$(x) \ \bar{y}/y = y/x \supset x \in \ ST$$

since not all particulars are even linguistic, let alone singular terms. I suspect that you are confusing

$$(x) \ x \in ST \equiv \bar{y}/y = \ y/x$$

with

$$(x) \ x \ is \ particular \equiv \bar{y}/y = \ y/x$$

which is, on my "object language" analysis of the categorizing expression 'particular', a definitional truth. A comment on 15(b) insofar as it concerns Frege's ghost will come at the end, because at this point it would constitute a lengthy digression.

Ad 16. It should now be clear from what I wrote in *Ad* 7., that I quite agree with you that "… that Jim is [·f·] is relevant not to what Jim pictures [i.e. the object of which Jim, as being an ·a·, is the linguistic representative], but to what Jim pictures it *as*".

You sum this up by saying that

Jim pictures a *as f* by being [·f·]

and express the suspicion that this takes us back to the "Fact pictures fact" model, which I have rejected. Once again I refer you to the passage in the Russell paper in which I address myself to this issue. But I really believe that it is all in N&S and T&C—though, perhaps, somewhat in the manner in which the oak is in the acorn.

Ad Frege's ghost. According to my PMese lights

$$p = q$$

where 'p' and 'q' represent object language sentences, says no more, and no less, than

$$p \equiv q$$

[in PM it is provable that p **Eq** q $\equiv$ p $\equiv$ q, where '**Eq**', to speak informally, is reflective, symmetrical and transitive]. Thus I would not object to introducing the categorial predicate 'is propositional' as follows

$$p \text{ is propositional} =^{df} \overline{q}/q \equiv q/p$$

or, to use variables which don't seem to beg the question,

$$a \text{ is propositional} =^{df} \overline{\beta}/\beta = \beta/a.^8$$

But, of course, the context

$$\overline{\beta}/\beta \equiv \beta/\text{Socrates}$$

would be ill-formed, as would

$$\overline{\beta}/\beta = \beta/\text{snow is white}$$

given the Leibnitz-Russell definition of '='. For the latter would entail

Snow is white = snow is white

and this, unless it is construed as

Snow is white $\equiv$ snow is white

(in which case, *caedit quaestio*), would expand into

(F) F(snow is white) $\equiv$ F(snow is white).

If we construe 'F' as a variable for genuine predicates, which is implied by extending the L-R definition of identity to this context, the expression is ill-formed, since 'Snow is white' is not a singular term. If, on the other hand, we construe 'F' in terms of contexts (open sentences) in which sentences (as opposed to singular terms) can occur, then

Snow is white = snow is white

would turn out, as before, to be a rewriting of

Snow is white $\equiv$ snow is white

and not to be an identity statement at all.

But all this, of course, simply reflects my commitment to a Tractarian interpretation of PM. It belongs here simply as a way of exorcising *some* appearances of Frege's ghost, and, less metaphorically, as a warning against a piecemeal introduction of Fregean considerations into contexts governed by PM-Tractarian assumptions.

---

[8] The corresponding definitions of 'is particular' and 'is predicative' with neutral variables—after all, the burden of the definition is carried by the logical forms—would be

$$a \text{ is particular} =_{df} \overline{\beta}/\beta = \beta/a; \quad a \text{ is predicative} =_{df} \overline{\beta}/(\gamma)\beta\gamma\text{v} \sim \beta\gamma/a$$

Well, this was written in haste and there will certainly be some repenting at leisure. But I hope it achieves its immediate purpose, which is to carry our dialogue a step further before I am engulfed by the term (and so much else). See you next month.

Cordially, Wilfrid Sellars

ROSENBERG TO SELLARS: SEPTEMBER 28, 1972

Dear Wilfrid,

1. Thanks for the super-quick response to my last letter. Would that I could be as prompt, but I haven't yet achieved Distinguished Professorial leisure, and continued upward mobility is time consuming. Thanks, too, for "Reply to Quine" which I will digest at my earliest opportunity (probably July of 1978). For all that, I do have a few thoughts which can't wait, so here they are:

You're quite right to be puzzled by my

$$(x)\ x \in ST \equiv \bar{y}/y = \ y/x.$$

2. I suspect that my reasoning (what there was of it) involved something like:

$$(x)\ [x \in ST \equiv (z)(x \text{ represents } z \equiv \bar{y}/y = y/z)]$$

(i.e., All and only singular terms represent particulars) and that the 'x represents z' part got lost. But that's just a guess. What I *wrote* was certainly false.

3. One thing I'd like to chew on a bit in your latest remarks occurs in "*Ad* Frege's ghost". There occurs the following argument (I put 'fa' for 'Snow is white'):

The context $\bar{\beta}/\beta = \beta/$fa would be ill-formed, given the Leibnitz- Russell definition of '='. For the latter would entail
$$fa = fa$$
and this, unless it is construed as
$$fa \equiv \ fa$$
would expand into
$$(F)F(fa) \equiv \ F(fa)$$
If we construe 'F' as a variable for genuine predicates, which is implied by extending the L-R definition of identity to this context, the expression is ill-formed, since 'fa' is not a singular term.

Well, what am I to make of "since 'fa' is not a singular term", given all that has gone before? My natural inclination is to read it as:

[·f·]·a· s are not singular terms.

But *that* can't be right, [·f·]·a·s *are* singular terms (though not *mere* singular terms). Still, I can't think of any *other* plausible reading of " 'fa' is not a singular term" and, that being so, your argument is not complete and Frege's ghost refuses to lie down and be quiet.

4. But still bigger games are afoot. Let me explain. In section VII of "Abstract Entities" (AE) you pose the question

Are there any abstract entities which are not objects?

and answer that *of course* there are abstract entities which are not objects. Again, on page 68 of "Towards a Theory of the Categories", you argue that it would be correct and non-paradoxical to say that *there are entities which are not individuals*.[9] I used to be convinced that you'd successfully established these claims. In terms of recent developments, I now think that you haven't—and that they're false.

5. The example you give in AE are, roughly these:

    (a)   Lionkind is a kind and not an individual

(i.e. (a1) The ·lion· is a common noun and not a ST) and

    (b)   Triangularity is a quality and not an individual

(i.e. (b1) The ·triangular· is a predicate and not a ST).[10]
The problem is created by the fact that you address these questions *before* you make good the "still more basic oversimplification" which comes from not considering languages of the Jumblese sort. When the smoke from *that* fire has cleared, the reconstruction of 'triangularity' is no longer 'the ·triangular·' but rather 'the [·triangular·] INDCON'.[11]

6. Similarly, drawing on "Classes as Abstract Entities ... ", the purified reconstruction of 'lionkind' will not be 'the lion' but rather

    the [· $\in_1$ lion·] INDCON.

If this is right, then (a1) and (b1) above become:

    (a2)   The [· $\in_1$ lion·] INDCON is a common noun and not a ST
    (b2)   The [·triangular·] INDCON is a predicate and not a ST.

And these unpack, as a first step, into

    (a3)   [· $\in_1$ lion·] INDCONs are common nouns and not STs
    (b3)   [·triangular·] INDCONs are predicates and not STs.

7. Well, you can see what's coming:

    [· $\in_1$ lion·] INDCONs are INDCONs

---

    [9] 'Particular', 'object', and 'individual' seem to be interchangeable in our discussions to date and in many of your writings. There are, of course, differences—though I'm not sure we'd agree completely about what they are—but they don't seem crucial for present purposes. I'll continue to use them interchangeably as material mode counterparts of 'singular term' until it becomes important.

    [10] I abstract from the distinction between *distributive* individuals and others, since it is not essential to what I'm up to. I can grant that triangularity and lionkind aren't distributive objects, but they may turn out to be *objects* for all that.

    [11] I'm sticking with the bracketing conventions you use at the beginning of your first letter (25 July). I take it that both English *triangular(a)*s and, say, Jumblese *a*s would be [·triangular·] INDCONs. In AE, it's

    the ·triangular· INDCON

in "Classes as Abstract Entities ... " it's

    the ·triangular· [INDCON]

and, if I recall my quick and cursory reading of "Reply to Quine" it there becomes

    the ·[*triangular*]· INDCON.

You really ought to pick *one*, don't you think?

INDCONs are STs

Ergo, [$\cdot \in_1$ lion$\cdot$] INDCONs *are* STs

and, similarly,

[$\cdot$triangular$\cdot$] INDCONs are INDCONs

INDCONs are STs

Ergo, [$\cdot$triangular$\cdot$] INDCONs *are* STs.

The conclusions transcribe the material mode claims: "Lionkind is an object" and "Triangularity is an object", and are inconsistent with (a3) and (b3).

This I shall interpret as the cash value of the ancient maxim that everything which *is*, is particular.

8. Of course, [$\cdot \in_1$ lion$\cdot$] INDCONs and [$\cdot$triangular$\cdot$] INDCONs are not *mere* INDCONs and, hence, not *mere* STs. But I don't think that we can save 'kind' and 'quality' here. For if we ask what *else*, besides STs, [$\cdot \in_1$ lion$\cdot$] INDCONs and [$\cdot$triangular$\cdot$] INDCONs are, the answer it seems to me, has to be:

[$\cdot \in_1$ lion$\cdot$] INDCONs are not mere STs but *PROPs*

and

[$\cdot$triangular$\cdot$] INDCONs are not mere STs but *PROPs*.

These are the formal mode counterparts of "Lionkind is a state of affairs" and "Triangularity is a state of affairs". Both of these look wrong.

9. Well, time for some morals. What I take these animadversions to show, among other things, is that the *correct* transcription of

Triangularity is a quality

is *not*

The [$\cdot$triangular$\cdot$] INDCON is a predicate

(which is false), but rather, the *original*

The $\cdot$triangular$\cdot$ is a predicate

which is true. To speak of triangularity, in other words, is—as I see it now—to make reference to a linguistic role which *can* only be filled by *auxiliary* signs. (While Jumblese contains [$\cdot$triangular$\cdot$] INDCONs, it contains no $\cdot$triangular$\cdot$s.) It is this essentially *auxiliary* character of $\cdot$triangular$\cdot$s, and not the non-illustratingness of "[$\cdot$triangular$\cdot$] INDCON" which becomes the truth behind Frege's insight that functions are essentially *ungesättigt*.

10. Notice that, in your account of the semantics of language *in general*—the account which covers both PMese type and Jumblese type languages—both 'common noun' and 'predicate' as linguistic role designators have disappeared. They turn out to be *parochial* linguistic roles rather than *essential* linguistic roles. And this, surely, is as it should be, for Jumblese contains neither predicates nor common nouns. We wind up with two and only two *basic* semantic categories: INDCON and PROP. This is quite consistent with the *Tractatus*. In fact, as I read it, it *is* the *Tractatus*. Wittgenstein's semantics includes only 'name' and 'proposition' as basic categories.

11. This way of looking at things entitles us to say

  1. There are abstract entities which are not particulars

(because, although [·triangular·] INDCONs are STs, ·triangular·s are not); gives us an interpretation of

  2. There *really are* no abstract entities

(because the only *basic* semantic categories are INDCON and PROP); and commits us to

  3. Everything which *really* is, is particular

(because PROPs are STs, though not *mere* STs).

12. Now I'm not yet sure that I'm entirely *happy* with

  PROPs are STs (though not mere STs)

and the resulting commitment to

  Everything which really is, is particular

especially with Frege's ghost still lurking in the shadows, but I'm going to let these go until I have your reactions to what I've done in this letter. I guess it's heretical enough to warrant some comment.

13. See you in a couple of weeks. By the way, is there any chance that you could arrive here a day early or leave here a day late for Colloquium, so that my seminar could have a few hours' discussion with you? Your honorarium would be adjusted accordingly.

Anxiously awaiting your next letter.

Cordially, Jay Rosenberg

SELLARS TO ROSENBERG: JANUARY 16, 1973

Dear Jay.

I have been pondering long and hard about the questions you raise in your letter of 28 September. While they have not led me to change my views on any point of substance, they have convinced me that the way in which I have formulated them in print is in certain key respects inadequate and misleading. Above all they have forced me to clarify my views on the status of qualities, kinds and, last but not least, states of affairs. I will not attempt to summarize the outcome, but will let it emerge, such as it is, in my remarks on the specifics of your letter. I will avail myself of the numbered breakdown on which we agreed during my stay in Chapel Hill.

Ad 1. I hope I can get some reaction to this letter in the not too distant future, preferably before "July of 1978". I begin to hear "Time's winged chariot" loud and clear, and would like to get these things straight before it catches me. Some more "few thoughts which can't wait" would keep the dialogue rolling. This letter has turned out to be monstrously long, but not quite as long as it looks, since it is quite repetitious.

Ad 2. No comment.

Ad 3. Things are beginning to warm up; but why doesn't the distinction between STs and *mere* STs provide the answer? Surely what combines with predicates to form statements are *mere* STs. This would rule out, as intended,

  F(fa).

Ad 4. This section sets a general theme which recurs throughout the remainder of your paper. Since it contains no argument, I will not discuss it here. I will, however, return to it after commenting on your criticism of my treatment of qualities and kinds and its compatibility with the idea that they are examples of entities which are not objects.

Ad 5. We are now in the kitchen when, in the latter part of AE, I changed from equating Triangularity with the ·triangular· to equating it with the [·triangular·] INDCON, my aim was to interpret Triangularity as something that could be expressed in Jumblese as well as PMese languages. Since Jumblese contains no predicates,[12] it obviously contains no ·triangular·s. Thus, the metalinguistic sortal,

[·triangular·] INDCON

as used in this connection, could no longer imply that the items to which it applies consist of a ·triangular· and an INDCON. It was now (informally) characterized as a common noun which applies to expressions in any language, whether Jumblese or PMese, which do the job done in *our* PMese language by INDCONs which are concatenated with a 'triangular', and in other PMese languages by INDCONs which are concatenated with auxiliary expressions which function as does our 'triangular'. My reason for shifting to

·[*triangular*]· INDCON

in my "Reply to Quine" was to stress the auxiliary role of the design *triangular* in our PMese language. However, in using this new mode of representation, I should have remembered that when I first introduced the bracket notation I placed them around adjectives to indicate that they were being used to form a common noun out of a common noun; thus the brackets in

[white] dog

represented that the whole expression is a common noun formed from the common noun 'dog' and the adjective 'white', and has the sense expressed by the phrase

dog which is white.

However, when I used this device in metalinguistic contexts I soon began, without explicit awareness of what I was doing, to construe the brackets as implying concatenation. According to this line of thought

[*triangular*] 'a'

would apply, by virtue of the brackets, to 'a's which are concatenated with a *triangular*. In this respect, the brackets played the role of the standard symbol for concatenation, '^'. The result was a sad muddle.

The above explains (without justifying) my placing the dot quotes *outside* the brackets in

·[*triangular*]· INDCON

for I wanted this to apply to Jumblese INDCONs which, though not concatenated with an auxiliary expression corresponding to *triangular*, nevertheless were the Jumblese counterparts of expressions in our language which consist of INDCONs concatenated with a *triangular*.

---

[12] Predicates, as I have emphasized since "Naming and Saying", are auxiliary expressions, and are linguistic conveniences rather than necessities.

Clearly I must straighten out my notation. I have ideas about how to do this, largely based on my study of recent theories of grammar, but they will have to wait until another occasion. In the meantime, I will return to my initial use of brackets and informally characterize

[·triangular·] INDCON

as a metalinguistic sortal which applies to

INDCONs which have a character by virtue of which they function as do INDCONs which are concatenated with a ·triangular· in PMese languages, and, in first instance, as do INDCONs concatenated with an *triangular* in *our* PMese language.

Obviously this puts a tremendous informal burden on the expressions inside the brackets. Far too much metalinguistic information is left without explicit representation; or, to put it somewhat differently, the dot quotes are playing a much richer role than that of forming a common noun which applies to inscriptions in any language which do the job done in our language by the inscription which appears between the dots.[13]

But enough of this brooding about a perspicuous notation. Without further ado I shall follow your example and use

[·triangular·] INDCON

in the intended generic sense in which it applies to PMese and Jumblese items alike.
Ad 6 and 7. You are quite right to insist that if, after reinterpreting Triangularity as the [·triangular·] INDCON, I had continued to assert both of the following

(a)   Triangularity is a quality
(b)   The context '____ is a quality' is the material mode for (roughly) the context
'..... is a one place predicate'[14]

I would have been committed to the nonsense

(c) The [·triangular·] INDCON is a predicate.

---

[13] For PMese languages

[^triangular·] INDCON

might do, construed as applying to INDCONs which have the character of being concatenated with a ·triangular·. For something which applies to PMese and non-PMese expressions alike, we might try

[^*triangular*] INDCON.

Here the only *directly* illustrating component would be introduced by asterisk-quotes. The dot-quotes would, as always, serve to form a linguistic-functional expression; in this case an adjectival functional expression which, as indicated by the brackets, combines with 'INDCON' to form a common noun which applies to INDCONs in any language which have a character which is functionally equivalent to the character of being concatenated with a *triangular* in our language. The illustrating role of the dot-quoted expression as a whole would consist in the fact that it selects for functional scrutiny any sentence in our language which consists of an INDCON concatenated with a *triangular*, e.g. 'triangular a'.

[14] I say 'roughly', because, obviously, to capture in the formal mode the specific sense of 'quality' we must pick out a far more restricted class of predicates than simply those which are one-place. I shall not attempt to botanize predicates on this occasion, beyond contrasting those which *characterize* (roughly adjectival predicates) and those which *classify* (roughly common nouns). In other words, in what follows 'quality' has, roughly, the sense of 'attribute'.

Also, since, to use your example, Jumblese *a^*s are [˙triangular˙] INDCONs, and hence, on this new account, express Triangularity, by accepting (c) I would have been committed to the absurdity that in the Jumblese language in question

The 'a' is a predicate.

Now, it is quite true that after offering the above reinterpretation of Triangularity in the latter part of AE, I did not discuss its consequences for the earlier analysis of the categorizing statement, 'Triangularity is a quality'. Yet I would certainly have refused to pair this statement with

The [˙triangular˙] INDCON is a predicate

and I clearly equated Triangularity as reinterpreted, with

that something is triangular

which places it *somewhere* in the category of states of affairs. Exactly where, I left rather up in the air, though I did give the essential clues, which I shall spell out shortly. The fact remains, however, that in subsequent papers, however, I continued to "oversimplify" (as I put it in AE) and to equate Triangularity with the ˙triangular˙ and to pair

Triangularity is a quality

with

The ˙triangular˙ is a (certain kind of) predicate.

Obviously, therefore, I must face up to the questions,

(1) Is it correct to construe Triangularity as the [˙triangular˙] INDCON?
(2) If so, what sense can be made of 'Triangularity is a quality'?

As I see it, I am faced with the following alternatives:

(a) I can continue to construe 'is a quality' as material mode for 'is a (certain kind of) predicate', in which case qualities would be parochial, and it would be incorrect to construe Triangularity, for example, as the [˙triangular˙] INDCON.
(b) I can reconstrue 'is a quality' to fit the reinterpretation of Triangularity as the [˙triangular˙] INDCON. I can do this by taking 'quality' to be the material mode for something like 'is a characterizing PROP'. In this case, both PMese and Jumblese would contain expressions which stand for qualities.

Of these two courses, (a) is the one *you* recommend. I have no strong objections to it, since the point I wanted to make, mainly that we can define a sense in which a Jumblese expression can pertain to Triangularity, or, more generically, a quality, can be made in a way which is compatible with (a). On the other hand, the simplest way of explaining how a Jumblese expression can pertain to a quality, e.g. Triangularity, would be to adopt alternative (b).

The important thing to see is that on alternative (a) there is, in addition to 'Triangularity is a quality' another, but *non-parochial* categorizing statement, which is intimately related to it, and which alternative (b) construes as synonymous with it. This non-parochial statement can be unearthed by taking seriously the idea that [˙triangular˙] INDCONs, being PROPs—which of course they are—have as their material mode of speech counterparts, *states of affairs*. Thus the material mode of

_____ is a characterizing PROP

would have the form

.... . is a ϕ state of affairs.

What might we substitute for 'ϕ'? I see no reason for not using 'qualitative', provided that it is clearly understood that although the root of this term is (on alternative (a)) parochial, it would now be used non-parochially to apply to states of affairs which, though they can be expressed in Jumblese as well as PMese, are expressed in PMese by a concatenation of INDCONs with a predicative expression which stands for a quality—as contrasted, for example, with one which stands for a kind.

In first approximation, to make this move is to pair the categorizing statement

That something is triangular is a qualitative state of affairs

with

The [˙triangular˙] INDCON is a characterizing PROP

In section 7 you correctly point out that

[˙triangular˙] INDCONs are not PREDs but INDCONs

so that if Triangularly is construed as the [˙triangular˙] INDCON, it would be an object, whereas on my original interpretation, which construed it as the ˙triangular˙, it would not be an object. After pointing out that on my second interpretation, Triangularity and Lionkind turn out to be objects, you characterize this as

... the cash value of the ancient maxim that everything which *is*, is particular. [Ital. JR.]

Though you do not explicitly make the connection, I take it that you are referring back to section 4, and arguing that when my analysis is spelled out it is inconsistent with the claim that there are entities which are not objects.

Now I assume that by italicizing the 'is', you mean to isolate a *philosophical* sense of 'is' in which not everything which is, *is*.[15] Perhaps, then, you are prepared to admit that there is such an entity as Triangularity, which on *your* construction (as the ˙triangular˙) is not an object, while denying that there *is* such an entity. But what makes you think that when *I* claimed that there are entities which are not objects, I meant that there *are* entities which are not objects?[16] I shall return to this topic shortly. For the moment I simply note that although the context makes it look as though it is because Triangularity (as the ˙triangular˙) is parochial that you deny that it *is*, it later becomes clear that this is not your reason. Being parochial turns out to be, as it should, a sufficient but not a necessary condition for correctly denying that something *really is*. Thus, presumably, Disjunction (as the ˙or˙) and Two (as the ˙($\exists$ 2x) x $\in_i$ KIND) would be entities which are, but which *really are* not. Furthermore, they are entities which are not objects.

Ad 8. You point out that if Triangularity is construed as the [˙triangular˙] INDCON and Lionkind as the [˙ $\in_1$ lion˙] INDCON then, since

[˙ $\in_1$ lion˙] INDCONs are not mere STs but PROPs

---

[15] In one sense the statement that there are minds is non-controversial. But *are* there minds? The Cartesian says yes, the Strawsonian, no.

[16] See "Towards a Theory of the Categories", 68, the paragraph which immediately follows the claim in question.

and

> [˙triangular˙] INDCONs are not mere STs but PROPs

we would have, in the material mode,

> Lionkind is ... a state of affairs
> Triangularity is ... a state of affairs.

"Both of these," you write, "look wrong." You then go on in section 9 to draw the "moral" that "the *correct* transcription" of 'Triangularity is a quality' is ... the *original* 'the ˙triangular˙ is a predicate' ".

Now, while I share your intuition about the oddness of

> Triangularity is a state of affairs

I think I can account for it in a way which reconciles it with the interpretation of Triangularity as the [˙triangular˙] INDCON. The basic point is that what belongs in the context

> ———— is a state of affairs

is a that-clause which results from applying 'that' to a (descriptive) *statement*, whether atomic, molecular or quantified. Thus we have

> That a is triangular is a state of affairs
> That a is triangular or b is triangular is a state of affairs
> That something is triangular (i.e. that ($\exists$ x) x is triangular) is a state of affairs.

However,

> That something is triangular

as it occurs in the context

> That something is triangular implies that it is trilateral[17]

is *not* the result of applying 'that' to a statement. It is the material mode for (in first approximation)[18]

> The [˙triangular˙] INDCON.

Thus, while

> That something is triangular (i.e. the ˙($\exists$x) x is triangular˙) is a state of affairs

is unproblematic,

> That something is triangular (in the *second* sense) is a state of affairs

is incorrect, and must be replaced by

> That something is triangular is a kind of state of affairs

which (again in first approximation)[19] has as its formal made counterpart

> The [˙triangular˙] INDCON is a kind of PROP.

There are a number of points to be noted here. In the first place there are at least two ways in which there are kinds of PROP.

(1) There are sub-categories of PROP, e.g. atomic, molecular, general, etc. Thus we have

---

[17] See the discussion of this statement in AE, *Philosophical Perspectives*, 262 ff.
[18] The reason for the qualification will emerge shortly.   [19] See previous footnote.

The ['triangular'] 'a' is an ATPROP
The 'a is triangular or b is triangular' is a MOLPROP
The '($\exists$x) x is triangular' is a GENPROP.

(2) Corresponding to the many states of affairs which have in common the fact that each consists in some particular thing's being triangular, thus

That a is triangular, that b is triangular, ...

there are many PROPs which have in common the fact that each is a ['triangular'] INDCON$_i$, for a particular value of 'i'. It is the latter sense in which there are kinds of PROP which concerns us here.

Consider, now, the following:

(a)   That a is triangular is something's being triangular
(b)   Something's being triangular is a kind of state of affairs.

The first of these can be quite adequately construed as the material mode for

The ['triangular']'a' is a ['triangular'] INDCON.

But what of the second? The previous paragraph suggests that in some contexts the phrase 'something's being triangular' is to be construed as *containing* a variable (a metalinguistic variable), as contrasted with *mentioning* one (an object language variable) as does 'that ($\exists$x) is triangular.' This suggests that (b) has as its formal mode counterpart

(For all i,) the ['triangular'] INDCON$_i$ is a kind of PROP

which reduces to

(For all i,) ['triangular'] INDCON$_i$s are a kind of PROP

e.g.

['triangular']'a's are a kind of PROP.[20]

Notice that, as usual, the plural which occurs in the formal mode of speech, when we make the move from statements about (for example)

the 'or'

to statements about

'or's

does not occur in the material mode of speech. Material mode singular terms (e.g. Triangularity, that Tom is tall, etc.) yield plurals only when translated into the formal mode.

Thus, to get

['triangular']'a's are a kind of PROP

into the material mode, we must first go to

The ['triangular']'a' is a kind of PROP

which yields

That a is triangular is a kind of state of affairs.

Perhaps we can now understand why

---

[20] Compare 'Dogs are a kind of animal'.

Triangularity is a state of affairs

"looks wrong". For while, according to the above analysis, Triangularity belongs to the category of states of affairs, the correct formulation would have to be

Triangularly is a kind of state of affairs.

Equating, as I proposed in the latter part of AE, Triangularity with that something is triangular, our categorizing statement translates into the formal mode as

The [·triangular·] $INDCON_i$ is a kind of PROP.

Notice that to make this move we have had to reconstruct triangularity not as

The [·triangular·] INDCON

but as

the [·triangular·] $INDCON_i$.

The former contains the common noun 'INDCON', the latter contains the common noun *variable* '$INDCON_i$' which takes as substituends specific common nouns, e.g. '·a·' where

The ·a· is an INDCON

i.e.

·a·s are INDCONs.

Ad 9. The "essentially *auxiliary* character of ·triangular·s" is, of course, the key to the account of predication I have been stressing since "Naming and Saying". As auxiliary symbols, predicates have meaning only by virtue of the fact that by giving INDCONs the character of being concatenated with them, they turn them into PROPs. It is, indeed, as you say, the essentially auxiliary character of predicates which is "the truth behind Frege's insight that functions are essentially *ungesättigt*"—but remember what a miscellany Frege includes among functions (e.g. logical connectives). What baffles me is what led you to think that on *my* view it is "the non-illustratingness of '[·triangular·] INDCON' " which corresponds to this insight.

Ad 10. Again I can only say that *of course* both · $\in_1$ lion· and ·triangular·s play "*parochial* linguistic roles rather than *essential* linguistic roles". But what you must not overlook is that while Jumblese contains neither adjectival predicates nor common nouns, it does contain statements which say *how* an individual is as contrasted with *what* it is. It enables the expression of both *qualitative* and *sortal* states of affairs. It contains no count nouns, but it does contain enumerative statements.

The more important claim you make in 10 is that "we wind up with two and only two basic semantic categories: INDCON and PROP". This claim which you elaborate in 11 is clearly intended to tie in with the theme you announced in 4, and a discussion of it will give some measure of unity to this sprawling letter.

Ad 10 and 11. What are we going to count as semantic categories? And what is a *basic* semantic category? Are 'connectives' and 'quantifiers' semantic categories? Clearly they are categories, and clearly connectives and quantifiers are subject to translation, and have senses, i.e. are proper subject matter for the context

_____ means. . . . .
_____ expresses the sense. . . . .

yet they do not, as such, correspond to anything in the world, though statements involving them do. I can understand why you would want to say that 'connective' and 'quantifier' are syntactical *rather than* semantical categories, whereas 'proposition' and 'singular term' are semantical (as well as) syntactical categories. Provided that one recognizes (*pace* Quine) that the theory of reference is a branch of the general theory of meaning, the terminology can do no harm. You are quite right to point out that Wittgenstein held that only INDCONs and PROPs (in the first instance ATPROPs) correspond to anything in the world. Thus we can agree that "Wittgenstein's semantics includes only 'name' and 'proposition' as basic categories."

The strategy of my treatment of abstract entities has always been to pour nominalistic wine into platonistic bottles. In this sense I have argued for several decades that although there are abstract entities, there *really are* no abstract entities. My initial insights were, at best, fragmentary, but they all finally crystallized into the analysis developed in AE. Since I hold that while there are abstract entities, there *really are* no abstract entities (though you seemed to have missed this), I cannot object to the core of your section 11. The reason *you* give for saying that "there really *are* no abstract entities," namely

… because the only basic semantical categories are INDCON and PROP

strikes me as not so much wrong as misleading. One would almost expect you to conclude that there *really are* both particulars and (atomic) states of affairs, both INDCON and ATPROP being "basic". One reason why you don't might have been that you don't think of atomic states of affairs as abstract entities. Your actual reason, of course, is that although atomic states of affairs *are* abstract entities, they are, after all, INDCONs—though not *mere* INDCONs.[21]

Among the abstract entities I was considering were states of affairs, thus

That a is triangular.

Now,

That a is triangular is a state of affairs

is the material mode for

the [·triangular·]·a· is a PROP

i.e.

[·triangular·]·a·s are PROPs.

And when I argued that while there are states of affairs, there *really are* no states of affairs, it was on the ground that statements about states of affairs are paraphraseable by statements about conceptual tokens. And in general, my reason for saying that everything which *really is*, is particular, was not that all conceptual items which directly represent something in the world are basic singular terms, *even atomic propositions being basic singular terms* (though not *mere* basic singular terms), but rather that *all* abstract entities, including states of affairs, turn out to be distributive objects, the putative names of which are DSTs. Thus the state of affairs

---

[21] I suspect you also have in mind the categorial grammar of Ajdukiewicz, according to which the basic grammatical categories are 'noun' and 'sentence', *predicates* being expressions which concatenated with a noun yield a sentence, *connectives* being expressions which turn sentences into sentences, etc. But the relation between this distinction between basic and derivative categories to the semantic problems we have been discussing remains to be clarified.

that a is triangular

turns out to be

the [·triangular·]·a·

and is reducible to

[·triangular·]·a·s.

In other words abstract singular terms turn out to be metalinguistic *predicates*.

Let me spell this out more precisely, so that its implications will be clear. The material mode existence statement

There are states of affairs, e.g. that a is triangular

translates into

There are PROPs, e.g. the [·triangular·]·a·.

Again,

The [·triangular·]·a· is a PROP

which is the formal mode counterpart of a statement which has the surface grammar of a singular subject predicate statement, namely

That a is triangular is a state of affairs

reduces to

[·triangular·]·a·s are PROPs.

From this point of view, the statement

There are states of affairs

which appears to have the form

(∃x) x is a state of affairs

turns out, when translated into the formal mode, to have the form, not as one might expect

(∃x) x is a PROP

but rather

(∃K) Ks are PROPs

which involves ∃-quantification of a metalinguistic *predicate* variable and doesn't assert the existence of PROPs. To do the latter we must make the *additional* step of asserting

(∃x) x is a PROP

which tells us that there are propositional tokens.

This can be summed up by saying that the idea that there "really are" no abstract entities amounts to the idea that abstract singular terms dissolve into metalinguistic predicates which are true of *concreta*.

But although in this sense, there "really are" no states of affairs, we can draw another distinction between abstract entities which "really are", and others which "really are not". It is this distinction which, as I see it, lies behind your remarks. The theme to begin with is *indispensability*. For example, Negation would be indispensable whereas Triangularity (interpreted as the ˙triangular˙) would not. Again, definable entities would be dispensable in favor of their *definientia*. But, to come to the heart of the matter, and focusing our attention on entities which are "in the world", we can zero in on the question with which the *Tractatus* opens: Can we dispense with atomic states of affairs in favor of entities which are not states of affairs? To this question the answer is clearly no. A linguistic representation of the world cannot consist of *mere* names, and the relevant non-(*mere* names) are ATPROPs. Thus, although a monadic ATPROP is a name, it is not a *mere* name, but a name which is ϕ, where 'ϕ' stands for a linguistically relevant characteristic which may or may not involve the use of an auxiliary expression. Thus we have

> ATPROPs are BSTs (basic singular terms), but not mere BSTs; they are BSTs which are thus-and-so (e.g. concatenated with a ˙triangular˙)

which corresponds to

> Atomic states of affairs are particulars, but not *mere* particulars; they are particulars which are such-and-such (e.g. triangular).

Thus whereas our former line of thought led to the conclusion that there "really are" no atomic states of affairs, this second line of thought leads to the conclusion that there "really are" atomic states of affairs. But the two conclusions are quite compatible, for the latter simply amounts to the indispensability of ATPROPs in representing the world.

Ad 12. Notice that it is not just the fact that PROP is a basic semantical category on which you are relying in section 10, for it is only ATPROPs which are STs though not mere STs. Thus, to take a previous example,

> ˙($\exists$ 2x) x $\in_1$ KINDs are PROPs, but they are *not* STs.

Two is an entity which is not an object at all, let alone a *mere* object.

Only in the context of the lines of thought developed above concerning entities, objects and semantic basicness, does

> ATROPs are BSTs but not mere BSTs

illuminate the claim that everything which *really is*, is particular. Yet there is a sense in which, representing, as it does, the correct interpretation of predication, it is the keystone of the system. For it embodies the basic truth that we say how a particular, say *a*, is by inscribing its name in a certain 'style', thus by inscribing a [˙triangular˙]˙a˙ and *not* by concatenating its name with the 'name' of an abstract entity. This focuses our attention on the *two* dimensions of matter-of-factual connection between atomic propositions and the world: (1) the connection by virtue of which the name is hooked up with a certain object, thus ˙a˙s with *a*; (2) the connection by virtue of which names inscribed in a certain style, thus [˙triangular˙]˙a˙ are hooked up with certain objects, thus triangular objects.

One final point remains to be elaborated. I argued in *Ad* 3 that what combines with a PRED to form a PROP is a *mere* ST. It is an ˙a˙ *simpliciter*, and not, for example, a [˙triangular˙]˙a˙ which combines with a PRED token, e.g. a ˙red˙ to form a PROP. Thus

> (a is triangular) is red

is ill-formed, even though it is true that

> 'a is triangular's are ˙a˙s (but not *mere* ˙a˙s).

In other words, a theory of material mode categories must be careful to distinguish a sense in which atomic states of affairs, *are* objects (though not mere objects) from a sense in which they are *not* objects, *but* states of affairs.[22]

What has been stressed up until now is the by no means unimportant sense which atomic states of affairs, unlike numerical states of affairs *are* objects. For, as noted above, whereas

[˙triangular˙]˙a˙s are PROPs by virtue of being STs (i.e. ˙a˙s) though not mere STs

has as its material mode counterpart

That a is triangular is a state of affairs by virtue of being an object (i.e. *a*), though not a *mere* object,

the following,

˙(∃ 1x) x ∈₁ pope˙s are not STs, *but* PROPs

becomes, in the material mode,

That there is one pope is not an object *but* a state of affairs.[23]

I *think* that the above is relevant to the fact that you are "not quite sure" that you are "entirely *happy* with

PROPs are STs (though not mere STs)

and the resulting commitment to

Everything which really is, is particular

especially with the Frege's ghost still lurking in the shadows ...". To the extent that your uneasiness is due to Frege's ghost, I hope that I have laid them to rest with my remarks in *Ad* 3 and the above elaboration. They suggest that when, in the theory of predication, we get down to the nitty gritty of ontology, the objects of which predicates are true are *objects as such*. Platonists like Bergmann construe this to mean that predicates are true of *bare particulars*. But on a correct theory of predication, it implies nothing of the sort. All 'object as such' rules out, as pointed out above, is such strings as

(a is triangular) is red[24]

i.e. strings of the form

F(fa)

where 'F' represents a genuine predicate and not any old 'open sentence', e.g. 'not____', for, of course,

not (fa)

---

[22] Jeff Sicha, in a personal communication, has emphasized the care with which a system of categorial classification, with its *contrastive* pigeon holes, must be worked out to avoid paradox.

[23] It must be remembered that there is another sense (one more step up the semantic ladder) in which it is true that
    That there is one pope is an object.
In this sense it is the material mode for
    The ˙the ˙(∃ 1x) x ∈₁ pope ˙˙ is an ST (i.e. a DST).
See the discussion of levels of abstract entities, *AE*, 250 ff. in *Philosophical Perspectives*.

[24] This is not, of course, to be confused with: a, which is triangular, is red.

is as well formed as can be. Thus, the theory of predication in question enables us to understand why

a is triangular

doesn't assert that a nexus of exemplification obtains between a bare particular and a character. There really are triangular objects (as contrasted with objects which are merely tied to another object named Triangularity). Thus, when we say that "everything which really is, is particular", this must be construed as compatible with

There really *are* states of affairs.

And this can be done along the lines I sketched above where it was emphasized that the representation of the world by ATPROPs cannot be reduced to its representation by *mere* INDCONs, and that the non- (*mere* INDCONs) which are necessary are the ATPROPs themselves.

To sum up:

(1) There really are atomic states of affairs

is true, as the material mode formulation of the indispensability of ATROPs in representing the world.

(2) Atomic states of affairs are particulars, but not mere particulars

reminds us that ATPROPs are BSTs which are of a linguistically relevant character over and above that by virtue of which they are the BSTs they are. And, finally,

(3) There *really are* no states of affairs

is the material mode formulation of the fact that the singular terms which ostensibly name states of affairs turn out, in the formal mode, to be metalinguistic predicates.

Ad 13. I had a most enjoyable stay in Chapel Hill and, in particular, found the experience of meeting with your seminar both challenging and rewarding.

Cordially, Wilfrid Sellars

Master Bibliography

Alston, William P., [SMG], "Sellars and the 'Myth of the Given'", *Philosophy and Phenomenological Research*, 65 (2002), 69–86.

Baum, L. Frank, [WO], *The Wizard of Oz* (Bobbs-Merrill Co.; Indianapolis, IN: 1899).

Brandom, Robert B., [AR], *Articulating Reasons* (Harvard University Press; Cambridge, MA: 2000).

_____ [KSA], "Knowledge and the Social Articulation of the Space of Reasons", *Philosophy and Phenomenological Research*, 55 (1995), 895–908.

_____ [MIE], *Making It Explicit: Reasoning, Representing, and Discursive Commitment* (Harvard University Press; Cambridge, MA: 1994).

_____ [PRC], "Perception and Rational Constraint", *Philosophy and Phenomenological Research*, 58 (1998), 369–74.

_____ [PRC0], "Perception and Rational Constraint: McDowell's *Mind and World*", in Villanueva, [PPI], 241–59.

Carroll, Lewis, "What the Tortoise Said to Achilles', *Mind*, 4 (1895), 278–80; variously reprinted.

Castañeda, Hector-Neri, and Sellars, Wilfrid, [Corr.], "Correspondence between Hector Castañeda and Wilfrid Sellars on Philosophy of Mind" (1961–2), http://www.ditext.com/sellars/corr.html.

Castañeda, Hector-Neri (ed.), *Action, Knowledge, and Reality: critical studies in honor of Wilfrid Sellars* (Bobbs-Merrill; Indianapolis, IN; 1975).

Chastain, Charles, "Reference and Context", in Keith Gunderson (ed.), *Language, Mind, and Knowledge*, Minnesota Studies in the Philosophy of Science, 7 (University of Minnesota Press; Minneapolis, MN: 1975), 194–269.

Cornman, J. W., "Sellars, Scientific Realism, and Sensa", *Review of Metaphysics*, 23 (1969/70), 417–451.

Davidson, Donald, [T&M], "Truth and Meaning", *Synthese*, 7 (1967), 304–23.

_____ [VICS], "On the very idea of a conceptual scheme", *Proceedings of the American Philosophical Association*, 17 (1973/4), 5–20.

Delaney, C. F., "Sellars' Grain Argument", *Australasian Journal of Philosophy*, 50, (1972), 14–16.

_____ Loux, Michael J., Gutting, Gary, and Solomon, W. David, *The Synoptic Vision: Essays on the Philosophy of Wilfrid Sellars* (University of Notre Dame Press; Notre Dame. IN; 1977).

Dennett, Daniel C., [MTE], "Mid-Term Examination: Compare and Contrast", in *The Intentional Stance* (Bradford Books, MIT Press; Cambridge, MA; 1987), 339–50.

deVries, Willem A., *Wilfrid Sellars* (Philosophy Now) (Acumen Publishing/McGill-Queen's University Press: 2005).

deVries, Willem A., and Triplett, Timm, [KMG], *Knowledge, Mind, and the Given* (Hackett Publishing Co.; Indianapolis, IN: 2000).

Feyerabend, Paul, [AM], *Against Method* (Humanities Press; London: 1975, and Schocken; New York: 1978).

Feyerabend, Paul, [HBGE], "How to be a good empiricist—A plea for tolerance in matters epistemological", in B. Baumrin (ed.), *Philosophy of Science: The Delaware Seminar*, 2 (1962/3).

Goldman, Alvin, "Folk Psychology and Mental Concepts", *ProtoSociology*, 14 (2000), 4–25.

Gordon, Robert M., [SRR], "Sellars' Ryleans Revisited", *ProtoSociology*, 14 (2000), 102–14.

_____ "How to Think about Thinking", in M. Davies and T. Stone (eds.), *Mental Simulation* (Blackwell Publishing; Oxford: 1995).

Hall, Everett, *Philosophical Systems* (University of Chicago Press; Chicago: 1960).

Hanson, Norwood Russell, [PD], *Patterns of Discovery: an inquiry into the conceptual foundations of science* (Cambridge University Press; Cambridge: 1958).

Harman, Gilbert, "Enumerative Induction as Inference to the Best Explanation", *Journal of Philosophy*, 65 (1968), 529–33.

_____ "Inference to the Best Explanation", *Philosophical Review*, 74 (1965), 88–95.

Heal, Jane, "Understanding Other Minds from the Inside", *ProtoSociology*, 14 (2000), 39–55; repr. in A. O'Hear (ed.), *Current Issues in the Philosophy of Mind* (Cambridge University Press; Cambridge: 1998), 83–99.

Hooker, C.A., "Sellars' Argument for the Inevitability of the Secondary Qualities", *Philosophical Studies*, 32 (1977), 335–348.

Kant, Immanuel, *Critique of Pure Reason*, trans. Norman Kemp Smith (Macmillan & Co., Ltd. & St. Martin's Press; New York:1929 & 1965); also ed. and trans. Paul Guyer and Allen W. Wood (Cambridge University Press; Cambridge and New York: 1998).

Kripke, Saul, [N&N], also [NN], "Naming and Necessity", in G. Harman and D. Davidson (eds.), *Semantics of Natural Language* (D. Reidel Publishing Co.; Dordrecht, Holland: 1972), 253–355; repr. as *Naming and Necessity* (Harvard University Press; Cambridge, MA: 1980).

Kuhn, Thomas, [SSR], *The Structure of Scientific Revolutions* (University of Chicago Press; Chicago, IL: 1970).

Kukla, Rebecca, [MMM], "Myth, Memory and Misrecognition in Sellars' 'Empiricism and the Philosophy of Mind'", *Philosophical Studies*, 101 (2000), 161–211.

Lauden, Larry, "A Confutation of Convergent Realism", *Philosophy of Science*, 48 (1981), 19–49.

Leplin, Jarrett, "Reference and Scientific Realism", *Studies in History and Philosophy of Science*, 10 (1979), 265–84.

McDowell, John, [HWV], "Having the World in View: Sellars, Kant, and Intentionality", *Journal of Philosophy*, 95 (1998), 431–91.

_____ [KI], "Knowledge and the Internal", *Philosophy and Phenomenological Research*, 55 (1995), 877–893.

_____ [KIR], "Knowledge and the Internal Revisited", *Philosophy and Phenomenological Research*, 66 (2002), 97–105.

_____ [MW], *Mind and World* (Harvard University Press; Cambridge, MA: 1994, 1996).

_____ [RB], Reply to Brandom, [PRC0], in Villanueva, [PPI], 290–8.

_____ [RC], Reply to Commentators, *Philosophy and Phenomenological Research*, 58 (1998), 403–9.

O'Shea, James, *Wilfrid Sellars* (Key Contemporary Thinkers) (Blackwell/Polity Press: 2006).

Peirce, Charles Sanders, *Collected Papers of Charles Sanders Peirce*, ed. C. Hartshorne and P. Weiss, 6 vol. (Harvard University Press; Cambridge, MA: 1931–5).

Pitt, Joseph C. (ed.), *The Philosophy of Wilfrid Sellars: Queries and Extensions* (D. Reidel Publishing Co; Dordrecht, Holland; 1978).

—— *Pictures, Images, and Conceptual Change: An Analysis of Wilfrid Sellars' Philosophy of Science* (D. Reidel Publishing Co.; Dordrecht, Holland; 1981).

Putnam, Hilary, [MM], "The meaning of meaning", in Keith Gunderson (ed.), *Language, Mind, and Knowledge*, Minnesota Studies in the Philosophy of Science, 7 (University of Minnesota Press; Minneapolis, MN: 1975), 131–93; repr. in *Mind, Language, and Reality* (Cambridge University Press; Cambridge and New York: 1975).

—— [R&R], "Realism and Reason", *Proceedings of the American Philosophical Association*, 50 (1977), 483–98.

—— [WR], "What is realism?", *Proceedings of the Aristotelian Society*, 76 (1975/6), 177–94; repr. in *Meaning and the Moral Sciences* (Routledge & Kegan Paul, Ltd.; London and Boston: 1978).

Quine, W. V., [EN], "Epistemology Naturalized", in [OROE], 69–90.

—— [OR], "Ontological relativity", *Journal of Philosophy*, 65 (1968), 185–212; repr. in [OROE].

—— [OROE], *Ontological relativity, and other essays* (Columbia University Press; New York: 1969).

—— [TDE], "Two Dogmas of Empiricism", *Philosophical Review*, 60 (1951), 20–43.

—— *Word and Object* (MIT Press; Cambridge, MA: 1960).

Rorty, Richard, [PMN], *Philosophy and the Mirror of Nature* (Princeton University Press; Princeton, NJ: 1979).

—— [WWL], "The world well lost", *Journal of Philosophy*, 69 (1972), 649–65.

—— "Pragmatism, Davidson, and Truth", in Ernest Lepore (ed.), *Truth and Interpretation: Perspectives on the Philosophy of Donald Davidson* (Blackwell; Cambridge: 1986), 333–68; repr. in *Objectivity, Relativism, and Truth* (Cambridge University Press; Cambridge and New York: 1991), 126–50.

Rosenberg, Jay F., [AK], *Accessing Kant: A Relaxed Introduction to the Critique of Pure Reason*, (Clarendon Press; Oxford: 2005).

—— [BF], *Beyond Formalism: Naming and Necessity for Human Beings* (Temple University Press; Philadelphia, PA: 1994).

—— [CLC], "The Concept of Linguistic Correctness", *Philosophical Studies*, 30 (1976), 171–84.

—— [CRCP], "Coupling, Retheoretization, and the Correspondence Principle", *Synthese*, 45 (1980), 351–85.

—— [DIT], "The Dispute on the Indeterminacy of Translation", in M. Dascal et al., (eds.), *Sprachphilosophie/Philosophy of Language*, vol. 2 (Walter de Gruyter; Berlin and New York: 1996), 1050–57.

—— [GHTI], "The 'Given' and How to Take It–Some Reflections on Phenomenal Ontology", *Metaphilosophy*, 6/3–4 (1975), 303–37.

—— [KSUP], "Kantian Schemata and the Unity of Perception", in Alex Burri (ed.), *Language and Thought* (Walter de Gruyter; Berlin and New York; 1997), 175–90.

Rosenberg, Jay F., [LR], *Linguistic Representation* (D. Reidel Publishing Co.; Dordrecht, Holland: 1974, 1981).

_____ [NPT], "New Perspectives on the *Tractatus*", Dialogue, 4 (1966), 506–17.

_____ [OW], *One World and Our Knowledge of It* (D. Reidel Publishing Co.; Dordrecht, Holland: 1980).

_____ [PSI], "Philosophy's Self-Image: A Reply to Rorty", *Analyse & Kritik*, 4 (1982), 114–28.

_____ [RFOS], "Russell and the Form of Outer Sense", in G. W. Roberts (ed.), *Bertrand Russell Memorial Volume* (George Allen & Unwin, Ltd.; London: 1979), 285–303.

_____ [RTSH], "Red Triangles and Speckled Hens: Critical Notice of BonJour and Sosa on Epistemic Justification", *International Journal of Philosophical Studies*, 12 (2004), 463–77.

_____ [SEALA], "Science and the Epistemic Authority of Logical Analysis", in N. Rescher (ed.), *Reason and Rationality in Natural Science* (University Press of America; Latham, MD: 1985), 1–26.

_____ [SEL], "Synonymy and the Epistemology of Linguistics", *Inquiry*, 10 (1967), 405–20.

_____ [SSSN], "On Strawson: Sounds, Skepticism, and Necessity", *Philosophia*, 8 (1978), 405–19.

_____ [SU], "Spontaneity Unchained: An Essay in Darwinian Epistemology", in Ralph Schumacher (ed.), *Idealismus als Theorie der Representation?* (mentis Verlag; Berlin: 2001), 181–209.

_____ [TAK], *Thinking About Knowing* (Oxford University Press; Oxford: 2002).

_____ [TAR], "Transcendental Arguments Revisited", *Journal of Philosophy*, 72 (1975), 611–24.

_____ [TS], *The Thinking Self* (Temple University Press; Philadelphia, PA: 1986)

_____ [WHPL], "What's Happening in Philosophy of Language Today", *American Philosophical Quarterly*, 9 (1972), 101–6.

_____ [WSC], "Wittgenstein's Self-Criticisms, or 'Whatever Happened to the Picture Theory?'", *Noûs*, 4 (1970), 209–23.

_____ [WTLP], "Wittgenstein's Theory of Language as Picture", *American Philosophical Quarterly*, 5 (1968), 18–30.

Röska-Hardy, Louise, "Self-Ascription and Simulation Theory", *ProtoSociology*, 14 (2000), 115–44.

Russell, Bertrand, [PLA], "The Philosophy of Logical Atomism", in *Logic and Knowledge; essays, 1901–1950*, ed. R. C. Marsh (George Allen & Unwin, Ltd.; London: 1956).

Seibt, Johanna, *Properties as Processes. A Synoptic Study of Wilfrid Sellars' Nominalism* (Ridgeview Publishing Co.; Reseda, CA: 1990).

Sellars, Wilfrid, [A&E], "Actions and Events", *Noûs*, 7 (1973), 179–202; repr. in [EPH], 189–213.

_____ [AE], "Abstract Entities", *Review of Metaphysics*, 16 (1983), 627–71; repr. in [PP], 229–69.

_____ [ATS], "The Adverbial Theory of the Objects of Sensation", *Metaphilosophy*, 6 (1975), 144–60.

_____ [CAE], "Classes as Abstract Entities and the Russell Paradox", *Review of Metaphysics*, 17 (1963), 67–90; repr. in [PP], 270–90.

_____ [CE], "The Concept of Emergence" (with Paul Meehl), in H. Feigl and M. Scriver (eds.), *The Foundations of Science and the Concepts of Psychoanalysis*, Minnesota Studies in the Philosophy of Science, vol. I (University of Minnesota Press; Minneapolis, MN; 1956), 239–253.

_____ [CIL] "Concepts as Involving Laws and Inconceivable Without Them", *Philosophy of Science*, 15 (1948), 287–315; repr. in [PPPW].

_____ [CL], the Carus Lectures = [FMPP].

_____ [EAE], "Empiricism and Abstract Entities", in P. A. Schilpp (ed.), *The Philosophy of Rudolph Carnap* (Open Court; LaSalle, IL; 1963), 431–68; repr. in [EPH], 245–86.

_____ [EPH], *Essays in Philosophy and Its History* (D. Reidel Publishing Co.; Dordrecht, Holland; 1975).

_____ [EPM], "Empiricism and the Philosophy of Mind", in H. Feigl and M. Scriver (eds.), *The Foundations of Science and the Concepts of Psychoanalysis*, Minnesota Studies in the Philosophy of Science, vol. I (University of Minnesota Press; Minneapolis, MN; 1956), 253–329; repr. in [SPR], 127–96.

_____ [FMPP], "Foundations for a Metaphysics of Pure Process" (The Carus Lectures for 1977–78), *Monist*, 64 (1981), 3–90.

_____ [GEC], "Givenness and Explanatory Coherence", *Journal of Philosophy*, 70 (1973), 612–24.

_____ [I], "… this I or we or it (The thing) which thinks", *Proceedings of the American Philosophical Association*, 44 (1970/1), 5–31; repr. in [EPH].

_____ [IAMBP], "The Identity Approach to the Mind-Body Problem", *Review of Metaphysics*, 18 (1965), 430–51; repr. in [PP], 370–88.

_____ [ICP], "Is Consciousness Physical?", Lecture 3, pp. 66–90, of [FMPP].

_____ [IILO], "Imperatives, Intentions, and the Logic of 'Ought' ", *Methodos*, 8 (1956), 228–268.

_____ [IKTE], "The Role of Imagination in Kant's Theory of Experience", in Henry W. Johnston, Jr. (ed.), *Categories: A Colloquium* (Pennsylvanian State University; College Park, PA: 1978), 231–45.

_____ [IV], "Induction as Vindication", *Philosophy of Science*, 31 (1964), 197–231; repr. in [EPH], pp. 367–416.

_____ [KPT], *Kant and Pre-Kantian Themes: Lectures by Wilfrid Sellars*, ed. Pedro Amaral (Ridgeview Publishing Co.; Atascadero, CA: 2002).

_____ [KTM], *Kant's Transcendental Metaphysics: Sellars' Cassirer Lecture Notes and Other Essays*, ed. Jeffrey F. Sicha (Ridgeview Publishing Co.; Atascadero, CA: 2002).

_____ [KTE], "Some Remarks on Kant's Theory of Experience", *Journal of Philosophy*, 64 (1967), 633–47; repr. in [EPH].

_____ [KTI], "Kant's Transcendental Idealism", *Collections of Philosophy*, 6 (1976), 165–81.

_____ [LA], "The Lever of Archimedes", Lecture I, pp. 3–36, of [FMPP].

_____ [LCP], "On the Logic of Complex Particulars", *Mind*, 58 (1949), 306–38.

_____ [LT], "The Language of Theories", in H. Feigl and G. Maxwell (eds.), *Current Issues in the Philosophy Science* (Henry Holt, Rhinehart and Winston; New York, NY; 1961); repr. in [SPR], 106–26.

_____ [LTC], "Language as Thought and Communication", *Philosophy and Phenomenological Research*, 29 (1969), 506–27; repr. in [EPH], 93–117.

Sellars, Wilfrid, [MCP], "Metaphysics and the Concept of a Person", in K. Lambert (ed.), *The Logical Way of Doing Things* (Yale University Press; New Haven, CN: 1969), 219–52; repr. in [EPH].

_____ [ME], *The Metaphysics of Epistemology, Lectures by Wilfrid Sellars*, ed. Pedro Amaral (Ridgeview Publishing Co.; Reseda, CA; 1989).

_____ [MEV], "Mental Events", *Philosophical Studies*, 39 (1981), 325–45.

_____ [MFC], "Meaning as Functional Classification", *Synthese*, 27 (1974), 417–37.

_____ [MGEC], "More on Givenness and Explanatory Coherence", in George Pappas (ed.), *Justification and Knowledge* (D. Reidel Publishing Co.; Dordrecht, Holland: 1979), 169–82.

_____ [N&O], *Naturalism and Ontology* (Ridgeview Publishing Co.; Reseda, CA: 1979).

_____ [N&S], "Naming and Saying", *Philosophy of Science*, 29 (1962); repr. in [SPR], 225–45.

_____ [NI], "Notes on Intentionality", *Journal of Philosophy*, 61 (1964), 655–65; repr. in [PP], pp. 308–20.

_____ [OPM], "Ontology and the philosophy of Mind in Russell", in George Nakhnikian (ed.), *Bertrand Russell's philosophy* (Duckworth and Barnes and Noble, 1974), 57–100.

_____ [P], "Particulars", *Philosophy and Phenomenological Research*, 13 (1952), 184–99.

_____ [P], "Phenomenalism", in [SPR], 60–105.

_____ [PP], *Philosophical Perspectives* (Charles C. Thomas: Springfield, IL; 1967); repr. in 2 vol., *Philosophical Perspectives: History of Philosophy* [PPHP] and *Philosophical Perspective: Metaphysics and Epistemology* [PPME] (Ridgeview Publishing Co.; Reseda, CA; 1977).

_____ [PPPW], *Pure Pragmatics and Possible Worlds— The Early Essays of Wilfrid Sellars*, Jeffrey F. Sicha, ed. (Ridgeview Publishing Co; Reseda, CA; 1980).

_____ [PSIM], "Philosophy and the Scientific Image of Man", in Robert Colodny (ed.), *Frontiers of Science and Philosophy* (University of Pittsburgh Press; Pittsburgh, PA; 1962), 35–78; repr. in [SPR], pp. 1–40.

_____ [RNWW], "Realism and the New Way of Words", *Philosophy and Phenomenological Research*, 8 (1948), 601–34.

_____ [RQ], "Reply to Quine", *Synthese*, 26 (1973), 122–45.

_____ [S&M] also [SM], *Science and Metaphysics: Variations on Kantian Themes* (Routledge & Kegan Paul Ltd; London, and The Humanities Press; New York; 1968); reissued (Ridgeview Publishing Co.; Atascadero, CA: 1992).

_____ [SK], "The Structure of Knowledge" (The Matchette Foundation Lectures for 1971), in H.-N. Castañeda, ed., *Action, Knowledge, and Reality*, pp. 295–347.

_____ [SPR], *Science, Perception and Reality* (Routledge & Kegan Paul Ltd; London, and The Humanities Press: New York; 1963); reissued (Ridgeview Publishing Co.; Atascadero, CA: 1991).

_____ [SRII], "Scientific Realism or Irenic Instrumentalism: A Critique of Nagel and Feyerabend on Theoretical Explanation", in R. Cohen and M. Wartofsky (eds.), *Boston Studies in the Philosophy of Science*, vol. II (Humanities Press: 1965), 171–204; repr. in [PP], 337–69, and [PPME], 157–89.

_____ [SRLG], "Some Reflections on Language Games", *Philosophy of Science*, 21 (1954), 204–28; repr. in [SPR], 321–58.

_____ [SRPC], "Some Reflections on Perceptual Consciousness", in R. Bruzina and B. Wilshire (eds.), *Crosscurrents in Phenomenology* (Martinus Nijhoff; The Hague: 1978), 169–85.

_____ [SSIS], "Seeing, Sense Impressions, and Sensa: A Reply to Cornman", *Review of Metaphysics*, 24 (1970/1), 391–447.

_____ [SSMB], "A Semantical Solution to the Mind-Body Problem", *Methodos*, 5 (1953), 45–82.

_____ [T&C], "Truth and 'Correspondence' ", *Journal of Philosophy*, 59 (1962), 29–56; repr. in [SPR], 197–224.

_____ [TA], "Thought and Action", in Keith Lehrer (ed.), *Freedom and Determinism* (Random House; New York: 1966), 105–39.

_____ [TTC], "Towards a Theory of the Categories", in L. Foster and J. W. Swanson (eds.), *Experience and Theory* (University of Massachusetts Press; Amherst, MA: 1970), 55–78; repr. in [KTM].

_____ [VR], "Volitions Reaffirmed", in M. Brand and D. Walson (eds.), *Action Theory* (D. Reidel Publishing Co.; Dordrecht, Holland: 1976), 47–66.

Sellars, Wilfrid, and Castañeda, Hector-Neri [Corr.], "Correspondence between Hector Castañeda and Wilfrid Sellars on Philosophy of Mind", 1961–2, http://www.ditext.com/sellars/corr.html.

Sosa, Ernest [MG], "Mythology of the Given", *History of Philosophy Quarterly*, 14 (1997), 275–87.

Strawson, P. F., [I], *Individuals* (Methuen & Co., Ltd.; London, 1959).

Villanueva, Enrique (ed.), [PPI], *Perception: Philosophical Issues, 7* (Ridgeview Publishing Co.; Atascadero, CA: 1996).

Wittgenstein, Ludwig, [PI], *Philosophical Investigations*, trans. G. E. M. Anscombe (Macmillan; London and New York: 1953).

_____ [TLP], *Tractatus Logico-Philosophicus*, trans. D. R. Pears and B. F. McGuinness, (Routledge & Kegan Paul, Ltd.; London: 1961).

Williams, Michael, [ATG1], "Mythology of the Given: Sosa, Sellars and the Task of Epistemology", Part I of "Are There Two Grades of Knowledge?", *Proceedings of the Aristotelian Society*, supp. 77 (2003), 91–112.

Ziff, Paul, *Semantic Analysis* (Cornell University Press; Ithaca, NY: 1960).

Index

Concepts

Names

Abbreviations
in Formulae